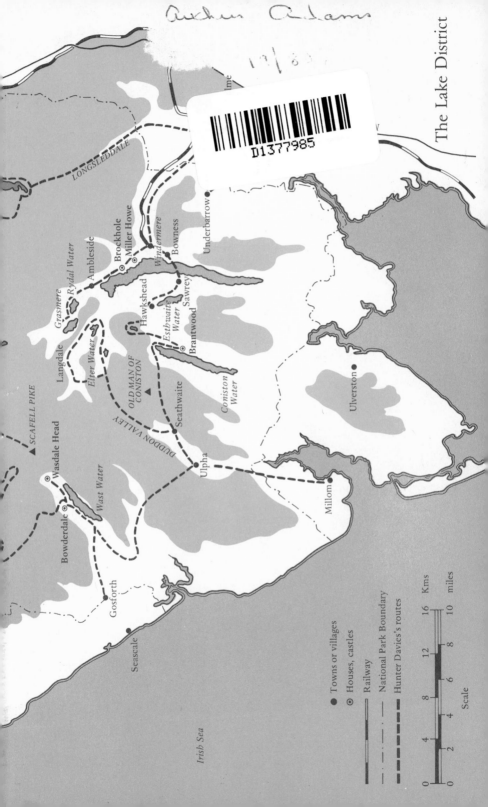

Arthur Adams

The Lake District

D1377985

LONGSLEDDALE

Brockhole
Miller Howe
Windermere
Bowness
Ambleside
Underbarrow

Rydal Water
Grasmere

Hawkshead
Esthwaite Water
Sawrey
Brantwood

Langdale

Elter Water

OLD MAN OF CONISTON

Coniston Water

Ulverston

SCAFELL PIKE

Seathwaite

DUDDON VALLEY

Wasdale Head

Ulpha

Millom

Wast Water

Bowderdale

Gosforth

Seascale

Irish Sea

● Towns or villages
◉ Houses, castles
    Railway
    National Park Boundary
    Hunter Davies's routes

Kms
0   4   8   12   16
0   2   4   6   8   10
                      miles
Scale

A Walk Around the Lakes

A Walk Around the Lakes

Observations
relative chiefly to the
Picturesque Beauty,
for those desirous of being guided to the
Lake District
in the North-West of England;
particularly the
Lakes, Mountains and Valleys,
made on a pedestrian tour in the year 1978;
and a
Consideration
of the many
Eminent and Literary Personages
associated with Cumbria,
particularly
Mr William Wordsworth
by

Hunter Davies, BA

Weidenfeld and Nicolson
LONDON

For Margaret,
a true Cumbrian...

CONTENTS

Contents

ILLUSTRATIONS

INTRODUCTION

THE LAKE DISTRICT IS UP IN THE TOP LEFT-HAND CORNER OF England, a round blob on the map, usually in dull brown to indicate that it's hilly. It's bordered on the right-hand side by the M6 motorway and if you were driving fast you could be past it in half an hour and hardly have realised. Even inside the Lake District, if you got up early and walked really well you could be right across it in a day. It's only forty miles from side to side. As walks go, it's not very far.

The hills are hilly for England, but Scotland has more and bigger; and compared with the Alps or the Himalayas, they're just wrinkles in a rather small rug. The lakes are large for England, but only drops compared with lakes in the United States of America. So what's all the fuss. Why, for two hundred years, has there been an incessant stream of guide books. Why has such a small patch attracted so many famous people. Why do millions of the unfamous go to the Lakes for their holidays each year and dream of perhaps one day living there. Why has more poetry and prose been written about the Lake District than about any other single district of England.

'I do not know any tract of country in which, in so narrow a compass, may be found an equal variety in the influences of light and shadow upon the sublime and beautiful features of the landscape.'

So wrote William Wordsworth in his *Guide to the Lakes*, which dates back to 1810. He was a local, born and bred, but when he wrote those words he had seen most of Europe's beautiful features. He was still convinced that Lakeland was supreme.

The variety is extraordinary. In one small plot you have everything of England: lush pastures, twee cottages, stately castles, romantic valleys, lakeside resorts, hidden tarns, smooth hills, wild fells, sudden waterfalls, open heather, rough moorland, frightening crags, dramatic snow-clad mountain tops. It's nature's miniature kingdom. The peaks rarely get above three thousand feet but, despite their size, enough people fall off them each year, finding them not as cuddly as they may look. Because of the unusual geological and climatic conditions, you can experience almost everything in a very short space and in a very short time, going sometimes from a Mediterranean heat to sub-arctic conditions in just a two-hour climb. Yet the scale is all so manageable. There is no place you can't escape from and be in complete isolation in half an hour, even on the busiest bank holiday.

I have spent the last year wandering round the Lakes. I thought I knew it well, having been brought up in Carlisle, the area's biggest town, but now I know how much I still have to learn. It was a planned wandering. The Lakes are roughly circular so I set myself to wander roughly in a circle, taking in every famous lake, climbing most of the best-known mountains, visiting the best-loved valleys and villages. I wanted to guide those just beginning and yet satisfy those who already know it well.

I talked to those who have their life and living in the Lakes, from shepherds to squires, as well as to tourists and preservationists, and heard their problems and their pleasures. On my journey, I made sure I visited or observed those distinctly Cumbrian activities, like fell running and wrestling, so that by the end of the book, I hope, there emerges a fairly rounded picture of life in the Lakes today. I didn't simply want topographical listings, dehumanised walks, places without people. The book stalls are crammed with those.

At the same time, I followed the past. I visited and tried to recapture the lives of those famous people – most of them writers – who came to the Lakes and who in turn gave the Lakes to a wider world, such as Beatrix Potter and John Ruskin. Most of all, I followed the steps of William Wordsworth and that group known to the world as the Lakes' Poets.

Wordsworth's life was long and at times rather dramatic and I've used him as a secondary narrative, splitting his life into chunks, which is what happened anyway, as he moved round the Lakes. It's a common device in fiction, to have two running stories, one in the past and one in the present, but not in non-fiction, so I hope you will forgive what may be an early clumsiness, until, I hope, the two stories blend together. I believe that some knowledge of Wordsworth is vital to a real appreciation of the Lakes.

I took almost a year over the journey, wanting to experience the different seasons and the different sorts of activities, and I split it into sections, researching and then investigating. I took trains and cars and boats as I popped up and down and back and forth but it is essentially a walking book. I covered the route itself on foot. Sometimes I had some of my family with me, as I wanted to share such pleasures as getting to the top of Scafell Pike, but mostly I was on my own.

I could do it all again. I now know the valleys I never saw; the people who were out when I called; the rows I never saw resolved. But it was only one year in the life of the Lakes. The nicest year I have ever spent.

London NW5
January 1979

3

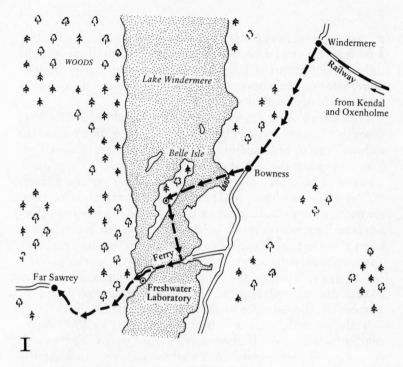

I

WINDERMERE

On arriving at England's largest lake.
A discovery on Belle Isle. Some strange
adventures on the Bowness ferry.

I GOT OFF THE INTER-CITY TRAIN AT OXENHOLME WHICH IS far from a city and far from anything at all but, if you get the right mainline train to Glasgow from Euston, you can be dropped there, right on the doorstep to the Lakes in three and a quarter hours. Isn't British Rail wonderful.

They didn't think railways were so wonderful, back in 1844 when this branch line was first proposed. They didn't want the railway to go from Oxenholme right into the heart of the Lakes. You never knew the sort of people it might attract. Wordsworth was one of the chief campaigners against this Lakeland railway and wrote furious letters and pamphlets, warning the public that the native gentry would be driven out and that the new industrialists from Lancashire would be 'flitting to and fro between their fancy villas and the homes where their wealth was accumulated'. Even worse than the second-homers would be the working classes on day trips. 'Look at the little town of Bowness in the event of such railway inundations. What would become of it, not the Retreat but the Advance of the Ten Thousand!'

Today the little local railway goes only as far as Windermere, thanks to Wordsworth and his fellow protestors. The railway was never allowed to go further into the Lakes to reach Ambleside and Grasmere and disturb the peace and tranquillity of Wordsworth's own home at Rydal Mount where he was then living, a grand old man in his late seventies, recently made Poet Laureate, a revolutionary who had been confirmed as a reactionary and was raging against most changes in the Lakes. He was of course proved correct. When it's a fine bank holiday in Bowness today, it seems more like the Advance of the Ten Million.

But it was early January when I got on to the local train at Oxenholme, the second day of a new year. The passengers from Euston had all seemed businessmen, severe in their suits, sitting silently alone studying their statistics, or loudly in threesomes discussing office politics, re-organising their firm, the whole industry, promoting themselves to the top. I could still hear their voices as they sped off towards Carlisle taking the twentieth century with them and leaving me in a toy-town station with an empty train to Windermere, or so I had imagined. It turned out to be almost full. Huge rucksacks had appeared from nowhere and hanging on to them were students in the inevitable shapeless orange and blue anoraks. Students as a whole have changed drastically in the twenty years since I was one, in looks and attitudes, but these ones, spending their Christmas holidays in the Lakes, just as I used to do, looked exactly the same: scruffy, spotty, rather serious. The Lakes must attract a special breed. The label on the rucksack of the student beside me said the owner came from King's College, Cambridge. And the name was female. I didn't want to inspect too closely, as it would take some delving into the depths of her tent-like anorak to find absolute proof of her sex, but I wondered what Wordsworth would have thought, having girls at his old university. Think of the pamphlets of complaint he would have written.

We trundled through Kendal, climbing all the time, and in half an hour we had reached Windermere where the rucksacks got off, closely followed by their owners. I'd hoped for snow, as the radio at home in London had said there was snow in Carlisle, but the sun was forcing its way through. Windermere was gleaming, sharp and empty, with the streets gently shining from some overnight rain.

You have to start at Windermere for any tour of the Lakes. Everybody does and always has done. Even before the railway, it was the way into the heartland. Windermere is the biggest lake in the Lake District, some ten miles long and a mile wide, and is by far the best known and the most glamorous. Glamour in the North of England? Several other lakes are more beautiful, some are more mysterious, many are more hidden and undiscovered, but Windermere has definite Hollywood appeal. All those industrialists whom Wordsworth feared built palatial summer houses on the slopes of the lake and today it looks a bit like Beverly Hills. And there is still a lot of money around. You can feel it in the landscaped trees and gardens that protect these luxury houses from the eyes of the day trippers.

Down on the lake, especially on the eastern side, all the bays and promontories bristle and bustle with very smart yachts. Even in the winter, enough lie at rest to make you think you're at the real seaside. With the sun shining through the pine trees at the edge of the blue lagoons, it can look positively Mediterranean.

The small town called Windermere, where the railway ends, is not on Windermere itself. Until 1847, when the Kendal and Windermere line was opened, it was a little hamlet called Birthwaite. You have to go down the hillside for about a mile in order to reach the lake. But it burst into commercial life with the arrival of the railway, becoming a booming holiday resort, full of hotels and guest houses; it now has a population (with Bowness) of 8,500. There's nothing nicer in winter than a seaside resort which is what Windermere basically is – but even in the height of the summer Windermere can still be attractive. There are indeed hordes of cars, caravan sites, bulging caffs, and almost standing room only on the lake itself. When all the big yachts and motor boats come out to play, the little rowing boats have to struggle like tadpoles in the shallows round the edges. Windermere might then appear vulgar to some eyes but it's never flash or scruffy or strident. It's been carefully commercialised. The tourists are not vile, nor are the amenities. Only the cars are truly horrid. And as with absolutely everywhere in the Lakes, you can quickly leave people behind.

The steamers weren't running yet, the ones run by British Rail which go up and down the lake, from Ambleside down to Lakeside at the southern tip of the lake, taking in Bowness as the halfway mark. They run from late May to mid-September, plus the Easter holiday weekend, and have been a great feature of Windermere for the last hundred years. At one time, before British Rail, there were rival steam companies who fought out noisy battles to attract customers, offering cut-price fares and brass bands. (It could be said, therefore, that Windermere is *less* vulgar today. Monopolies do tend to go quietly about their business.)

In the middle of Windermere is an island called Belle Isle. In the summer, a little boat runs a private service, taking tourists across to visit the thirty-eight-acre island. On the island is a unique stately home, the only truly circular house in the country, one of the best-known features of Windermere for the last 200 years. I'd marked it down as my first visit. The owner, Edward Curwen, had kindly agreed to come across in his boat to Bowness to pick me up.

The Romans are thought to have used Belle Isle and there was a house of sorts there during the Civil War when the owner was a Royalist and got himself blockaded on the island by the Roundheads for ten days. The present, circular house was built by a Mr English in 1774 – according to Wordsworth he was the first man to settle in the Lake District for the sake of the scenery – and his architect was John Plaw, later a master builder in Westminster, responsible for Montague House, Portman Square. The house is an exact circle, fifty-four feet in diameter, with the portico over the front door being the only point which projects. Architects always have great fun inspecting it, working out how he got rid of the sewage (there's an unseen pit under the house) and how he disguised the flues and chimneys (they're brought up to the middle of the house, forming a dome at the top which also contains the window lights to the main stair well; very cunning).

The locals of the time were not impressed, hating the new house and the way the island was being landscaped and laid bare to give maximum views. Mr English got fed up with all the moans and in 1781 sold the island and house, on which he'd already spent £6000, to Isabella Curwen for £1720. She was sixteen and the heiress to Workington Hall and the Curwen estates, a member of an ancient local family, which had made a fortune out of the west Cumberland coal mines. She put back the trees and appeased the locals and the house today is almost as it was built.

Mr Edward Curwen is her great-great-great-great-grandson. Until ten years ago his name was Edward Chance, a member of another equally illustrious Cumbrian family. His mother was a Curwen and when she died he inherited the Curwen estates, on two conditions. He had to change his name to Curwen and he had to take on the Curwen coat of arms, which meant getting the Queen's signature. In return he got Belle Isle and 3000 acres in west Cumberland, half of which he had to sell off to pay the £300,000 estate duties.

Five years ago, to help pay the running costs, Mr Curwen and his wife opened it to visitors. In the season, she and his mother-in-law act as guides while he's the boat man, ferrying trippers back and forward at 60p a time, something of a change for a man who, when he inherited the island, was a Lieutenant Commander in the Royal Navy. The house has been much loved by artists over the centuries and inside there's a Reynolds and two Romneys, amongst others. The best known Romney, of Isabella Curwen, is now in the Smithsonian, Washington, sold off in the 1930s for estate duties. 'I saw it myself quite recently, going round Washington as a tourist. They have a room stacked high with Romneys, four or five deep, with about thirty on a wall. As an Englishman, it rather grieved me.'

We went round the twenty-bedroomed house, which is bigger inside than it appears, with hidden staircases, meant only for the servants. There are no corridors, as it's circular, and the rooms all connect. The furniture was especially built and fits so cleverly that you're hardly aware that all the main rooms have a curved side. Mr Curwen is philosophical about having to open it up (receiving 6000 visitors in 1977) and sees the continuing growth of tourism as inevitable. 'It's like an avalanche that cannot be reversed. The planning people are always ten years behind with their predictions.' The lake is now heavily polluted in summer, with all the motor boats, and he wouldn't dare let his children swim in it. Then there's the drone of the engines which can be heard all season. He hates all that. But the romance of it all, living in a circular house on your own island. Terribly Arthur Ransome. Wasn't that worth it? He seemed unaware of actually living on an island, treating his boats (they're a five-boat family) like motor cars which have to be driven back and forward to the shops, just like anywhere else. Getting oil and coal delivered to the island, that was a problem, and getting in and out of the boats on rainy days, but that was about all. No, he didn't feel at all remote or cut off. Civilisation was all too close, though he feels that Bowness and Ambleside, as tripper traps, aren't anywhere as bad as Keswick. (In Keswick, people will tell you that Keswick is nowhere as bad as Bowness and Ambleside.)

William Wordsworth's son John married a Curwen so I asked what relation that made him to the poet. He had no idea. But hold on, he said, he had found a handwritten sonnet in an old trunk which he'd never got round to showing to any expert. He dug it out and I opened it with great excitement, copying down the first few lines, 'Geordano, verily thy pencil's skills...'

It wasn't good poetry, not even by late Wordsworth standards, but this was my first visit on the Wordsworth trail and it looked as if I'd stumbled on an unknown sonnet. What a beginning. I'd already done some Wordsworth research and, judging by the date (Rydal Mount, Feb. 11, 1846) and a note at the top saying the poem had been inspired by his son returning from Italy with a painting (doubtless the same son who married a Curwen), I was already pretty sure it was a genuine Wordsworth sonnet. I said I would tell the experts when I got to Dove Cottage.

Take it with you, he said, thrusting it at me. That day I'd already lost my best biro and a map, so I made an excuse and declined. As he ferried me back to Bowness, I told him I had written down enough information to tell the experts. He should keep the sonnet safe till they arrived, that's if they were interested. You know what experts can be like.

Back at Bowness, I walked slowly round the lake shore, heading for the ferry right across the lake. This ferry runs all the year round, though it had been closed the previous day, being New Year's Day bank holiday. It's such a vital link for those who live on the west of Windermere, connecting them, whether they like it or not, with the civilised world, that they must feel rather isolated when it's not running. In the height of the season it must be even more annoying, having to queue up to get across. The ferry has always been one of the arteries of the Lake District, connecting the old Westmorland, which used to be on the east of the lake, with the north-west tip of Lancashire, on the west of the lake. Since 1974 it's all been Cumbria.

There were only four cars on the ferry. The water was calm and quiet and the boat hardly seemed to move, which isn't too surprising as it's not a conventional motor boat. It pulls itself across the lake on two chains. It always therefore keeps a straight line. To the right I could see Belle Isle and through the trees I could just make out a bit of the house.

I did a spot check on the four cars on board the ferry. In the first car was a young couple from Oxford who were driving from Inverness, where they had spent Christmas They seemed a long way off their route but they said they always made a detour to take in the Lakes. If the rain held off, they would walk round Esthwaite Water. If not, they'd have a poke round Hawkshead. In the next car was a marine biologist, heading for the Freshwater Biological Station across the lake, beside the ferry landing stage. They analyse the water in all the lakes, count the plants, examine the fish and other amusements. He said he had previously been in Kenya but much preferred living in the Lakes.

In the next car was an Australian couple who'd arrived in the Lakes only minutes earlier, having just booked into a hotel in Windermere, and were now off on their first exploration. They had driven up from Liverpool that morning where they'd visited his mother. They thought it was all really wonderful, what they'd seen so far anyway. The fourth car was a mini-bus, a twelve-seater Transit van which had emblazoned on its sides 'Mountain Goat'. I thought at first it must be from New Zealand, mistaking the drawing of the goat for a kiwi. It was empty but for the driver who said he was called Chris Taylor and the operator of a mini-bus service round the Lakes.

Scientifically, it wasn't much of a controlled sample, though

I'm sure Ph.Ds have been written on less than a random group of four, but it was an interesting winter cross-section. Two visitors (one of them from abroad) and two locals, both of whom worked in the Lakes, though neither was a native. No doubt the Cumbria Tourist Board could feed the figures into a computer and have a lot of fun.

I tried to chat to the ferryman but only got his name, Harold Gidman. He said he wasn't allowed to give out information about the running of the ferry. No, he couldn't talk without permission from the very top. Had I stumbled on a branch of MI5? Perhaps that Freshwater Biological Station was in it as well. It certainly looked very suspicious. Perhaps everyone on the ferry was a spy.

The Mountain Goat man had been watching me and was highly amused at the ferryman's reluctance, telling him not to be so scared. At last the ferryman said he would ring his superiors, when he had the time. There's no phone on board but on the next crossing he might be able to stop long enough to get to one. I decided to leave him for the way back and went off with the Mountain Goat. He offered to drive me to a pub just up the road which he could highly recommend: The Tower Bank Arms. It's unusual as pubs go, in not only being owned by the National Trust, which isn't too rare as they own bricks and mortar all over the country, but also managed by the National Trust. Jean Williams, the lady behind the bar, is an employee of the National Trust and had previously worked in one of their country parks. She said the new life was lovely. The ferry limits the arrivals, delivering them a load at a time. 'It would be murder if there was a bridge across Windermere.'

We sat round a huge log fire and had real ale from the wood and generous sandwiches and Chris Taylor talked about his herd of Mountain Goats. He's from Sussex, went to school in Yorkshire and did odd advertising jobs, in London and in Australia, before coming to the Lakes five years ago when his parents retired up here. His grandparents had their holiday home on Windermere, part of that very grand industrial squirearchy who knew how to holiday, back in the good old days. His grandfather was a director of a chemical firm that went to form ICI and in the twenties he would take two coaches on the train up from Liverpool, one for his family and one for the servants. They would get off the train at Lakeside, at the foot of Windermere, and then go up the lake by steamer where their family coaches would be waiting to take them all to the big house for the whole of the summer. It was the highlight of the year for all the children. Chris, now aged forty, had come back to the Lakes to try and recapture some of his childhood memories, though at the time he had no idea how he would earn a living.

When he heard that Ribble Buses were giving up one of their routes from Windermere to Glenridding, he thought he'd apply for the licence and do it himself, despite opposition to his application from rival firms. He bought a second-hand mini-bus for £2000, christened it Mountain Goat, and drove it himself for six months. Now, five years later, he has seven Mountain Goat mini-buses and three large buses and a staff of sixteen. His brother has joined him, looking after their newly formed holiday side. The Mountain Goat holidays seem an excellent idea. Anyone who has ever walked in the Lakes knows the drag of getting to the starting point of your walk. Getting back afterwards is even worse, thanks to the poor local bus service. The ideal is to plan a round walk, but very often you have to come back almost the way you went. What Mountain Goat holidays do is provide drivers and mini-buses and guides who take you to the beginning of the good walks, guide you across if so desired, and then pick you up at the end. They also provide hotels for an inclusive price. So far they seem mainly to attract the elderly but I'm sure young people would like them as well. End of commercial.

The bus side of the business, running a scheduled service, had proved very hard work. 'I'm always in danger of doing the schedules so tight that I leave no time for the bus to stop and pick up.' But it was now running at a small profit. 'We can't rely on the locals to pay for the scheduled service. We need the tourists in the summer to make it possible.' The holiday side looked a winner, after only one season, though they had got carried away and printed 20,000 brochures – 10,000 of which they still had left. Chris has his own offset printing press and designs and prints his timetables and brochures, a bit of experience and knowledge left over from his advertising days.

They still have some opposition from rival firms, including the big ones who have long since abandoned the country services that he now provides. 'They oppose my tours by describing it as "abstraction of traffic" which means they're scared I'm taking their passengers away.' Another of his problems is that he can't have priority or make any advance bookings on the ferry. It only takes twelve vehicles at a time so he has to wait in a long queue in the summer, like everyone else. He therefore can't build any schedule round the ferry, which cuts off half of Windermere.

He was very pleased on the whole with his new life, though he wished he didn't have to work so hard and could spend more time playing the banjo. He didn't look like a banjo player, being tall and very public schoolish with short hair and gentlemanly manners, but then what do banjo players look like? He also sings and is a member of a pub group in Bowness, the New Hall Jazz Band. His ambition is to retire early and go sailing every day.

I said I had better get back to the ferry, just in case MI5 had given permission for the ferryman to spill the beans, though I knew from long experience of chatting up minor officials that the time spent in persuading them is always in inverse ratio to what they finally have to say.

While waiting for Mr Gidman I poked my head into the entrance hall of the Freshwater Biological Station, a handsome building. It did seem strange. I studied a list of the scientists and officers which included Professor Fogg, Dr Droop, Mr Woof, Dora Wappett, Mrs Heron, Dr Hilda Canter, Dr Crisp and J. A. B. Bass. If it wasn't MI5 then it must be Beachcomber. A young lady asked if I needed any help so I bought a booklet, 'A Key to the Nymphs of The British Species of Ephemeroptera' by T. T. Macan, price 60p, which I thought might provide some light reading for the train back to London.

I was proved wrong when at last Mr Gidman appeared. I had a most interesting chat with him on the way back across Windermere on his ferry. He'd looked a worried, nervous figure on the way across but he grew in stature as he told me about his previous job – working on the Wall of Death at Belle Vue, Manchester. Before that he was a speedway driver in Bradford and before that he was a trapeze artist in the circus. Life must seem so boringly safe, being pulled across Windermere on a couple of chains all day long. His parents, who had had a garage in Cheshire, had retired to Sawrey and he had been staying with them when he had spotted the advertisement in the local paper for the ferry job. That was six years ago. In the summer there were two men on duty to cope with the crowds, but he was on his own in the winter and he liked that much better. 'I have more time to chat to people.' His private life is still fairly eventful. He'd rowed to the Isle of Man the previous summer, in an ordinary little rowing boat, with a French man, a friend of his with whom he goes hang gliding. They'd previously tried to row all the way to Ireland but after fourteen hours gave up when halfway across. Why does he do it all? 'Well,' he said slowly, 'You could say it's for the achievement, that's why I do it.'

The lights were sparkling in the dusk as we approached the Bowness side of Windermere. Once again I thought how luxurious the hillside looked with its proud country mansions of the Lancashire cotton kings, many with their private piers and landing stages, currently changing hands for at least £100,000. Like so much of Lakeland, from the ferryman to the Mountain Goat, developments big and small are so often run by outsiders, people attracted for a variety of reasons to live and work or just retire to the Lakes. Thank goodness that Lakeland's best-known resident was a true native.

2

HAWKSHEAD

Mr Wordsworth's birth and hard times. His happy school days. Hawkshead revisited. An interesting connection.

WILLIAM WORDSWORTH USED TO TAKE THE FERRY ACROSS Windermere every term when he went from home in Cockermouth or Penrith to school in Hawkshead. It wasn't of course the same boat, but the ferry was in the same place, making the same daily trips and no doubt Wordsworth looked back and wondered at the posh houses springing up on the lakeside at Bowness.

I was on the trail of Wordsworth, following his life and his mysteries, as well as making a pilgrimage round all the lakes. I wanted to visit most of the places associated with famous people and famous events but Wordsworth and his circle would provide the main fascination, as he has done for the last 150 years, ever since people first came specially to the Lakes to gape at him.

Wordsworth was born in Cockermouth on 7 April 1770, the second eldest in a family of five. His father John was a lawyer who worked as a steward for Sir James Lowther, one of the richest landowners in the North of England. The Wordsworth house, in the main street of Cockermouth, was, and still is, the handsomest house in that very pretty west Cumbrian town. You can go round it today and admire its beautiful Georgian front and imposing gate piers, inspect the fine rooms and furniture, much of it owned by Wordsworth himself, and look at the excellent portraits of Wordsworth and the other Lakes' writers. There's even a fine landscape by Turner who once stayed at Cockermouth Castle with his patron, Lord Egremont. But the house itself was never owned by the Wordsworths. It came with the job and was always owned by the Lowther family. The precise financial relationship between John Wordsworth and the Lowthers has never been made clear. From the records it looks as if John Wordsworth never paid any rent. At the same time, he didn't get much of a salary, if any. He worked himself into an early grave for the Lowther family and got very little for his trouble. Sir James Lowther controlled nine parliamentary seats and one of Wordsworth's father's jobs was to go round at election time, keeping the voters sweet with money and other favours. He had a small property of his own which brought in a small income. He was also coroner of Millom, a position he got through Lowther influence.

Wordsworth's mother was Ann Cookson, daughter of a

linen draper in Penrith, on the east side of Cumberland. The Cooksons lived over the shop in the market square. They had some landed relations and considered themselves as belonging to the 'Penrith upper classes', despite being only shop keepers. Penrith, then as now, is a little market town with a decided lack of upper-class folk, though the surrounding area is still rich in squirearchy.

William went for a time to school in Cockermouth where one of the pupils was Fletcher Christian, of mutiny on the *Bounty* fame. The Christians were neighbours of the Wordsworths in Cockermouth. (It's interesting to note that during this period Cockermouth, for all its smallness and isolation, produced three people who, in completely different ways, went on to national recognition – the other being John Dalton who produced the theory of the atom in 1808.)

There are few records of Wordsworth's school days in Cockermouth but quite a lot about the dame school he later attended in Penrith, his mother's home town. At this school William and Dorothy, his only sister who was twenty-one months younger, became close friends of the Hutchinson children. From his mother, Wordsworth was taught a love of the countryside and they went on picnics and expeditions to places like the Penrith Beacon, the local landmark. Wordsworth's father is a more shadowy figure, forever travelling round Cumberland on his master's business, but he taught William to learn chunks of Milton and Shakespeare by heart and introduced him to the novels of Fielding.

Wordsworth was unhappy with his Penrith relations, with whom he was forced to spend so much of his early years. They had aspirations to gentility and considered him wild and unruly, too full of animal spirits. Even his own mother found him a handful and predicted that William would be memorable—'either for good or evil'. Dorothy, in later years, remembered many tears being associated with their time in Penrith and how their uncles disliked William.

It all became worse in 1778 when William was almost eight and his mother died. It looks as if she caught pneumonia which had been caused, so the family thought, by sleeping on a damp bed while on a visit to London. Dorothy was sent away to live with other relations, firstly in Yorkshire, and was very upset to be separated from William. In 1779 William and his brothers were sent away to school at Hawkshead, on the other side of the Lakes, where he was free at last of his Penrith relations and where he found for himself a substitute home.

Hawkshead was in those days a prosperous market town, a centre for the wool and cloth trade. This local industry, which centred round Kendal, had been flourishing since the fourteenth century, though the industrial revolution was eventually to move the factories south to Lancashire and Yorkshire. Industry as a whole was booming in Cumberland and Westmorland, a factor which is forgotten today. The west coast, where Wordsworth's father did most of his work, was in at the beginning of the coal and shipping and early industrial boom, thanks to the investments and developments by the Lowther family. In 1780, Whitehaven was the second port in the land, coming after London, but before Liverpool, Bristol and Newcastle.

The little grammar school in Hawkshead had been founded in 1585 by Edwin Sandys, Archbishop of York, a native of the parish, and was noted for its scholarship. Education was free, except for an annual entrance fee of one guinea for those who came from outside the immediate area. Twelve local charity boys got everything free, including board and lodgings. The boys ranged from sons of professional people, such as the young Wordsworths, to the sons of humble yeoman farmers. The masters were all clerics, mostly graduates of Cambridge, and there were a hundred boys in the school in Wordsworth's time, some having come from as far away as Edinburgh and Hawick, though the great majority were from the valleys and villages of the surrounding Lake District.

Wordsworth and his brothers boarded while at Hawkshead school with Ann Tyson, a joiner's widow, who looked after the motherless boys with great love and affection. Each boy paid twelve guineas a year for his lodgings which didn't leave much for many luxuries. Each boy was charged extra for candles, coals, sugar and tea.

Wordsworth was now living in the heart of the Lake District (Penrith and Cockermouth are on the fringes), right beside Esthwaite Water, but also within easy walking distance of Windermere and Coniston. Even at the age of ten, in his first winter in Hawkshead, he was out roaming the fells half the night. He was allowed absolute freedom outside school hours and spent his time fishing, skating on Esthwaite Water, bird watching and birds' egg stealing. His love of skating stayed with him all his life. It was during these school years at Hawkshead, between the ages of nine and seventeen, that he first started to have his visions. On his long walks up the valleys and over the fells, he often entered dream-like trances when he felt himself at one with nature. This retreat into a spiritual communion with nature is today thought by some Wordsworth watchers (especially the Freudian ones) to be a direct effect of his mother dying and his unhappy times with his Penrith relations. This state is not uncommon amongst sensitive adolescents, at least for a while, but it was a state Wordsworth never forgot. He started writing poems at school, encouraged by the headmaster who was a great lover of poetry, and his first known verses were written in 1785 to commemorate the school's bicentenary.

In 1783 his father died. He was riding home at Christmas time from Millom where he had been conducting an inquest when he lost his way on Cold Fell, spent the night without shelter on the exposed hillside and never recovered. From then on, not only was Wordsworth an orphan but he was beset with endless money problems. His father had died with his affairs hopelessly complicated and with Sir James Lowther (who became Earl of Lonsdale in 1784) owing him £4700 in legal and political fees. Various uncles took over the guardianship of Wordsworth and his brothers and they tried hard, with no luck, to get the money out of the Lowther family. They were strict and severe and still didn't care much for William personally, especially all that wandering round the fells spouting his own poetry, and he in turn never got on with them. The only nice family event around this period was the rediscovery of Dorothy, during his last year at Hawkshead, whom he met again when she returned to live with their relations in Penrith. They hadn't seen each other for nine years.

In 1787 Wordsworth went up to St John's College, Cambridge. His Uncle Richard advanced £400 for his education at Cambridge, a debt which Wordsworth worked hard for many years to repay, not finally settling it till 1813. Despite going up to Cambridge, he returned to Hawkshead in the holidays, going back to Mrs Tyson and his old digs, the only real home he had. Ann Tyson's account book records the purchase of velvet at 5s 6d and silk at 4s 9d for William, who needed a fine velvet coat for evening wear at Cambridge.

At Cambridge, the image of young William had taken on quite

a transformation. He had gone up an intense, very serious scholar, miles ahead in Euclid, having promised his guardian, who had forked out the money for his university education, that he would be ordained and then try for a college fellowship, thus insuring his financial independence. Hawkshead Grammar had a fine tradition of producing such scholars – and Wordsworth's younger brother Christopher became one. Wordsworth's whole university career is a bit short on detail, and surrounded in some mystery, but it is recorded that he quickly dropped mathematics altogether. In his exams in the first term of his first year he was placed in the first class – but from then on he went downhill, preferring to devote himself to other interests. He had the feeling, so he wrote, that at Cambridge he was 'not for that hour, nor for that place'. He violently disliked the compulsory twice daily chapel attendance and attacked the system, much to the displeasure of his guardians. He was also against competitive examinations. Instead of concentrating on his Latin and Greek, he got himself private lessons in modern Italian. His guardians were naturally incensed, seeing him as a young man wasting his time and their money.

When he arrived back in Hawkshead for his holidays, he was very much the Cambridge dandy, prancing around in his fine clothes which he refers to in a line in his vast autobiographical poem, 'The Prelude' – 'my habiliments, the transformation and the gay attire'. He did put on his old clothes when he went back to his former pleasure, walking round the lakes and fells. It was during this holiday that he began to write 'An Evening Walk', which became his earliest published poem.

At Cambridge he took up dancing and spent a lot of time during his Hawkshead holidays at smart country dances. He would come home at four in the morning, weary with pleasure, and pass the farm workers going to the fields. After one country dance at a farm two miles from Hawkshead, he described the evening as having been a 'promiscuous rout, a medley of all tempers'.

Wordsworth's later image, which he did a lot to encourage by carefully missing out certain early episodes in 'The Prelude', is of a very serious and terribly upright gentleman. But it seems obvious that as a young student he acted very much as so many young students have always acted, running up debts, living a gay social life, disliking the academic system, prancing about in his holidays. He always enjoyed coming home to Hawkshead. His first love was a local girl, though little is known about her. Hawkshead had been his real home for most of his life, from the age of nine until he was nineteen, and so naturally he was very fond of it. Today in Hawkshead, they're quite fond of him.

Hawkshead is probably as prosperous as ever it was in Wordsworth's days, thanks to tourism. It's the most beautifully preserved small town in the whole of the Lakes with interconnecting little squares, overhung seventeenth-century timber-framed buildings, narrow cobbled streets and some very handsome houses, formerly the homes of the wool merchants. There are several old coaching inns, where the horses were watered and rested after their ride up from the ferry, and a whole host of olde-worlde tea shoppes and gifte shoppes, all in genuinely olde buildings, but selling the usual Lakeland tourist tat. In the season Hawkshead gets very crowded, but they have made a large car park at the edge of the town, beside a rather nasty-looking modern restaurant called The Norseman, which at least encourages visitors to explore the town on foot, as it should be done.

I went first to look for the grammar school and was amazed by its smallness. It's largely as Wordsworth knew it, yet it seems impossible to believe that a hundred boys were ever taught there. The ground floor is one huge classroom, with the original pews laid out as they used to be. Wordsworth's desk is still in its old position, carved with a mass of initials of long-since-forgotten pupils. It has a glass cover, just in case anyone should be tempted to add to it. The room is dark and scholarly and it takes time to get accustomed to the gloom. It still has the atmosphere of the eighteenth century, of long hours spent learning the classics by rote. On the walls are mementoes of Archbishop Sandys, the founder, and his sons who were amongst the backers for the Pilgrim Fathers' voyage to America. This school produced many notables, apart from Wordsworth, such as Sir Daniel Rawlinson who became a Lord Mayor of London.

There are fine collections of contemporary books, the ones Wordsworth read and was taught from, and details of the school work of himself and his brothers. I noticed that a reference to his younger brother Christopher which said, wrongly, that he had gone on to Trinity College, Dublin, had been carefully altered by hand to Trinity College, Cambridge.

I was alone in the school that day and I tried to chat to the caretaker, an old, rather wheezy man who returned to reading his paperback in a dark corner after I paid my 5p. It was a thriller called *Died in the Wool*, rather apt for such a town. There was no literature to buy and a complete lack of any commercialisation. When you think how few eighteenth-century schools there are in such excellent condition, compared with the number of eighteenth-century churches which positively bombard you with leaflets and mementoes, you'd have thought they'd have tried harder. He said he was just helping out his wife. She was the proper caretaker. He wasn't personally interested in Wordsworth. 'I got enough of him at school.' The upstairs classrooms were locked and he said I would have to write to the trustees for permission to view them. Then he agreed that as there was no one else around, he'd lock the downstairs room for a few minutes and take me upstairs, which was very good of him.

He led me into two dusty classrooms, crammed with book cases, which looked as if Wordsworth and the other pupils had only just popped out, perhaps gone away for the holidays. In one of the rooms I noticed a pile of Brownie and Guide badges and belongings, obviously a store room or meeting place for the local troop.

I next went round to the parish church, St Michael and All Angels, which Wordsworth described in 1788, coming home on his first vacation from Cambridge. 'I saw a snow white church upon a hill, sit like a throned lady sending out a gracious look all over her domain.' There is still a fine view over the countryside, though it's now been un-whitewashed. Inside, everything is in excellent condition, beautifully cared for, as is everything else in Hawkshead. It is hard to imagine that in 1548 a local vicar so upset the people of Hawkshead that he had to barricade himself in what is now the Old Courthouse for two days while a 'tumult of insurrection' armed with swords, bucklers, staves, bills, clubs, daggers and other weapons demanded that he come out so that they 'would have one of his arms or legs before going away'. It is not recorded what he'd done to annoy them.

I came across a nice inscription on the gravestone of a certain Thomas Cowperthwaite who died in Hawkshead in 1782 – while Wordsworth was still at the school. 'His facetious disposition,' so the stone reads, 'together with his other good qualities made him respected.' It's the use of the word facetious I like. Presumably in those days it could also mean happy.

I had a salad for lunch in a fifteenth-century building called the Minstrels' Gallery, resisting the temptation to go into a pub which was boasting Pheasant in the Basket. On the way out, I noticed a cottage for sale, Ross Cottage, so I rang the agent, out of interest. Well, it was more than interest as I was beginning to half look for a cottage, like millions of others who visit the Lakes and can't get over its beauty. After all, I needed a base for the year, especially since I'd seen the price of rented cottages. One I'd recently taken at Bowness had cost £90 for one week. Ross Cottage was only £10,500 which sounded reasonable, for such a desirable little town, though it obviously needed work done on it. But it was already under offer.

My last visit in Hawkshead was to Ann Tyson's cottage. The town as a tourist centre isn't all that Wordsworth conscious, what with the grammar school being so under-promoted and few references in the local literature to all the years he lived there, but Ann Tyson's cottage is well signposted and most shops have postcards which say that Wordsworth lived there. Alas for the postcard buyers. Wordsworth didn't live in that house, not according to the latest scholarship.

The cottage in Hawkshead marked as Ann Tyson's cottage was at one time lived in by Ann Tyson, but, by the time Wordsworth came to live with her, she had moved to another cottage about half a mile away, in the nearby hamlet of Colthouse. This piece of investigation was first done by a local sheep farmer called Mrs Heelis in the 1930s. She found the evidence in Ann Tyson's ledgers in a barn which she happened to be clearing. References in 'The Prelude' fit the Colthouse cottage theory much better than they do the Hawkshead cottage – such as a brook running through the garden and Wordsworth catching hold of a tree on his way to school. Hawkshead, then and now, is very much a built-up town.

Mrs Heelis, the lady behind the discovery, is better known to the public as Beatrix Potter. No visitor to the Lakes, especially one who has just come over the Windermere ferry, should miss her home. Wordsworth may be the greater writer and we'll be reaching his days of greatness in a later chapter, but in at least one way Beatrix Potter is today the greater attraction.

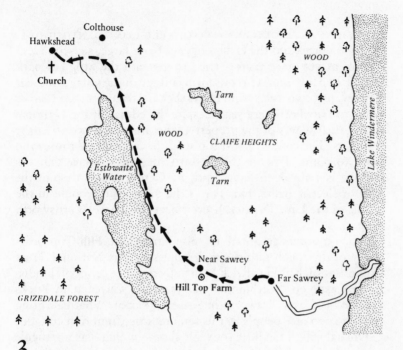

3
SAWREY

The strange tale of Beatrix Potter. An interesting meeting with an old shepherd.

THERE WAS A LOUD BRAYING OF SELF-CONFIDENT MIDDLE-class voices and the crash of gears from large, self-confident Volvos as yet more visitors tried to get into the little car park at Hill Top, an unpretentious farm cottage in the village of Near Sawrey, just two miles from Hawkshead. Around 70,000 visitors come to Hill Top every year, despite the efforts of the National Trust, the owners of the property, who are trying to restrict the numbers. The cottage is just too small to cater for all those who want to come. Despite these efforts, despite the fact that the cottage is only open from April to October, and despite the lack of electric lights, Hill Top is the most visited home in the whole of the Lake District. It even beats the three Wordsworth homes.

When it comes to a national popularity poll, Hill Top beats many of the much grander and more spacious National Trust properties such as Hardwick Hall in Derbyshire (47,000), Lindisfarne Castle in Northumberland (51,000), Cliveden in Bucks (39,000) and even Petworth in Sussex (38,000). What can bring those 70,000 nice people to this remote little Cumbrian cottage?

Once through the little souvenir shop – which was a struggle as the well-bred kids were fighting to buy postcards – you go up a little garden path to the front door. The outside is rather dull with its murky grey rough-cast walls and its dark slate roof. Inside, the house was much more attractive. The kitchen, the first room you enter, has a stone flagged floor and a large fireplace, complete with roasting spit, a spinning wheel and a rag rug. The house dates back to the seventeenth century, a modest example of Lakeland vernacular architecture. By the fireplace are a pair of clogs, as if laid out for someone's return. The clogs were once worn by Beatrix Potter.

Hill Top Farm is the farm where Jemima Puddleduck lived. It was also the setting for Tom Kitten, Pigling Band, The Roly Poly Pudding, The Pie and the Patty-pan, Ginger and Pickles. Beatrix Potter set six of her books in Hill Top but many others contain views of Sawrey or are in some way connected with this gentle, rolling corner of the Lakes. Decades of children, in nurseries throughout the civilised world, have been brought up hardly realising that in their formative years they, too, were growing up in Hill Top Farm. No wonder there is such a scamper every year to see where the author of Peter Rabbit once lived.

Beatrix Potter was born in London in 1866, the child of rich and very conventional middle-class parents. Her father Rupert was a barrister but he never practised. Both he and his wife had inherited Lancashire cotton fortunes. Her grandfather had been a self-made cotton tycoon, a friend of Cobden and Bright, and was at one time Liberal MP for Carlisle, but Beatrix's parents considered they had moved away from such things as trade and industry, never soiling their hands with any actual work. Rupert spent his days in soft cultural pursuits, visiting museums, dabbling in photography, and passing his evenings at his club. Beatrix's mother concerned herself with undermaids and second butlers and all the Upstairs Downstairs problems of running a large Edwardian household. The house where Beatrix and her younger brother Bertram were brought up was 2 Bolton Gardens, South Kensington. 'A dark Victorian mausoleum, complete with aspidistras', so one of her cousins described it. (It was demolished by a land mine during the Battle of Britain') Bertram went away to school but it wasn't considered proper in their circles for girls to be educated so Beatrix was kept at home, living her life in the nursery quarters, under the care of governesses.

The one bright spot in the year was their annual holiday. Mr Potter, complete with family, tons of luggage and lots of servants, would decamp for three months to a rented house in Scotland or the Lake District. They didn't take little country cottages but grand residences such as Wray Castle on the shores of Windermere. Beatrix would bring back pet animals from her summer idyll, rabbits and hedgehogs, and keep them with her in her bedroom in Kensington. She gave them names, like Peter Rabbit or Mrs Tiggy Winkle, and would draw them and observe them and they would be her friends, her only friends, in the long days and nights spent in the third-floor nursery in Bolton Gardens. The only excursion she was allowed was to the Royal Academy. Even then, she didn't go alone, being taken in the family coach by the family coachman. She never thought of rebelling. She treated her parents with the utmost respect and deference, just like a true Victorian daughter.

Apart from her pet animals, her only refuge was a secret diary where she recorded her private thoughts and impressions. This was not discovered until after her death (it was found in an attic in Sawrey), and was not decoded until 1966, thanks to some ingenious detection work by Leslie Linder (*The Journal of Beatrix Potter*, Warne, 1966). She had secretly written 200,000 words, from the age of about ten until she was almost middle aged, which give minute details of her everyday life, a life that was silent and lonely, highly privileged, yet completely impoverished. Through her secret journal we see her tender aspirations, trying naïvely to find a career for herself, hoping that her interest in drawing animals would somehow turn itself into a proper job. She gets an introduction to the Royal Botanic Gardens at Kew and hopes that on the strength of some delicate drawings of fungi, she might be given some sort of position. But she has no education, no scientific training of any sort. It all comes to nothing.

So life creaked on in Kensington, staying at home with her parents, till she was well into her mid-thirties. One summer, during their stay at Wray Castle, they became family friends of Canon Rawnsley, then vicar of Wray, one of Lakeland's earliest and greatest activists. He was endlessly waging war against people who were ruining Lakeland, such as developers and railway companies. He wrote countless books, including several on the Lakes, became a Canon of Carlisle, a friend of Tennyson, a campaigner against naughty postcards, and a great organiser of bonfires. For Queen Victoria's Jubilee in 1887, 148 of his Lakeland bonfires could be seen from the top of Skiddaw. Canon Rawnsley's name lives on in Lakeland life but his greatest action, and one for which the whole nation should be truly grateful, was the founding of the National Trust.

Canon Rawnsley was one of the few people in Beatrix's family circle who enthused about her interest in nature and animals and actively encouraged her to do little drawings. It was he she turned to for advice when, in 1901, she thought of printing at her own expense a book for children called *The Tale of Peter Rabbit*.

For many years she had entertained the children of friends and relations by drawings and stories about the doings of her pet animals, such as Peter Rabbit and Mrs Tiggy Winkle, animals who were still her constant friends, who travelled with her on holiday in special baskets.

In letters to the children, she wrote about Jeremy Fisher, Tabitha Twitchet and her other animals. The letters were so popular that the idea eventually struck her of printing them as a book. She sent Peter Rabbit off to a publisher, Frederick Warne, a well-known publisher of children's books, but it was returned. Six other publishers also said no. So in 1901, with Canon Rawnsley's encouragement, she found a printer herself and he produced

250 copies at a total cost of £11. She sold them, price 1s 2d, to doting aunts and uncles for their nephews and nieces and then by word of mouth to friends of friends. Dr Conan Doyle was one of the first people to buy a copy for his family. It sold so well that she did a second edition of *The Tale of Peter Rabbit* and then she brought out a second book, *The Tailor of Gloucester*, again doing it privately. However, by the time she had published *The Tailor of Gloucester* in 1902, Warne had come back to her, saying they would, after all, do *Peter Rabbit*, but they wanted it in colour, not black and white as she had done. They became her publishers from then on.

Her third book, in 1903, was *The Tale of Squirrel Nutkin*; then came *Benjamin Bunny*, *The Tale of Two Bad Mice* and, in 1905, *Mrs Tiggy Winkle*. Tiggy Winkle was her pet hedgehog, the one she still travelled with on holidays, holidays spent in the Lake District with her parents, even though by now she was a lady approaching forty. Back in London, armed with sketches of Lakeland scenery, she worked on the book. She propped Tiggy Winkle on her knee so she could draw her – but she was too fidgety a model when it came to wearing a mob cap and apron. Instead she made a cotton-wool dummy which she dressed up, though Hunca Minca, her pet mouse, was always pulling out the stuffing.

In 1905 she was proposed to by Norman Warne, the son of her publisher, who had shown great personal interest in her books and whom she had consulted on every detail. For the previous three years she had spent a lot of time in his company. He too loved children and made dolls' houses for his favourite nieces and nephews. Her parents were very upset by the engagement. He was considered to be 'in trade' and therefore beneath Beatrix. But she went ahead and became engaged, the first time in her life she had disobeyed her parents' wishes. But in the summer of 1905, just a few weeks after their engagement, Norman Warne fell ill and died of leukaemia. In that same summer of 1905 she bought Hill Top Farm.

Beatrix Potter had seen Hill Top on holidays with her parents. She now had a bit of money from her books and she bought it as her bolt hole, a little place to escape to from London and her parents. Perhaps she had hoped to move there secretly and marry Norman, so defying her parents completely. Her brother Bertram had married secretly, going off to be a farmer on the Scottish borders. She remained the dutiful daughter, however, emotionally and physically still part of her parents' life.

For the next eight years she was based in London, still spending the main holidays with the family, only managing to spend a few months every year in Hill Top. She had a manager living in one part of the cottage, running the farm, while she lived in it herself when she could get away from London and her family. It was in these eight years, in stolen weeks at Hill Top, that she wrote the bulk of her books.

The thirteen books produced during these eight years were all good sellers, being translated into French and produced in America in pirate editions. Right from the beginning her creations were merchandised – a development which we tend to think of as being very modern. Sanderson's brought out a nursery frieze, based on Peter Rabbit and her other animals, which has sold steadily, in revised versions, for the last seventy years. She herself tried to market Peter Rabbit dolls but couldn't find a British manufacturer to produce them – the market had already been flooded with cheap German versions, pirated copies of her characters.

With her growing income Beatrix started buying up chunks of Sawrey, adding to Hill Top Farm and acquiring cottages and increasing her stock of animals. In 1909 she bought Castle Cottage, a property just across the road from Hill Top, and in so doing used local solicitors with offices in Hawkshead, W. Heelis. William Heelis was around her age, a tall, quiet bachelor who was said to look a bit like Wordsworth. They communicated when she returned to London. He kept an eye on her Sawrey properties and kept her in touch with local affairs. They became engaged, much to the displeasure of her parents. Once again, they thought he was beneath their family, being only a country solicitor. Despite attempts to dissuade her, however, they got married in October 1913 and moved into Castle Cottage. It was a bigger and more convenient farm cottage than Hill Top. Two weeks after her marriage she was called to London by her mother who wanted help with a new parlourmaid. She was by now forty-seven years old. But still she went, being the obedient daughter, leaving her husband behind.

Castle Cottage became her home for the next thirty years. She left Hill Top as it was, with the farm manager in one end. Her part of the cottage was unlived in, but kept full of furniture and possessions, exactly as she had had them. Every time she bought old plates or oak furniture or other local relics, she moved them into Hill Top. Hill Top became a personal museum – and in fact her life as Beatrix Potter, spinster author of children's books, became a museum piece. On moving into Castle Cottage she became Mrs Heelis, woman farmer. She did write a few more books over the next thirty years, mainly emptying old sketch books, but to all intents and purposes she had ceased to be a writer. She said she had no ideas. Her eyes weren't good enough to draw. She didn't have the time. The latter was certainly true. She gave herself to her property which grew enormously as she bought up farm after farm, not just around Sawrey but throughout the southern Lakes.

In 1923 she bought an estate of 2000 acres around Coniston. She became a passionate conservationist and, spurred on by the example and encouragement of Canon Rawnsley, she gave generously to the National Trust. Whenever a parcel of land came up for sale which the Trust needed to complete a section, she often bought it and gave it to them, usually anonymously.

Her speciality as a farmer was Herdwick sheep, Lakeland's own breed. She became one of the best-known breeders of Herdwick sheep in the Lakes, as well as a judge and successful exhibitor. She would talk about sheep but not of her life as Beatrix Potter, refusing interviews and trying to avoid admirers who arrived at her cottage – except for Americans. She appears to have been flattered by their serious, academic approach to her books, whereas the silly questions of English admirers tended to annoy her. But her life as Beatrix Potter was really over. It had been a means of escape from her overpowering parents and her highly restrictive upbringing. Now she was fulfilled as a farmer and as a solicitor's wife and was able to live her life completely in her beloved Lakes. As is so often the way with strangers, off-comers as they are called, she became more passionate about preserving the Lakes than many of the natives.

She spent a lot of time at sheep fairs, with her shepherds and with her sheep and walked her fells in all weathers – looking as if she walked the fells in all weathers. As she grew older, she became more and more like Mrs Tiggy Winkle in her old, poorly fitting clothes. She wore several layers of old tweed, a battered bonnet on her head, a stick in her hand and metal-shod clogs on her feet. On several occasions she was mistaken for a potter, the local term for tinker or gypsy. She was fond of telling a story against herself about an old tramp who met her as she was toiling up some fell to see her lambs, dressed in her usual rag-bag clothes and sack over her shoulders. He shouted a greeting to her: 'It's sad weather for the likes of thee and me.'

She died in 1943, aged seventy-seven, spending her last nights sitting up in bed interviewing shepherds. She left £211,636. Her flock of Herdwick sheep went to the National Trust, as well as 4000 acres. The copyright of all her works went firstly to her husband and then to a favourite nephew of Norman Warne.

It's when you go upstairs at Hill Top Farm today, passing through the bedrooms full of her stuff, her cups for her prize-winning Herdwicks, the long case clock she drew in *The Tailor of Gloucester*, that you come perhaps to the biggest attraction for all Potter lovers – the originals of her books. This is in a special gallery in which all her water colours are on display. It's a lovely sight.

I left the house and was walking in the fields beside Hill Top Farm when I came across an old man standing beside an awful smelling bonfire. He said he was burning wellingtons. We stood chatting, me being an expert on wellies and their myriad qualities, and he turned out to be an expert on Beatrix Potter. I hadn't realised there were any locals left who had worked for her, as the National Trust goes to some lengths to restrict publicity about Hill Top Farm. He said his name was Tom Storey and that for eighteen and a half years he'd worked for Mrs Heelis as a shepherd and then farm bailiff. He was aged eighty-two but looked a good twenty years younger.

In 1943, on her death, she left him £400 and instructed that, though the farm was to go to the National Trust, he should take over the tenancy. This he did, farming Hill Top Farm till he retired – handing the tenancy over to his son. He's eternally grateful for her kindness though, being a true Lakelander, there was no trace of slobby sentimentality about his memories of her.

Even now, he's surprised by the success of her books. She gave his children autographed copies of the *Fairy Caravan*, the first copies from the press, which they still have. 'You can read them all in twenty minutes,' he said, turning over the ashes of the wellies. 'Yet she made all that money from them. I can't understand it.'

In the standard biography of Beatrix Potter by Margaret Lane, it says her fellow farmers sought her opinion on Herdwicks at sheep fairs and that she was 'one of the shrewdest farmers in the Lake Country'. Other publications about Beatrix Potter speak equally highly about her great farming expertise.

'Just a fallacy,' said Mr Storey. 'What could she know about farming, coming out of London? She liked Herdwicks, right enough. She'd look at no other, but she could make mistakes when judging them. I could give you examples, but I don't like to. It wouldn't be fair, after all these years. I'll tell you just one. At Keswick Show one year we'd won everything and she was taking someone round. "These are the ewes we won with, aren't they Storey?" They weren't. They were Willy Rigg's. Ours were in the next pen...

'She wasn't a bad farmer, I'll say that. We had our flaps. We differed over some things but I didn't take much notice. I just got on with it. When you've gone through it all as a boy, you just carry on.

'I told her many a time that she'd be better off having some cattle instead of all Herdwicks. She was losing money by having just Herdwicks and I once got very worried. "Don't you worry, Storey," she told me. "It's only a hobby."'

Despite her privileged London background, which in Storey's eyes could never make her a farmer, he said she had a plain voice, not a Kensington one, and she loved to hear the real Westmorland dialect. He was obviously quite proud of her habit of dressing like an old farm hand, not displaying her wealth.

After she died on 22 December 1943, Mr Storey was having his Christmas Dinner when Mr Heelis walked into his house. 'He said "Here's the ashes, you'll know what to do with them." I'd promised her I'd scatter them. Nobody else was to know the place, not even her husband. We'd discussed it several times. I talked to her the night before she died.

'So I got up from my dinner and went off and scattered them, in the place she'd chosen. I've never told anybody where the place is. She wasn't daft. She knew folks would go and look at the place if they knew. I was sorry when she died. She was a good woman. I intend to tell my son the place before I die, so there will always be someone who knows.'

4
WORDSWORTH ABROAD

Young Mr Wordsworth's affairs in France and the West Country. A happy return to the Lakes.

WILLIAM WORDSWORTH DIDN'T COME BACK TO HAWKS-head during his last long vacation at Cambridge. He went off instead with a friend on a three month 'pedestrian tour' of France, Switzerland and northern Italy. This sort of student trip is commonplace today, at least the hitch-hiking variety, but in 1790 it was rare for young gentlemen to venture off alone round Europe, especially *walking* round Europe. The norm for young gentlemen who wanted a grand tour was to go in their own coach or, if they didn't have the money, to get themselves a job as tutor or companion to someone who did have the money and the transport. Wordsworth and his friend set off with £20 between them, a light overcoat each, an oak stick and their belongings in a large pocket handkerchief. Most of their friends thought they were mad. Wordsworth wisely didn't tell his guardians, or even Dorothy, not at least until he had arrived in France.

France was in the first heady stages of Revolution. The Bastille had been destroyed and the absolute monarchy put to rout, and Wordsworth and his friend watched many of the celebrations. 'The whole nation was mad with joy', so Wordsworth wrote to Dorothy. They walked twenty miles a day, joining in the fun at every stop. Like all right-thinking students, they approved of the Revolution and its aims.

When they got to Switzerland they found it very dull by comparison – and already being spoilt by tourists – but they loved the Italian lakes, especially Como. On the way home, they went up the Rhine by boat and took in Belgium, where again they ran into more great events – a revolution against the Belgian Emperor. It must have been a highly exciting trip for both of them. In our present times, students flocked from all over Europe to Lisbon when the Portuguese Revolution took place in 1974, just to join in the marches and demonstrations. But imagine seeing and joining in the French Revolution as it was happening. Wordsworth made copious notes and later wrote extensively about his travels, in verse and in travel essays. It had a huge effect on his early writing and thinking. In fact, judging by the excitement in his letters to Dorothy, he never enjoyed an experience more in his whole life.

> Bliss was it in that dawn to be alive,
> But to be young was very Heaven!

Then came boring old reality back in England. What was he

going to do for a living? He got his degree in 1791, but a poor one, without honours. He couldn't face the thought of the church or of the law, both of which had been vague ideas at one time, so once again, doing the full student bit, he bummed around London, spending months cadging beds and meals, doing nothing in particular. Then he bummed round Wales, staying firstly with the Cambridge friend with whom he'd gone walking in Europe. A cousin offered to fix him up with a curacy, but he refused. What he really fancied being was a tramp, just walking round for ever, if only he could find someone to supply him with £100 a year. 'I am doomed to be an idler through my whole life,' he said in a letter to a friend.

Money problems had hung over him ever since the death of his father. The legal battles continued with Lord Lonsdale, trying to get him to pay up the money which the Wordsworth family maintained he owed. At last the case came up at Carlisle Assizes in August 1791, and the family won – Lord Lonsdale being ordered to pay £5000 owed to Wordsworth's father. Divided amongst the five children, and properly invested, William worked out he would get his £100 a year after all – but Lord Lonsdale refused to pay. The case dragged on again, with the legal costs mounting in such a way that the family feared that, even if they got the money, there would be little left to distribute.

In November 1791 William decided to go back to France, on his own this time, no doubt trying to recapture the good times he had had eighteen months previously. This brings us to one of the most intriguing incidents in Wordsworth's life, one that never became public till over a hundred years later, one that you never hear about when you're learning Wordsworth at school.

He went first to Paris, where he watched the Legislative Assembly in action and visited the Jacobin club, and then in December moved to Orleans which in pre-Revolution days had been a popular city in which young Englishmen could learn French. He had an introduction to a lady writer living in Orleans – but she had gone by the time he arrived. He had very little money, leaving England with only £20, but he found some cheap digs in Orleans and got a young French girl to give him French conversation lessons – for free. The girl was called Annette Vallon, aged twenty-five, four and a half years his senior, and they fell madly in love. She became pregnant and moved back to her home village of Blois. She had only been in Orleans on a visit, staying with her brother, a noted monarchist supporter who later narrowly missed the guillotine. Annette was a Catholic, from a staunch Royalist family – her father, a surgeon, was dead – and here she was, getting mixed up with a poverty-stricken, out of work, travelling Englishman, a Protestant with strong Republican leanings. She spoke no English and Wordsworth's French wasn't much good, despite the free lessons, or perhaps because of the free lessons.

He followed her back to Blois and took digs there secretly, not being very popular with Annette's family. In December 1792 Annette moved back to Orleans, presumably because of the displeasure of her family, and had her child by William, a girl called Caroline. Two months before the birth Wordsworth had gone. He left her ostensibly to go back to England, perhaps hoping the Lonsdale money had come through, planning to return and marry her when he could support her. He went back via Paris, however – and spent *two months* there, watching and joining in other revolutionary activities – before eventually getting himself back to England.

Was it just a one-night stand, a passing, if rather passionate affair, wild oats sown by a young student having his first fling, which he had no intention of continuing once he was back in England? There is no evidence, earlier or later, of Wordsworth being a ladies' man. Did she seduce him – an older woman, picking up an amusing foreign boy? Whatever the circumstances, Wordsworth never forgot her, or his commitments. But for the fact that war soon broke out between England and France, and continued for twenty years, save for one brief lull, he would certainly have returned. He definitely planned to and if he had done so his whole life could have turned out very differently.

Annette wrote regularly to William during the war between France and England, but most of the letters were never delivered, though she never knew that at the time. They were confiscated by the French police, since they were sent to a foreign power, and lay in local French archives till they were discovered about 130 years later, which was when the whole story first became public. These letters are very tender and loving, telling him all about his daughter, hoping that very soon he can return and they will be married.

William doesn't appear to have written very often, but he confessed everything to Dorothy on his return and she wrote regularly to Annette, looking upon her as her sister, and Annette wrote to Dorothy in equally loving terms.

Meanwhile, back in England, Wordsworth had a fairly miserable time for the next two or three years. He still had money problems, his guardians were not very pleased with him, and he was torn between France and England. His guardians must have heard something of the Annette incident, if not of the baby, and Dorothy tried but failed to get permission for him to marry Annette. He hung around London and thought at one time of becoming a political journalist, but feared that as he suffered from 'nervous headaches' he wouldn't be able to stand the noise at parliamentary debates. He played a lot of cards, did a lot of late-night talking, wrote away at his poetry and other bits and pieces.

Wordsworth's first poems were published in 1793, 'An Evening Walk' (which was set in the Lakes) and 'Descriptive Sketches' (about his pedestrian tour to the Alps – the first trip, not his Annette encounter). He hoped to make some money from them, but they sold badly and were not well received, at least by the London critics. Several young men of taste, however, were very impressed by Wordsworth's talent and by his desire not to take an ordinary job but to devote himself to his genius. Some even helped with loans and gifts, just when he needed them. His best bit of luck was when he was left a legacy of £900 in 1795 by Raisley Calvert, a young friend from the Lakes whom he had helped to nurse during an illness.

In 1795 he decided to leave London. He was disappointed at the reception of his poems and felt the call of the countryside, to live simply and get back to nature. He didn't head for the Lake District, as one might have imagined, but to the West Country, purely because that was where he was offered some free, or very cheap accommodation. He went with Dorothy, his sister, and they set up house together, an idea they'd discussed for many years. Was there a feeling of guilt about the Annette affair and the mess he'd got himself into in France? Did he feel safer with Dorothy? Dorothy, anyway, was absolutely delighted.

It was here, by chance, that Wordsworth met Samuel Taylor Coleridge and formed a friendship that is one of the legends of Eng. Lit. They came together, dazzled together, shone together like two bright stars, brought out the genius in each other and even though the fizzling out stages were to be rather sad, they had an effect on English poetry which has probably never been equalled.

Coleridge was born in 1772, two years after Wordsworth, in Ottery St Mary, Devon. He was the youngest of ten children, nine boys and one girl, and his father was a scholarly but unworldly vicar and school master who died when Coleridge was eight. Like Wordsworth, his home life was disrupted, and he was sent away to school at Christ's Hospital, not returning home for eight years. He was brilliant at Greek, captain of the school; then he fell in love with the sister of a school friend, with whose family he spent most of his holidays.

He went up to Cambridge and won awards and medals, but then ran into debt. His girl friend finally rejected him, so he ran away and enlisted in the Light Dragoons under the name of Silas Tomkyn Comberbacke. He made a rotten soldier, falling off his horse and losing his rifle, but eventually his Cambridge friends and his brother tracked him down and bought him out. He returned to Cambridge but left without taking a degree.

During his last long vacation Coleridge went to Oxford and met Robert Southey and they moved together to Bristol, writing poems, discussing philosophy, making plans for a new and better life. Their big scheme was called Pantisocracy. They intended to go to America and start a commune, based on mutual love and mutual ownership, all very idyllic, living off the land, though not doing too much work as, according to their reading of Adam Smith, three hours' work a day should do it. There were twelve young men, all of good education, and they were taking a suitable number of young ladies. There was some intellectual argument about whether marriages should be lasting, or whether you could, in their new ideal state on the banks of the Susquehanna River, break a marriage when you felt like it. But marriage seemed the most sensible system, at least to Robert Southey who was planning to marry one of three sisters who were going on the voyage, the Fricker girls. He married Edith Fricker and his friend Coleridge was set to marry Sara Fricker.

However, the proposed Susquehanna scheme never got going. They couldn't get the money and they started to fall out, all blaming each other. It was just at this moment, when Coleridge and Southey had fallen out, despite the fact that Coleridge had married his Fricker sister and they were all now related, that Coleridge met Wordsworth, yet another young idealistic poet.

39

Coleridge, like Wordsworth, had been given some cheap accommodation by admirers – at Nether Stowey, Somerset. He had read and loved Wordsworth's first poems and they were introduced by a mutual friend, a bookseller in Bristol. William and Dorothy were staying at Racedown in north Dorset, not too far away, and they immediately made plans to meet again.

There's a nice description of Coleridge's first visit to them at Racedown, given by Wordsworth forty years later. Coleridge was in such a hurry to see William and Dorothy that he 'did not keep to the high road but leapt over a gate and bounded down a pathless field'. Coleridge had so admired Wordsworth's poems on his first reading that he was already calling him 'the giant Wordsworth' and referred to him as 'the only man to whom at all times and in all modes of excellence I feel myself inferior'.

William and Dorothy decided to move to Alfoxden in Somerset to be nearer Coleridge and all three of them as good as set up house together, living almost joint lives, talking all day, writing and reciting, walking half the night. Coleridge was of course married and soon had a child, Hartley, born 1796, but Mrs Coleridge tended to get left behind. It was always William and Dorothy and Coleridge who were out on their nocturnal tours.

Coleridge had been as fortunate as Wordsworth with his friends. He had a pension of £150 a year from Tom and Josiah Wedgwood, of the pottery family. It enabled him to devote himself to poetry so that he would not have to go into the ministry as his family wanted. The Wedgwoods also loaned Wordsworth some money when he, Dorothy and Coleridge went off on a tour of Germany. These private patrons of the arts, who gave money to struggling young poets, have completely gone from Britain today. Lucky old Wordsworth and Coleridge to meet them – but how touching that people had such faith in them when they were so young and had done so little and, as far as their own middle-class families were concerned, they were just a load of weird-looking spongers. Drop-outs and hippies they would be called today and in many ways they were exactly the same, with their refusal to conform, going off to live in the wilds.

There's a well-recorded episode which took place when they were living in Alfoxden. Wordsworth had already bemused the local residents by walking the fields at all hours, carrying his little pocket telescope and speaking poetry aloud. It had been thought more than once that he was trying to bewitch the cattle.

Joined by Coleridge, and of course the ever-present Dorothy, Wordsworth led a strange-looking trio. Dorothy had a very dark complexion and looked wild and foreign. Wordsworth had long given up his Cambridge dandy days and dressed like a tramp.

One day a local resident passed on complaints to the Home Office about their behaviour. 'A very suspicious business concerning an emigrant family ... the Master of the house has no wife with him but only a woman who passes for his Sister. The man has Camp Stools which he and his visitors take with them when they go about the country upon their nocturnal or diurnal excursions and have also a Portfolio in which they enter their observations which they have been heard to say they should be rewarded for ... These people may possibly be under-agents to some principal in Bristol.'

England was of course at war with France and the three of them did discuss politics a great deal, especially French politics, as Wordsworth told Coleridge all about his French exploits. The report also mentioned their strange accents. Amongst other suspicious circumstances was their habit of 'washing and mending their cloaths all Sunday'.

The Home Office sent down a detective who took up quarters at a local inn and began to spy on them, hiding behind sand dunes and trying to listen to their conversation. He heard them discussing someone called Spy Nozy, which convinced the Home Office detective he was on the right track. Wordsworth did have a rather large nose. (They were in fact discussing philosophy, and the writings of Spinoza.) The Home Office man, a Mr Walsh, decided that they were not French but 'a mischiefuous gang of disaffected Englishmen'. He turned in copious notes about their meals, how many visitors turned up, what they looked like, what they ate, what they argued about, the sort of information that has proved invaluable for their biographers. Wordsworth's name went into the Home Office's black books and it was probably one reason why his lease on the Alfoxden house was not renewed.

The major result of the friendship of Wordsworth and Coleridge was the appearance of *Lyrical Ballads*, first published anonymously in 1798. The final spur for its publication was the thought of getting money to finance their proposed trip to Germany. They got thirty guineas each for their work, though all but four of the poems were Wordsworth's. Coleridge's main contribution was 'The Rime of the Ancient Mariner'. *Lyrical*

Ballads, though it created little fuss at the time, is now considered to be one of the turning points in the history of English poetry.

Wordsworth explained that the poems were deliberate experiments, trying to use the language and conversation of ordinary people, writing about ordinary topics, especially the humble and rustic. Many reviewers were outraged by 'The Idiot Boy' but there was general approval for 'Tintern Abbey'. It was a complete break-away, in subject matter and form, from the heavy, metrical poems of the eighteenth century. Wordsworth had been influenced by other contemporary poets, people like Burns whom he greatly admired, but he was showing genuine originality in linking the spiritual with nature, writing personal poetry which had its origins in his own 'emotion recollected in tranquillity'. These early poems had a profound effect on countless young men of the day, who, when they discovered them, suddenly saw a new meaning in language and poetry.

On their arrival back from Germany, in 1799, Wordsworth decided to return to the Lakes; so many of his poems had sprung from his Lakeland memories, in subject and in feelings. He'd written about the Lakes while in the West Country and in Germany he'd started the 'Lucy' poems.

He and Dorothy came back to Hawkshead in November 1799, the first time for ten years. Ann Tyson had died three years earlier, aged eighty-three. They spent just one night in Hawkshead and then moved on to Grasmere, the vale of his dreams, where he decided he most wanted to live. He was now aged twenty-nine. He had seen a great deal of the world, but he had never spiritually left the Lakes. He was to live there for the rest of his long life – trailing just a little cloud of glory at this stage, but a whole host of golden friends and followers who were soon to make up what the world came to know as the Lake Poets.

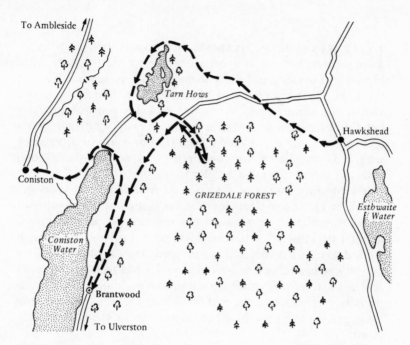

5
CONISTON

*A visit to a beauty spot. Mr Ruskin and his
home at Brantwood. The body in the lake.*

I LEFT HAWKSHEAD, HEADING FOR CONISTON, AND VERY
soon there were signs everywhere urging me to go to Tarn
Hows, so I decided to follow them. It's a very famous place in
the Lake District and I had often heard it talked about and
visited and admired and mentioned on every tourist's itinerary
but I'd never been and, shame to say, I wasn't quite sure what
it (or they) is (or are). Could it be a lake or a hill or a house or
what? 'To the Tarns', another notice said, so that was a good
clue. Whatever it is must be plural.

It's a beauty spot, that's what it is. And as beauty spots go,
it looks it. I have to restrain myself from being snotty and superior
about it, which is what snotty and superior people usually are
about Tarn Hows. You have to shield your eyes from the glare on
a good day, as it looks as if it's jumped straight off a chocolate
box. It's so beautiful it doesn't look real – and technically it isn't
real. It's a stretch of beautifully sculptured parkland with a sensa-
tionally pretty tarn in the middle. There are pine trees around
the edges, smooth fells rising behind and terrific views from every
point.

There's only one tarn, despite that plural, and it was created
in the nineteenth century by damming a stream and joining what
were three rather swampy pools. Wordsworth, writing in 1810,
mentions going past Tarn Hows farm but says nothing about
any water, though he does admire the view. 'By this road is seen
much the best view of Coniston Lake from the south.' (I don't
understand the reference to south – Tarn Hows is to the north of
Coniston. Perhaps it's an 1810 misprint?)

The National Trust looks after Tarn Hows very efficiently,
providing excellent car parks, a nature trail with a well-written
guide, but in a good year the park can get over three quarters of
a million visitors and the human erosion is now becoming a big
problem. I later took my children to see it in their school
holidays, which was a terrible mistake, though they loved it,
racing round the little peninsulas and inlets, wading to the pine-
clad islands, throwing fir cones at each other. But the crowds.
It was about as rural as the Serpentine on August bank holiday.
On no account visit it during school holidays – keep it for the
early spring or late autumn. The colours anyway are at their best
at these times.

Before heading down to the slopes of Coniston Water, I spent
some time exploring Grizedale forest which lies between Coniston

and Esthwaite Water, but I didn't like it. The Forestry Commission are trying hard these days, wanting everybody to love them, welcoming visitors and laying on nature trails. There's a wildlife centre and a big camping site, and most surprisingly of all, a Theatre in the Forest. This almost earns as many signposts in the surrounding area as Tarn Hows and no doubt deserves it as in the summer it attracts internationally-known musicians. It was a wet and dismal day when I was there, which didn't help.

However, I explored deeper and deeper into the forest as I had the address of a cottage to let. I'd spoken on the phone to the owners, a Manchester couple, who said they were in residence and would provide tea when I arrived. I eventually found it but they were out so I opened the door and poked round the kitchen, guessing from their Habitat kitchen utensils and their pine table and straw matting what sort of couple they must be (late thirties, perhaps a solicitor, probably Didsbury). I never met them as the whole place was so dripping in damp and so claustrophobic that I did a coward's trick and just closed the door again and never ever told them I'd turned up. I hope they're not still waiting.

Grizedale forest used to have a German prisoner-of-war camp at one time – officers of course – and they were always trying to escape. No wonder, though they rarely made it. I bet they were confused by the maps. As in many instances in the Lakes, you get different places with similar names. Grizedale forest, for example, has no connection with Grisedale Pike (which is miles away, near Keswick) or with Grisedale Tarn (which is miles the other way, near Helvellyn). I was glad to leave it and hit open land on the shores of Coniston.

I was aiming for Brantwood, on the eastern side of the lake, the home of John Ruskin for the last twenty-nine years of his life. It was February, and out of season, but I had been told the house could be seen by appointment so I had rung up and arranged to be shown round. I knocked at the door of the lodge, as instructed, and it was opened by a tall, gaunt-looking man who glared at me suspiciously. 'I thought you were coming next week,' he said, closing the door again. I wandered round a yard and after five minutes he opened up again and said, with not much enthusiasm, that he would show me round the house. I was very lucky, he said. Ten minutes later he wouldn't have been in.

'Ugly place,' he muttered, as we entered Brantwood. 'And it's freezing. There's no heat on so we'll go round quickly.'

The gentleman was Derek Phippard, manager of Brantwood, one time manager of a sports shop, who did warm more to me and his subject as he took me round the house, though it was hard going. The house is pretty cheerless and has a morbid atmosphere. The pre-Raphaelite paintings and furniture are equally stark and uncomfortable, but I enjoyed noticing Ruskin's hair, handkerchief, tie, baby chair and other personal delights. In Ruskin's bedroom, Mr Phippard pointed out a little turret which Ruskin had built in the corner, providing excellent views of the lake. 'It gave him nightmares so he moved out of this bedroom.' I nodded my head wisely in reply, saying that of course Ruskin did go mad in the end.

'Who said he went mad,' declared Mr Phippard, turning on me. 'I go mad if I hear people saying Ruskin went mad.'

'Well, several books say he went mad,' I said.

'He wasn't mad. He just did so much writing in this house that he had a mental blockage. He was a bit eccentric, that's all he was. I don't believe all these tales about him being mad.'

'And what about him being impotent,' I said, deciding to get all the scandal over in one go. A new book had come out that very week which alleged that Ruskin was impotent, but Mr Phippard would have none of it.

'Rubbish,' he said.

John Ruskin was born in London in 1819 and first visited Coniston as a young boy of five, a visit he never forgot. His father was a very successful wine merchant and was in partnership with Domecq, the sherry people, and it was his custom in the early days of his business to take his wife and family on his tours with him. He would stay at local hotels or houses with his family and servants and visit local houses and beauty spots. In 1830, when Ruskin was eleven, they had three weeks in the Lakes. One day they took the Windermere ferry to Hawkshead and Ruskin wrote a poem about driving by coach to Coniston and having dinner there – a rather witty poem, for a boy of eleven:

> When dinner was over, as still it did rain,
> We thought that we scarcely need longer remain:
> So, ordered the carriage, and with no good will,
> We ordered the pest of all travels – the bill.

Ruskin's father was a great lover of the arts and the countryside and encouraged his son to paint and write poems about his travels – which soon took them all over Europe. His mother, a highly religious woman, decided his precocious genius should be sheltered. At seventeen he fell in love with Adele Domecq, the daughter of his father's partner, but the affair was frustrated and it was this emotional failure which is supposed to have had a great effect on his subsequent love life. He went up to Oxford in 1836 where his social life was a bit constrained by the fact that his mother took lodgings nearby to keep an eye on him. His father gave him a very generous allowance and it was while at Oxford that he started to collect paintings by Turner who was then under attack because of his abstract style. This led to the first volume of his great classic work, *Modern Painters*, which appeared in 1843, when Ruskin was only twenty-four. It was a great success, though Turner was slightly embarrassed by the passionate defence from such a young man.

Ruskin was a great patron of the arts and a champion of many social and economic causes. He wrote books, gave lectures, collected and encouraged painters, using his private wealth to buy their works when the world at large was against them, as with the pre-Raphaelites. He was a great friend of Rosetti, Burne-Jones and Millais and was an eminent artist in his own right.

In 1848 he married Effie Gray, the pretty young daughter of a Scottish friend of his family. It sounds a strange marriage. On their holidays, Ruskin took lusty young men with them, such as the young Millais. The marriage ended in 1854 with Effie running off with Millais. London society was shocked when she gained the annulment of her marriage to Ruskin on the grounds of her husband's impotence. She was examined by doctors and declared a virgin – the dreaded words 'incurable impotence' appearing in the documents. Ruskin maintained he could prove his virility, if need be, but didn't want her back now anyway.

Ruskin subsequently had another unhappy love affair with a young Irish girl, Rose La Touche, whom he first met when she was only ten. When she was sixteen, he declared himself to her parents who were horrified. He seemed to be attracted to very young girls and was always writing letters to them, carrying on intense relationships. In his forties he did some lecturing at a girls' school in Cheshire where he was very fond of playing blind man's buff in his classroom – with him blind-folded and having to tell by touching which girl was which.

In 1871 he bought Brantwood for £1500. He admitted in letters to friends that it wasn't all that pretty, calling it 'dilapidated and rather dismal' but it was the views he'd bought it for. 'I've bought a small place ... with on the whole the finest view of Cumberland or Lancashire ... Here I have rocks, streams, fresh air and, for the first time in my life, the rest of the purposed home.'

The house, little more than a large cottage at the time, had been famous for its views for almost a century. It had had literary associations before, being the home of William Linton, a printer and engraver whose wife wrote Victorian novels with exciting titles like *Grasp Your Nettle*.

Ruskin moved into the house with his cousin Joan Severn (he never re-married) and began rebuilding, putting on twelve rooms and his fancy bedroom tower, and adding to the estate till eventually it covered almost 500 acres, including Fir Island in the lake. He was fifty-two when he moved in and it was his home till he died, aged eighty, in 1900. He wrote many books there, including his autobiography, *Praeterita*, and was visited by many other eminent Victorians, such as Burne-Jones, Holman Hunt, Charles Darwin, Coventry Patmore, Marie Corelli, Kate Greenaway. He had the house full of paintings, by himself and his contemporaries, including many priceless Turners. He took a great part in local activities and was very much a Wordsworthian, loving nature and Lakeland life. His final years were overshadowed by mental illness and depression, a sad ending for such an original spirit. 'One of the most remarkable men,' so Tolstoy described him, 'not only of England and our time but of all countries at all times. He was one of those rare men who think with their hearts.'

He left the house to his cousin Mrs Severn and her husband – and this is where Brantwood's troubles began, which perhaps helps to make it rather an austere place today. He wanted the Severns to 'accord 30 consecutive days in every year to strangers to see the house and pictures as I have done in my lifetime' but they refused, putting up a notice saying they were not a museum and not open to the public.

When Mrs Severn died in 1924, her husband moved back to London, to a house given them by Ruskin, and started to sell off the treasures of Brantwood, including the Turners. There was a remarkable series of sales starting at Sotheby's in 1930 in which all the best items from the house, paintings, furniture, books and manuscripts, were individually sold. Luckily, a wealthy collector and disciple of Ruskin, J. Howard Whitehouse, went round buying back all the Ruskin possessions he could find. He had founded the Birmingham Ruskin Society and a boys' school in Bembridge, Isle of Wight, in 1919 which he ran on Ruskin's educational principles.

The Bembridge connection is where Mr Phippard, my friendly guide, comes into the story. He was educated at Bembridge school before the war and had lectures by Whitehouse about Ruskin. 'At the time I thought what a mess Ruskin's work seemed to me, but the education was considered very progressive for those days. We had woodwork and printing which boys' schools didn't do then. I remember being taught that in life you should use your head, hands and eyes – that was a Ruskin principle.'

It wasn't until seven years ago that Mr Phippard came to Brantwood, after working most of his life in the sports-goods' field, doing particularly well with pogo sticks. There were fourteen staff when he arrived and the house was used for educational courses but these have now ceased. His main job is to look after the house and property and guide visitors in the season. (The official curator lives at Bembridge.)

They got almost 20,000 visitors in 1976, a record number, but dropped to 12,000 in 1977. 'I blame the Queen's Silver Jubilee – and also the fact we didn't have an exhibition that year.' Brantwood tries to be self-supporting, but they find it a bit of a struggle. One of the big problems is putting over exactly who Ruskin was. The general public, even the educated public, are a bit confused. If only Ruskin had done only one thing and not involved himself in so many activities he would have been easier to identify.

'Your Wordsworth was a wonderful bloke,' said Mr Phippard. 'People keep on telling me that. Folks flock to his cottage. He wrote some poem about daffodils, didn't he? Well, we've got daffodils here. Thousands of them. Compared with a bloke like Wordsworth, Ruskin did much more. It's a pity the public don't know more about him, but what can you do?

'Only twenty-five per cent of the people who come here are interested in Ruskin – the rest are just curious. I try to interpret his life so that tourists can understand. Did you know he thought up Green Belts, Smokeless Zones, free schools, free libraries, the National Trust, Rent Restriction Act, Town Planning? I'd like to

organise an exhibition of his life in simple picture-and-caption,
like a cartoon, but how do you illustrate the Rent Act?'

I queried his founding of the National Trust, as it was Canon
Rawnsley and two others who are generally credited with doing
that, but Mr Phippard would have none of it. 'That's the National
Trust for you. They don't talk about it! But they change their tune
when they want something. I was very short to them on the
phone the other day. They are preserving the *Gondola*, the old
boat that used to run on Coniston – Ruskin used to catch it
across the lake to get his train to London. Anyway, they asked
me if they could build a pier at Brantwood. I said they had to
admit first what Ruskin did for them.'

He kindly offered to arrange an introduction to the man who
runs the Ruskin Museum in Coniston village, though he worried
at first about ringing him. 'I was a bit rude to him the other
day. He rang me to ask if I could show an American round
here but I refused.' Before I left I paid Mr Phippard £2.50 for a
bottle of John Ruskin Sherry, one of his little sidelines which he'd
just begun. He assured me it had been bottled especially for
Brantwood by Domecq, Ruskin's father's old partner. It turned
out to be a pleasant Amontillado, quite presumptious, an amusing
memento from a rather sad house.

The walk round Coniston was delightful. At the head of the
lake there's a most tremendous view. You see right up the lake
at almost water level, as if you are swimming, with the water
stretching for ever into the distance. Wordsworth loved the view
from this end and there used to be near Brantwood a Wordsworth
Seat, so called because he was always recommending friends to
use the spot for the best views of Coniston. Coniston Old Man
towers over the lake and in February it was snow clad and most
dramatic.

Coniston Water is now much quieter than Windermere, but in
its day it was a veritable highway – in fact it still is in law a
public highway. From Norman times there was considerable
charcoal burning in the area and iron ore was often brought up
the lake to be smelted. There were copper mines around Coniston
for centuries, the last ones closing after the First World War. You
can still see little rows of miners' cottages around the village of
Coniston. There was a railway line from Furness to Coniston,
opened in 1859, which brought crowds of trippers before the
coming of the motor car, but it is now closed.

Most of the shores of the lake are open to the public, thanks to such large tracts being owned by either the National Trust or the Forestry Commission. There are three islands, in the care of the National Trust, and one of them, Peel Island, is Wild Cat Island in Arthur Ransome's *Swallows and Amazons*.

I went to call on the curator of the village's Ruskin Museum, Basil Bilton, a retired chemist, who took me into his cottage to let me admire a copy of one of Ruskin's books which had just been published in Polish. Mr Bilton, a rather retiring, rather whimsical gentleman, knew nothing about Ruskin till he was asked to help out and keep an eye on the museum. The museum is operated by turnstiles and is unmanned, but he pops in every day in the season to make sure there's no vandalism. Most people, he says, wrongly suppose that Ruskin actually lived there. 'He was a queer fellow, from all accounts,' said Mr Bilton. 'I'm interested in his paintings – and I'm interested in his interest in young girls. He was fascinated by them, but so are lots of chaps, aren't they?' He took me to see a display of letters written by Ruskin to some of his young girls.

The Ruskin Museum is part of what's known locally as the Institute – though more properly it should be called the Coniston Mechanics Institute and Literary Society. It was founded in 1852, part of that sudden splurge of educational and cultural institutes which spread across the country in the mid-Victorian age, designed to bring cultural and intellectual facilities to the workers. In those days, Coniston had a population of 1300 (a third more than it has today) of whom 600 were employed in the copper mines. John Ruskin, naturally enough, became a pillar and patron of the Institute when he moved to Brantwood in 1872 and helped its expansion. On his death, they lost their most eminent patron – and with the Severns being so bolshie about opening Brantwood to the public, it looked as if Coniston could lose completely its Ruskin connection. W. G. Collingwood, Ruskin's secretary, worked to set up a Ruskin Museum at the back of the Institute as a place to preserve any Ruskin mementoes they could get their hands on and in 1901 the new building was opened by Canon Rawnsley – who else.

They get a great number of visitors every year – around 10,000 – almost as many as Brantwood, yet it's little more than a village hall, an endearing if rather amateurish collection of bits and pieces that once belonged to Ruskin. It brings in around

£900 a year in entrance fees – enough to keep the Institute going. There's a lovely collection, made by Ruskin himself, of local geological specimens, all carefully polished and arranged, a nice thing to have in a village which has such a stirring mining history. There's also his birth certificate, his Bible, his painting box and his funeral pall. Ruskin had encouraged the local linen trade and so when he died the local linen ladies decided they would stitch his pall themselves. It took some months, as they hadn't done one before but, having got the hang of it, they then went on to do Tennyson's when he died, stitching that one in three days flat.

Then of course there's his letters to the little girls. 'I don't think he was impotent,' said Mr Bilton when, just by chance, I'd brought the subject up. 'Come and look at this.' In a locked alcove he produced a book about Ruskin in which there were several paintings of him. 'Look at this one of Ruskin with a terrific erection – and there's more. Here's a naked lady admiring herself in the mirror.' I pointed out that the paintings were all imagined, and done recently, but Mr Bilton said they were based on a lot of research. Well, if your job is caring for someone's museum, you're bound to feel jealous of his reputation.

In the middle of the little Ruskin Museum is what at first sight seems an incongruous intrusion – a set of photographs of a motor boat disaster on Coniston Water. They are a memento to the other great name for ever associated with Coniston – a gentleman who has nothing at all in common with Ruskin, apart from the fact that he too happened to die there. Donald Campbell made his last attempt on the world's water speed record on Coniston in 1967 when he somersaulted at a speed of some 300 miles an hour. He had been a frequent visitor to Coniston over the years. The lake is five miles long, without the curves and bays or pleasure craft of Windermere and Ullswater, and therefore ideal for speeding.

Ruskin is buried in Coniston churchyard and his grave is marked with a large decorated cross, carved out of Coniston stone from a local quarry at Tilberthwaite. Donald Campbell has no grave. The disaster happened in the upper reaches of the lake. His body and most of the wreckage have never been recovered. Coniston is a very deep lake.

6

WORDSWORTH AT HOME

Life at Dove Cottage. Passion and poetry.
Mr Wordsworth and his women.

WILLIAM AND DOROTHY STARTED THE NEW CENTURY IN Dove Cottage, Grasmere, having moved in at the end of December 1799. Dove Cottage is known to millions of people round the world as the home of Wordsworth and every year it attracts around 53,000 visitors – yet the Wordsworths never knew it as Dove Cottage. It didn't have a name when they arrived and they never gave it one. Their address was simply Town End, Grasmere, which was the collective name for the group of cottages at the southern end of the village. The cottage had at some stage previously been an inn called The Dove and Olive Branch and this is where its present-day name has come from.

'We were young and healthy and had obtained an object long desired,' wrote Dorothy later. 'We had returned to our native mountains, there to live.' It was a fairly humble cottage, and still is, with two rooms downstairs, plus a back kitchen, and four little rooms above. Dorothy papered one of the little rooms with newspapers to try and keep it warm.

Dorothy and her brother lived here for over eight years and they had a constant stream of relations and visitors who stayed for weeks at a time. Goodness knows where she put them all. Coleridge almost immediately followed them up to the Lakes. He stayed with them in April 1800, and then Dorothy found him a house to let at Keswick, Greta Hall, where he moved in with his family, to be followed not long afterwards by the Southeys. Coleridge and Southey had, of course, married sisters and a third sister also moved into Greta Hall with them. Coleridge, however, seems to have spent most of his time in the first few years with the Wordsworths, walking the thirteen miles or so to take tea then staying for weeks.

Wordsworth's younger and much loved brother John, who'd gone to sea, stayed with them for long stretches when he was between voyages. The Hutchinson sisters, Mary and Sarah, childhood friends of Dorothy and William's from their Penrith days, also came for long holidays.

But the basic unit, in the early Dove Cottage years, from 1800–1802, was Dorothy and William. They lived in the cottage alone and together they built up the garden, growing runner beans and peas, creating a hut in one corner (still to be seen) which she planted with mosses and rock plants, found on the fells. There were no houses in front of the cottage at the time (now there is a hotel and a terrace) and William could lie in bed and see Grasmere lake. Dorothy was his housekeeper, cooking and cleaning, and his secretary, writing his letters, copying out his poems. Wordsworth's habit was to compose aloud, out in the garden or out on the fells, reciting as he walked, polishing and declaiming at the same time. Later he would recite it to Dorothy who usually had the task, a beloved task, of writing it all down.

Dorothy was also his inspiration. Her own love of natural objects, like butterflies or daffodils, helped William to write poems about them. She kept notes and descriptions in her own Journals, details of what she and William had seen and felt together, people they'd met on their walks, and he would make her read them out later, to remind him of what they'd done. 'I wandered lonely as a cloud,' the best-known Wordsworth poem to the general public (and almost the least-mentioned poem in every academic book about Wordsworth) owes a great deal to Dorothy's original description, in prose, of daffodils they had seen by the shore of Ullswater. 'I never saw daffodils so beautiful. They grew among the mossy stones about and around them, some rested their heads upon these stones as on a pillow for weariness and the rest tossed and reeled and danced and seemed as if they verily laughed with the wind that blew them over the lake ...'

Dorothy was also his best friend, his soul mate, his kindred spirit. She had a natural and original intelligence, despite a lack of formal education, though she was well read. Wordsworth was never close to his eldest brother Richard who sounded rather boring and conventional and became a lawyer. Christopher, the youngest of all, was academically the brightest and did all the right things at Cambridge which William didn't do, going on to join the church. He was very close to John, the sailor, but he was so often away. Dorothy was his first love and they clung to each other throughout the family troubles, despite being separated for so long. They felt the same way about life and nature. Most of all, they both agreed on William's god-given genius.

But was Dorothy also something else? Could she have been William's lover? The storm caused in the 1920s by the discovery of the Annette scandal and the illegitimate baby kept the Wordsworth scholars going for years – looking for further evidence, arguing about how it influenced his life and his work. They are still at it today, trying to prove that certain girls referred to in his poems were really based on Annette. But in the 1950s, the suggestion that he and Dorothy had had an incestuous relationship caused an even bigger stir. It had been hinted at, very gently, by previous writers but in 1954, F. W. Bateson, a noted Wordsworth scholar and Fellow of Corpus Christi College, Oxford, produced a book called *Wordsworth – A Re-interpretation* which spelled out the possibility very clearly indeed.

Their relationship was definitely very intense, not to say strange, and Dorothy herself has given us enough clues in her Journals. She kept a short Journal when they'd lived together in Alfoxden in 1798 and a much fuller one from 1800 to 1803 in Grasmere. There's nothing more after this date – unless it's been destroyed or lost. The Journals are delightful and well worth reading (they're now in paperback by Oxford University Press), though they are infuriatingly short of real explanation or any human insights. She records their daily doings, meals eaten, walks taken, the countryside changing, beggars arriving at the door, passersby met on their walks, visitors who stayed, books read, illnesses suffered from. It's all charmingly done and Ernest de Sélincourt, a noted Wordsworth scholar, said she was 'probably the most remarkable and the most distinguished of English writers who never wrote a line for the general public'. Her prose is certainly better than old William's, who is almost without exception deadly dull in his letters.

When William was away on a visit without her, even a local one, Dorothy was completely dejected. 'My heart was so full that I could hardly speak to William when I gave him a farewell kiss. I sate a long time upon a stone at the margin of the lake and after a flood of tears my heart was easier.' On this occasion, he had only walked into Yorkshire with his brother John. She walked miles every day to Ambleside, sometimes going twice, in the hope of a letter from him and was distraught if there was none. While he was away, she often slept in his bed. 'And I slept badly for my thoughts were full of William.' There are many references to physical contact, albeit harmless, but obviously of great pleasure to her. 'I broiled the Beefsteaks. After dinner we made a pillow of my shoulder. I read to him and my Beloved slept.' Another time she hugs to herself a blanket which William has used. When William once returned unexpectedly, Dorothy wrote in her Journal that 'the surprise shot through me. I believe I screamed.'

William hasn't left any journals of his day-to-day thoughts, as he didn't go in much for such writing, but there are many love poems which he admitted were written for Dorothy, based on incidents which had happened between them, such as the poem which begins 'Among all lovely things my Love has been.' The poem 'Strange Fits of Passion have I Known' is also thought to have a Dorothy connection.

Dorothy was dotty about him – and did love him physically – but there is no real evidence that William loved her in more than a very strong, brother–sister sense. Writing love poems to your sister doesn't prove you slept with her. Poets must be allowed a bit of licence. Families at that period did show more affection to each other than they do today, especially ones who had been orphaned and only had each other. It's not just scandal-mongering, however. If Wordsworth was a man of genius, as most English Literature experts think, then all his actions must be examined.

While William shared many intimate times alone with Dorothy, there were other ladies in his life, particularly the Hutchinson sisters. The Wordsworths, both William and Dorothy, had known Mary Hutchinson and her sister Sarah from their childhood in Penrith. Over the years they had made frequent visits to each other's houses. Mary had visited them in the West Country. William had gone to see her at her family home in Yorkshire. The sisters both came to stay during the early heady days at Dove Cottage, from 1800–1802, and took part in expeditions, usually in a party of five or six. There would be William and Dorothy, Mary and Sarah Hutchinson, John Wordsworth the sailor, plus Coleridge. They had day and night walks, reciting poetry, discussing nature and life. They had in-jokes, in-references, like Sarah's tree, places that meant something special to just their little gang. They all carved their initials on a rock by a road near Keswick – WW, MH, DW, STC, JW, SH. It remained there for many years but was destroyed during road improvements. The Great Canon Rawnsley, defender of the Lakes and Beatrix Potter's friend, tried to save it in vain. (There is today in Dove Cottage a water colour of the rock in its original setting.)

Mrs Coleridge didn't join the party, not caring for walks or their company, which is just as well because Coleridge had taken a fancy to Sarah Hutchinson. He and Southey had fallen in love with sisters – now it was happening again, only this time it was him and Wordsworth and a different set of sisters. Sarah doesn't appear to have returned his love – she appears, if anything, to have fancied Wordsworth. Just to complicate the circle, Dorothy might have been in love with Coleridge, though this could have been simply a projection of her Beloved's love for Coleridge, just as she took to calling William's Annette her sister without ever meeting her. They were all, in fact, in love with each other, which you can read any way you like.

Personally, I would not be surprised at anything that might have happened in this little circle. The locals, as in the West Country, looked upon them as very strange, with mysterious nocturnal habits, living a weird life, with no apparent means of support. They weren't just early hippies in their communal life style – there was also a drug connection. Coleridge himself took opium, for his health at first and then because he liked it; Wordsworth never took it. Wordsworth didn't touch strong drink. He was strictly a child of nature, sticking to water for his thirst and the countryside for his spiritual highs. He was very much a man of animal spirits, not an intellectual, like Coleridge, or a great book-man like Southey. His main reading was travel books. His observations and philosophy of life was picked up by his experiences – which soon led him to be rather dogmatic – but as a young man he was full of vitality and natural enthusiasm.

Dorothy actually *looked* wild and several friends wrote of her 'Gypsy tan from constant exposure to the sun and winds – and her eyes wild and staring.' Wordsworth, in one of his poems about her, also refers to 'thy wild eyes'.

Coleridge valued both her mind and her heart.

Wordsworth and his exquisite sister are with me. She is a woman indeed; in mind, I mean, and heart; for her person is such that if you expected to see a pretty woman, you would think her ordinary; if you expected to see an ordinary woman, you would think her pretty! ... Her manners are simple, ardent, impressive. Her eyes watchful in minutest observation of nature; and her taste a perfect electrometer. It bends, protrudes, and draws in, at subtlest beauties and most recondite faults.

As for poor Mary Hutchinson, she has had a very poor press. The few surviving scraps of contemporary description of her make her sound very dull.

A woman neither handsome nor even comely according to the rigour of criticism – nay generally pronounced very plain ... but angelic, of simplicity, purity of heart speaking through all her looks, acts and movements. Her words were few. In reality she talked so little that Mr Slave-Trade Clarkson used to allege against her that she would only say 'God Bless you.' Certainly her intellect was not of an active order.

Dorothy had always been a good friend of Mary, just as William had, but her Journal indicates what agonies she went through every time William went off to visit Mary in Yorkshire or Penrith. It's all done very flatly, isolated panics and fears and headaches mixed up with mundane events like making pies, but you can see the effect it had on her.

The engagement of William and Mary happened suddenly, at least that's how it appears in Dorothy's Journal. They get up one day and she and William are off South, making for London. No explanation is given. They cross Westminster Bridge, where Dorothy makes notes of their impressions which William later turns into one of his finest sonnets. Then they head for Dover. Where are they going? You've guessed. They're off to see Annette. Now that he has become engaged William, ever the gentleman, wants Annette to be the first to know.

There had been letters back and forward for some years, with Dorothy doing most of the corresponding to Annette. Some at least must have come through because Dorothy remarks in passing in the Journal that amongst the letters one day is another one from France. It's safe to assume that William told Mary about his affair with Annette, confessing everything, once they got engaged.

The trip to France lasted in all four weeks and they seem to have spent most of it on the Calais sands. 'We walked by the sea shore almost every evening,' notes Dorothy in her Journal, 'with Annette and Caroline, or William and I alone.' It was now August 1802, and the Peace of Amiens had at last brought a temporary settlement between France and England. William hadn't been to France for ten years or seen his daughter Caroline who was now ten (unless there was a secret trip during his London bumming-around days). Dorothy gives absolutely nothing away about the nature of the discussions. She describes a few buildings, says that William one day went swimming but she didn't swim as she had a bad cold, and that's about all.

In his discussions and explanations with Annette, William possibly promised her some money. Lord Lonsdale, the bad 'un who had been so horrid to the Wordsworth family, had died earlier in 1802, without ever paying up any money, but they felt certain that the new Lord would settle the scores. The thought of this might have spurred on the marriage. William felt he could now support a wife and family, and also Annette, or at least do the decent thing by her and give her some money.

The marriage took place almost immediately after their return from France in October 1802. Mary's family, the Hutchinsons, weren't too keen on the marriage, considering William some sort of wandering vagabond, with no profession. It was a very quiet affair in Yorkshire, perhaps partly out of consideration to Dorothy. She appears to have been in a state of collapse throughout and Mary is almost forgotten as they have to revive Dorothy. In fact it looks from her own description in her Journal that she couldn't even face the little ceremony.

At a little after 8 o'clock I saw them go down the avenue to the Church. William had parted from me upstairs. I gave him the wedding ring – with how deep a blessing! I took it from my forefinger where I had worn it the whole of the night before – he slipped it again onto my finger and blessed me fervently. I kept myself as quiet as I could but when I saw the two men running up the walk, coming to tell us it was over, I could stand it no longer and threw myself on the bed where I lay in stillness neither hearing or seeing anything, till Sara [Mary's sister] came upstairs to me and said 'They are coming'. This forced me from the bed where I lay and I moved faster than my strength could carry me till I met my Beloved William and fell upon his bosom.

Well, it sounds more like hysteria than sisterly love. Dorothy gave up her Journal almost immediately after the marriage as all three of them settled down together in Dove Cottage. She still adored him as much but perhaps she now got over her deepest, more intense physical passion for him. She and Mary henceforth jointly devoted themselves to William's every desire. Perhaps she didn't have to write her Journal about William's daily doings any more because she had Mary, his wife, under the same roof. Together, they could discuss William all day.

William had now two ladies to help him write down his poems and mop his fevered brow when the creative passions took him. And his creative passions were now at their height. A new edition of *Lyrical Ballads* came out, this time with only Wordsworth's name on it, and it sold quite well. He had a little money at last and some passing fame, with his poems becoming better known, and literary types of the day started coming up to the Lakes just to see him and his friend Coleridge down the road.

The Lakeland group was becoming talked about in London literary circles and Charles Lamb, knowing this, played a trick on Wordsworth just after his marriage. They all came straight back to Grasmere for their threesome honeymoon (William, Mary and Dorothy), arriving on 6 October 1802. On 9 October the following surprisingly detailed wedding announcement appeared in the *Morning Post*:

Monday last, W. Wordsworth, Esq, was married to Miss Hutchinson of Wykeham, near Scarborough, and proceeded immediately, with his wife and his sister, for his charming cottage in the little Paradise Vale of Grasmere. His neighbour, Mr. Coleridge, resides in the Vale of Keswick, 13 miles from Grasmere. His house (situated on a low hill at the foot of Skiddaw, with the Derwent Lake in front and the romantic River Greta winding round the hill) commands perhaps the most various and interesting prospects of any house in the island. It is a perfect panorama of that wonderful vale, with its two lakes, and its complete circle, or rather ellipse of mountains.

William was furious at it – and if you read it carefully you can see why. Firstly, there's the reference to Dorothy going with them on their honeymoon. Then there's all the purple prose, meant satirically presumably, aping an estate agent's advertisement. William was very hurt in case anyone thought he'd put in such details about himself and his cottage – as if he and Coleridge were turning themselves into tourist attractions, giving out details to bring in the trippers. The blame was put on Lamb who had been to Dove Cottage, and to Coleridge's house, and it was very much his sense of humour. It increased London gossip about Wordsworth and Coleridge, tales of their women, and their little Lakeland poetry commune.

It could of course have been Coleridge doing a double bluff, putting himself in to distract attention. It certainly wasn't Wordsworth. There is no trace of him ever having that sense of humour.

The joke of course turned out to be a true joke. Lamb, if it was Lamb, was simply being the first to draw attention to the Lakes as a tourist trap for those desirous of soaking up some of the very wonderful, very literary atmosphere in beautiful Lakeland, as made famous by the very wonderful Lakeland poets. It still goes on.

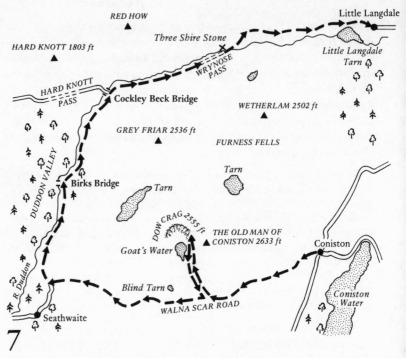

7

DUDDON VALLEY

*Lost on Coniston Old Man. A nasty
experience in the mist. A warm welcome
in Little Langdale.*

WITH THE WORDSWORTHS SAFELY ESTABLISHED IN Grasmere, I set off on my first long walk, the sort they loved to make, heading for the Duddon Valley and the Langdales. So far on my present-day journey I'd been wandering mainly round the Windermere–Coniston area, but now I was approaching the high fells.

Coniston village didn't look so bad in the rain. On the previous visit, in bright sun, the grey-green slates had looked harshly mineral but they had softened in the rain and I could now see why it's such a popular place. I had a last look at the church-yard, filling in time, and noticed that beside Ruskin's grave were some Severns (his cousin-housekeeper) and Collingwoods (his secretary), and that on his memorial, the one built in local stone with the pre-Raphaelite engravings, was a swastika. The swastika, of course, was a well-known symbol long before the Nazis took it over.

The rain was obviously set in so I decided to get started, climb-ing very steeply up a little road behind the village, past the Sun Hotel and the old railway station, heading for the Walna Scar Road. This isn't a road, despite its name, but an old packhorse route which climbs up and round Coniston Old Man. If it had been a brilliantly sunny morning, I would have gone up the Old Man, just for the views, and then cut back to my route. On a clear day, you can see Morecambe Bay from the top of the Old Man. On an even clearer day, you can see Blackpool Tower. On such clear days, you can't get moving for scores of hikers, all trying to see Morecambe Bay and Blackpool Tower. Coniston Old Man is 2633 feet high and as the southernmost major fell in the Lakes, it does command terrific views, but not on a rainy day.

This was famous mining country and the Old Man itself is like an old cheese, full of holes and mounds where man has been hack-ing it about over the centuries. Today the copper mines are closed, though the spoil heaps are still there and the names linger on, like Coppermines Valley.

As I climbed higher, I could see the dark, volcanic rocks above, the craggy, spiky outcrops that are so typical of the southern fells – so different from the smooth slopes and rounded tops of the North. The red bracken and the rocks mingled in the mist and rain before my eyes and it was almost like being in a volcanic eruption. I began to imagine that molten hot lava was pouring out all round me. Then the mist completely descended and I could see nothing.

One of the pleasures of climbing is to look back, see how well you've done, give yourself a pat on the back. In the Lakes, the view turning back is always a delight. Even another few steps can alter a view, change the perspective, move mountains, bring lakes out of the hat, makes houses disappear, alter the shape of valleys. Certainly you're not resting. You're admiring the view. But now all views had gone completely. I should have brought my compass. I'd got one for my birthday from my wife but had left it behind.

There was a sense of excitement in first realising I was lost. It was me against the world. I had seen no one at all since leaving Coniston some two hours previously, not one walker, which was strange – though not so strange, now I thought about it. I was the only daft one climbing up the fell that morning. I kept on measuring my steps, just to see if the mist was lifting, but it was getting worse if anything. I tried to shelter behind some big rocks to consult my map but the rain and wind made it impossible to unfold. The path had turned into a stream and I was walking up a torrent, picking my way over little waterfalls. I was glad, as ever, for my wellingtons.

Was it a path, I began to think to myself. All paths on steep hill sides become streams in rainy weather, so that didn't alarm me too much, but I couldn't believe that packhorses had ever climbed this way, yet a path of sorts did seem to have been made up through the rocks. I was glad I was on my own. My wife and I would have been screaming at each other by now, arguing about who had made the mistake, who had said this was the way. Alone I could put my mind to going forward, not going back over how such a mess had happened. I felt terribly clear, light-headed almost. Then it faded and I got depressed. How would anyone ever find me? I had told my wife I was going over Coniston to the Duddon Valley that day, but she was in London. The inn I was heading for knew I was coming, but didn't know when. I've always wondered how a mountain rescue team works.

Suddenly I realised I had been following a line of cairns. They were definite little mounds of stones, which seemed random at first, till I could see they'd been planted at regular intervals beside the rough streamy path. How marvellous the men must have been who built them. How marvellous in snow they must be when the path completely disappears. How marvellous not to be lost. My spirits reflated again. I wished my wife was with me. There you are, I've done it again, after all your moans. Just trust me. All the lives these cairns must have saved. Every twenty yards they appeared – just the length of my vision. Now I wouldn't fall down an old mine, which had been my worst fear, though I had hardly allowed myself to think it.

The cairns kept going, though the path was now non-existent. I realised with excitement that I was now on the top, at least on the top of something, a plateau of some sort, if not the top of the Walna Scar route over the Old Man. Then at my feet there suddenly appeared water, deep water, not a stream this time. I managed a quick glance at the map, a quick fight with the wind and the rain, and could see no tarn marked on my route. It must be flooding, I thought, or perhaps a little tarn, too small to appear on my map. I explored the side of the tarn, climbing over large boulders, wading through the edges, but I could neither see the tarn's size nor shape because of the mist. I had no idea if it was small or big, long or fat. I could have hit the North Sea for all I knew.

I struggled round the edge for fifteen minutes – and still the tarn went on. It must be a known tarn, not a temporary bit of flooding, so I got the map out again and realised with horror that I'd gone completely off my route. A tarn this size must either be Blind Tarn, a most appropriate name, or Goat's Water. I got to the end of the tarn at last, whichever it was, and found myself climbing again – this time up some sheer rocks. For the first time I did genuinely panic. I realised from the map that whichever of the two tarns I had just passed, I was any moment now going to find myself falling over the edge of Dow Crag – which I knew to be some of the steepest and most dangerous crags in the Lake District, one of the spots where rock climbing in this country had begun. The range of climbs, according to the experts, go from 'difficult' to 'severe'. My wellies certainly weren't up to that. The moment this awful thought struck me, I turned round immediately. My mind had begun to go fuzzy again, being hypnotised by the murky tarn and the nothingness around, but the thought of Dow Crag stopped me short. I was definitely going back this time. Better to lose a day than lose my life.

On the way down, slowly retracing my steps, I caught a smell of Bovril. I hadn't consciously been thinking of how nice a big steaming mug of Bovril would be, but I must have been. Later on I felt sure I could smell aniseed. Had I trodden on some aniseed-smelling plants or perhaps hit an old hound trail or was I maybe going bonkers. Coniston Old Man is supposed to have this effect on you. There is a dotty religious sect who actually worship the Old Man, believing he's charged with spiritual energy, though I had failed to find any details of them in Coniston village. It was on Coniston that one of the earliest photographs of a UFO was taken. And you know how dotty they are.

Anyway, I concentrated my mind on the cairns. Having cursed them for leading me astray on the way up, I would have been lost without them on the way down. I stumbled and slipped and it was almost a mile before I hit a definable path. Consulting the map, now the wind and mist had slackened a little, I realised that it must have been Goat's Water I'd hit by mistake, the furthest away and more isolated of the two tarns on the west flank of the Old Man. I thought for a moment of continuing to retrace all my steps, right back to the village, but I was sure I was now on the real Walna Scar packhorse route at last. I came to a little stone bridge, in very good condition, which looked almost brand new. There was a raging mountain stream below which alarmed me for a moment as it wasn't on my map, but the discovery of it gave me confidence that I'd hit civilisation. Then I came across a set of fresh boot prints. Not just bridges – people. I almost crashed into the owners of the fresh boot prints a moment later, coming on them in the mist, aquaplaning in my wellies. They were walking in silence, a group of about ten school boys in the usual orange anoraks.

I could only get grunts out of them. They just stared at me, as if I was a yeti out of the mist. One of them moaned that they were all soaked to the skin. They had the usual huge boots on, the real climbers' boots, so I naturally boasted about my dry feet in my wellies. The leader, a dour, bearded Irishman, said it was their own fault. They had insisted on wading every stream. I wanted to tell them about my adventure on Dow Crag but they were too dispirited to listen to me. They were from County Durham, on some local authority adventure holiday, heading for Black Hall youth hostel. I walked with them for a hundred yards but they were not inclined to chat any more and as they were going slower and slower, weighed down with their packs and their waterlogged boots, I went on ahead, saying that if I fell on any rocks they could pick me up. In seconds, they disappeared in the mist.

I was thinking how bad weather can so easily put off young people in the Lake District when I hit an identical-looking party, coming towards me this time, another ten young people in orange anoraks. They were on a similar educational holiday. The Lakes these days are full of school and student parties. Most local authorities from the North-East and North-West seem to have some sort of residential centre in the Lakes where they lay on climbing, walking and boating holidays for their pupils. This party was from Rochdale and they were extremely cheerful with a young, friendly leader. I was just on the summit of the Walna Scar path when I met them and they asked me how far to the top. They all cheered when I said ten yards. They soon disappeared into the mist but I could hear their excited chatter drifting down after me.

Once over the top, the descent was quick and grassy and suddenly I was into fresh air again, with a sky above and a view beyond and the plateau of darkness only a bad memory, though my eyes took time to focus after the monotone of the mist. I came down a hillside stream above Seathwaite and so into the Duddon Valley, one of the most beautiful valleys in the Lake District. There's a narrow road right through the valley, which twists and turns and goes round little hummocks.

The road was deserted and for an hour I saw neither vehicle nor human being. Lakeland roads, the minor ones of course, are a pleasure to walk, as long as you don't choose to walk them on Easter Sunday. They follow the contours yet they're above the contours. You can look up and down and all round without having to bother to watch your feet the way you do on the fells. Fell walkers scorn roads of any sort – which is silly. It's traffic which is terrible not tarmac.

The walls and houses of the Duddon Valley looked so different from the Coniston area. In a few hours, I'd left the slates behind and I was into stone again, soft and rounded. The rain was still pouring down and I realised that, finally, my Peter Storm anorak and trousers, my lightweight weather-proof clothes that I'd worn for four years without ever getting wet, were letting in rain. Perhaps I'd damaged them falling around on Dow Crag or the seams just hadn't been up to such a constant battering of rain. Real oil-skin clothes are better but they're like suits of armour. I sheltered by a bridge over the Duddon – before realising it was Birks bridge, one of the most photographed and painted bridges in the whole of the Lakes. The river forces and polishes its way through a little rock gorge and the hump-back stone bridge seems itself to be a work of nature, blending and melding so well with the rocks either side. There's a very nice car park nearby, and very neat signposts. How considerate our public bodies are these days. How eager to show what kindly people they are, always willing to help blind preservationists across the road.

The road started to flatten out and the valley became broader which was a surprise. I was heading up the river, towards its source, so you would normally expect it to get steeper and nar-rower. But it was the fattening before the thinning. Wrynose Pass was getting near, my final and ultimate haul up and over to the Langdales, and I was feeling pretty exhausted. So much for boast-ing how much I liked long walks. I turned right at Cockley Beck bridge for Wrynose – looking left towards Hard Knott Pass which loomed equally menacingly. A car came from that direction, the first I had seen for hours, and I gave it a half-hearted thumb, half wanting it not to stop so that I wouldn't give in and break my day's hiking. It didn't stop – and I was furious. The rotten lot. Only one other human in the universe and he charges right past. I walked on, now counting every step forward as an extra penance. If hitch-hiking hadn't crossed my mind I would have plodded on quite happily, thinking of the days Wordsworth strode this way. He wrote in his long poem, 'The Excursion', about 'Wonderful Walker', a nineteenth-century parson who lived in the Duddon Valley for sixty-six years, managing on a stipend of £5 a year, yet feeding the poor, treating the sick, bring-ing up his own large family and dying at ninety-two, leaving £2000. But I was getting a bit too tired for such reveries. All I could think of was the narrow, switch-back road, a barren moun-tainous landscape without trees or houses and, worst of all, no signs of a car.

Wrynose, one of the steepest and most difficult roads in the Lake District, was unsurfaced till 1939. During most winters, as the one just passed, it can still be closed for many weeks because of snow. Then a Mini sneaked up behind me and suddenly stopped. A door was opened and a little puff of confetti blew on to the road, sucked out by the gale-force wind and rain. It was a honeymoon couple, a glowing, cuddlesome, very healthy couple, both with bright red hair and wearing very clean chunky white polo-neck sweaters. Yes, they said they'd give me a lift to Little Langdale, wherever that was. They had been to Ravenglass for the day to look at the steam railway and were heading back for their hotel, the Red Lion in Hawkshead. What a nice place for a honeymoon, I said, having stayed there myself. They were from Blackburn, Lancashire, and said they were delighted by the Lakes, despite the weather. On the top of Wrynose, right at the very summit beside the three shires stone – which marked the meeting point of the three old counties, Cumberland, Westmorland and Lancashire – we got a sensational view down the other side of the valley and the first glimpse of Little Langdale Tarn. They jumped out, still glowing, handed me their camera and I took their photograph as they held hands in the rain, with the Little Langdale Tarn in the distance behind them. I wonder if that picture ever came out.

It's the journey not the arrival which is supposed to appeal most to travellers but I think the most concentrated pleasure is getting into a hot bath at the end, all movement stopped, lying there completely exhausted, knowing you've made it, the limbs and soul having somehow survived together. Thought you'd got me, didn't you, old Dow Crag. Can't catch me now, lying in my bath in the Three Shires Inn. I found the inn in the *Good Food Guide*, which isn't always reliable when it comes to accommodation. The welcome was warm, the tea which instantly appeared on my arrival was hot and the bath was scalding. What more can one ask after a day in the rain on the fells? My sodden garments were whipped off silently to an airing room. No doubt years of wet walkers had taught them the way to their hearts.

Later that night I discovered that Mr and Mrs Price, the owners, had opened only two days previously. It was their very first hotel. For the previous three years they had been in the Middle East. Where else, after all, can someone with no capital go today and amass some tax-free money. John Price is a civil engineer by profession and he saved hard during his three years with the Arabs. Added to some money they made by converting and selling a cottage in north Wales, his home area, they had accumulated enough to come home, buy a small hotel and start a completely new life. His wife Mavis had always liked cooking, but neither had had any experience of running a hotel.

There was much scurrying round the two nights I was there,

trying to find keys, how to switch the light on in the telephone booth, working out ways to run their new little empire. There were only four other guests in the hotel, two young couples, and the Prices joined us for coffee and drinks by the log fire in the sitting room after they had served us dinner. All seven of us sat boozing, cut off from the outside world in a remote little valley, the rain lashing outside, telling our life stories. All that was missing was Agatha Christie to bump one of us off. Next morning I did wonder if we were all playing parts, making up our reasons for happening to be in the Three Shires Inn, Little Langdale, on the night of 13 March 1978. Did we tell the truth? Now I think about it, could someone, even in this day and age, save up enough by working for the Arabs to buy a Lakeland hotel which must, in my estimation, have cost at least £80,000. Hmm. And what about that funny bloke who arrived in wellies, said he'd walked over Coniston Old Man and then started interrogating everyone. Said he was writing a book about Wordsworth and the Lakes. Very suspicious.

8
GRASMERE

A Mr De Quincey writes a fan letter. The home life of the dear Wordsworths. Rows, arguments and some dreadful gossip.

IN 1803 WORDSWORTH RECEIVED A STRANGE LETTER FROM a strange young man called Thomas De Quincey. It was a fan letter sent on by Longman's, publishers of the two-volume edition of *Lyrical Ballads*, and the writer described in highly passionate terms about how he had been enslaved by Wordsworth's poems for two years. 'The whole aggregate of pleasure I have received from some eight or nine other poets that I have been able to find since the world began falls infinitely short of what these two enchanting volumes have singly afforded me.'

Just the thought of meeting Wordsworth had rescued him from despair during the last two years, but what chance had he to meet him? 'What claim can I urge to a fellowship with such a society as yours, with genius so wild and magnificent?' He added that he was just a boy, but that 'my life had been passed chiefly in the contemplation and worship of nature'.

De Quincey was indeed only a boy, nearly eighteen, but the use of the word 'nature' was a little bit sweeping. He had been living for many months with the down-and-outs in London, consorting with drug addicts and prostitutes, until his money had run out. He was born in Manchester, the son of a wealthy merchant who had died when De Quincey was seven. He went to Manchester Grammar School, where he'd been brilliant at Latin, but had run away. Now, in the summer of 1803, he was waiting to go up to Oxford. Wordsworth was so impressed by De Quincey's sensitivity and language that he wrote a letter in reply, adding an invitation to visit him at Grasmere. It was probably the first letter of this kind that Wordsworth had ever received.

Nearly three years later, during which time De Quincey had continued to rave to fellow students about Wordsworth and Coleridge, he made an attempt to take up the standing invitation. He got as far as Coniston, where he spent the night in an inn, but gave up out of shyness and returned to Oxford.

In 1807, however, he managed to get himself introduced to Coleridge who was staying with friends in Somerset. The first flush of excitement at being all together in the Lakes was temporarily over. William, Dorothy and Mary were as cosy as ever in Dove Cottage, but there had been some coldness between William and Coleridge. Coleridge's addiction to opium had become worse and he was already ill. His marriage was collapsing, much to the distress of the Wordsworths, who didn't approve of his behaviour or his habits.

Coleridge, then, had left the circle and was wandering abroad, doing odd reviewing jobs, visiting old friends in the West Country when De Quincey managed to meet him. De Quincey knew all Coleridge's work by heart and they had three hours of great philosophical and intellectual discussion. Despite being the much younger man, De Quincey was a great reader and was almost as learned as Coleridge.

To De Quincey's surprise, Mrs Coleridge appeared. He had heard stories of the marriage problems, but she was down visiting Coleridge with her children. He realised the coldness between them, but he was quite taken with her. Lord Byron had recently lampooned Coleridge and Southey for having married two such boring sisters, describing them as 'two milliners from Bath' which young De Quincey thought was a vile insult.

De Quincey liked both of them and arranged to make an anonymous gift of £300 to Coleridge, doing it through a third party, saying it was 'from a young man of fortune who admired his talents'. Coleridge had to go to London, to do some lecturing, so de Quincey offered to squire Mrs Coleridge and the children by coach back up to the Lake District. And so, in November 1807, De Quincey at last met Wordsworth – almost five years after being first invited.

Their first stop in the Lakes was at Dove Cottage. The three Coleridge children – Hartley nine, Derwent seven and Sara five – were all very excited and Hartley ran ahead as they approached the gate. De Quincey could hardly contain himself. 'This little cottage was tenanted by the man whom, of all men from the beginning of time, I most fervently desired to meet; that in less than a minute I should meet Wordsworth face to face. I did tremble.'

De Quincey's description of the great meeting is in his *Recollections of the Lake Poets*, perhaps the most readable, if rather bitchy, observations ever written about Wordsworth.

He was, upon the whole, not a well made man. His legs were pointedly condemned by all female connoisseurs in legs; not that they were bad in any way which would force itself upon your notice – there was no absolute deformity about them; and undoubtedly they had been serviceable legs beyond the average standard of human requisition; for I calculate, upon good data, that with these identical legs Wordsworth must have traversed a distance of 175,000 to 180,000 English miles – a mode of exercise which, to him, stood in the stead of alcohol and other stimulants; to which indeed he was indebted for a life of unclouded happiness, and we for much of what is excellent in his writings. But, useful as they have proved themselves, Wordsworth's legs were certainly not ornamental; and it was really a pity, as I agreed with a lady in thinking, that he had not another pair for evening dress parties – when no boots lend their friendly aid to mask out imperfections from the eyes of female rigorists.

The Wordsworths had three children by now: John aged four and a half when De Quincey arrived, Dora aged three, and Thomas aged one. De Quincey was excellent with the children, thinking up games and amusements for them. He was also very good with the womenfolk, chatting them up, accompanying them on little trips, squiring them on social occasions when William wouldn't go. On his first visit he stayed for a week.

Dove Cottage soon became far too small for their growing brood, plus all the relations and friends who seemed permanently to be staying with them, and in May 1808 the Wordsworths moved out of Dove Cottage into a bigger house nearby in Grasmere, Allan Bank. It was a new house, and Wordsworth had watched furiously as it was being built. 'A temple of abomination,' so he'd described it, 'the house will stare you in the face from every part of the Vale and entirely destroy its character of simplicity and seclusion.' But as it was the only house available when he came to move, he ate his words and took it over.

Dorothy was thrilled that at last they would have a room each, but it was she who had all the trouble of the removal. Mary was pregnant with her fourth child. Sarah Hutchinson (Mary's sister), who had become almost a permanent resident, was ill and William himself, though master of the house, was no help. 'He you know is not expected to do anything,' wrote Dorothy in a letter. They soon discovered that the fireplace had been badly built, so William had been right in alleging that it was jerry built, and filled the house with smoke. It was so cold one winter's day and the fire so unworkable that they all took to their beds in the middle of the afternoon, with the baby in the centre to keep it warm.

De Quincey took over Dove Cottage when they moved out – and he had the tenancy of the cottage for the next twenty-eight years. Dorothy made him curtains and his arrival was re-membered for 'the never ending books that continued to arrive in packing cases for several months in succession'. He was very proud to be a resident of Grasmere, one of the literary Lakers at last, and thrilled by the beauty of Dove Cottage and life in Grasmere.

When the lake froze over in winter, he watched the Wordsworths going skating. William loved skating and was very proud of his skills. They all went as a family – Dorothy and Mary on chairs, holding a baby each in their arms, while William with a relative or some other adult, skated behind, pushing them across the lake. It's a sight you rarely see in the Lakes today. None of the lakes ever seems to freeze right over, the way they did in the early nineteenth century. Esthwaite Water, particularly, the one beside Hawkshead, was always freezing over in William's school days. Today, our winters are positively Mediterranean by comparison.

De Quincey, ever observant of William's physical appearance, wasn't as enchanted by William's skating as William himself was. 'He sprawled upon the ice like a cow dancing a cotillion,' so De Quincey rather acidly comments in his book.

He was fascinated by William's marriage and his whole attitude to women. He just couldn't imagine Wordsworth ever being head over heels in love with a woman.

I could not conceive of Wordsworth as submitting his faculties to the humilities and devotion of courtship. That self surrender seemed a mere impossibility. Wordsworth, I take it upon myself to say, had not the feelings within him which makes this total devotion to a woman possible. There never lived a woman whom he would not have lectured and admonished under circumstances that should have seemed to require it; nor would he have conversed with her in any mood whatever without wearing an air of mild condescension. Wordsworth, being so, never could in any emphatic sense, have been a lover.

If only De Quincey had known about Annette! What a surprise he would have had. He surely didn't, because in his *Recollections* he mentions Wordsworth's stay in Orleans, without a hint of the affair. And De Quincey, who repeated and enlarged on every bit of gossip, would certainly have used it in his book as he spared nobody's feelings. But this was how he now found Wordsworth – a prematurely aged and rather stiff, self-centred man in his late thirties, surrounded by doting women.

Whatever De Quincey may have thought of Wordsworth's personality, he always had a very high estimation of his work and rejoiced in all his success and good strokes of fortune. 'A more fortunate man, I believe, does not exist than Wordsworth.'

But there were some bad bits of luck. The first death that seriously upset Wordsworth, as an adult, was the death of his beloved sailor brother John in 1805. John had become captain of the *Earl of Abergavenny* which sank off Portland Bill. He had life savings, worth around £20,000, invested in the cargo and had planned to return to the Lakes on the proceeds, to live with William and Dorothy and give up the sea for ever. The whole family was distraught for months.

Two of Wordsworth's five children died while very young, both in the same year, 1812. Thomas was only six and died of pneumonia following measles and Catharine, aged four, after a seizure. It happened at the Parsonage, yet another Grasmere house, one equally damp and uncomfortable, which the Wordsworths moved into in 1811.

De Quincey had been particularly close to little Catharine and she'd been very fond of him. 'The whole of Grasmere is not large enough to allow of any great distance between house and house and as it happened that little Kate Wordsworth returned my love, she in a manner lived with me at my solitary cottage; as often as I could entice her from home, walked with me, slept with me, and was my sole companion.'

De Quincey appears almost to have been mentally deranged by her death, stretching himself every night for two months on her gravestone in Grasmere churchyard, convinced that he could see her walking. It was only when he left the Lakes for a while, going back to Bristol, that he eventually got over her.

The closeness of their lives in Grasmere, living so much in each other's laps, did tend to swing them from one extreme to another, usually over something petty, though those first differences between Wordsworth and Coleridge were eventually patched over. After wandering around elsewhere, Coleridge came back to the Lakes in 1808 and moved in with the Wordsworths in Grasmere, staying with them almost non-stop for eighteen months, which didn't in the end endear him to them very much.

The really big row, when it came, the one which led to a real estrangement between Wordsworth and Coleridge, was about something Wordsworth was supposed to have said. According to a mutual friend, Wordsworth had described Coleridge as having become 'an absolute nuisance in the family'. He was now 'a rotten drunkard' who had 'rotted his entrails out by intemperance'. Wordsworth now had a perfectly respectable family life, with a loving wife and children, and perfectly respectable friends, like the new Lord Lonsdale.

Coleridge, however, had gone downhill – or had continued as he'd always been, depending on your point of view. His marriage had finally collapsed and he was even more dependent on drugs and other stimulants. Wordsworth was therefore glad to get him out of his house where he had lived for so long, moaning and complaining. Sarah Hutchinson was part of the household, acting for a while as his secretary, until finally she refused to have anything more to do with him.

Wordsworth, after he had gone, denied he'd used such a phrase as 'rotten drunkard', but Coleridge didn't believe it. Letters and accusations flew back and forth, getting terribly confused and exaggerated in the process. It was a typical Victorian literary row, the sort that both Dickens and Thackeray got mixed up in, with people denying things they were supposed to have said. When Coleridge did make a return trip to the Lakes to see his children, he drove straight through Grasmere, passing the Wordsworth house, without even stopping. That story was soon all round London.

They had lived almost as one family in Grasmere for over ten years – and before that in the West Country. In his notebooks Coleridge wrote that he had given Wordsworth fourteen years of 'consummate friendship' and been 'enthusiastically watchful' over his literary fame. 'Yet the events of the last year have now forced me to perceive – no one on earth has ever LOVED ME.' He concluded that Wordsworth had only ever given him the 'semblance of friendship'.

Then came a row with De Quincey, which, when it eventually happened, was equally convoluted. The specific trouble, according to the Wordsworths, was that De Quincey cut down the moss hut in the back garden of Dove Cottage to give the apple trees more light. The real affront, as others saw it, was moral and social. De Quincey had taken to opium and, having been through all that with Coleridge, the Wordsworths couldn't stand it any more. He had also taken up with a local girl, Margaret Sympson, by whom he had a child. He married her the following year, in Grasmere church, and made it all respectable (which Wordsworth, in his youth, never did) but the Wordsworths tried to make him give her up and were upset by the marriage, much to De Quincey's resentment.

Reading between the lines in De Quincey's *Recollections*, it seems that the real trouble was that Wordsworth never treated young De Quincey as an equal. He was willing to concede points to Wordsworth, but Wordsworth would never concede anything to him, dismissing his opinions as childish, or just ignoring them. 'Having observed this human arrogance, I took care never to lay myself under the possibility of such an insult. Systematically I avoided saying anything, however suddenly tempted into any expression of my feelings, upon the natural appearance whether in the sky or upon the earth. Thus I evaded one cause of quarrel.'

In the end, so he maintains, he couldn't put up with Wordsworth's over-bearing attitude any longer. He would always admire him as a writer but no longer as a person. There was no alternative but to leave.

So the Grasmere days ended in some disagreeable times. It had all begun so wonderfully, with their idyllic little group. It was the most creative period in Wordsworth's poetic life, but the changes in Coleridge greatly saddened him. He was never as close to Southey, who stayed on at Keswick, working away in his library, well out of all the squabbles. The outside world thought they were one tight little group of writers, as they still do, even when De Quincey went off in a sulk and started pouring out the real truth, or at least the gossip. Not that Wordsworth really cared. He was by this time installed beside the next lake, in a large handsome house on Rydal Water, his last home where he was to spend the next thirty-seven years of his life. His most successful days were yet to come.

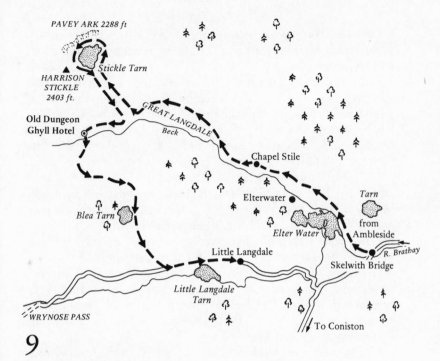

9
LANGDALE

Mr Norman Nicholson, Lakeland's resident poet. A walk up Great Langdale. Not a Co-op van driver but a potter.

LAKELAND HAS ONLY ONE POET TODAY. ONLY ONE PERSON has spent his whole life in Lakeland and managed, somehow, to survive simply on his writing. It's a remarkable feat. Even Wordsworth moved away for those few years. Norman Nicholson has never had a job. He's not known nationally to the general public, like Betjeman, and recognition, even by the poetry public, has been slow in coming, though in 1977 he was awarded the Queen's Gold Medal for Poetry and in the same year the Arts Council awarded him a grant of £3000.

He's sixty-four and wears bushy, mutton-chop grey whiskers which give him a Wordsworthian look. He's neat and painstaking, in himself and in his conversation, explaining things very carefully. He's lived an enclosed life, acquiring his knowledge in his own way and in his own time, a self-educated, self-formed, original almost innocent figure. Most of us have had to work with others, in offices or factories, and been formed by our environment, taking our chance in conversation, bouncing as we are pushed. Norman Nicholson therefore can strike an outsider as rather didactic. He would probably have become a teacher, if circumstances had been different.

I went down the Duddon Valley to see him, in the little terrace house in Millom where he was born and still lives. Millom is in south Lakeland, in the Furness area, not a place that pulls the tourists; at one time it repelled them as Millom was a smoky industrial town, with iron works that boomed and roared for almost a century, right from the day that local iron ore was discovered in 1843. The collapse was terrible. Millom was left a shell. Unemployment in the 1930s was about the worst in the country. Today, there is still a certain sadness about the town, a left-over feeling, but the grimness and grime have gone, the old works flattened – which Nicholson for one regrets, as he liked the structure of the old iron works – but to a stranger, such as myself, coming down the Duddon Valley and seeing the sea is a delightful surprise. I had never realised the Duddon sands were so beautiful. When the tide is out the sand stretches for ever. There are several lush little valleys that come down from central Lakeland and they seem to walk straight into the sea – a strange visual juxtaposition. The eye is used to the still waters of a lake with the fells behind but not as part of the open, moving, living sea.

His little street is right in the middle of the town, surrounded by grocers, betting shops and small supermarkets. Next door there is an Oxfam shop. His house was a shop at one time and still retains the old shape, except that the main shop part, down-stairs as you come in, is now his entrance hall. His father was a gents' outfitter and this was his shop until his death in 1954. Norman was the only child and it was discovered at sixteen that he had TB. He attended the local secondary school in Millom and his parents had hoped that he would go on, possibly to university or a training college, but instead they had to put their savings together and send him for two years to a sanitorium in the New Forest. They knew that the chances were that he would remain an invalid all his life.

'I was very ill indeed. I spent fifteen months in bed, staying in a little chalet on my own. It was my form of university. I read three books a day. My generation was now on to Lawrence but I was working my way through Wells, Bennett and Shaw. I learned about nature. From my bed I identified fifty species of birds.'

He came back to Millom as a semi-invalid, having to rest and do special exercises, and spent the next ten to twelve years at home with his parents, doing little apart from trying to recover. There was no possibility of being fit enough for a job. 'My parents had made big sacrifices for me by sending me away. My first duty was to get well.'

In 1935 his imagination was awakened dramatically when he read T. S. Eliot for the first time. He says it was the shock which jolted him into trying to write. For seven years he attempted to write poetry, mainly working Eliot out of his system, with no success, still being completely supported by his parents, then in 1944 his first book of poems, *Five Rivers*, was published and won the Heinemann prize.

He's gone on since then to produce several other volumes of poetry as well as verse dramas and has led a busy writing life, without ever having much money. Looking back, he's amazed how he survived for so long. His chief means of support, from his father, looked as if it had disappeared on his father's death in 1954 but in 1956 he married a local teacher, providing himself – as he admits cheerfully – with another bread winner to augment his income. His wife Yvonne was teaching at Millom Girls' School and they met when she came to see him while she was studying for a diploma which had one of his verse dramas, *The Old Man of the Mountains*, as a set book. She has now retired from teaching.

Apart from poetry, he has written five topographical books, all about Lakeland. He's probably better known for these. They've certainly made him more money, especially *Portrait of the Lakes*, produced in 1963, which is still selling well and is now in paperback. His style and presentation of writing about Lakeland has been much admired, and much copied. They tend to be a type of anthology, looking at different aspects of Lakeland life, based on great research and first-hand knowledge, and written in a polished, tight, personal prose style. They are probably the best of the post-war books on the Lakes.

'I'm not planning any more books on the Lakes. Books about the Lakes come out so rapidly, about one a month I should think. I like to think I've influenced other writers on the Lakes, drawing their attention to specialist subjects, like geology, which has long been ignored. Poetry is now the thing again. If I have anything else to say, I'll say it in poetry.'

It was surprising to discover, having read his topographical books, that he hadn't actually been on top of all the heights he so vividly describes. Since the onset of TB at sixteen, he's been unable to do any hard climbing, though he's managed nonetheless to view almost everywhere in Lakeland. Relatively late in life, his health seems to be improving, which is good news. 'I could do more in my fifties than I could do in my forties and now in my sixties I can do even more.' He has no plans for discovering the rest of the world. He's only ever been abroad to one place and that was to Norway. 'My compass always turns North. I would never go South. I'm extending my knowledge of Cumbria by going to see the Norsemen. I'm very insular.' He does a bit of lecturing and gives readings of his own poetry, but mostly in the North of England.

Unlike Wordsworth, he's never had any private patronage, except for a cheque for £100 which once came through the post to his publishers, Faber and Faber, from an anonymous reader. The Arts Council money (which is taxable) has come a bit late in life, though nonetheless welcome. In the end he did get a degree, an honorary MA from Manchester University.

'I've never been tempted to move away. I find this area exceptionally satisfying. My forefathers lived and died here and I feel a sense of continuity. As an industrial community, the town has died but it will endure as a place to live.

'If I'd been in medicine or the church, someone of my standing would have been quite well rewarded by now. As a poet, I've always lived a modest life. I've been exceptionally fortunate. Falling ill was probably the luckiest break I had because through that I found writing.'

As one might imagine, he is an admirer of Wordsworth, having written of and been influenced by the same Lakeland scenery. 'Wordsworth was an enormous poet but I used to resent him at one time. I worried I might seem like a second-hand version of him. He wasn't a perfect technician, in fact he could be clumsy, but he is one of the three or four key people in the history of English literature.

'In my opinion, it wasn't principally his concern for nature that makes him so important. There was something else. Up to the end of the eighteenth century, England was a homogeneous society. When Pope wrote, all the educated people of the day felt as he did and knew and agreed with what he was writing about. Today, unless you are writing for a specific group, whether it be Marxists, Mormons or nudists, you simply can't expect people to agree with you. What a poet does today is write about himself.

'Wordsworth was the first to realise that a poet's most important subject is himself. He's given us an absolutely authoritative account of how the poet felt. He said to himself, what is the thing I know most about, and the answer was himself. On the whole, this is what poets have written about ever since. "The Prelude" was his epic work, all about himself.'

Like Wordsworth, Norman Nicholson is very fond of the Duddon Valley, not just because it's local and he knows it best but because there is so much variety in it. As I went back up the valley, heading for the Langdales again, I thought again how little it has changed over the centuries. Little Langdale has hardly changed either, which is a surprise, as it's so popular, but Great Langdale, where I was heading next, can get completely over-run in the summer.

Great Langdale is much bigger and broader and has long been one of the country's chief climbing centres. This is where the professionals come, loaded down with their hardware, not the sort who get lost in the mist in their wellies. The valley starts very gently, almost suburbanly, at Elter Water. I didn't notice any swans on the strangely shaped little tarn, though I looked hard through the reeds. The name comes from the Old Norse and means 'swan lake'; but I did spot a huge flock of orange-coated, greatly-crested youth hostellers, getting their nesting materials on their backs and coating their feet in several tons of thick leather and nails. In the season, when you meet them swarming all over the long, flat-bottomed valley, you can't believe there'll be enough rocks for them to fall off.

You can see the Langdale Pikes for miles around and I'd been following them and marvelling at their distintive, spiky silhouettes for weeks. They're perhaps the most impressive-looking crags in the whole of the Lake District and easily the most loved by decades of climbers and walkers. Well, perhaps Borrowdale is equally popular, but it's a close-run thing. It would be interesting to know the best-walked paths, the most-climbed crags, the most-savoured views. The National Trust and the National Park people know the well-frequented parts of the Lakes – erosion is the give-away. In Great Langdale they are particularly worried that some paths, even on the high crags, will disappear under the weight of numbers and they're making great efforts to re-direct the hordes.

I gave myself an easy climb, this being climbing country, and headed up the valley side to Stickle Tarn. There are some terrific water falls on the way up Stickle Ghyll, all nicely fenced in, the paths laid with poles, viewing stations beaten flat by generations of gapers. The Victorians loved all waterfalls and these and the nearby Dungeon Ghyll waterfalls were an enormous attraction.

The path beside the Ghyll climbs incredibly steeply and I was soon into rough scree and rocks. If you fell, no one would hear your screams for the sound of the waterfalls. All the way up, the beck roars and screeches as it throws itself in a suicide fall over rock faces and I was grateful for the times the path veered away, just to give my ears a rest.

Stickle Tarn came as a sudden and beautiful surprise and I almost exclaimed in excitement. I had been turning round every few yards on the scree slopes, admiring the changing view below. It had started with a view back down Great Langdale. Then slowly as I got higher, I caught glimpses of Coniston Water. Higher still, Coniston appeared to be suspended wholly in mid-air, as if I could stretch over and touch it. So it was a surprise, turning away from all those fine views, to find myself facing the tarn. Such calm, still water, so smooth and inviting, with behind, rising sheer out of the tarn, the tremendous rock face of Pavey Ark.

I had never done this walk before and I hadn't realised from the map how the tarn would look. The mass of the rock is so awe-inspiring that you forget how small the Lakes' mountains are, compared with the Alps or the Himalayas. The scale might be small, but once you're up amongst them, the effect is gigantic. The sky always seems so close in the Lakes that the hills appear to dominate the universe. Anyway, the result that morning was breathtaking. A poet could not but be gay. With his heart leaping up so many times, no wonder Wordsworth worked so hard to describe it all.

They all have such strange names, the Pikes in the Langdales. To my left I could see Harrison Stickle, a great block of crystal gingerbread, stuck on the end of Pavey Ark. Then there's Pike O'Stickle and Gimmer Crag. I could see a glimmer of several paths ahead but they disappeared in a covering of light snow which had fallen overnight, covering the rock faces. I stuck to my plan of walking round the tarn and not attempting anything too clever. I'd leave the real rock climbs for the professionals. They can spend all day on one slab, gripping it, searching its hidden crevices, its secret orifices, waiting and caressing, coupling and poking, inserting and pulling, their ropes stiff and taut, working themselves slowly into position as they jerk themselves forward in fits, in starts, till the moment of supreme climax when they reach their peak and lie exhausted on the top, all passion spent, their lifelines dangling limp and lifeless. Not my idea of fun, or even sublimation. Give me a grassy path along the fellside any old day.

I met hordes of people on my way down, all struggling up the scree to the tarn. There was a large school party, as ever, rather out of breath but very cheerful. They were handicapped kids, so the teacher said, from a special school in Wigan. He brought a party of them up to the Lakes by mini-bus every Wednesday. Now that the M6 has brought the Lakes to the doorstep of Manchester, he could be here in a couple of hours, spend a long day in the hills, and be back in time for bed, with none of the problems of carting luggage, and getting accommodation.

I was aiming for Dungeon Ghyll Falls which, according to the map, were very near. I crossed the beck on some stepping stones but I couldn't see anything of the waterfalls. They must be higher up, or perhaps the first lot of waterfalls I'd admired were the Dungeon Ghyll Falls. Much as I love reading maps, they can splatter emotive words in huge letters, or in what seems huge letters, and you rush to inspect exciting things – like Roman Fort, Prehistoric Circle, Piles of Stones (the Ordnance Survey is especially fond of Piles of Stones), Old Quarries, Climbing Hut, Waterfalls, Springs, Bloomery (which is where they smelted iron), Maiden Castle (where they burned maidens?), Mound (which might be anything) and, best of all, PH meaning public house. But very often when you get there, all you can find is nothing at all.

I gave up looking for the other waterfalls and hit a nice easy path along the side of the valley which brought me out above Old Dungeon Ghyll Hotel, a busy-looking hotel, at the end of Great Langdale. This is where the road stops, should you be the sort of cheapskate who brings a motor car to the Langdales, tut tut. After that, you have to walk, though there is still some easy walking ahead up two smaller valleys, till you're completely surrounded by the towering fells and crags, the sort which true climbers dream about, slaver over when they're back in industrial Lancashire. Bowfell, Crinkle Crags, Rossett Pike, Scafell Pike, Great Gable. This is the way the real climbers go, up up and away.

Behind the hotel, I came across a mass of well-painted signposts in a secret, climbers' language, which took me some time to decipher. 'Path for NDG, Pavey, Far East,' said one sign. I knew that Pavey was short for Pavey Ark and at length I realised that NDG must be New Dungeon Ghyll. But Far East might mean anything or everything.

The signs were beside a mountain rescue hut – which was where the map said it would be – and it announced on the wooden door that it had been opened by Chris Bonington. I hoped to meet him, later on my journey, and I wondered if he would speak a climbers' language I wouldn't understand. Well, every subculture has to have its little ways, its private dress and gear and words and mating calls. Inside the bar of the Old Dungeon Ghyll Hotel it was pretty easy to understand what kind of language climbers speak, once they've stopped climbing. It's called throwing things. There was a huge notice saying 5p deposit on every glass. I was alone and the lady behind the bar could see from my wellies and my lack of pick-axes that I wasn't one of the heavies but, even so, she made a big performance of *not* charging me 5p deposit on my glass of draught Guinness, letting me know what a big favour she was doing.

'No, I wouldn't say the climbers always go wild,' she said, watching the white froth slowly rise. 'A bit enthusiastic perhaps.' The bar was spartan and primitive, with stone floors and white-washed walls and little cattle byres where the drinkers can herd together. The most mischief they could cause would be to each other, if they did get a bit too enthusiastic. There were some climbers' cartoons on the wall, all very sixth form and equally primitive. The punch line in most of the jokes seemed to be Piss Off.

In the hotel proper, it was surprisingly comfortable and attractive. I got a brochure and the terms looked reasonable – £6 for bed and breakfast, so it said for 1978 – and I made a note to come back some day. The property is owned by the National Trust, as is much of the Great Langdale Valley, most of it being left to them in 1928 by that great benefactor, G. M. Trevelyan, the historian. Did he come here of an evening for a spot of glass throwing? As seaside hotels boast a sea view in their brochure, so the Old Dungeon Ghyll Hotel has a very Lake District attraction in clear letters in its brochure: 'A large Drying Room is available in the cellar.'

There's a regular Ribble bus service right to the front door of the hotel (as I discovered when I went outside) from Ambleside, via Skelwith Bridge and Elter Water, four times a day. How nice to think that such an isolated place should have a bus service – all thanks to its being a mecca for climbers.

I turned left and headed across the valley towards the little winding road that climbs up and over into Little Langdale. At Wall End, just as I started the climb, I inspected a lovely barn, a dry-stone barn, made of stone and layers of slate. I could see no trace of cement, even where it had been repaired. Dry-stone walls are commonplace but I hadn't seen a dry-stone building before. Put that on your map, Mr os.

On top of the road, which is usually impassable in winter, you catch the first sight of a lonely tarn called Blea Tarn. It has a pretty setting amid pine trees and with a bit of landscape cheating and fiddling could easily be another Tarn Hows, should the great British public want another Tarn Hows. I'm sure the local farmers don't.

The road down into Little Langdale was rather marred by a succession of empty polythene bags that kept blowing towards me, the sort which are all the rage with farmers these days. They contain feeding blocks, full of magnesium, which farmers leave in the fields, especially in lambing time. They open one side of the plastic bag, exposing the block, which soon takes on the appearance of a very large cow pat. When it's eaten up, the bags just blow away, unless the farmer goes round again and collects them. The ones I picked and tried to hide were marked RUMEVITE. The National Trust should get on to the manufacturers and suggest they make the bags in edible plastic. Then every farmer could have a conservational glow.

In the bar of the Three Shires in Little Langdale, I met a Co-op delivery man called Tom Wilson. His little Co-op van was outside and he said he was collecting orders from local farmers' wives for the Co-op in Chapel Stile. Wouldn't it be easier if they rang their orders through? Farmers these days do have telephones. But he said no. It was a tradition round here. Farmers' wives liked to be called upon. Most of them didn't have a car and were stuck at home all day. Anyway, he wasn't really a proper Co-op salesman. It was just a temporary job, for a few weeks. 'I'm a middle-aged drop-out from the rat race, that's what I really am.'

Four years ago he was working as the manager of a wallpaper machinery factory in Cheshire and had a good salary, a nice semi and he and his wife ran two cars. 'We became upset at our young son's materialism. Simple presents weren't enough. He had to have a new bike or a hi-fi on his birthday, or else he felt his friends looked down upon him. I realised we were all living to keep up with the Joneses. My wife had a part-time job in order to afford the second car which she needed in order to go to her part-time job. It was a vicious circle. Yet we didn't seem to be getting much pleasure out of it. We hardly met. I came home at six and she went out at six to work.'

Now they have a rented cottage in Great Langdale and for a year he's been trying to set himself up as a full-time potter. 'Driving the Co-op van is just an interlude. Overlook that, will you. I bought myself a kiln which has cost £1000 and I need a regular job to manage the payments. My old friends think I'm a nut, but we love it. Our son is happy at the local school. I worry slightly that he's a bit remote from other boys his age, living in an isolated cottage, but he now writes poetry, something he never did before.'

They live a very simple life, he and his wife and twelve-year-old son. Frugal was the word he used. They eat a lot of toast. 'We do eat less well than in the old days but we tell ourselves how healthy it all is, how we'll live longer. We buy very little. We have no drink in the house. We have no fuel bills because we only use wood for heat and we gather all that ourselves from the fields and the fells. You're allowed to pick up any fallen branch under six inches in circumference. Our son keeps on trying to break up big bits but I tell him to search around, there's enough little bits waiting to be gathered. That's on Sunday afternoon, when we do our weekly wood-gathering session. In the morning we go for our weekly swim at Windermere, in the Lakes School pool. It's a big day for us, Sundays.

'Socially, we have a terrific time. You think at first there must be nothing happening in Langdale, just a few cottages, but there's endless dances and lectures. We've had a Windscale scientist to talk to us, someone on red deer, how to make furniture, how the mountain rescue teams work. All fascinating. And all free. Then there's cheese and wine parties, Young Wives' dos. My wife is very active in the Young Wives and puts on plays in the school hall. It's a more social life than in Cheshire. We just didn't have the time then. We were too exhausted working.

'I shall succeed as a potter. In fact I wish I'd never mentioned the Co-op job. I've got a feeling I'm going to make it. I look around, trying hard to be unbiased, and I tell myself that this time next year I'll be out of the clag, out of the shite. I'm very critical by nature but when I look at my stuff, I'm very happy. My sort of work will break through. I just know it. A friend of mine sold four the other day in London – just on photographs and to another pottery! Can you imagine it. Another potter buying my work. That was a fantastic sign. I felt great for days.

'What I specialise in is little Welsh dressers, only four inches high, but they have all the shelves and plates on them. Sometimes I put a bit of cheese on the plate, the sort of thing you might leave lying on a Welsh dresser, or an old newspaper, or a cat curled up on the top shelf. Each is different and unique. I number them. They'll be collectors' items one of these days. I know it. I used to be an instrument maker, that's how I was trained. I love small things. I love small women. So we'll forget the Co-op. I'm a *potter*.'

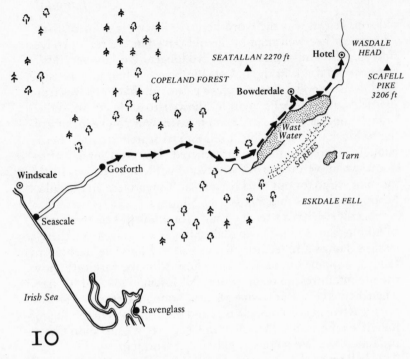

10

WAST WATER

The life of a world champion. The amazing Herdwick sheep.

I THEN MOVED ON TO WAST WATER, THE HOME OF ONE OF Lakeland's best-known living residents, Joss Naylor. If you live in the Lakes you are bound to have heard of him. He holds many world records. They just happen to be records that most of the world has never heard of.

Joss Naylor is not just well known in the Lakes – he's well liked. They don't always go together. Cumbrians, like most rural types, suspect anyone who becomes too successful or too well known. They look out for people becoming 'lost', too big for their boots, too flash and full of themselves. Joss Naylor is known for doing something which requires that much admired quality, hard graft. He runs hard and he works even harder, combining a tough life as a sheep farmer on the high fells where it's surprising anything can live, with running up and down peaks or combinations of peaks, sometimes all day and all night, depending on the particular madness of the race he's running.

Fell running is a sport so easy to admire. You can *see* the peaks. You know how hard it is to walk up them. So imagine tearing up – and down – seventy-two of them in twenty-four hours, just for the fun of it. World-class marathon runners have failed to beat Joss, not aware of the variety of terrain which has to be covered, the complexity of pacing yourself, of knowing how to run over swamp and rocks, how to avoid hidden peaty holes and leap over bracken, what sorts of grass and moss to trust. It's not just long-distance running – it's long-distance, obstacle running.

His home is in Wasdale, overlooking the banks of Wast Water. It's probably the most dramatic valley in the whole of the Lake District yet approaching from the coastal plain, as most people do, it starts off soft and rather lush, till you reach the lake itself, when life and nature narrows and becomes tough and unrelenting. It's an isolated, hidden valley with a one-way road. You can't drive into it from central Lakeland. You have to work your way right round the coast to get in, so most tourists never see it.

Almost at the end of the lake, on the left-hand side, you come to an isolated farm called Bowderdale, the home of Joss Naylor. The road itself peters out in another mile or so at Wasdalehead, a little tundra of no man's land, like an Alpine oasis, with, towering behind the peaks of Scafell and Great Gabel, the highest mass of mountains in the whole of the Lakes.

You can just see his farm house from the little road – but you can't imagine how anybody farms there. The surrounding fells seem to be sheer rocks and scree. There appears to be nothing for the sheep to eat. It would take a rural alchemist, turning base rock into pasture, to scratch any sort of living.

Joss weighs only nine and a half stone, yet he's not much short of six feet high. His face is spare and seems to be all bone with deep-set eyes. Most surprising of all is his walk, as if every step was agony. It is only on the fells that the speed of his walk is apparent, his long legs eating up the yards.

For most of his life he has indeed been in agony. He's had disc trouble since the age of nine and has spent many years undergoing operations and wearing corsets and special strait-jackets. He had two discs removed from his back when he was twenty but then he fell and had fifty-four months off work, six months in all in a surgical jacket. Many nights he's had no sleep at all and it's only been in the last few months that he's had any pain-free hours. He's been told constantly over the years by doctors and surgeons to give up sheep farming and fell running and find an easier life.

Joss Naylor was born in 1936 in Wasdalehead, just a mile from his present house, where his father was a tenant farmer of Middle Row Farm. The Naylors had originally come from round Parkend in John Peel country. He went to elementary school at Gosforth, the village some eight miles away towards the coast, the school which his two younger children now attend. He played a bit of football at school, did a bit of Cumberland and Westmorland wrestling, but his back always handicapped him. He left at fifteen and became a shepherd, working for his father and on other farms. His disability got him out of National Service. But for his fell running, which has now taken him on trips round Britain and as far away as Colorado, he's lived and worked in Wasdale.

His wife Mary comes from Newcastle – a city girl who came one summer to work for two months for Joss's mother who, like Joss and his wife today, takes in paying guests in the holiday seasons. They got married in 1962 and the same year Joss applied to be the tenant of Bowderdale which has just become empty. He offered £166 a year for it, the same rent as the previous tenant had paid. There were higher offers but they decided to let a local shepherd have it who would know how to run it. The rent is now a lot higher, but he won't say how much. You have to work hard to get Cumbrians to discuss money.

For his £166 a year, he got a farm of 140 acres, only eighteen acres of which are workable, though even those are only good enough for hay not arable. The sheep graze almost entirely on the open high fells, some 2000 acres of Red Pike, High Fell and Scoatfell which go up 2700 feet, most of it today owned by the National Trust. For his £166 he also got 150 stock sheep, all Herdwick. If and when he ever gives up the farm, he must leave the same number and type of sheep. It took him ten years to build up his own stock of sheep to over 1000 which is what he has today.

He's a one-man sheep farmer, having no help, even at the height of shearing and lambing seasons, which makes his fell running all the more surprising. In order to get away for a big race, he has to work round the clock for weeks before, getting ahead with his jobs. It's impossible to get a stand-in shepherd, though, when he's desperate, his brother will keep an eye on things. Nobody's daft enough to be a sheep farmer today, not on these fells.

He's awake each day at dawn, has a mug of hot water from the Aga stove which is permanently on, and then starts the day. The first job is to milk the cow which he does by hand. She gives about three gallons and he puts it in the fridge. The family drink the previous day's milk on their breakfast cereal. They have three children. The younger two, Susan ten and Paul nine, go eight miles on the school bus from the road end to Gosforth. The eldest, Gillian, has to go to the secondary modern school at Keswick where she boards during the week.

Depending on the time of the year, he spends most of each day on the fells, working till it's too dark to work. He has six dogs, all Curs, who go with him – Scamp, Laddy, Bob, Gip, Speck and Patch.

He never eats anything during the day. All he takes with him is a Mars bar. If he gets hungry, he might have a few mouthfuls of spring water on the fells. Hunger soon passes if you drink. When he comes down from the fells, he has a scrub down in the beck. In the summer, he gets in up to his waist but in the winter he just takes his boots and socks off and freshens his legs.

When he was building up his stock, a ewe in 1962 cost him around £4. Today, a Herdwick ewe will cost him £20 while a Swaledale will cost £25. He has mainly Herdwicks, which are most suited to the rough land, plus some Swaledales and Rough Fell Crosses. The reason why a Swaledale ewe comes dearer than a Herdwick ewe is that a Swaledale is ninety per cent sure to produce lambs while a Herdwick is only sixty per cent.

He has about 400 lambs a year, all things being equal, and he goes on to sell all but six of the males who are kept as rams for breeding. The rest of the males are castrated – at birth rubber rings are fitted on their testicles which drop off after six weeks. – then fattened up and sold. All the ewes are kept for breeding, eventually replacing the older ewes which either die or get too old to withstand the life on the high fells.

There's a technical language amongst sheep farmers, passed on from generation to generation by word of mouth. Gimmer t'winter is the name for a two-year-old ewe. Wether t'winter is the equivalent male. He's sold off all his male lambs by the time they're three years old, selling them at fat-stock sales in Cockermouth in October and November.

For their first winter, all the lambs are kept near the farm house, in the inbye land, as it's known in Cumbria. But as Joss has so little suitable winter pasture, he sends at least 100 lambs every winter away further down the valley – which costs him £7 a lamb.

The adult ewes spend most of the year on the high fells, usually coming to the inbye land for mating in November and December (they start breeding at three years old) and again in April for lambing. By May, most of them have returned to the fells with their lambs. A good ewe can keep producing lambs till she's eight or ten years old. Joss has one of eighteen who came with them from Wasdalehead, a favourite sheep who had her last lamb only two years ago at the age of sixteen.

He knows all his sheep individually and can tell you sagas about almost each of them, accidents and births and parentage. Sheep all look the same to the outsider but I had slowly come to recognise a Herdwick from a Swaledale. The Herdwick has been grazing, or at least existing, on the Cumbrian fells for 400 years. They're supposed to owe their origins to Spanish sheep ship-wrecked on the Cumberland coast during the Armada, but this is a matter of contention. They are a breed which is special to the Lake District, almost these days verging on a rare breed, and are supposed to be the hardiest sheep in the world. When they have absolutely nothing to eat, they eat their own wool.

Herdwicks are white-faced, thick-set and only the males have horns. Swaledales are finer-bodied, dark-faced (with a light nose) and both males and ewes have horns when fully grown. The tradition of inheriting a flock of stock sheep when you take on a new letting, as Joss did, is a sensible one. Flocks become acclimatised to an area and have a strong homing instinct, travelling miles to return to the inbye land when the going gets really rough or when they are in lamb.

Herdwicks don't make a lot of money, never growing big and fat, which is why it was an indulgence of Beatrix Potter to keep so many of them down in her lush, lowland pasture. The money comes from selling off the lambs, usually as three-year-olds when, at present, they fetch around £20 each. They either go direct to the butcher though, coming from high fells like Joss's, they usually go via a middle man, lower down, who fattens them up for the slaughter. The other income is from wool. When he started he got 12p a pound for black and 14p a pound for white. Now it's gone up to about 80p a kilo. The Government gives a subsidy of £3.50 per ewe to encourage sheep farmers to keep sheep on the fells. Otherwise, most would give up.

It was the strong, very tough Herdwick wool which laid the early foundations of the wool trade in places like Hawkshead. Local farmers would do their own spinning, having little spinning galleries where the wool was hung out to dry. (There's one at High Yewdale, near Coniston.) The Herdwick has been very much part of Lakeland life for centuries, in songs and traditions. On the other hand, Herdwick, like all sheep, have also been spoiling Lakeland life. They crop so closely and leave the ground open for erosion and they put nothing back in the way of manure, as cattle do. All the minerals they take from the soil go into their wool. After sheep have grazed heavily, land once fit for oaks, which is how it once was, is only good enough for bracken. The Forestry Commission, for all that people complain about their plantations, are doing an important reclamation job, as they will always tell you, quick as a flash.

Despite the famed hardiness of the Herdwicks, if the snow goes on for months they can die of starvation, like any sheep. Foxes can get them. Then there's disease. Maggots breed in summer and the sheep can get eaten alive. They can get foot rot in the supposedly good inbye land when the fields are heavy with rain. A sheep farmer these days has to be a walking pharmacist, having all the modern aids to keep his sheep alive – both the adults up on the top and new-born lambs in the fields. Lack of constant care at lambing time, plus bad luck and badly nourished mothers, can result in twenty per cent of lambs being lost at or around birth. All hill farmers use vaccines to control infection, drenches to kill worms, dips and insecticides to control the external parasites.

A one-man sheep farmer like Joss can never think in terms of a weekly income, hardly an annual one. His money is in his flocks. Even in a good year he might not have much more than £2000 left for himself. At that moment he was running one and a half tractors – the half tractor being broken as he wondered how he could afford £4000 for a new one.

He has his own identification mark, or smit, on each of his sheep, a mark which goes with the flock he inherited. Each area has a shepherds' guide book, listing all the local marks. His mark in theory should be a blue blob and a dash on the tail bones but it used to so cripple him holding them between his knees, thanks to his bad back, that he's now simplified it to just the dash. He smits them by hand, using a special dye, and he also shears them by hand. One of the big occasions in a shepherd's year are the annual shepherds' meets which always take place in the same pubs. Traditionally this is the time to hand back stray sheep but it's also a big social evening with dialect songs and poems being performed. The other big social occasions are the sports.

Joss never ran as a lad. It wasn't till he was twenty-four that he ran his first race – and that was unofficial. They were holding a mountain trial at Wasdalehead, where he was working on his dad's farm, and at the last minute he joined in, still in his working boots. He was first to the first check-point on top of Yewbarrow, joint first to the next point, then he got cramp in both legs and gave up after eight miles. He entered for lots of races after that – and was last in many of them. It wasn't till he was thirty-one that he started to be any good. He thinks that was when his circulation improved and he stopped having cramp. Now, at forty-one, he's been ten years at the top in fell running and doesn't expect to get any better, despite his back giving him less trouble than it's ever done.

He set the first of his twelve current records in 1970. They include the Lakeland classic, the Twenty-Four-Hour Race, in which he has done seventy-two peaks of over 2000 feet in twenty-four hours, covering a distance of 108 miles and climbing in all 40,000 feet. It's a record no one can see being broken. He's won the Vaux's Mountain Trial nine times. The length, and route, of this varies each year but it's usually about twenty miles up and down fells, following grid references.

Outside the Lakes, he holds the national record for the Three Peaks – the three biggest in England, Scotland and Wales – Scafell Pike, Ben Nevis and Snowdon. You're allowed to drive between them, though when Joss set his record it was before the M6 was built which lost him time. He did the three in eleven hours, fifty-four minutes. He's also done the Welsh Peaks – fourteen peaks 3000 feet high – in four hours, forty-six minutes.

The figures are fairly meaningless on paper, unless you've actually been up and down a 3000-foot fell recently. There's no basic grid line against which other athletes can measure themselves, such as a hundred metres in ten seconds, or a mile in four minutes. Fell running records are not flat figures. They're three-dimensional. They have to be seen to be believed. Because of this, you wouldn't imagine it would be an expanding sport, yet not only is it growing, it's becoming overcrowded. Some of the popular ones are now like processions. Every year there's a thirty per cent increase in entries for almost every race. In 1950 the Three Peaks Race in Yorkshire had fourteen runners. Last year they had to limit it to 450 – having sent back 125 application forms.

It's not just lean and rugged shepherds but factory workers, professional people, office workers and expert athletes from other sports, such as Chris Brasher, the ex-Olympic hurdles' champion, who like to try out their legs and their lungs on the fells. It's probably part of the back to nature, health kick which so many town dwellers are following, trying to protect themselves from heart attacks. They start with jogging, then some move on to fell running, mainly for the fun of it, just to see if they can finish the course.

It's an amateur sport which to Joss is why it's such fun. There are indeed many professional runners in the North and in Scotland and many professional races and Joss could obviously make himself a bit of money – especially if he put money on himself with the bookies, as many of them do. He gets nothing, apart from an occasional pair of running shoes over the years from friends and fans. Recently when he went across to the Isle of Man for the Manx Marathon, he lost three days' work because of delays in the flights, and spent a lot of his own money in expenses and digs, all for no financial return.

For a big race he might be clipping solidly for two weeks beforehand, well into the night by lamp light, to get ahead with his work. He deliberately tries to delay his own lambing time, putting back the mating season, in order to fit in with his spring races. He had recently been in a marathon race at Crystal Palace in London, doing 132 miles in twenty-four hours.

His wife Mary loves the life of fell farming. On the outside, it might look lonely and rather deprived, stuck in the back of beyond, with so few modern conveniences. The nearest neighbour is over a mile away. They get no newspapers (except that the hotel keeps them a *News of the World* on Sunday) and have to go eight miles to the nearest village. But there is a great social life among sheep farming folk. They could be out every night if they wanted.

Although he is genuinely retiring and unpushy, Joss will help any local organisation out when they're stuck for a speaker. He can be out three or four nights a week round Cumbria, travelling surprisingly long distances, just to chat to a handful of people, always about fell running. He'd just been to talk to the Wigton Round Table at the Oddfellows Arms in Caldbeck – a trip right round the Lakes. He gets written-up in the *Cumberland News* and *Westmorland Gazette* and interviewed on Border TV when he wins a big race and people send contributions when he's taken on something particularly expensive, such as getting himself to America in 1975, to run in Colorado. In 1976 he was awarded an MBE.

Joss likes living where he does, but he's not exactly enamoured with the life of a sheep farmer. Given the choice, he would concentrate on his running, the biggest love in his life. But how else can he live, when what he knows best is sheep. The only possibility is through his family who have a little land at the end of the lake on better, lusher ground. One day, a bit of it will be his and he might be able to find an easier way to survive, perhaps opening a camping site, if he could get permission which is doubtful.

It rather ruined the romance of it all, to find the hardy son of the fells thinking of giving up sheep to cater for campers. Flocks of caravans would obviously be easier to tend than flocks of sheep, but not half as romantic. But then so much of the romance of actually carving a living out of the high fells is all in the mind of the beholder, especially those who live soft, easy lives in the towns.

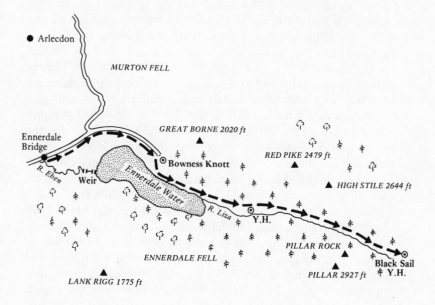

II

ENNERDALE

Walking with the poets. Down in the forest.
The threat to Ennerdale Water. A civilised
dinner with an atomic scientist.

THE LAKE POETS WERE THE FIRST OF THE FELL WALKERS, that's if you count a fell walker as someone who comes and walks the fells, purely for the pleasure of walking the fells, as opposed to shepherds like Joss Naylor who have to walk the fells to get their work done. Wordsworth, being a local lad, walked the fells from his childhood and continued walking throughout his life, but he preferred low fells and paths to the hard stuff. Southey was a softy. He had a very brief spurt of fell walking when he first came to the Lakes, but it didn't last long. Of the three poets, Coleridge was by far the champion. He only did it seriously for three years, but managed some amazing climbs.

Wordsworth first took Coleridge on a walk in 1799, doing what Coleridge satirically called in his notebooks a 'Pikteresk Toor'. Looking at the Picturesque was all the rage at the time. They climbed Helvellyn, visited Ennerdale and Ullswater, with Wordsworth leading the way, and pointing out how and what to admire. They inspected Castlerigg stone circle near Keswick and found the famous stones had been defaced with white paint. Vandals in 1799. (I always quote that incident when people moan about the present generation's hooligan tendencies.)

When Coleridge moved up full-time to the Lake District in the next year, he then started going off for long walks on his own. No doubt he was partly pleased to get out of the house, as his marriage had as good as collapsed, but the main reason was the joy he felt in roaming the fells. In his notebooks he is always stressing how much he enjoys walking the fells alone. 'I *must* be alone, if either my Imagination or Heart are to be enriched.' He used to take in Helvellyn, on his way from Keswick to visit William and Dorothy in Grasmere. He climbed Helvellyn one night by moonlight, which sounds a rather foolhardy thing to do, arriving at the Wordsworths' cottage when William was in bed. William put on his dressing gown while Coleridge read to him the latest part of his poem 'Christabell' and Dorothy cooked him a chop.

Coleridge later climbed Scafell Pike which is thought to be the first recorded climb of that mountain by an outsider. He carried, as always, a portable ink horn with him and wrote his notes or letters on the spot. This was during the years in which he had a passion for Sarah Hutchinson and on Scafell he got out pen and ink and added a few more paragraphs. 'Surely the first letter ever written from the top of Scafell.' It probably was, as only shepherds had ever climbed it before, as far as is known. He then came straight down, scrambling over a ridge, ignoring the easier ways.

'There is one sort of gambling to which I am addicted,' so he later wrote in his letter to Sarah. 'It is this. When I find it convenient to descend from a mountain I am too confident and too indolent to look around about and wind about till I find a track or other symptom of safety; but where it is first possible to descend, there I go – relying upon fortune for how far down this possibility will continue. So it was yesterday afternoon.'

It's sad to think that Coleridge's health began to suffer so quickly and that he lived almost the rest of his life on drugs and medicines, yet in these early years in the Lakes he sounds like Wilson of the *Wizard*, bounding over hill and dale, without a care in the world. When Wordsworth came to do Scafell, many years later, he and Dorothy took a guide, which was normal for the time.

Many of Coleridge's one-man expeditions lasted up to nine days and for one of them, in 1802, he described what he was taking with him: 'A shirt, crevat, 2 pairs of stockings, a little paper and half a dozen pens, a German book (Voss's Poems), a little tea and sugar, with my night cap packed up in my natty green oil-skin, neatly squared and put in my net knapsack and the knapsack on my back and the Besom stick in my hand ...'

Coleridge was particularly fond of Ennerdale, which was where I was now heading. He went there first in 1799, when Wordsworth was giving him that introductory tour, and he just missed seeing an eagle. A farmer told him how some eagles had stolen a live goose. 'One took off a full-fed Harvest Goose, bore it away, whelped when weary, and a second came and relieved it.' In 1802 Coleridge went there again, this time on his own, part of one of his marathon solo walks, and he heard tales of a pair of foxes and their five cubs who had managed to kill eight lambs.

Ennerdale Water is the most westerly of the Lakes and the valley that leads from it is one of the most remote and hardest to explore, so Coleridge did rather well. Even today, access is difficult. It's the only lake without a road. Every other lake has at least one side with a road running along it, even Wast Water, but Ennerdale has to be explored on foot. You can take your car to the edge of the lake, near Bowness Knott, but then the next ten miles of Ennerdale has to be walked. And you had better beware. No, it's not eagles who might gobble you up or wild foxes, but fierce foresters. Should you be so bold as to take your car past the car park at Bowness Knott, this is what will appear on your windscreen:

Dear Visitor,

As you will be aware, MOTOR VEHICLES ARE NOT PERMITTED IN THE FOREST under the Forestry Commission Byelaws 1971. I would be obliged if you would contact me to explain why you have found it necessary to disregard the Byelaws. If you are unable to provide an acceptable reason, or if I do not hear from you within the next three days, I shall have to consider whether to take proceedings against you for prosecution under the above mentioned Byelaws. – Signed – K. A. Hobson, Head Forester, 1 Forestry Houses, Ennerdale, Cumbria.

In 1977, thirty people received this warning – and one was subsequently fined £10 – a very small proportion when you consider that 25,000 people take their cars to Ennerdale every year and leave them, as instructed, in the Bowness Knott car park. Not that Mr Hobson is an ogre. He lets most offenders off with a warning, asking them if the Department of the Environment knows about their disability. What disability, they say. Inability to read, says Mr Hobson. They have a very school-masterly sense of humour, some of these foresters.

Ennerdale would be unrecognisable today to Coleridge and Wordsworth, even to anyone who was there only fifty years ago. Ennerdale is now a forest. The barren rough fellsides and tumbling scree slopes which Coleridge walked have been dramatically transformed into a sea of dark green. Down in the forest, a lot has been stirring these last fifty years, not least a certain amount of antipathy to the Forestry Commission, though when I walked round Ennerdale, another Baddy had just reared its head. The Forestry Commission, once so disliked, now looks like becoming almost a Goody.

The National Forestry Commission, a government-controlled body, was set up in 1919, mainly for strategic reasons, to build up a reserve of wood in times of war. In 1958, by which time it was clear that modern armies don't run on wood, they announced that their aims were now mainly economic – to increase wood production and provide employment in rural areas. In 1974, they once again proclaimed publicly what it was they thought they were doing with all that land – and the keynote now is conservation. They're still in it for the money, aiming for a return of three per cent on the funds they get given, but they consider that nature conservation, enhancing the landscape, providing recreational facilities, are equally, if not more important.

They took a terrible hammering from the self-appointed nature lovers a decade or so ago who screamed when they saw all those armies of conifers suddenly maturing and advancing over the land, all in strict, military order, not a tree out of step, betraying their original martial intentions. A most frightening sight, so many thought, and one that should be stopped. They are now trying to alter their original straight lines, putting in a few natural-looking curves and gaps, mixing the trees a bit more, genuinely trying to bring us all into the forests and enjoy the facilities.

The Forestry Commission is all over the Lakes, with forests in many areas, and it has in all about 30,000 acres. Ennerdale is its biggest single section with 8855 acres, but under half of that is actually forested. Grizedale, their show forest in terms of amenities, and Thornthwaite have both got bigger forests. The Commission's property at Ennerdale includes parts of Great Gable, Pillar Rock and a lot of higher fell which is leased to the National Trust and un-forested.

They started planting in Ennerdale in 1926, putting in mainly Sitka spruce, Norway spruce and larches, and stopped in 1950. It takes around fifty years for such softwoods to mature and in 1979 they started felling for the first time. The slowness of seeing any returns tends to keep forestry out of the headlines. There's no glamour in it for any thrusting politician who wants to announce huge increases in production the way, for example, it can be done with housing.

Ennerdale forest has some sixteen miles of forest roads which are open to walkers, plus many paths and bridleways, a well-marked forest trail along Smithy Beck which has a guide book and takes up to two hours, and a much longer nine-mile walk up the River Liza. Mr Hobson is very proud of these and cares for them most lovingly. He admits, if pushed, that on the nine-mile walk you spend a lot of your time hemmed in by trees and don't have much of a view and it can be rather oppressive, but he points out that it's a walk that can be done safely in all weathers. When you can't climb Pillar, or even see it, you can still get exercise by walking in the forest.

He's a civil servant and therefore isn't allowed personal views on the army of conifers which he controls. 'If the Government says cut them all down, we're building a rocket launching site, I would say yes sir, when do we start.' He did let slip, after I'd been with him for several hours, that his own favourite tree was a beech – and they have, surprisingly, a few of them dotted around – but I hadn't to take this as a criticism of his spruce and larch. 'They give excellent shelter for sheep in bad weather. I've seen sheep eat pine needles when they've been hungry.'

I started off my tour of Ennerdale at the Bowness Knott car park where I duly admired how most of it had been discreetly placed out of sight behind larch trees. It was so discreet that I had trouble finding my way there, but this is apparently the Lake District Planning Board's fault who don't want too many signs leading you to the forest, which seems daft. The Planning Board also doesn't care for the six or so little picnic spots, complete with home-made wooden benches and tables, which have been created in the forest. Oh, what petty little squabbles all these competing authorities manage to create. On the one hand the Forestry Commission is bending over backwards to bring people into Ennerdale – they even have traffic counters to see how well they are doing – while the Planning Board, who have overall authority, want to keep Ennerdale secluded, only for those who already know how to get there.

We came to a junction in the forest where there were about three signs, pointing to places like the youth hostel, and Mr Hobson stood fretting, worrying that he'd probably put up one sign too many and that at any moment somebody would complain and he'd have to take them down.

'Most complaints are just minor emotional responses from people who don't like the idea of change. A few years ago people were attacking us in Ennerdale for desecrating the valley – now we get compliments saying how nice we've made it. There was a piece of research done in one forest which showed that the same people who'd originally objected to planting forty years ago were now complaining because felling had begun! You can't win.'

His main worry that day was fire, which would appear to be a permanent worry for foresters but is only a real danger at certain times of the year. Each morning one of his first jobs is to work out the fire risk, deciding whether the danger is Nil, Low,

Moderate, High or Extreme. He bases this on the temperature, humidity, rainfall, number of people expected and the day of the week. Extreme days occur only two or three times a year and High days about twenty. This was a High day so he was very concerned, keeping an eye on all walkers for any idiot who might start a fire. High and Extreme days occur not in high summer, as one might expect, but from February to May, when the ground is still covered with dead vegetation which can easily ignite. Once the green shoots appear and the forest becomes lush again, the danger is much less, though of course in an exceptional, hot dry summer, like 1976, you can get Extreme days any day.

There are two youth hostels in Ennerdale, one beyond the lake and the other, Black Sail, right through the forest at the end of the valley. It's six miles from the nearest road and is the most cut-off hostel in the Lake District. You could easily miss it, dismissing it as a shepherd's hut, which is what it was. It has only three small rooms – in one the shepherd slept, in the other his horse and in the third he kept his wool clippings. Somehow, they now get in eighteen hostellers. There's no electricity and no phone and it's a ten-mile walk to the nearest shop in Ennerdale Bridge. We knocked at the door, and I felt like the wolf in *Goldilocks and the Three Bears*, or was it *Cinderella*, or am I getting all the stories mixed up; anyway, it was like a fairy story cottage. A girl came to the door to say the warden was in bed, not feeling very well, though we could come in and have a cup of tea, but we decided not to disturb him.

You get the best views from the end of the valley, once you hit open skies again, especially of Pillar, the 2927-feet-high fell which dominates the valley – and most of all, Pillar Rock which can be seen best from Ennerdale. This is a vertical chunk of rock, almost 600 feet high, which is said to be the tallest lump of vertical crag in England. I borrowed the Head Forester's binoculars to have a good look but have to say I was disappointed. I'd half expected an enormous stone phallus, from all the climbing books I'd read, as big and straight as the GPO tower.

So many of the famous spots in the Lake District have been so well photographed over so many years that the original doesn't have a chance. The image so often outdoes the reality. Taken in the best light from the best angle with the best equipment on the best day, there's nobody or no place that can compete with its best photograph.

Climbers do get terribly excited by the sight of Pillar Rock but to me it just seemed another big lump of fallen rock. Close-up, it probably is rather awesome. At one time it was thought unclimbable till a local shepherd, John Atkinson, did it in 1826. It's now done regularly, but only with the aid of ropes and all the tackle. Coleridge and Wordsworth never did it but they were regaled with tales of people who had lost their lives on Pillar when they were exploring Ennerdale. Coleridge, in his notebooks, tells of a shepherd on Pillar who had lain down and slept and then walked in his sleep, breaking his neck in a fall, with his staff remaining stuck in a cleft, staying there till it rotted away. Wordsworth, who was with him at the time, used the incident in his narrative poem, 'The Brothers'.

Pillar Rock has now been tamed but there is another awesome sight which true Lakeland lovers can hardly dare to contemplate – the raising of Ennerdale Water. Which brings us to the new Baddy on the scene.

Ennerdale Water has been used as a reservoir for west Cumberland for 130 years and has been used without much affecting the environment. The water is incredibly pure – you just have to walk round to see how clean it is, with no vegetation in sight, no reeds, little plant or bird life, little variety of fish, though it's always been popular with fishermen because of the trout. The water authority has had to do no more than put a small weir over the outlet river, the Ehan, and pipe down what they needed to Workington and Whitehaven.

Now, however, they want to raise the level by another four feet, doubling the amount of water they take out to twenty-six million gallons a day. This project will cost two million pounds. They could get the water from elsewhere, by using the River Derwent near Workington, which is outside the National Park, but that would cost over four million pounds. Naturally they want the cheaper system. They say they will landscape Ennerdale afterwards, at a cost of half a million pounds, so no one need get upset.

There had been intense argument about the whole scheme for months. The North-West Water Authority took a whole page in the *Cumberland News* the week I happened to be there, just to answer their critics. I read their explanations carefully but couldn't see exactly what raising the level would entail – there were few facts and figures about the damage that would be done, the paths or fields that would be lost, or what their half million landscaping would consist of.

As usual, a balance will have to be struck, but saving two million pounds by disrupting Ennerdale Water seems small beer compared with the six hundred million which is to be spent between now and the end of the century on developing Windscale. Even if there was only the slightest chance of Ennerdale Water ending up like Thirlmere or Haweswater, which have become dead lakes now that they are reservoirs, it should not be touched. We can't afford to lose any more lakes.

I walked round the edge of Ennerdale Water, deliberately looking for any signs of past spoiling by the water people, but could find very little. There is a small retaining wall, about four feet high, along the western shore, where the Ehan runs out, but this is the cultivated end anyway, with farm land going down to the water's edge. The weir itself looks as if it's always been there and the pump house is small and insignificant.

It was a calm soft evening in early summer and there were many fishermen around, all local lads, judging by the accents of the ones I talked to. Ennerdale, because of its situation, is very much a local, west Cumberland lake. I watched one young lad almost cycle straight into the lake, then throw his bike down just as he got to the water, and take out his rods. He'd come straight from work on a building site and was from Frizington. I thought carefully before making any comment. Frizington is perhaps the least attractive of a little string of left-over mining villages in west Cumberland, an area where it's almost impossible to believe lush Lakeland is only a few miles inland. It's not just the natural scenery, which is flat and boring, but the houses and the people seem deprived and left behind. However, I chose my words carefully, not wishing for a punch on the nose, and asked him what life was like in Frizington.

I thought at first he hadn't heard me. He was fixing together the parts of his rod, running his eye down the length, making sure it was straight. Eventually, he looked at me thoughtfully and replied with one word: 'Desperate'. Then he walked into the water and started casting.

Life would be desperate in west Cumberland today, if it wasn't for the handful of thriving new industries, many of them begun by refugees from Nazi Germany just after the war. They took great chances, moving into fields dominated by giant firms, such as chemicals and clothes, yet they succeeded and have given back much to the local community, in the way of theatres and cultural activities as well as employment.

The biggest employer, however, is the atomic plant at Windscale which employs over 6000. The site includes the first full-scale nuclear power station in the world which was opened in 1956. It is a nice coincidence that the father of the atomic theory, John Dalton, should have been born not far away – in Eaglesfield, outside Cockermouth. Windscale is just two miles outside the National Park boundary, but it dominates the view and the minds of many throughout the Lakes. It had been hogging the national headlines for many months in 1978, thanks to the official enquiry into the possible dangers from the dumping of nuclear waste (found to be minimal) but this was now over. It's only people outside Cumbria who refer to it as Windscale. Locals call the plant Sellafield, after the name of the village, while the people who actually work there call it the Factory.

I met one of the Windscale scientists on the train one evening, returning to London after a week in the Lakes. We sat opposite each other over dinner and I told him about my Lakes book and he told me about his life at Windscale. He invited me, when I reached Ennerdale on my tour, to come and see him as that was where he lived – so that evening, having walked the Ennerdale valley, I had dinner with him and his wife.

David Phillipson is originally from Sunderland but went to school in London. He's a chemist by profession and is now a Training Manager for the United Kingdom Atomic Energy Authority at Windscale. His wife Elsie is a local girl from White-haven. He's been seventeen years at Windscale, the first seven in a new house in Seascale, the little town near Windscale, but ten years ago they decided to move into the country, and bought a small farm of twenty-eight acres at Arlecdon, not far from the entrance to Ennerdale. This is a normal pattern – the longer people are at Windscale the more they tend to move out and settle in the non-scientist community, going for places near West Water or Ennerdale.

Their farm house is a handsome red sandstone building and has an enormous barn attached, some thirty feet by sixty feet, big enough to divide into three houses, which is what their friends always say to them. They're in their mid-fifties, with no children, and prefer to live very quietly. It's a listed building and he's produced his own printed pamphlet on its history. He sent one copy to the British Museum, thinking that was what you did with all publications, even private ones, and now gets libraries asking for copies. It's called *Bigcroft*. The *Big* part probably comes from the Norse word bygg, meaning barley. The building dates from 1827 but there was a previous farm building on the site. He lets the land to a local farmer and the barn is empty, but for three caravans, crouching rather lost in a corner, which he was keeping for friends. They'd had a hound trail on their land the day before I saw them, the second in ten days, which was rather worrying Elsie. She was concerned about some lapwings' nests being destroyed and a pair of herons being frightened away, but her husband assured her that two hound trails in ten days was exceptional. You had to let the locals have their sport.

He was concerned about an international conference he was involved with, organised through the Atomic Energy Authority, which was coming up the next week. The subject was Vibration and over 200 delegates were coming from over twelve countries. It was going to be held in Keswick, much to his pleasure, and he was looking forward to watching the foreign scientists, and their wives, discovering the Lake District. They had had some difficulty getting accommodation and a big enough meeting hall, but had taken over an old cinema, the Pavilion. I wondered what Keswick would make of such exciting topics as Fatigue Cracking on Gimbal Joint Bellows Shrouds, Tube Bundle Vibrations, Fuel String Dynamics or Transient Postfailure Pressure Waves – or what the Japanese, American, Russian, Czech, Bulgarian and other scientists would make of Kendal mint cake and Cumberland rum butter.

He said they were all very pleased at Windscale that the hundred-day examination under Mr Justice Parker – the longest assessment of its type in British history – had come out in their favour. The protesters and the scientists, despite publicly taking opposite sides, had got on very well socially during the examination, playing football, going to each other's parties, all very civilised.

Locally there was not much concern about nuclear dangers. People trusted the scientists and welcomed the work they brought, so he said. The scientists, after twenty years, were now part of the community, manning mountain rescue teams in their spare time, joining village drama societies. 'Everybody loves being up in

Cumbria. There's no sense of being sent out into the sticks. They end up being Cumbrians by adoption.'

They hadn't heard much local discussion either about raising the water level of Ennerdale. 'It must be for the good of the country,' Elsie said. 'I think the decision should be left to the experts. David and everyone at Windscale were put under great pressure because of their work, so I now feel a bit sorry for the water people.'

He felt, though, that it was right for public pressure to be exerted, so that everything possible should be known. 'They have a responsibility to explain what they're doing, just as we do at Windscale. This is the consensus of opinion today. The times when you could open a factory and just dump your waste any old where have gone. The public have a right to know and a right to protest. I've heard just recently that there's a plan to open up a coal seam at Frizington which I certainly would not like to see. I've written to ask for all the plans and I'll moan and groan if I don't get a proper reply. I believe that the Water Board need more water and that the best source would be Ennerdale but a balance will have to be met between industrial needs and the environment.'

As for the Forestry Commission, the other so-called enemy of Ennerdale, the Phillipsons weren't upset by what had happened. The straight lines didn't annoy them, though they would have liked a bit more variety in the trees. They admired, if anything, how well they'd done. 'We've tried and failed to grow conifers, so we know how hard it is.'

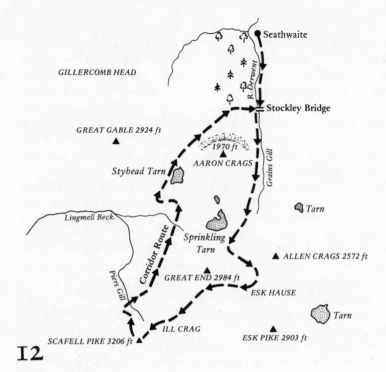

12

SCAFELL

Some interesting facts about the weather.
Down with climbing boots. Up Scafell Pike.

I HAD BEEN THINKING ABOUT SCAFELL PIKE FOR SEVERAL weeks. The worry was not mist, which had ruined my ascent of so many fells so far, but the sunshine. It was now early June, the Whit holiday period, and we'd had three weeks of brilliant sunshine and no rain – except for a sudden thunderstorm the night before, the first night of the World Cup which had been a very boring draw between Poland and Germany and the interference on the TV screen had hardly mattered. I didn't want to spend a whole day on Scafell Pike in blazing sun and end up with sunstroke. For a start, no one would believe it. You're supposed to have blazing rain in the Lakes. But I thought we'd try it. We could always turn back. Good weather stops play. That would be unusual for the Lakes.

I decided to climb it from Borrowdale, the longest way to climb it but, according to Wainwright's fell guide, the most exciting and most scenic. You can make it a round trip, if you do it from Borrowdale, going up one way and coming down the other, making it the 'finest mountain walk' – again according to Wainwright.

On the Ordnance Survey maps they always call it Scafell Pikes, which is very confusing, especially when you see another point which is marked simply Scafell. There is a separate mountain called Scafell, though it's part of the same massive range. The highest peak of all is known in common usage as Scafell Pike. And there is no argument about its claim to fame. At 3206 feet, it is the highest place in England.

We got to Seathwaite at the end of Borrowdale at ten in the morning – where it wasn't raining and didn't look like raining and didn't look as if it had ever rained. Seathwaite's claim to national fame, completely unsought, is that it is the wettest inhabited place in the whole country with 130 inches of rain a year. It's not that Seathwaite gets many more rainy days than some other places but that, when it does rain, it puts a lot of effort into it. They still talk about the terrible floods of 1966 when the head of Borrowdale became a lake with bridges damaged, roads ruined and the valley bottom littered with rocks washed down from the fells. But weather records are funny things. At Sty Head, at the very head of Borrowdale, rain fell for forty-eight consecutive days in 1903. In February 1932, on the other hand, there was no measurable rain *anywhere* in the Lake District. I'd obviously caught Seathwaite in another freak spell of consecutive dry days.

The Lakes has a very bad name for climate, especially rainfall, but what people don't realise is that, inside the Lakes, there are huge variations. While Seathwaite gets 130 inches a year, at Keswick, only eight miles away, the rain decreases dramatically to fifty-one inches. And if you go, say, twenty miles away, down the coast or the northern-eastern fells towards Carlisle, the rainfall drops to around thirty inches a year, which is better than south Devon. It's the high bits at the heads of valleys, such as at Seathwaite, that gives the Lakes a bad name for rain. They have five times the rainfall of the more sheltered Lakeland places.

'There can be very few pieces of country in the world where such variety from place to place, from day to day can be found in a short distance,' so Professor Gordon Manley, the country's leading expert on weather, has written about the Lakes. It's not just day to day but from hour to hour that you get such changes. And if you don't like it, move. Within half an hour's drive of anywhere in the Lakes, you can run out of rain and into shine. (Mind you, it works the other way, which isn't so funny, if you've started off in shine for a picnic and get there to find it's pouring down.) When I lived in Carlisle, I was always amazed to go to Silloth for the afternoon, or Caldbeck or Keswick, and have a rainy afternoon, yet come home and find the streets dry and everyone in the garden.

You never get any fog in the Lakes, as there's no pollution. You also get those lovely long light nights in the summer, with three-quarters of an hour more day to play with than in London and the South. The winters are surprisingly mild, milder than London, at least in the valleys, which is where the towns and villages are. It's once you climb up that you get all that rain, plus all that cold and wind. The summits are freezing – in fact, because of the low temperature and the meagre vegetation and animal life, they are classed as sub-arctic. You get no human settlements in the Lakes over 800 feet or so whereas in the Pennines they can live and farm at 1500 feet. (It's being so near the coast and those Atlantic winds that does it.)

Wordsworth always recommended people to come to the Lakes in May and June or in September and October, which are still the best two times. May and June are by far the driest months and September and October are the most colourful. He never mentioned anything about avoiding Seathwaite, but then they didn't start collecting rainfall at Seathwaite until 1844. They've been pretty busy since. That's the last remark about poor old Seathwaite's rain, except to say that they don't hold the record for the *greatest* amount of rain in one day. That's held by Weymouth in Dorset with over ten inches in a twenty-four hour period. Seathwaite manages only eight at its best. Those terrible thunderstorms which can suddenly hit the south coast of England rarely touch the North.

Seathwaite is an inhabited place but it's not really a village, more a couple of farm houses. It's just where the road ends and to prove it the place was jam-packed with parked cars. There was an air of great excitement as walkers and climbers unpacked themselves, got their kit on, took their kit off as they felt the sun in their faces and decided to make a break for comfort, just for once. I was in plimsolls (Dunlop Green Flash) and shorts with a light sports shirt, carrying a jumper and light anorak top in our little rucksack which also contained our lunch plus the os tourist map, Wainwright's *Southern Fells* (Book Four) and some strips of elastoplast. I'd never actually walked a whole day in the mountains in plimsolls and feared I might get blisters. I was with Jake, my eleven-year-old, and he was equally lightly clad, wearing training shoes. Stupidly clad, so the experts would say. But having climbed all winter in wellingtons, which the experts would also ban, I wasn't going to give in now the summer was here and buy those fearful climbing boots. Also setting off with us was my wife and five-year-old-daughter Flora, though they were only aiming to get half-way, to Sty Head Tarn. They too were in plimsolls.

Personally, I can see nothing wrong with wellingtons for wet weather and plimsolls or training shoes for dry weather, that's if all you're doing is fell walking. Climbing rock faces would be another matter, but then that's mechanical engineering, nothing to do with walking. There's no mystique about walking. Walking consists of placing one foot in front of the other, taking care when coming downhill that you look where you're putting the said feet, and that's all there is to it. You don't wear climbing boots to go up and down stairs at home so why wear them for walking up a hill? If you worry that you're going to twist your ankles, either going up stairs or going up Scafell, then by all means wear great huge clumping leather boots. To me, it's like taking another passenger.

I've studied the accident figures very carefully and I can see no correlation between accidents and clothing. The *Cumberland News* in March 1978 had full details of four people who'd been killed over the previous two months on the mountains and only one of the four was described as being 'ill equipped', though even he had fell boots on. The other three were all very experienced and had the professional gear, like ice axes and crampons. They'd simply been unable to stop their slide, once they had fallen, even using their ice axes.

The full, official report on accidents in 1977 by the Lake District mountain rescue teams lists 129 incidents, of all sorts, for which they were called out. This includes the mountaineering types as well as the Sunday-afternoon fell walkers. They give a description of the equipment worn by the people concerned, where it was known – and the figures show that most accidents happen to the well equipped. In thirty instances they used the term 'inadequate' as opposed to seventy-five whose equipment they described as being either 'adequate' or 'good'. (One of the inadequate was wearing open sandals, which even I wouldn't wear.) You can argue forever about what figures really mean. Most people, in my observation, do wear good strong clothes and boots, so naturally, when accidents happen, you're going to get a lot of well-equipped people involved, as they are in the majority. But the figures indicate to me that the so-called bad equipment, by which they specifically include things like wellingtons and plimsolls, can in no way be proved to *cause* accidents. The three main causes, which they also list, are slipping, getting lost or collapsing through some other human failing. You can slip in fell boots on an icy path just as easily as you can in wellingtons – and getting lost or collapsing has of course nothing to do with your footwear, nor has being hit by a falling boulder, another common cause of accidents.

So why do the vast majority of walkers wear those big hulking boots? Well, I do admit that big leather boots, however uncomfortable I might find them, last longer than plimsolls. So, you have to buy plimsolls more often. Another argument is that they protect your ankles. Personally, I don't think they need it. Ankles are pretty clever things, built to twist and turn and bend. Enclosing them can lead to problems, especially if you're not used to having your ankles enclosed. Footballers have long since given up wearing ankle-high boots, as they did in the old days, finding they get more control with the slipper type, yet they are well aware of the dangers of ankle accidents as it can ruin their whole careers. No, I'm still not convinced there's anything wrong with walking in wellies or plimsolls. I wouldn't wear really flimsy footwear, as you would feel every stone and they could be torn to pieces before your journey was over, but a reasonable pair of plimsolls, specially of the training-shoe variety, seems to me ideal for fine weather with wellies for wet.

I've gone on perhaps too much about footwear but then every guide book and leaflet does so, repeating the same old advice about climbing boots being the most important thing. Personally, I think telling people to take an extra jumper and some sort of waterproof is more important. You just can't tell what the weather will be like on top, even on a perfect day. And in winter, gloves are a good thing. My feet never got cold or wet all year, but my hands were often freezing.

As for the other things the experts tell you to take, I think most of them are superfluous. The mountain rescue booklet, having instructed you never to wear plimsolls or gumboots, tells you what to take: 'In addition to the usual sandwiches, take chocolates, dates, mint cake or similar sweet things which restore energy quickly. Equipment *must* include map, compass and at least one reliable watch in the party. A whistle, torch and spare batteries and bulbs and in winter conditions, an ice axe and survival bag are *essential*.' Ye gods, you'd think it was Everest. No wonder everyone you pass on the fells is so loaded down. No wonder they slip, get lost or collapse exhausted.

Accidents do happen, and there's around a dozen deaths a year in the Lake District fells, so it would be silly to say you should take no precautions. It seems to me that the real causes are bad luck (which is why it happens so often to experts, trying to chance their luck), and stupidity (which means it won't happen to you, will it). If you want to be safe, stay at home. If you want to go, there is only one word to bear in mind: comfort. If it rains, gets freezing, turns to scree, will you still feel comfortable? The answers are up to you. Don't let the experts clutter you with junk.

Now I think about it, you won't be safe staying at home. That's where most accidents happen. Get out on those fells and stay healthy. The incidence of carbon monoxide poisoning on the fells is very small, according to the most reliable statistics, and so is mugging, rape, being run over by buses, falling chimneys, runaway lorries, explosions, hijacks, bombs, terrorist attacks, junkies, madmen, football hooligans, gun battles, bank robberies and all the other common or garden events of modern urban living.

So, off we set for Scafell Pike, beautifully equipped with all the wrong things. My only little nagging worry was that, should something happen to me, through bad luck or stupidity or an act of God, the mountain rescue chaps would take one look at my feet and that would be it. No excuses would be possible. They wouldn't want to hear details of the bad luck, or the act of God, or my analysis of their statistics. I'd be damned for ever as a dope. Another Inadequate for their annual report. Their St Bernards wouldn't even give me a swig of brandy. We don't want your sort on our mountains.

We tore through the long lines of hikers ahead, many of them families with children, all of them loaded down, and in fact all day we were never passed by anyone. It's not a race, we kept telling ourselves. We just happened to bound along. We were soon bare-chested as indeed were many of the climbing gangs. The sun was hot but not clammy and the sky was unbelievably blue.

I got out my Wainwright, having decided to go up via Sty Head, and eventually we came to a little bridge, Stockley bridge, just as he describes it, a little old packhorse stone bridge over the River Derwent. We rested for a while, looking into a little pool, so perfect it seemed a mirage. It was deep and rounded with a flat bottom and the water was ice green. It looked the sort of phoney mountain stream you see in the advertisements for cigarettes, the ones on the back page of the colour magazines. It was so inviting that we didn't even contemplate feeling it. It was bound to be absolutely perishing. Far better to look and imagine but not touch or it might all be shattered.

The route became a bit complicated after Stockley bridge but I asked a couple of wizened walkers, loaded down with compasses and whistles and survival bags, no doubt full of mint cake ready to rot their wizened teeth, and they said yes, we were on the right path for Sty Head.

We passed several large parties of school children, all in their big boots, as instructed. Some were obviously never going to make the top. 'I wish I hadn't brought me bloody knife,' one little boy was saying to another. He had a huge sheath knife in his hand, big enough to kill himself a sheep, should he run out of mint cake. His companion, who was lying on the ground, sweating profusely, was fat and spotty. He was wearing a yellow t-shirt which announced: 'Carry me gently I'm a superstar.'

As we got higher and higher the climbers became fewer. They'd either turned back or taken different paths. I told Jake we would come to Sty Head Tarn, just at the top of that steep bit ahead. Trust me. I had been a patrol leader in the Boy Scouts after all. We'd then have our first proper halt at the tarn and share an orange. We got over the brow, and there was no tarn to be seen. Had Wainwright got it wrong for once? Ahead was a monstrous wall of dark grey unclimbable rocks, a mountain which didn't appear to be on my map. Don't say the Ordnance Survey had also got it wrong. I waited for a gentleman behind, climbing in a deer stalker so he must have been a gentleman, and he said Sprinkling Tarn was just over there to the right, but Sty Head Tarn, that was a good mile away. So we sat down, and I gave Jake the whole orange to keep him occupied, while I thought hard as I realised I'd been completely lost for the last hour. We should have turned right for Sty Head Tarn at the little bridge. Instead we had come straight up Grains Gill and were now at a little plateau at the top of the ravine, the route I'd planned to take on the way back.

So, it wasn't too bad. I now at least knew where I was. I could reverse our plans. It made no difference really, though it was worrying to have got it wrong on the easy stuff. Could I cope with the hard stuff when we got to Scafell Pike itself? The thing about Scafell Pike, and why Wainwright says you must allow six hours to get up and down from Borrowdale, is that, unlike Skiddaw or Helvellyn, Scafell Pike is a mountain stuck behind other mountains. You have to do a lot of climbing, up and down and over and round before you actually get to climb Scafell Pike. Old Samuel Taylor Coleridge did pretty well, climbing it on his own, back in 1802. And he was carrying his pen and a bottle of ink. I bet the mountain rescue chaps wouldn't approve of that.

We turned left, heading for Esk Hause, the topmost part of the plateau, and then we turned right, climbing up again. In effect, we were working our way up and round the huge chunk which had been in front of us. It turned out to be called Great End, a very good name indeed. Ahead we could see snow, large splinters of it, stuck fast in some deep crevices, hidden from the Mediterranean heat-wave we'd been experiencing. I could also see mist, swirling down from where Scafell Pike must lie, but going the other way.

I was now very grateful we'd come, by accident, the way we had come. The Esk Hause route had opened up beautifully and we soon seemed to be striding through so many summits. Then came the wonderful moment when we saw the top of Scafell Pike for the first time, just as we got on the slopes of Ill Crag. We were now up amongst the snow enclaves which at close quarters looked strange, rather scruffy and grey, melting at the edge like gutter snow, nothing like the stark whiteness of the view we'd seen from below.

We got faster and faster, almost running up and down the remaining cols and slopes. The grass had given out and it was now all rocks, but good-sized rocks in the main with only a little scree, easy to bound over in our plimsolls, like crossing stepping stones in a stream. The clod-hoppers in their boots were almost stationary, resting all the time. We bounded to the top, racing each other to the cairn, but when we got there, we found a queue. It's a very large circular cairn with flat slab steps up to it. Inside, eating sandwiches or studying their Wainwrights or picking out the view, I counted thirty-five people. We had to wait till some came down before we could get up. It had taken us only two-and-a-half hours to the top, coming the longest way, an hour quicker than Wainwright had said, so we felt rather chuffed. Jake thought they should sell badges, just to prove you'd done it. I thought Guinness would be nicer. We had our sandwiches, found the trig. point, inspected the cairn dedicated to the First World War dead, felt grateful to Lord Leconfield for having given over the land, and then studied the view for a long time. Wast Water looked incredibly near, as if you could dive down into it. Derwent Water also looked quite close. There was a large, long lake, much further away, and I couldn't work out if it was Windermere or Coniston. I decided it must be Windermere as, from that angle, the Old Man must obscure most of Coniston Water. Despite the brilliant sun, I couldn't see the Isle of Man. It must have been the heat haze.

We were so pleased to have done it, as I'm sure everyone is who has ever done it, all the hundreds of thousands of them. Most of all, I was pleased to have done it on such a perfect day. I hadn't needed my jumper. I had no blisters. We'd done no puffing. Boast, boast.

We fairly bounded down the scree-ridden summit slopes towards Sty Head Tarn, making for what's known as the Corridor

Route, confident that, having got to the top, coming down would be a dawdle, even by a different route. The first part of the descent was grim and rather boring, being all scree with little view and we were grateful again we'd come up the other way. We lost sight immediately of the top we'd just come from – and then that swirling mist we'd seen earlier suddenly hit us, but it was soon gone. We started meeting people on the way up that we'd passed two or three hours earlier. Something was bound to go wrong, I said, after all this boasting.

The Corridor wasn't as ominous or as corridor-like as the name suggests, just a path between rocky summits, very safe and easy to walk, though I did lose it at one time, finding myself looking down a huge ravine which I worked out was Piers Gill, not a place recommended for plimsoll wearers, in fact a place no one should wander into. Someone did in 1921, falling and breaking both ankles, and lay at the bottom for eighteen days. He was brought out alive, thanks to having landed beside a pool of water.

Jake and I had a good but careful look round the top of Piers Gill. It was near this spot, just two months previously (in March 1978), that an aeroplane crashed and three people had one of the luckiest escapes ever in the history of Lake District accidents. They were in a Piper Cherokee on a flight from Southport to Carlisle. They got caught in a storm over the Solway coast and went missing; RAF helicopters failed to find them and they were feared dead. Then two teachers with a party of children from Watford Grammar School, walking in a heavy mist on Scafell, stumbled upon a man who said he'd just crawled out of a crashed aeroplane. He led them to where his two companions were lying, both injured, but alive. All three survived. For the next few weeks, souvenir hunters were scrambling all over Piers Gill, looking for the wrecked plane, smashing bits of it with their ice axes. At one point, a National Park warden counted thirty-five people, crawling over the entrails. We could find no remains of the plane. The human vultures must have gobbled it all up.

Not long after Piers Gill, a man came running towards us over the rocks in a state of great agitation and we thought for a moment there had been another crash. (So much for saying that you should come to the fells to escape urban accidents.) He'd lost his camera, which had been his wife's twenty-first birthday present, somewhere between the top of Scafell Pike and Sty

Scafell

Head Tarn. We promised to look out for it. He gave me his name and address: K. Jackson of 24 Greengate Lane, Knaresborough. We never found it, Mr Jackson. I hope you did.

You get a terrific view of Great Gable, coming down to Sty Head Tarn, a beautiful, moulded, mountain-looking mountain, going straight up into the sky, the path beckoning ahead up its classical slope, the sort of hill you see in a child's painting of hills. Jake said it looked boring. Who'd want to climb a mountain that just went straight up.

As we approached Sty Head Tarn, I could see flashes of white all along the edges. It looked like white flowers of some sort, or perhaps some wild ducks had landed. It turned out to be socks. A party of climbers were lying exhausted on the sides of the tarn, their bare feet dangling in the water. Their heavy woollen socks had been discarded and were standing almost erect, breathing heavily and no doubt smellily. They looked the sort advertised as being sealskin-coated. We'd seen the party hours earlier, in the morning, and thought then that they didn't look as if they were going to make the top. We bounded past in our plimsolls.

Just below the tarn, we came upon the rest of our party, Margaret and Flora, which was a nice surprise. They'd had a marvellous day, going up to Sprinkling Tarn and then around to Sty Head Tarn, all without a map as we'd taken it, just by looking at the landscape and working out a round trip. They'd climbed well over 2000 feet which wasn't bad for a five-year-old.

We all came down together, all tra la la, with the sun shining and our faces glowing with satisfaction and smugness and all of us stood at Stockley bridge, staring longingly into the ice-green mountain pool. They too had wondered at it on the way up, but had decided not to try it.

We were under an hour from Seathwaite, almost home, having successfully completed our great climb, so what the hell. Jake and I stripped to our underpants and dived in. It was all true. The reality was as marvellous as the image. Flora joined us, naked, and other climbers came to watch, and they too joined in. It was the most pleasurable swim I've had in my life, rewardingly refreshing, sensuously satisfying, so clean and sharp. I would have been straight out, if it had been as cold as I'd feared, but it was soft and smooth and we played for a long time. What a nice way to end a nice day.

13
WORDSWORTH AND TOURISM

A history of books on the Lake District.
Wordsworth's guide. Tourism today.

COLERIDGE WAS THE FIRST PERSON TO WRITE ABOUT having climbed Scafell Pike but his notebook and letters, recording the event, were personal accounts, not meant for instruction. It's a wonder, really, that he didn't turn them into a guide book. Guide books to the Lakes, which had first started to appear towards the end of the eighteenth century, had suddenly become all the rage. It was left to William Wordsworth, whom one doesn't normally associate with cashing in on a trend, to produce a guide book to the Lakes which made him a good deal of money and put his name, and the Lakes, in the minds of a lot of people who had heard of neither. But it all happened very much by chance.

Until the middle of the eighteenth century, outsiders never visited the Lakes and the population at large, if they ever thought about the Lakes, had curiously medieval notions of a land of monsters and falling rocks, wild beasts and frightening legends. Adventurous gentlemen went instead to the Alps for their scenery but around 1770 (when Wordsworth was born) guide books and writings about the Lakes started to appear and it soon became fashionable to explore one's own native wild areas, such as Scotland, Wales and the Lakes.

The first visitors to the Lakes did look upon themselves as explorers, writing in their books about the terrifying sights, the horrible sensations, the valleys that simply couldn't be entered, the mountains that were impossible to pass, but very soon the explorers gave way to tourists. The first published description of a tourist visit to the Lakes was by a Dr Brown in 1770. It was in the form of a letter to a friend and concentrated mainly on Keswick.

Thomas Gray, the poet (of Gray's 'Elegy') published his journal to the Lakes in 1775 and did much to improve the image of Lake tourists, making it into a sensitive and lyrical experience, but the first of the guide books proper, and for decades by far the most successful, was by a Jesuit Father, Thomas West, with his *Guide to the Lakes* in 1778. West's *Guide* sold in enormous numbers and ran to many editions (ten editions by 1812) and Wordsworth knew it well. As we know, he never cared much for the intellectual books of the day, the sort which were bought and avidly read by Coleridge, De Quincey and Southey, but he was very fond of guide books which were his main light reading.

After West, the other big selling and highly influential early guide book was by another cleric, the Rev. William Gilpin. His book was called *Observations, relative chiefly to Picturesque Beauty, made in the year 1772, on several parts of England; particularly the Mountains and Lakes of Cumberland and Westmoreland*. It was first published in two volumes in 1786. I know the full title because I bought a copy last year price £30 at auction at Phillips in London.

They're exceedingly handsome volumes with hand-coloured aquatints of very idealised Lakes' settings. The whole object of Gilpin, and his followers, was to find the Picturesque, the sort of beauty which would be effective in a picture. Everything is described in strictly visual terms, deciding whether views should be painted or done in pencil, laying down hard-and-fast rules of what was and was not a picturesque view. He divided mountains according to their form and shape, their light and shade, saying whether they would make a good background to a painting or not.

This passion for the Picturesque – which Coleridge poked fun at and Wordsworth and De Quincey argued about – was a tremendous fashion at the turn of the century. Visitors would come to the Lakes, armed with guide books like Gilpin's and head for the 'stations' – the places he had decreed were the best viewing spots – and would admire the view, usually with a Claude glass, and then perhaps get out their painting materials, or pencils if Gilpin had decreed it was a better pencil view. A Claude glass was a special mirror for admiring the landscape and most guide books of the time expected you to use one. You turned your back on the view and peeped into the mirror over your shoulder, getting the sort of framed, perfectly-shaped view, which the experts had described. Today we have photography.

Gilpin was very quick to dismiss scenes and views he didn't like, at the same time betraying many of the medieval notions of the wildness of the Lakes which he'd been brought up on. His words, for example, on Dunmail Raise are very typical. 'The whole view is entirely of the horrid kind. With a view of adorning such a scene with figures, nothing could suit it better than a group of banditti. Of all the scenes I ever saw this was the most adopted to the perpetration of some dreadful deed.' He approved of Buttermere, and pointed out many picturesque spots, but didn't like the rocks at the head of the valley. 'As wild and hideous as any we have seen.'

Gilpin was obsessed by natural views but he took side swipes now and again at changes that were happening, criticising some landowners at Keswick for their 'barbarous methods of cutting timber'. He didn't mind woods being thinned carefully but not chopped down wholesale. Trees always seem to have exercised the minds and emotions of Lakes writers, from Gilpin and Wordsworth to Rawnsley and the present day.

Gilpin was himself a Cumbrian and was born at Scaleby Castle, near Carlisle, and educated at Cumberland's public school, St Bees, before going to Oxford. He took over a school at Cheam – an ancestor of the prep school which Prince Charles attended – and did so well out of it that he retired at fifty-three, having saved £10,000, and took a living in the New Forest. Every summer he did a long tour, to places like the Lakes or Scotland, which he turned into his books, giving the public the benefit of his judgements, marking Loch Lomond or Buttermere so many out of ten, criticising mountain tops for not being smooth or lakes for not having enough bends or islands for not being formal enough.

These and other early guide books brought in the first visitors and Wordsworth, when he returned to live in the Lakes in 1799, was often moaning about the number of tourists that were now arriving, longing for the good old quiet days before the Lakes had been discovered. This is a moan which has gone on *ad nauseum* ever since. Almost every new arrival over the last 200 years can look back, if only to last year, and complain that things are being ruined. In Wordsworth's case it was probably true – the first discovery of the Lakes by outside visitors did coincide with his birth and he could with some justification say that things were no longer the same. Nothing was being ruined as we think of despoliation today – if you forget that pot of paint on the stone circle – but the Lakes were never going to be the same again.

The closing of most of Europe from the turn of the century, due to the Napoleonic wars, meant that even more tourists came North for their holidays and excitement and to experience the Picturesque. The turnpike roads were being improved and hotels were growing up and the rush to the Lakes was soon being satirised in the London magazines and on the stage. In 1798 there was a comic opera in London called *The Lakers*, which was what the new breed of tourists were being called, and it contained the following song:

> Each season there delighted myriads throng,
> To pass their times these charming scenes among
> For pleasure, knowledge, many thither hie,
> For fashion some, and some ... they know not why.

After the Picturesque, the next craze was for the Gothic Horror when ruins were the big thing to go and see. Scott's novels and narrative poems helped fire people's imagination to look for old castles, haunted abbeys, and visit the scenes of ancient legends. If you didn't have an old ruin for visitors to gape at, you built a new ruin. In the Lake District there was a gentleman called Colonel Braddyll who built his own hermitage in his garden near Ulveston and employed a full-time hermit who lived in it for twenty years and never cut his hair. The same Colonel turned one of Derwent Water's islands into an eighteenth-century version of Disneyland, combining the fashion for the Picturesque and the Gothic by building a mock church and fort as well as his own Druids' circle, based on the Castlerigg stones.

Wordsworth, for all that he moaned about the tourists, did in the end do more than anyone else to pull them in. His guide book to the Lakes made him better known to many people than his poems. Matthew Arnold first told the story about the clergyman who asked Wordsworth if he'd written anything else – apart from his guide to the Lakes. The story has passed down through the decades and become legendary, but it probably did happen. His poems never sold all that well, compared with Scott, but his *Guide to the Lakes* was a best-seller.

Its origins go back to 1810 when Wordsworth wrote an anonymous introduction to a collection of drawings of the Lakes made by a Norfolk vicar. He had thought, off and on, of doing some sort of guide book and Mary had suggested it to him in 1807 after they had been on a tour of west Cumberland, to Ennerdale, Wast Water and Cockermouth. He never got round to it and it's not clear why, in 1810, he should have written the words for someone else's drawings, someone he didn't know and whose drawings he didn't actually like. In a letter to a friend, Lady Beaumont, he said that 'the drawings, or etchings, or whatever they may be called, are, I know, such as to you and Sir George must be intolerable. You will receive from them that sort of disgust which I do from bad poetry, a disgust which can never be felt in its full strength but by those who are practised in an art, as well as amateurs of it. They will please many who in all the arts are most taken with what is worthless.' No doubt Wordsworth simply needed the money, the lame excuse which writers, before and since, give when they write for something they don't approve of.

Dorothy was very aware of the money to be made from guide books and it was she who later suggested that he should write his own guide to the Lakes, using the introduction. 'It would sell better, and bring him more money, than any of his higher labours.' That's precisely what happened, the anonymous preface being expanded and emerging under his own name in 1820, firstly as part of some other writings, and then as a book on its own in 1822. At regular intervals he added to it, bringing out revised editions in 1835 and 1842.

In the very first version, back in 1810, he used a simile which has been used about the Lakes by many people since – even those who have never read his book. He asked the reader to imagine himself on a cloud, hanging between Great Gable and Scafell, and seeing 'stretched at our feet a number of valleys, not fewer than eight, diverging from the point at which we are supposed to stand, like spokes from the nave of a wheel'. Thousands of people since have looked at the Lakes – on maps and in the flesh – and likened their shape to a wheel.

As the editions went on, it's interesting to note Wordsworth tempering some of his earlier assertions, omitting, for example, an attack on Scottish scenery for being monotonous, compared with the 'exquisite variety' of Lakeland.

In the 1842 edition he included new chapters on geology and botany, which Wordsworth got others to write. He saw that the rival guide books, some selling better than his, had these sort of specialist sections. He didn't fancy doing this himself, finding it 'troublesome and infra dig', so he got experts to do it for him. The geology specialist was an old friend of his, Adam Sedgwick, professor of geology at Cambridge, who was born in Sedburgh (then in Yorkshire, now in Cumbria) and who had promised Wordsworth some twenty years previously that he would do him some geological notes, if ever required.

Wordsworth never knew that Professor Sedgwick privately preferred a rival guide book by Jonathan Otley. 'I wish with all my

heart,' he wrote in 1854, 'that my letters to Mr Wordsworth
on Geology of Lakeland had been printed in Otley's guide.' But
he had made his promise and kept it and his geological letters
were a vital part of the book's continuing success. What had
slightly upset Sedgwick, and all geologists of the day, was an
attack by Wordsworth in his narrative poem, 'The Excursion',
on geologists who hammered at the lichen-covered rocks.
Sedgwick referred to it as 'the poetic ban on my brethren of the
hammer'. Wordsworth tried to talk his way out of the criticism
by saying it was the character in the poem, the recluse, who was
against the pocket hammerers, and anyway, the attack was against
mineralogy not geology.

It is the 1835 edition of Wordsworth's *Guide to the Lakes*
which is generally looked upon as the definitive one – later
edited with an introduction by Ernest de Sélincourt in 1906 –
and later still, reprinted as a facsimile edition by Oxford
University Press in 1977. So, it's still selling well. Not bad for a
quickie, first written for someone else's book.

Wordsworth's guide book is a guide to Wordsworth's thoughts
and feelings and prose style as well as a guide to the Lakes. It's
rather didactic for modern tastes, but then that was the style of
guide books in those days. His running theme is the intrusion of
man in the Lakes. He quickly gets through the touring part of the
book, which he obviously found a bit of a bore to write anyway.
Only the first twenty pages are devoted to straightforward tourist
information as he takes readers (or, as he prefers to call them
'Persons of taste and feeling for landscape') quickly round the
Lakes. He suggests a start at Windermere, using the Bowness
ferry as the way to get the first feel of the lake. 'As much the
greatest number of Lake Tourists begin by passing from Kendal
to Bowness, upon Windermere, our notices shall commence with
that Lake.' Then he does Coniston, recommends going over Walna
Scar to the Duddon Valley and up Little Langdale to Blea Tarn
(working in a twenty-two-line extract from his own poem, 'The
Excursion', which is set at Blea Tarn). He moves on to Borrowdale and Keswick, admires the view from the Caldbeck Fells over
Bassenthwaite, fits in Buttermere, then works his way round to
Ullswater. It's very much the route I have followed in this book,
though he managed it in those twenty pages.

Having got rid of the tourist journey, he moves on quickly to
considering the Lakes under more general headings, such as the

Effects of Light and Shadow upon the Vales, Winter Colouring, Climate, Causes of False Taste in Grounds and Buildings – having a go in turn at his favourite hates. Even on the first page of his so-called Information on Windermere he is complaining. 'The view from the pleasure-house of the station near the Ferry has suffered much from the Larch plantations; this mischief, however, is gradually disappearing, and the Larches, under the management of proprietor Mr Curwen, are giving way to the native wood.' He keeps up his attack on larches all through the book. There was apparently a breed of new landowners moving in who were putting up larch plantations in mathematical shapes, which Wordsworth hated. He described the larch as a foreigner, preferring the sycamore (which in fact had been imported from Germany some 200 years earlier) and wanted at all times the native plants and trees to be preserved. Wordsworth in many ways was the first preservationist, though his ideas and views were not taken up formally until the National Trust and other bodies came into existence, over fifty years later.

Wordsworth was appalled, on moving into Dove Cottage, not only at the new visitors but at the new houses being put up. When he wrote the first version of his guide, he was living in Allan Bank, the new house in Grasmere he had always hated the sight of but had been forced to move into because of his large family. Nonetheless, he never lost his dislike of fancy new houses which he said disfigured the landscape by their prominence and were a primary source of bad taste. He hated them especially when they were put on the summits of naked hills, just to get the views. 'The craving for prospect which is immoderate, particularly in new settlers.'

He hated white-washed houses which were then becoming common. This had started as a way of keeping out rain, rough-casting the bare stone as a protection, then white-washing over it. Wordsworth thought that just one white-washed cottage on a hillside could ruin the view completely. 'I have seen a single white house materially impair the majesty of a mountain.' He recommended that if houses must be painted over, a stone colour should be used.

'The objections to white, as a colour, in large spots or masses in landscape, especially in a mountainous country are insurmountable. In Nature, pure white is scarcely ever found but in small objects, such as flowers, or those which are transitory, as the clouds, foam of rivers and snow. Mr. Gilpin has also recorded the just remark of Mr. Locke that white destroys the *graduations* of distance.'

Mathematically-laid-out conifers are still hated today, but it's strange that no one now seems to be against white-washed cottages. The opposite is probably true, judging by the way they are used in posters and advertisements, a stylised country scene being incomplete without a white-washed cottage. When did the change take place? Who led our eyes to view them differently? Fashions in fashions is a study in itself. It's not just that views change in the Lakes – we also change in how we look at them.

Wordsworth considered himself an expert on such things and maintained that he had a calling for three professions – poet, art critic and landscape gardener. He persuaded others of his inherent genius in visual things and at Rydal he was constantly on call to advise on building materials and chimneys, which were his particular speciality. 'Houses should be gently incorporated into the scenery of Nature.'

His great love for the Lakes shone through all he wrote, despite the changes he despised, and he did much to create an awareness of the landscape amongst the new breed of inhabitants. He claimed all the beauties for the Lakes, and he had first-hand knowledge (as he described at length in his guide) of the Swiss Alps and the Italian Lakes.

The big rush came with the beginning of railways – and this is where Wordsworth felt decided unease, perhaps even panic. The early tourists, as the guide books hoped, were people of taste, but the railways changed all that.

After the success of the Liverpool–Manchester passenger service in 1830, Britain in the 1840s was in the grip of railway mania, with lines being planned everywhere. Wordsworth quite enjoyed travelling to London on a train, and had nothing against them as such, but when they planned that line almost to his doorstep, he was up in arms, writing to Gladstone, writing to the local papers, doing anything to stop the Kendal and Windermere railway. There he was, making money out of a guide book to the Lakes, championing the life of the underprivileged in his poems, yet when the uneducated wanted to come and look at his Lakes, he recoiled in horror, writing that the poor would not benefit 'mentally and morally' from the Lakes and that they would ruin it for the educated classes, 'to whom such scenes give enjoyment of the purest kind'. No reactionary today would use such emotive, class-ridden language and indeed Wordsworth was criticised by the press and some of his friends, including Crabb Robinson, for his outbursts.

There's a vivid description by Thomas Arnold (son of Wordsworth's great friend, Dr Arnold) about the day he caught Wordsworth in full steam.

My mother and I paid a morning call at Rydal Mount ... presently the Poet entered, having a sheet of paper in his hand; his face was flushed and his waistcoat in disarray as if he had been clutching at it under the stress of fervid thought. 'I had been writing a sonnet,' he said. After a few more words, standing up in front of the fire he recited to us; it was the sonnet 'Is there no nook of English ground secure from rash assault.' The force and intensity with which he uttered the lines breathed into his hearers a contagious fire and to this hour I recollect the precise manner and tone of his delivery more exactly than in any case of any verse I ever heard ...

Tourists in the Lakes and elsewhere are still looked upon in some quarters as being rather vulgar, though the Lakes, on the whole, has fewer vulgar tourist attractions than the seaside resorts, such as Blackpool. For some reason, Lakeland has never had Royal patronage. Wordsworth did have one Royal visitor, as we shall see, but Queen Victoria and Albert preferred rushing up to Scotland for their hols. (They were great guide book addicts. An inventory of the library at Balmoral in the 1860s showed '26 guide books, 32 Ladies of the Lake and 12 Rob Roys'.)

Today over three million people a year spend a holiday of at least one night in the Lakes with the average holiday being four nights. They spend seventy million pounds and the vast majority of them, eighty-one per cent, come by car. Only six per cent come from overseas, though this number is growing. In socio-economic terms, you get a nice class of tourist in the Lakes. In 1977, twenty-nine per cent of all tourists were in the AB class (senior and middle managers) and twenty-six per cent in C1 (junior managers, clerical). Only thirty per cent were C2 (skilled manual) and fifteen per cent semi-skilled and unskilled. (For other exciting tourist facts and figures, see appendices.)

The people responsible for compiling these figures, and a lot else, are the Cumbria Tourist Board. They have offices above the library in Windermere where they have a staff of twelve and produce a constant stream of excellent maps, leaflets, books, guides, as well as fascinating facts and figures. They're an autonomous body, but directly related to the English Tourist Board, financed by Cumbria County Council, the ETB and a trade membership of some 800 Lakeland firms and organisations.

They've been going only since 1969 when the Development of Tourism Act was passed and the regional tourist bodies were set up. Tourism has been with us since Wordsworth's time, yet it's only in the last ten years that it's been recognised officially as an industry, one which needs Government encouragement, proper planning and controls. There aren't many industries in Britain, after all, which are expanding at such a rate.

Their aim is very simple – to improve and help the prosperity of tourism in Cumbria. They hope to create jobs and bring wealth but, as they have no teeth, no legal powers to command new hotels to be built, no ways of actually shifting a few 100,000 cars off the main roads, no way of sending the charabancs to Carlisle instead of Keswick, then they naturally have a very hard job. And they don't get a lot of credit for it.

Many residents were tourists themselves once – and they are the worst when it comes to considering tourism in the future. They don't want any more. They want customs barriers set up on the boundaries, the roads closed and trains halted and every outsider turned back. I did see one letter in a local paper during the year which wanted all cars stopped at the National Park boundary and only those with proper climbing gear allowed in. You just have to look at the figures for what the three million visitors a year put as their favourite activities to realise that climbing and fell walking are not, alas, the top attractions. These are, in order of preference: driving round the area, sightseeing in towns and villages, shopping for presents, visiting pubs, climbing and fell walking, visiting historic buildings, visiting exhibitions and museums, going to the beach, and, finally going on a lake steamer. So if you only let in those equipped for climbing, almost everyone would be kept out and the Lake District economy would collapse overnight.

At the same time, the Tourist Board resists any attempt to provide attractions which are not natural to the area – such as amusement arcades – or those which will spoil other amenities. The Board is forever turning down fancy propositions by smart promoters. One last year wanted a cable car up Scafell, as it's so hard to get to, which would be nice for the infirm or the lazy, but rather spoil the view for everyone else.

With the opening of the M6, there are now fourteen million people within three hours of Windermere. A frightening thought. The Board's current plan is to try to spread things out – in time and space. They encourage visitors to come, not in the peak summer months, but in May and June which anyway has the best weather, and to be more adventurous and try to discover places like Maryport, Carlisle, the Pennines and the Solway.

One of the most frequent criticisms against the Board is that 'they'd come anyway'. They're doing something that needn't be done. They have facts to prove that is not so, according to Roger Gouldsworthy, the Board's public relations officer. They did make a deliberate attempt in 1974 to push places like the Eden Valley and so didn't spend so much time and money pushing Grasmere and Ambleside. There was then a drop in holiday-makers in Grasmere and Ambleside – and complaints from them that the Board wasn't doing the job they were paying them to do. Now they try to promote the periphery and the centre at the same time.

'I can't see any other industry which will create such wealth in this area as tourism,' says Gouldsworthy. 'Mines and factories and quarries won't do it – and they ruin the landscape. Tourism does less visual damage to the environment than any other industry.'

One of the things they always proudly point to is the fact that tourism revives and stimulates local crafts and industries which would otherwise die or falter. It is true, if you turn over the stuff in the local gifte shoppes, that a lot of it is locally made. They also maintain that tourism helps farming, which might at first seem a contradiction, when you hear farmers moan about walkers leaving gates open, or about farm workers leaving the land to work in the tourist towns. But they have figures to show that the hill farmers are directly subsidised by their bed-and-breakfasts in the season. Joss Naylor is a good example.

The anti-tourist lobby point out that residents don't need all those gift shops. They want butchers and bakers and shoe makers. They argue that tourism increases the traffic, wears out the roads, unbalances the economy, gives only seasonal labour, brings in immigrant labour. You have to make up your own mind whether it's all worth it – and naturally it will depend on where you are sitting. Personally, I'm all for tourism.

Over the last 200 years, tourism has grown well beyond the worst fears of Wordsworth, but the Lakes can't really be said to have been ruined. They are still there to be appreciated, even by those who don't understand the Picturesque.

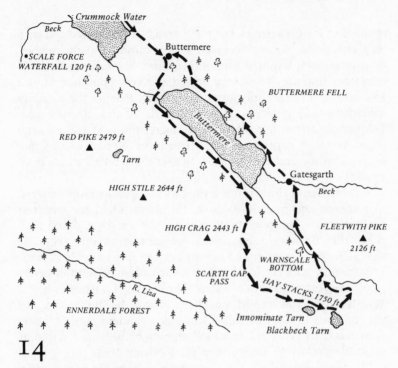

14

BUTTERMERE

*Beauty and the Beast. A walk round
the lake. An eventful climb up Haystacks
and a nice piece of gingerbread.*

THE LAKE DISTRICT IS FULL OF STIRRING LEGENDS ABOUT Celtic gods, Norse princesses, wicked fairies, ghostly knights, ghastly miners, haunted mountains, mounted haunts, haunted huntsmen and they're all very boring and very complicated and I've steered very carefully away from them. I've got them on my list, along with geology, as aspects of Lakeland life to avoid. But here is a *true* tale about Buttermere, the next stage in my journey, which captivated the attention of Wordsworth, Coleridge, Southey and De Quincey, in fact the whole nation, back in 1802.

A gentleman calling himself the Hon. Augustus Hope arrived in Keswick and took lodgings at the Royal Oak, the smartest place in town. He rode about in an elegant carriage, dined with the quality, flashing his impressive visiting cards, telling everyone that he was the brother and heir to Lord Hopetown. He became very friendly with the local wealthy, such as Mr Crump, a Liverpool lawyer who built Allan Bank, the Grasmere house Wordsworth later moved into. Surprisingly, he didn't seek out the company of Mr Coleridge, Keswick's eminent man of letters who was then living at Greta Hall, though he became a welcome guest almost everywhere else in the Keswick area.

He decided to take a few days' respite from his hectic social life and went for a short fishing holiday on Buttermere, taking up accommodation at a little inn by the lakeside. There he was served by a fine young woman of eighteen years of age, daughter of the house, who acted as a waitress. She was a noted beauty in the Buttermere valley and Mr Hope, immediately entranced, soon desired her hand in marriage. Permission was given. After all, he was the brother of a lord and had a smart carriage and his letters franked with his own name, a special Post Office privilege which in 1802 was only granted to the great and the wealthy. He married Mary Robinson, as the Beauty was called, on 3 October 1802, and off they went on a round of the smart hotels in the Lake District, moving mainly between Buttermere and Keswick.

One day, the police arrived at the place they were staying. All was then revealed about the Hon. Augustus Hope. He was no more than a wicked swindler and confidence trickster, not a lord's brother, but a failed commercial traveller who had left broken hearts, abandoned wives and countless fatherless children all over England. What a beast.

He was in due course tried at the assizes in Carlisle and the case was a sensation, splashed over every newspaper, one of nature's all-time Sunday paper stories. Amongst his belongings were found all the heart-breaking letters from the ladies that he had left. Wordsworth and Coleridge, who happened to be near Carlisle at the time, both asked to see him, fascinated by the case and agog to see the letters and the man who caused such anguish. He agreed to see Wordsworth and they had a long chat but for some reason he wouldn't see Coleridge.

The man's identity was never conclusively revealed, but his original name was thought to have been Hatfield, and that he had come from the West Country. De Quincey, in his *Recollections*, hazarded the guess that he feared that Coleridge, coming from the same area, might recognize him, which was why he had avoided him in Keswick. Anyway, Coleridge did eventually read all the juicy correspondence and wrote a great deal about them. What particularly struck Coleridge about the case was that though the man was a blackguard, 'with the litany of anguish sounding in his ears from despairing women and famishing children', he could still find it possible to 'enjoy the calm pleasures of a Lake tourist and deliberately hunt for the picturesque'.

The crime he was accused of was not bigamy but defrauding the Post Office. In those days, it was a capital offence to frank your own letters without authority. The Carlisle jury weren't all that keen to hang someone, just for cheating on a few postage stamps, but when they heard what he'd done to poor Mary, and countless others, he was sentenced to death and duly hanged in Carlisle on 3 September 1803.

The melodrama of the Beauty of Buttermere passed into popular legend and several plays were performed on the London stage, based on the story. Wordsworth uses the incident, calling her the Maid of Buttermere, in the seventh book of 'The Prelude' ... 'unfaithful to a virtuous wife, deserted and deceived, the spoiler came and wooed the artless daughter of the hills, and wedded her, in cruel mockery'.

In a fictional Victorian melodrama, she would have been ruined for ever, but Mary of Buttermere turned out to be not so artless after all and made the most of her encounter with the wicked spoiler. Hordes of tourists rushed to Buttermere, just to see the Beauty, and stayed at the inn where she remained for some time, a figure of national attention. De Quincey, being a true rubber-neck, went to stay there, and so did many others. 'Shoals of tourists crowded to the secluded lake, and the little homely cabaret, which had been the scene of her brief romance.'

De Quincey, picking his words as carefully as ever, obviously didn't find her all *that* sensational looking. 'I saw her repeatedly and shall say here a word about her personal appearance as the Lake poets all admired her greatly. Her figure was, in my eyes, good, but she was none of your evanescent, wasp-waisted beauties ... Everything about her face and bust was negative; simply without offence ... but she was what all the world would have agreed to call "good-looking".'

On another occasion, De Quincey was staying at the inn, just for another look, in the company of Southey. According to De Quincey, 'Southey was incapable of wounding anyone's feelings' and in his presence Mary flowered much more. He adds, rather elliptically, that Southey was of course well known to Mary 'by kind attentions and, I believe, some services'. Whatever could that have meant?

I set off for the Buttermere valley, wondering if De Quincey was hinting at some scandal about Southey which has never since come to light, but he was probably just stirring it up. The services, whatever they were, were no doubt very innocent.

Buttermere is the only valley in the Lake District with three lakes and I approached it deliberately from the Cockermouth end, wanting to take them in order, never having been there before. Loweswater is the first lake and it opens up like a secret valley, an ancient water colour of a lake, all misty and moody, the sort of idyllic sylvan eighteenth-century scene which very smart antique shops in Cockermouth try to sell you, for a large sum, yet which you never seem to see in real life. There are houses around, with TV aerials, and fields going down to the lakeside, yet it still seemed so unspoiled and unreal. The surrounding hills looked so strange, isolated, very independent, newly painted hills, acknowledging no connection with any other, plonked down by hand to give each the maximum effect. Normally in the Lake District the lakeside fells are in ranges, making it hard to see where one starts and the other ends, despite the map throwing individual names over every bump.

Crummock Water, the next one, is very different. It doesn't look at all like Loweswater. It's so wild and Scottish, which suits its name, with no fields in sight and the bare fells going straight down to the water's edge. It's over three miles long, about the same length as Derwent Water, twice as big as either Loweswater or Buttermere.

Then there's Buttermere, star of the show, top of the bill, head of the vale, which has a mixture of the prettiness of Loweswater and the wildness of Crummock, without being a copy of either. All three lakes are owned by the National Trust which probably helps the whole valley to have a uniformity of spirit, a natural tranquillity, despite the tourists.

There are two rather handsome inns at Buttermere village today, the Fish and the Bridge Hotels, but I'm not sure if either was the scene of the Beauty of Buttermere drama. Nobody I spoke to in either hotel had heard of her. I poked my head into the bar in each one, only to be met by notices telling me on no account to bring in any rucksacks or wear climbing boots. Buttermere is an extremely popular, and very pretty village, an excellent centre for walks and expeditions. It's a place loved by the regulars, the knowledgeable walkers, and is fortunately missed by many of the car-bound day trippers, who stick to the Windermere–Keswick race track.

Buttermere would be an easy valley to seal off, should you be in the business of sealing off valleys, and it's not surprising that the Beast of Buttermere thought he would be safe here to go about his wicked ways. Before him, well, quite a few centuries before him, the English made it their secret headquarters when they were being overrun by the Norman conquerors. They manned a counter-attack from the valley and Buttermere was one of the few northern valleys the Normans never managed to capture.

There's some lovely parking. Really, quite delightful, to the right of the Fish Hotel, beside a little stream. We connoisseurs of Lake District parking spaces can recognise a good'un when we see it. (Not quite the nicest parking place in the North because that distinction goes to Steel Rigg car park beside Hadrian's Wall. Ask to see its awards.)

The village is in a little alluvial plain between Crummock and Buttermere lakes and you have a choice of walking round either, a choice made very easy by the excellent walking leaflets which the National Park has provided. I had my family with me, as Buttermere looked an excellent place for family walks, and as we set off, following the arrows for the lakeside, it seemed as if the whole world and his family were taking the same route that bright, early summer day. We made little pointed stops, to admire views, hoping the other parties would disappear past us into thin air, which didn't work as everyone else was doing the same. There is this Lake District abstract gaze one soon perfects, staring into the middle distance, working out a very hard route, pretending that one is alone in the universe, far from the roars of kids getting their anoraks on and the clump of the climbing boots, noises that can hardly ever be avoided at every good starting point.

However, most people soon turned towards Crummock and Scale Force, the highest waterfall in the Lake District. I always suspect every fact about every waterfall in the Lake District, but Scale Force is said to have a drop of 120 feet. We were set to walk round Buttermere, very easy, a five-mile walk which almost anyone can do in two hours. The path went quickly into some sweet-smelling pine woods where the kids gathered fresh pine cones, great heaps of them, till I realised that I was meant to carry them and we'd just started, so I said no, only a handful each.

We had our picnic at the end of the lake and then lay down on some rocks beside a stream and sunbathed. As I lay there, I realised that the craggy silhouettes above us at the dead end of the valley looked strangely familiar, so I got out my map, identified the crags and it was Haystacks. It's just a minor fell, not one with any great height or any great lineage, in fact I'd never even heard of it until, a few days previously, I had read Wainwright's *Fellwanderer* book. He comes out at the end with the surprising statement that it's on Haystacks that he wants his ashes scattered. As Mr Wainwright has climbed and written about every fell in the Lake District, he must be heeded.

'I'll just be a couple of hours,' I told my wife. 'Up and down, no messing, you lot wander back around the lake and I'll catch you up. I've just got to see it.' There was a lot of moaning because for once I'd agreed to make it a quiet family day, do none of my usual cramming in of everything, in and out of sight. 'And on such a lovely sunny peaceful day as well,' she said. 'You promised.' But I was off, haring up the hillside towards Scarth Gap Pass, a modern Beast of Buttermere, selfishly neglecting his dear family, all for the sake of a mysterious beauty on the horizon.

I hadn't got my Wainwright book with me, the one in which he gives umpteen ways of climbing Haystacks, front, back and sideways. I'd never done anything, gone anywhere, since starting the year without first spending weeks reading and digesting every conceivable piece of literature. This time I was unprepared – and I'd also had too much picnic. My stomach soon ached as I hurled myself too quickly and too suddenly up the hill.

I stopped at the first brow on the Pass for a rest, had a quick drink from a tumbling beck beside the rocky path, and a quick shout down below to the valley bottom where I could see the family like little matchstick men, moving jerkily through some bright green fields, past some bright orange tents, towards Gatesgarth. To my amazement, they must have heard my shouts for they all stopped and looked up – at least their faces turned on top of their heads as if I was seeing them all in a plan elevation. They were waving their arms, and probably shouting as well, but I could hear nothing.

The path didn't lead to the gap I thought it was going to lead to; it suddenly moved round a hump I hadn't seen before, taking me to another gap, but it was all clear and easy, if rather rocky, and I was soon on a ridge, with Haystacks on my left and High Crag on my right. I knew I'd reached the top of the correct gap because the land fell steeply away and below I could see the beginning of Ennerdale, but I could see no way up Haystacks, though the only map I had with me clearly had a dotted line going straight up this side.

The family would be miles away now. I couldn't stand there all day. So I made a right angle with the top of the gap and headed straight up, sliding straight down again. I hadn't realised the scree was so loose. A couple in a hollow at the top of the gap, whom I hadn't noticed before, had been watching me and were clearly very amused. I'd told my wife I'd only be two hours, and I'd already spent one hour just getting to the foot of Haystacks. I did another run up and quick grab, looking for some bracken that would take my weight, and eventually I got going. I managed to find some zig-zag sheep tracks, running in parallel lines along the sides of the fell, dragging myself up to the next one every time they started to go down. I had on my wellies, as I'd expected rain, but the sun was hot and my wellies were on fire and I was scared I would split them to shreds or lose my foothold and slide completely down the fellside. It was more like a spoil heap, a left-over mining tip, than a wonder of nature. Wainwright must be a nut, I thought, to want to get buried up here. The surrounding views were terrific but how can you ever see them if you have continually to watch every footstep? I think I'll have my ashes scattered on a grassy slope, just like Beatrix Potter.

Far below me, the forest of Ennerdale looked enormous, with the River Liza snaking through it like an Amazon jungle where no man had ever been, except of course it was full of Forestry Commission little men, worrying about signposts, calculating the fire risks. It was strange to see it from the air. It looked much wilder than it had done from ground level. Across the valley were the heights of Pillar and Kirk Fell with not a flash of orange anorak between them, just as nature intended. I suppose it's this remoteness, the lack of any lush little Beatrix Potter roly-poly fields or little cottages which appealed to Wainwright, though I still couldn't share his enthusiasm.

At long last I pulled myself over the final stretch of scree and almost fell on to a hidden plateau, a secret land of its own with strange tarns and paths, patches of heather and thick bracken, marshes and rocky outcrops. After the monotonous grey of the scree it seemed to be in technicolour, deep purples and browns, bright greens, sparkling rainbow waters. I had thought the views down to the Ennerdale slopes had been good but these new views were magnificent – enormously extensive, down and over other plateaux and fells, and still with no signs of civilisation. They weren't valley views, looking down a dale with a lake below, the normal pretty fell-top views, but horizontal views. I'd got so used to climbing to a top and looking down. The subtlety of Haystacks is that you climb up – and then keep looking up and over. It's surrounded by much higher fells, such as Great Gable and Pillar, each a good 1000 feet higher than Haystacks which is only a mere 1900 feet, too small to get in most guide books. This is why Haystacks is relatively unknown to the general walker. Factually, there's very little to say about it. It's too insignificant to rate a mention on any expert's list of best climbs. Even Wainwright himself, at the end of Book Seven, in listing his six best fells, doesn't mention Haystacks because it hasn't got the height.

I'd meant to come straight down again, having got to the top, to rejoin the family, but I found myself being drawn along its mysterious, broad ridge towards a strange gleaming tarn which seemed to have three little islands on it, stepping stones for giants to walk on. This is Innominate Tarn, so called because it hasn't got a name (Old Cumbrian joke). I sat down and was quite mesmerised by it.

At length I moved on to another tarn, Black Beck Tarn, and just to the left, in a gap between the crags, I caught a glimpse of a magnificently framed view, sheer down the valley sides to Buttermere and Crummock. Very picturesque. I went nearer to savour it, thinking I might go back that way, but the view that hit me was so stunning I had to sit down. I felt suddenly dizzy. I'd almost wandered over a sheer drop. It was the view I'd seen from below, the sharp silhouette of the line of the ridge of Haystacks. It had been hard enough scrambling up the scree from the other side, but from this side, up the rock face, it would have been impossible. Later, when I got home, I read Wainwright's notes. 'The only advice that can be given to a novice lost on Haystacks in mist is that he should kneel down and pray for safe deliverance.' Thank goodness it was such a brilliant, sunny day.

There were some walkers coming along the ridge top towards me – including two girls who couldn't have been more than six. The walk from the Borrowdale direction must obviously be much easier. I could see paths ahead of me, and other walkers, and I headed for one particularly clear path that disappeared for a while, skirting a little fell, then re-opened and zig-zagged down into Warnscale Bottom, the end of the Buttermere valley which had looked impossible from below.

It was a great walk down, with waterfalls and ravines, sudden grassy paths, then rocky climbs, screes and streams, yet all very clear and easy to follow, though I was glad I was going down. Going up I might have been more worried about missing the correct line of cairns and falling over some strange, overhanging, dead-looking trees which beckoned menacingly on the sheer sides of Warnscale.

Halfway down I overtook an old couple, taking their time, stopping every few steps to admire the way they'd been. What with six-year-old girls and now with oldies, I obviously hadn't done so marvellously as I'd thought. They were from Northampton and were very knowledgeable and said that the way I'd come up Haystacks was hard to find, but I should have seen a line of zig-zag cairns. As the three of us stood talking together on a very narrow ledge, with me pointing back the way I thought I'd been , and the couple following my eyes, the old lady suddenly fell over.

I was horrified, blaming myself for distracting her, but her husband kept on talking. Yes, he was saying, he too had read Wainwright on Haystacks and he agreed with him. I bent down to try and help the lady up but she refused my arm, saying she'd be OK. It was just a dizzy spell. It would pass. Yet she still lay there in a heap. I had visions of me having to rush off to bring the mountain rescue teams.

'You went to school with Wainwright's children, didn't you dear,' she said at last, gasping for breath. 'No no,' he said rather irritably, 'that was Harold Abrahams's children. I've told you before.'

'Oh,' I said. 'Harold Abrahams the Olympic runner?'

'No, no, the bookshop owner.'

As I stood there, trying to think of any bookshop called Abrahams, the lady slowly dragged herself to her feet. She still looked dazed but assured me she had recovered. I shouldn't wait for them. They'd be all right. So I slowly continued on down the path, their voices gradually fading in the distance.

Looking back up the sides of Warnscale, when I eventually got to the bottom, was a thrilling sight. It's the complete dead-end of the Buttermere Valley, a defiant, prison-like halt. Go no further, the world stops here. Viewed from below, it was hardly possible to believe that any human could ever get up the sides, yet I'd left a couple of seventy-year-olds, casually chatting about shopkeepers, unless they'd both collapsed by now and their bodies would come bumping down any moment.

The valley bottom was very narrow, only a few hundred yards wide, but almost immediately it turned to rich green fields and meadows, though still with that isolated, end-of-the-world feeling. When I got to Gatesgarth, at the end of the lake itself, I was back to normal country life again, with neat notices and tidy car parks. Above a mountain rescue post there was a rather bossy notice saying 'Take Your Litter Home. Litter Spoils Beauty.' I hurried along the lakeside path, knowing I'd never catch the family up as they must have been back in Buttermere village hours ago, getting fed up waiting for me. It was a pretty, park-like, meadow walk, neatly laid out. At one point it suddenly goes through a tunnel, about fifty feet long, which was a surprise. I wondered who'd gone to the enormous expense of blasting a tunnel through a little outcrop of rocks when a path round or over would have been so simple. If I'd done my usual research, I might have known the answer.

The family weren't waiting in the car park, lovely though it still was, but I found them in the nearby Croft Farm tea room. Ah ha. I might have guessed. I'd raced like mad down Warnscale and along the shore of the lake and I was now quite out of breath. I took my wellies off, and my socks steamed like kettles, but the two ladies in charge of the tea room didn't seem to mind. I had two cups of tea, one after the other, and two enormous slices of home-made gingerbread, one after the other, cut from a huge tray. I complimented one of the ladies on the gingerbread and she said that Marjorie had made it fresh that morning, as she does every morning. I took them to be sisters, large, handsome, farm ladies. De Quincey would have been a bit catty about these present-day Buttermere Beauties. They certainly weren't any of your evanescent, wasp-waisted beauties, but anyone who could make such mouth-watering gingerbread must certainly be called good-looking.

Until I'd been to Buttermere, I would have said Ullswater was my favourite lake. Now, after such an unexpected, unplanned but wholly delightful day, would Ullswater ever compete?

15
SOUTHEY

*Life on the Keswick ant-hill. Some
famous visitors. Mr Wordsworth takes
over from Mr Southey as Poet Laureate.*

As I HEADED FOR KESWICK I THOUGHT AGAIN HOW SUR-prising it was of Southey, coming to gape at the Beauty of Buttermere. The impression I had picked up about him, mainly from reading the memories of the Wordsworth group, is of a stodgy old literary gent, forever stuck in his study in Keswick with his millions of books.

Robert Southey, when he's thought about today, which is rare, is presumed to have been a close member of the Wordsworth set. In fact he ran a power-house of his own, a rival literary factory, with its own characters and fringe figures, relations and hangers-on.

But it was the combination of the two of them, Wordsworth in Grasmere and Rydal, Southey in Keswick, that for almost fifty years turned the Lake District into a centre of English poetry, where young poets and writers went to worship and hope-fully meet the Greats, and where Grand Old Men from all professions did their ritual state visits, just to say they had seen the Lakes and met the poets.

The London smart set might have turned rather scornful of them, when they became disgusted by the changes in once-radical and brilliant men, but the new poets tended to die young, like Shelley and Keats, while Southey and Wordsworth ploughed on, still dominating their profession. Sir Walter Scott's poetry sold better and Byron pleased the intellectuals, but it was with Southey and Wordsworth both being in the Lakes and both being prolific for so long – never mind quality, admire the length – that made the Lakes synonymous with poetry throughout most of the century.

It's surprising they were so successful, managing to live on their writings and support huge families, while resolutely living 300 miles away from London. Even today, writers often think they'll never manage, never get contacts or jobs or acclaim, if they're not in the London swim. Publishers, newspapers and magazines, as today, were all in London, except for a few in Edinburgh. There were no phones and the railways arrived late in their lives. Until then, the 300-miles coach journey to London could take four days – forty-eight hours at best, if you got the right coaches and the right weather. They were never flush, never without a need to watch the pennies, but they survived and in turn took all the honours. Most surprisingly of all, at least in the judgement of posterity, Southey took the honours first.

Coleridge, as we have seen, left the Lakes relatively quickly.

It was he who first took on Greta Hall in Keswick, renting part of it from a self-made local carrier, who had worked hard and decided to build himself a suitable, Georgian-style pile beside the River Greta. Dorothy had found it for him and he moved in with his wife and children in 1800, but almost immediately he was rushing across to Grasmere, neglecting his family, to be with William and Dorothy, or going on his mammoth hikes.

In 1801 Coleridge persuaded his brother-in-law Southey to come up and share Greta Hall with them, though he warned him not to bring the third Fricker sister, Mrs Lovell, but to pension her off. Southey, ever the gentleman, ignored the advice. When he arrived he soon found he had all three sisters to look after – his own wife, the widowed Mrs Lovell, plus the abandoned Mrs Coleridge and her family. For the rest of his life, Southey made his home in the Lakes.

Southey had been born in Bristol in 1774, four years after Wordsworth, and, like Coleridge and Wordsworth, he too had had a disturbed childhood, being brought up by an eccentric spinster half-aunt in Bath who made him share her bed. She went to bed late and slept till ten in the morning and he wasn't allowed to disturb her. An uncle paid for him to go to Westminster School where he was expelled for an attack on corporal punishment in a radical and unauthorised school magazine, *The Flagellant*. He went to Oxford where he met Coleridge – two years younger – on a visit from Cambridge and they became young radicals and idealists together. It was with Coleridge, and ten others, that he had intended to drop out and form that utopian, agrarian community in the USA. His dotty aunt was very upset by this, saying she would give him no money, never accept him back in her house – and she never did.

Coleridge, rather ungallantly, used to maintain later that he'd only married his Fricker sister for Southey's sake, that he had been conned into it when it looked as if they were all going off to America. Southey's own marriage wasn't all that romantic, at least the ceremony wasn't. He left his Fricker sister at the church door and went straight off to Lisbon, presumably on the rebound from the abandoned American trip, where he spent the next six months with an uncle who was chaplain to the British community. It was on this trip that he started his life-long interest in Portugal and its empire. He then came back to his wife, made the marriage public, and looked around for a job, refusing family

1 A late eighteenth-century drawing by William Burgess of
Windermere Ferry with Belle Isle in the background.
Wordsworth used to cross by the ferry on his way to school.
For centuries it has been one of the main routes for travellers
in the Lake District, and is still in use today – though engines
have replaced horses.

2 Belle Isle as it is today.
Built in 1774, it is said to
be the only circular house
in England.

3 Mrs William Heelis, otherwise known as Beatrix Potter, Lakeland sheep farmer and landowner, lived at Sawrey, near Windermere, from 1905 until her death in 1943.

4 Hill Top Farm, the home of Beatrix Potter – and of Jemima Puddleduck. Six of her children's books were set in and around the farm. Today it is the most visited house in the whole of the Lake District.

5 Canon H. D. Rawnsley, who encouraged Beatrix Potter to publish her first book, was one of Lakeland's greatest conservationists. He was Vicar of Crosthwaite, Keswick, from 1883–1917, an active lighter of bonfires, campaigner against rude postcards, preserver of houses associated with the Lake Poets, and in 1895 was a co-founder of the National Trust, today the biggest landowner in the Lake District.

6 John Ruskin, writer and artist, lived at Brantwood on
Coniston from 1871 until his death in 1900.

7 A. Wainwright, the elusive but inimitable friend of all walkers. In 1952, aged forty-five and Borough Treasurer of Kendal, he decided to give himself thirteen years to climb every fell in the Lakes, making notes for his own amusement. Today, his seven *Guides to the Lakeland Fells* have sold half a million copies, the best selling books ever on Lakeland.

8 Mary, the Beauty of Buttermere. She was wronged by a blackguard in 1802 and the story got national coverage. Even the Lake Poets came to gape at her. (See chapter fourteen for full details...)

9 Chris Bonington, author and mountaineer. Everest is a bit higher than any Lakeland fell, but Bonington has chosen to make Cumbria his home.

10 Tom Harrington (*left*) and two of his brothers, dressed in their best for the 1978 Grasmere Sports, the highlight of Lakeland's sporting year. Cumberland and Westmorland style wrestling holds its own world championships. Tom has held three world titles at one time, a record not bettered in the four-hundred-year history of the sport.

11 Joss Naylor, sheep farmer and champion runner. Fell running is one of Lakeland's native sports. Joss Naylor has run up and down seventy-two Lakeland peaks of over two thousand feet in twenty-four hours – a record no one expects ever to be beaten.

12 William Wordsworth, Lakeland's greatest son, as seen by Haydon in 1818. He was born in Cockermouth in 1770 and died at Rydal in 1850. He made Lakeland famous throughout the world and a focal point of the Romantic movement. The writers associated with him, the Lake Poets, dominated English poetry for almost fifty years.

13 Dove Cottage, Grasmere, Wordsworth's home from 1799–1808, and a shrine today for the world's Wordsworth worshippers. The second most-visited house in Lakeland.

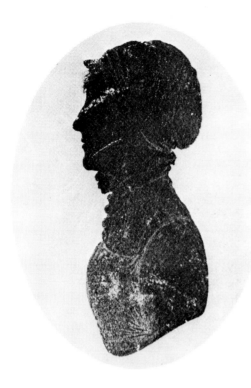

14 Dorothy Wordsworth, the poet's sister and lifelong friend, companion and inspiration.

15 Mary Wordsworth, the poet's wife, painted by Margaret Gillies. She married William in 1802 and joined him and his sister at Dove Cottage. All three spent the rest of their lives together. Mary died in 1859.

16 Samuel Taylor Coleridge, co-author with Wordsworth of *Lyrical Ballads* in 1798, followed Wordsworth to the Lakes in 1800, and made his home in Keswick. Finally left the Lakes in 1810, after a row with Wordsworth.

17 Robert Southey followed his brother-in-law, Coleridge, to Keswick in 1803. Poet Laureate in 1813.

18 Greta Hall, Keswick, home of the Coleridge and Southey families from 1800. Today it is a school.

19 Thomas De Quincey, author and opium-eater, wrote a fan
letter to Wordsworth in 1803 and subsequently moved to the
Lakes, taking over Dove Cottage from the Wordsworths, and
renting it until 1836.

20 Rydal Mount, the final home of Wordsworth, who lived
there from 1813 until his death. He became Poet Laureate in
1843 on Southey's death.

21 Jonathan Wordsworth (*right*), a descendant of the poet, and Hunter Davies, enjoying a literary cup of tea beside Grasmere Church.

pressure to take holy orders, just as Wordsworth had done. Like Wordsworth, after several attempts at different jobs in different parts of the country, an old friend, Charles Wynn, impressed by his literary talents, made him an annuity of £160.

The specific reason for Southey's decision to come up to Greta Hall was the loss of their first child Margaret, born after seven years of married life. Southey felt it would be a comfort for his wife to be with her sister, who also needed comforting. Coleridge, who wrote glowing reports to Southey about Keswick, denying that it rained a lot, probably realised the Southey would be a good rent-payer, and also provide company for his wife.

For the next forty years, Southey took over the responsibility of supporting an ever-increasing flock of little Frickers. There was, for a start, the three Coleridge children – Hartley, a child genius, brilliant way beyond his years at all academic subjects; Derwent, who was clever but more normal, and Sara, yet another gifted Coleridge child, with a definite literary talent.

Poor old Wordsworth must have been quite jealous to hear about them blossoming while his brood were in the main turning out very slow at their books. Wordsworth didn't visit much, but he helped with money towards Hartley's education and he heard about the latest Greta Hall chat from Dorothy and Sarah Hutchinson who were always close friends with the Greta Hall ladies. Sarah particularly was a universal aunt, acting at different times as secretary to Coleridge, Southey and Wordsworth and helping out with all the children. 'Send for Sarah,' was the cry whenever there was a domestic problem of any sort. She was a marvellous woman, who devoted her life to all three families. It is thought that at one time she might have married John Wordsworth, the brother lost at sea, but she remained a spinster to the end.

Then there was Southey's own offspring. He had eight in all, though two died in infancy. After a run of six girls, he had a longed-for son, Herbert, who was another child prodigy, being almost as clever as Hartley Coleridge, knowing Greek, French, German and Latin by the time he was nine, but he died aged ten in 1815. They had a final child, a son Cuthbert, in 1819 when Mrs Southey was forty-seven.

Southey also had adults to support – his wife and her two sisters lived full-time in the house and they were joined now and again by ever more Fricker sisters, two maiden ladies called

Martha and Eliza. Southey himself had two brothers who were always leaning on him for money. With up to twelve people at any one time to support, it's little wonder he worked round the clock. His complete published works – poetry, history, biographies, book reviews, articles and translations – would fill a hundred volumes. He started on a history of the Portuguese Empire when he moved up to Keswick, though he only ever published three volumes of it. This was the *History of Brazil*, the first published history of that country. Amongst his biographies was one on Nelson which did much to make him the public hero he still is today.

His income from his writings was surprisingly good. From the *Quarterly Review*, for many years his chief sources of regular money, he got, at his height, up to £100 an article. (Over 150 years later, someone writing articles for today's literary magazines would still consider themselves doing well to get such a price.) And from a publisher, he could expect between £600 to £1000 – which is what he got for his *Peninsular War*. Again, these sorts of prices are still being paid by publishers today, though naturally at the top end of the market the income can be rather more.

In 1817, *The Times* offered Southey a staff job at £2000 a year, which again sounds a huge salary for those days, but it meant going to London, so he refused. Presumably, he was already making up to £2000 a year by then from his books. Southey's poems never made him much money. For 'Kehama', which was well thought of at the time, he got only £75 in all, nothing compared with the thousands that Scott made from the 'Lady of the Lake'.

Southey became Poet Laureate in 1813 (Scott having declined) which brought in £90 a year, but in 1835 declined an offer from Peel of a baronetcy. He also got an unexpected legacy in 1834 on the death of Thomas Telford, the great Scottish bridge builder, with whom he had been friendly for many years and whom he'd joined on a long if rather rough journey round Scotland. It's nice to think of the literati of the day being friendly with the great engineers and scientists – Sir Humphry Davy, for example, was a friend of both Coleridge and Wordsworth. The two cultures today are much further apart.

Southey, despite all the hard work, didn't neglect his family. There's a nice description in a letter from Mrs Coleridge of a

typical day during the school holidays at Greta Hall in 1814 –
with all the adults lending a hand to teach the children of the
house, then ranging in age from eighteen to two. She says they
had organised themselves like bees in a hive from 9.30 to 4 with
Mrs C. herself doing writing, sums, French and Italian in the
dining room; Mrs Lovell doing Latin and English in her bedroom, while Southey was doing Spanish and Greek in his study.
The ladies, for those days, were highly educated, though
naturally they'd never been to university. They saw to it that their
daughters were given as many opportunities as their sons, even
if it all had to be done at home. Young Sara Coleridge was
translating French from an early age. Whenever any of the
children were ill or weakly in the Greta Hall homestead, as they
often were, there were wise mutterings and noddings of heads
over in the Wordsworth enclave, blaming it all on 'too much of
that studying'.

Normally, Southey was at work on his own writings from
waking up to going to bed, except for an hour's exercise around
midday. During this hour, he walked round Keswick and Derwent Water with a book in his hand, unless it was raining too
hard. At the age of fifty-six, he boasted that he could still walk
at three miles an hour and read the smallest print. If he had to
put his book in his pocket, he then did four miles an hour. Time
was money and he was loath to leave his pen or his researches.
Wordsworth lived his life in the open air, and was out for hours
every day and often at night. They must have made strange sights
– one poet walking deep in a book, the other walking and
shouting his head off as he practised new lines.

All the same, Southey was very generous with his money –
endlessly sending sums to relations or remote friends. He also
gave time to help new writers with their first books, writing or
editing for free, answering at length all his admiring letters,
entertaining young literary visitors. Charlotte Brontë got a long
letter from him when she wrote for advice about following a
literary career – and she wrote back to thank him for his kindness
in not saying 'that what I write is utterly destitute of merit'.

Shelley was one of the young aspiring writers who came up
to the Lakes, living in Keswick during the winter months of
1811–12 with his young bride. In 1811 he wrote that Southey's
'Kehama' 'is my most favourite poem'. He got himself an invitation to Southey's home and, having got to know him and been

his guest, he rather changed his mind, deciding he was a reactionary old bore, who was forever spouting chunks from books he had read. Shelley was just nineteen at the time.

'Southey had a large collection of books,' so Shelley wrote later. 'The shelves extended over the walls in every room of his large, dismal house in Keswick; they were in the bedrooms and even down the stairs. This I never saw elsewhere. I took out some volume one day as I was going down the stairs with him. Southey looked at me, as if he was displeased, so I put it back again instantly, and I never ventured to take down one of his books another time. I used to glance my eye eagerly over the backs of the books, and read their titles, as I went up or down stairs. I could not help doing so but I think he did not quite approve of it.'

Southey was always buying books, wherever he went, and once sent back nine hundredweight from a trip to Holland. In the end he had amassed 14,000 books, so much so that they feared for the floors. He was jealous of his books, and wouldn't think of lending them to someone careless, like Wordsworth, as De Quincey had once done, getting back a precious book all covered in jam. But once having pointed out a certain section to a young visitor, getting the book down himself, Southey allowed you to study it for as long as you liked, if your hands were clean. He got the children of the house to cover many of his books, cutting up their old dresses to do so, and his library was known in the family – and still is known to scholars today – as the Cottonian Library.

Southey struck many outsiders as living only in his books, though he was courteous and kind. De Quincey says he found him the nicer person, but really rather uninteresting, compared with Wordsworth. Yet at home with his family he was full of jokes and awful puns. He referred to Greta Hall as 'the ant-hill', which it was in both senses, being a hive of industry and a place where every lady was addressed as Aunt. He did a lot of writing for children, some of it very entertaining and witty. There's a nice bit of doggerel, written in a notebook, about a trip through France:

> Here we call for bread and butter
> Thanks for it in French we utter
> Better bread was never broken
> Worser French was never spoken.

It's ironic that of all the millions of words he published for adults his only well-known work today, apart from the Nelson biography, is one he wrote for children, *The Three Bears*. Even so, today's readers of *The Three Bears* are probably unaware that Southey was its author. In Southey's original version, which is delightful, it's an old woman who takes their porridge and sleeps in their beds. Goldilocks is a much later addition by someone else.

Southey loved picnics and outings with his large family. In 1815, to celebrate the victory at Waterloo, he organised a huge party to the top of Skiddaw to light a celebratory bonfire. Almost all the Southeys, Coleridges and Wordsworths were there – and there are amusing letters about it from several of those who took part.

Although Southey and Wordsworth had never been deep friends, perhaps even unspoken if respectful rivals, they came closer over the years. The connections between the two households were never broken, thanks to people like Sarah Hutchinson and Dorothy, but it was the next generation, the girls of the three poets, who finally brought them all together. They became each other's best friends and as Southey and Wordsworth each admired the other's daughters, the bonds grew stronger. When Sara Coleridge got married in 1829 the priest who performed the ceremony, at Crosthwaite Church, in Keswick, was the Rev. John Wordsworth, William's eldest child. The bridesmaids included three Southey girls and Dora Wordsworth, William's beloved daughter. For the second generation running, it had all become rather incestuous – using that term, of course, in its most harmless sense ...

In so many ways, Southey and Wordsworth had grown alike. The great young radicals, the student revolutionaries who, each in their way, had opposed the system, were now grand old reactionaries, forever laying down the law on every subject. Southey didn't get mixed up in politics, unlike Wordsworth, but there was one nice occasion in 1826 when Southey arrived home to Keswick, having been abroad, to find the town band and a whole posse of notables to greet him, congratulating him on being elected an MP. In his absence, he had been put up and won the seat at Downton in Wiltshire. This, of course, was in the days of rotten boroughs, before the Reform Acts. Southey swiftly declined the honour.

Perhaps the most interesting similarity between them was that each had, in essence, three wives. Southey had the three Fricker sisters living with him practically all his married life and Wordsworth had the two Hutchinson sisters and one Dorothy. All the ladies devoted their lives to their respective patriarchs, which must have been nice for them. It naturally gave the London clever clogs lots of chances for cheap jokes, especially Byron. Coleridge, even when he was still supposedly Wordsworth's bosom pal, poured scorn on the situation in a private letter to a friend, probably out of jealousy, being unable to get even *one* lady to devote herself to him.

'I saw him more and more benetted in hypochondriacal Fancies,' wrote Coleridge of Wordsworth, 'living wholly among *Devotees* – having even the minutest Thing, almost his very Eating and Drinking done for him by his Sister or his Wife. I trembled lest a Film should rise and thicken on his moral eye.'

A mutual friend, a Miss Barker who lived in Keswick, made the comment that Southey and Wordsworth were both spoiled by having their three wives, 'but that Wordsworth's were much preferable to Southey's'. This seems true. Despite their learnings, the Fricker sisters sound rather dreary, unattractive ladies and it's hard in any of the memoirs and notebooks of the day to find anyone with a good word for them – while everybody always raves about Dorothy and both the Hutchinson girls were greatly admired.

Coleridge has left the worst testament against his wife Sara, but then he would, calling her frigid, saying that nothing affected her with either pain or pleasure. 'If any woman wanted an exact and copious Recipe, "How to Make a Husband completely miserable" I could furnish her with one. Ill-tempered Speeches sent after me when I went out of the House, ill-tempered Speeches on my return, my friends received with freezing looks, the least opposition or contradiction received with screams of passion – all this added to the utter negation of all which a Husband expects from a wife.'

All the same, there was an endless stream of visitors to Greta Hall in Keswick so they must have found the Southey ladies welcoming enough. Charles Lamb and his sister were one of the first, staying three weeks and climbing Skiddaw. William Hazlitt came, and painted some portraits, but was driven out by irate locals after some amatory indiscretion. A recent letter in *The*

Times Literary Supplement started a heated row when it alleged that Hazlitt had raped the girl. (I mention this, not to drag in more scandals, but as an example of the endless fascination, 170 years later, which the lives of our Lake Poets and their friends still hold for so many scholars.)

Walter Scott made three visits to Southey, and one of the literary greats of the day, now hardly remembered, Walter Savage Landor, was also a visitor. The non-literary visitors included Canning in 1814 and William Wilberforce in 1818. Sir Humphry Davy visited Southey, as well as Wordsworth, and, according to Southey, was 'stark made for angling'. John Stuart Mill found Southey a 'remarkably pleasing and likeable man' and so did Robert Owen, the Scottish social pioneer. Owen tried to interest both Wordsworth and Southey in his schemes but he got a poor reception from the Wordsworth household. 'He is a good Man and a great enthusiast,' wrote Sarah Hutchinson, 'but must be a little cranky.' However, Southey was a bit more interested and went with Thomas Telford to look at Owen's model factory at Lanark, but his basic Tory principles made him suspicious of the socialistic overtones.

It was Southey's by now well-seated Tory views which made him absolutely furious when a rotten trick was played on him in 1817. A hitherto unpublished radical sketch about Wat Tyler, which he had written over twenty years previously in his rebellious youth, was illegally published and led to questions and rows in the House of Commons, with one MP accusing Southey, the Poet Laureate, of being a renegade. How they must have chuckled in the Kensington salons.

Southey was terribly self-righteous and everyone enjoyed the spectacle of him having to talk his way out of it, though Coleridge, then writing for the *Courier*, did come to his defence. He was also rather vain, boasting that his *History of Brazil* would 'win more permanent praise than Gibbon'. He was also very moralistic, condemning the loose living of many of the younger writers, branding Byron as the leader of what he called the Satanic School of Poetry.

Byron, like so many others, had been an admirer of Southey when he was young and in 1813, after their first meeting, had said that 'his appearance is epic and he is the only existing entire man of letters'. Southey had equally liked the look of Byron and his writing, but by the 1820s they had become opponents, attacking what each other stood for in articles and books. Much of it was little more than the usual literary quarrels, which both enjoyed, till Southey in the *Courier* accused Byron of being arrogant and Byron challenged him to a duel, though his second never got round to delivering the challenge. That would have been interesting. Life with the Lake Poets did have almost every other form of excitement and drama, from awful rows and sudden deaths to insanity, illegitimate births, rape and possible incest, but I haven't come across a duel in any of the notebooks.

However, the post-Byron generation were being brought up with some affection for the dear Poet Laureate, and also Daddy Wordsworth. There's a nice little poem written by John Ruskin, whom we last met back on the banks of Coniston. He wrote these lines in 1831 when he was just twelve, during a trip round the Lakes with his wine merchant father.

> Now hurried we home and while taking our tea
> We thought Mr Southey at Church we might see!
> Next morning the Church how we wished to be reaching,
> I'm afraid 'twas as much for the poet as preaching.
> His hair was no colour at all, by the way,
> For half o't was black slightly scattered with grey.
> His nose in the midst took a small outward bend,
> Rather hooked like an eagle's and sharp at the end!

Southey's own family life was always a pleasure to him despite the size of it and the need to work so hard, but it ended rather unhappily. He himself kept in excellent physical health, boasting that he was hardly ever ill, and was always cheerful, if ironic, about the normal passing ailments that any large household has to suffer. 'We are all well,' he wrote in one letter, 'except that I am lame, and that my son, my three younger daughters and Sara are settled in the whooping cough – bating these things with Bertha's toothache and Isabel's cold and Edith's sore throat and a few others, etc. Why, thank God we are all as well as can be expected.'

His wife Edith had always had depressive tendencies and in 1834 she began to show signs of insanity and died in 1837. Southey was much affected by this and became a recluse for a while and very depressed but in 1839 he surprised, and greatly annoyed, many people by marrying for a second time. His new wife was Caroline Bowles, a minor literary lady, some twenty years his junior, who had been a friend of the family for some time. The family was split down the middle. His brother and one daughter approved of the marriage but most of the daughters were against it and so was Wordsworth. Caroline, the new Mrs Southey, was very upset by the opposition to her, especially as she had become more of a nurse than a wife as Southey's own mental and physical powers were fast beginning to fade. He died at Greta Hall in March 1843, aged sixty-eight, and was buried at Crosthwaite Church, Keswick. Family quarrels about his second marriage led to the erection of three different memorials. Wordsworth wasn't invited to the funeral by Caroline, having been against her, but he turned up, uninvited, and wrote the words for one of the appreciations. So ended the literary life of Greta Hall, for forty-three years one of the most fascinating houses in the history of English literature.

Coleridge, its first literary inhabitant, had died some ten years previously in Highgate, London, where he had eventually ended up, after much wandering and ill health. His last years were in fact rather happy, since he was taken in by a doctor's family and worked again as a critic and essayiest. He never had the discipline of Wordsworth or Southey, yet in many ways he had a better mind.

'All other men whom I have known,' said Southey of Coleridge, 'are mere children to him, and yet all is palsied by a total lack of moral strength. He spawns plans like a herring. He will leave nothing behind to justify the opinion of his friends to the world.' Southey was wrong on this last point – he himself is the one almost forgotten. Coleridge's life and works are still studied today, far more than Southey's, though nothing like Wordsworth. But then the Wordsworth industry is something of a phenomenon. Only Sara Coleridge carried on the literary torch for the Coleridge-Southey household. She moved to London after her marriage and produced several books and edited her father's works, but of her five children, only one reached maturity. She died, aged forty-nine, from cancer.

Hartley Coleridge, the child prodigy, went to Oxford and became a Fellow, but then it all collapsed. He lost the fellowship after a year, for intemperance, then tried journalism and schoolmastering without success, returning to the Lakes to live in a series of rented rooms and houses, drinking too much, talking too much, borrowing money from the Wordsworths and other old friends of his father's, yet he was loved by everyone for his cheerful nature, his charm and his good conversation. He died in 1849 in Nab Cottage, his final digs, the cottage beside Rydal Water where De Quincey's wife had once lived.

Derwent, the less spectacularly clever of the Coleridge children, turned out the happiest and most successful, becoming ordained, then a headmaster and then the first Principal of St Mark's Training College, Chelsea.

None of the Southey children appears to have had any literary or academic careers of note. Mrs Lovell, the widowed Fricker sister, whom Coleridge said should be pensioned off but whom Southey brought to Keswick, outlasted all her sisters and contemporaries and was looked after by one of Southey's daughters, Kate, till she died aged ninety-one.

Literary Lakeland life still carried on, after Southey's death, over in Rydal, where it had always been at its most inspired and original. Mr Wordsworth was still physically very much in his prime, hard at work, involving himself in many projects. He at first declined the office of Poet Laureate on Southey's death, but Peel talked him into it. So in 1843, William Wordsworth became Poet Laureate, confirmed at last as the first figure in English poetry.

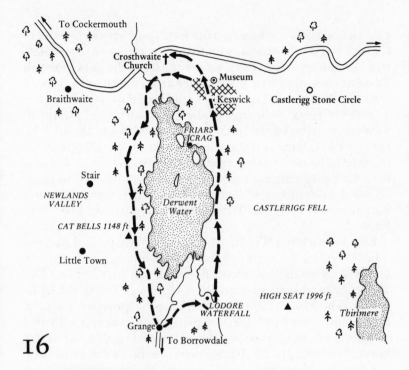

16

KESWICK

*Musical stones and a 500-year-old cat.
What the girls now do in Mr Southey's
bedroom.*

KESWICK TODAY LIKES TO THINK IT'S THE HEART OF LAKE-land and it probably is. Windermere is bigger – 8500 population as opposed to Keswick's 5000 – and it has the railway which Keswick no longer has. But Windermere is a bit of a sprawl, eating up Bowness and spreading itself along the lake, and there's a feeling of being at the *edge* of the Lakes, rather than in them. Keswick has the better situation, surrounded on all sides by famous lakes, famous climbs and famous views. It appears on the map to be rather stuck away in northern Lakeland, but it is in fact a better centre for exploring Lakeland. Getting to those secluded western Lakes, such as Wast Water, Ennerdale, and Buttermere, is hell from Windermere but relatively easy from Keswick.

Both Keswick and Windermere, being the two major Lakeland tourist centres, are pretty awful in high summer and you can hardly walk on the pavements or find a seat in a caff, yet I've always been able to park in Keswick, which biases me in its favour. The Moot Hall in the market place provides a central focal point, a very handy meeting place if you have kids who tend to wander off, and it looks suitably olde worlde and attractive. It's not really all that ancient, having been completely rebuilt in 1813.

Keswick's Moot Hall today houses the Information Centre where a bossy woman just inside the entrance told me to close the door and then got very snotty after I slowly looked through some guide books and maps on her counter, sighing heavily as she folded them back in the correct folds. They were rotten guides anyway – full of adverts. Further inside, though, there are some good displays of local scenes and an excellent selection of National Park leaflets and booklets.

Culturally, Keswick definitely has the edge over Windermere. The Royal Oak, where the Beast of Buttermere stayed, has a set of stained-glass windows in the dining room, each dedicated to a Lake poet including Shelley, which is straining it a bit, though he did live in Keswick for a while. It's hard to think of any literary or artistic figures who settled in Windermere, but Keswick is packed with literary connections, closely followed by Ambleside.

Apart from Southey and Coleridge (the two most obvious examples), Keats, Scott, Hazlitt and John Ruskin all visited Keswick and were very impressed. Charles Lamb perhaps over-did it, remarking that 'we thought we had got into fairyland'. Who, anyway, could resist a town which gave pencils to the world. Pencils for writers as well as those desirous of capturing the Picturesque.

The world's first pencil factory was opened in Keswick in 1566, using a rich deposit of graphite found in Borrowdale. Local graphite ran out in 1880 but the pencil industry is still going strong and Cumberland pencils are used the world over. The factory of the Cumberland Pencil Company is about the biggest building in Keswick. There's also a pencil museum, a mecca for pencil lovers everywhere. It was closed both days I went to look at it. Curses.

The town has always been very culturally conscious, as can be seen in the history of the Keswick Lecture Society, founded in 1869, which is in itself a microcosm of Lakeland life over the last century. All the topics and arguments of the day, from the worthy to the positively dotty, from the national to the obscurely local, are reflected in its annals. It was founded for 'mutual improvement' with members reading prepared essays to each other, or listening to essays by eminent guests. In its first season, 1869–70 the lectures included Ten Days in Ireland, Gypsies, Coal, the Telescope, the Suez Canal, the Local Antiquities of Crosthwaite Parish and a debate on the subject 'What are the best means for securing and maintaining a sufficient supply of food for the increasing wants of the nation?'

The year 1874 was jam-packed with particularly exciting lectures, what with Mr Grayson speaking on 'Umbrellas, their antique origin, history, humour and general importance', followed by Mr Ward on 'The Ear, its structure and development'. Imagine getting your dates mixed up and arriving to hear the wrong lecture. But the star performer of that year was probably Mr Fothergil on 'What is likely to be the effect of introducing flogging as a punishment for men who kick their wives and others'.

When times are hard, and the Society has had its lean years, with little money or interest, the lectures have been little more than what-I-did-in-my-hols. In 1878, they had a real flop with Mr Thomas Bakewell's paper on 'The History of Shorthand'. The minutes, very honestly, described what happened. 'When the time arrived the attendance was so small only nine persons beside the chairman being present, that Mr. Bakewell very properly declined to bring forward his paper, rightly considering that after the trouble he had taken in preparing the subject, providing

Diagrams, etc., such a miserable attendance amounted to a slight if not something more.'

The Society's biggest turnout in one evening was for Chris Bonington in 1962 when some 700 turned up to hear his account of climbing the Eiger. They also paid him the biggest fee they'd ever paid a lecturer in over a hundred years – £30, though that did cover two lectures in the one evening. Bonington was bang in the news having just returned from the Alps, but what was the big attraction back in 1908 when 400 people assembled to hear the Rev. Dr Dallinger talk on 'Spiders: their work and their wisdom'? That was an incredible turnout, especially considering, so the minutes record, that Dr Dallinger had travelled up from Eastbourne with a bad cold and 'it was evident that he spoke under great disability and many regretted that they were not able to hear all that was said'. Yes, the Keswick Lecture Society has witnessed some stirring times.

Perhaps, their all-time star lecturer, certainly the most indefatigable, was our old friend Canon Rawnsley, as ever at the heart of Lakeland life. Crosthwaite is the parish church of Keswick and he became vicar there in 1883 and was a staunch member of the Society until his death in 1920. He became President of the Society and in all presented over thirty lectures. The first and the last, in 1883 and in 1920, was on John Ruskin. In between, he delighted the members with Reminiscences of Wordsworth among the Peasantry of Westmoreland (later published), Some Royal Mummies, Some More Royal Mummies, Memories of the Great Paris Exhibition, The Inhabitants of the Bass Rock, What I saw of the Coronation of the Czar, The History and Reminiscences of the Jubilee Bonfires, A Visit to Italy, American Experiences, A Day at Rothenberg, The Excavation at Pompeii, Lord Nelson, German Miners at Keswick, Allan Bank (bought by Rawnsley in 1915) and the League of Nations.

The Keswick Lecture Society, over the decades, has not only attracted some eccentric lecturers but collected some eccentric objects. Most of them are today in the town's Fitz Park Museum, one of the most amazing museums in the Lake District.

'Don't look at the musical stones,' shouted the curator from his little ante-room, as I entered the Fitz Park Museum and was standing looking at the first exhibit, some musical stones. 'They're the least important exhibit! Start at the far end. Look at the Southey manuscripts first. They're the most important!'

I obeyed his command, though it was hard to drag myself away from such a fascinating object, and headed for the far room where, true enough, there were letters and manuscripts by Southey, Wordsworth, Ruskin, De Quincey and others. The Southey collection (most of which is not on show, but is available to scholars) is enormous. If Southey had today the following which Wordsworth has, you wouldn't be able to get moving for the screech of Ph.Ds being written. As it is, the manuscripts which are on show are in glass cases under green cloths and are rather boringly presented, though they do try to capture passing interest by displaying an original copy of *The Three Bears*. I watched as a party of school kids lifted the covers and then quickly dropped them, heading straight back for the musical stones, stopping on the way to climb on the edges of a massive relief model of the Lake District, which clearly warns visitors not to touch it. This huge model was built by a Mr Flintoft, an emigré who settled in Keswick in 1823. It took him six years to build. The Keswick Lecture Society bought it at an auction in 1878 for £160 and it's been one of their prize possessions ever since, appearing in all the old guide books to the Lakes.

The museum also contains a painting of the Beauty of Buttermere, some pleasant Lakeland water colours, geological specimens and a rather nice old English oak chest which has a notice on top announcing, '500 year old cat – lift lid carefully!' Inside, there is what it says – well, the skeleton of an ancient cat, preserved in a glass box.

And so back to the entrance, to the musical stones. The curator, Mr Norman Gandy, must obviously get bored with their endless fascination for visitors, specially as everyone insists on trying to play a tune on them – and everyone is welcome to try. They're genuine stones, scoured from the Skiddaw area by the Richardson family between 1827 and 1840, arranged in layers like a xylophone. When struck, each gives out a different note. In the nineteenth century they were trailed all over Europe and performed in public as a truly amazing oddity. They were played at a command performance before Queen Victoria in Buckingham Palace in 1848 – but she wasn't particularly amused by them.

I had a go and easily played a scale but they're hard on the knuckles. When they were played professionally, hammers were used, but very sensibly the Museum doesn't leave hammers around for kids to strike each other with. Almost every one of the Museum's 15,000 annual visitors has a go and, according to Mr Gandy, eighty per cent of them play one of six tunes. The most popular of all is the Do Ray Me tune from *The Sound of Music*. John Peel is also quite popular, with visitors no doubt trying to think of something Lakelandish. He couldn't actually name the other four most popular tunes. He just recognises the sounds.

'I'm not interested in music. If I could play music, I wouldn't play them. It wouldn't be like music, would it? It would be like playing dust-bin lids or glasses of vodka. They're not at all important, but as there's only six sets of musical stones in the world, all of them from this area, I can see the interest.'

Curators and guides in the Lake District come in two sorts – rather dozy ones, who don't quite know what it is they're guiding you round, and the characters, the ones with strong and in-dividual opinions. Mr Gandy is one of the latter breed.

He comes from Lancashire and, unlike so many off-comers to the Lakes, doesn't go around raving about every aspect of Lakeland life. 'Keswick people hate me saying this, but I think Keswick's like Blackpool. In fact, I prefer Blackpool. I like seascapes best.'

I could see what he meant, with all the trippers and the souvenir shops, but Keswick is surely so much cleaner and more tasteful, more discreet, not nearly as tatty as Blackpool.

'Hmm, you think so. Wait till August bank holiday. Then you'll see the kids vomiting in the doorways.'

Keswick has lots of easy walks, straight from the town centre, the most popular being along the shores of Derwent Water to Friar's Crag, the rocky promontory that sticks into the lake, one of the most photographed chunks of rock in the Lake District. There are two memorial stones, one to John Ruskin and the other to Canon Rawnsley, one definitely a founder of the National Trust and the other not so definitely, though don't say that if you visit Brantwood.

Cat Bells, along the western shore of Derwent Water, is my favourite little fell in the whole of the Lake District and I have lots of boyhood memories of climbing it. It's not really a climb, more a dawdle. It's very popular with children and old people. You often see the elderly with tears in their eyes, climbing it for possibly the last time, reliving all their old climbs, wondering if they'll be able to manage it again. As for children, it's a perfect beginning to fell walking.

The gentle, humpy slopes of the Cat Bells stand out for miles around, a child-like progression of easy heights. You get to the first top so easily, yet you get instant and terrific views. On so many fells, the first apparent top turns out not to be a top at all but a joke top, showing you that you've done nothing yet. No wonder Beatrix Potter loved Cat Bells. Perfect for Mrs Tiggy Winkle.

Sir Hugh Walpole also loved Cat Bells. His novels made him a fortune between the wars but are now sadly out of fashion. He settled in the Lakes in 1924, buying a little house called Bracken-burn, 'a little paradise on Cat Bells'. His early successes had been with stories of London life but he turned with even more success to novels set in Cumberland – *Rogue Herries, Judith Paris, The Fortress* and *Vanessa*. Perhaps they'll be done on TV some time and he'll be revived once again just as Galsworthy has been. He died at his home beside Cat Bells in 1941 and is buried in St John's churchyard at Keswick. 'That I wasn't born a Cumbrian isn't my fault,' so he wrote in the preface to his Herries series, 'that Cumbrians in spite of my "foreignness" have been so kind to me is my good fortune.'

I then went round Derwent Water to do the Lodore Falls, all part of the Keswick tourist trail. People are always moaning how the Lakes have been ruined in recent years by all the amenities being laid on for holiday makers, but when Southey visited the Lodore Falls in 1802 he found something which must have been exceedingly annoying for the residents of the day.

At a little public house near where the key of the entrance is kept, they have a cannon to display the echo; it was discharged for us and we heard the sound rolling round from hill to hill, but for this we paid four shillings. It is true there was an inferior one which would have cost only two shillings and sixpence, but when one buys an echo, who would be content for the sake of saving eighteen pence, to put up with the second best, instead of ordering at once the super-extra-double superfine?

In 1809, Southey wrote to his brother about the Falls. 'Tell the people how the water comes down Lodore? Why, it comes thundering and floundering, and thumping and plumping and bumping and jumping and hissing and whizzing and dripping and skipping and grumbling and rumbling and tumbling and falling and brawling, dashing and clashing and splashing, and purring and roaring and whirling and curling, and leaping and creeping, and sounding and bounding, and clattering and chattering, with a dreadful uproar – and that way the water comes down at Lodore.'

He wrote a poem about the Lodore Falls some thirteen years later, using almost the same words, and Victorian school children were very fond of learning and reciting the tongue-twisting lines, but I prefer his original prose version.

There's still a special entrance you have to go through, behind the hotel, to get at the Falls today. You put 2p in a turnstile and of course my family didn't have enough 2p pieces so we all had to jam in at one go, which led to a lot of cramming and damning, huffing and puffing, cursing and bursting, moaning and groaning, breathing and heaving, fighting and biting ...

The Lodore Falls are well known for being disappointing. People go there in the height of the summer and are furious to find only a trickle. We'd recently had rain so there was quite a bit of gurgling and splurgling, pattering and nattering, etc., but nothing to roar home about. It was in the nineteenth century that they were so passionate about waterfalls, making pilgrimage places out of the best Lake District ones. Most of the old guide books have lovely engravings of places like Lodore, Aira Force, Dungeon Ghyll, Scale Force and the others, with little Victorian gentlemen at the foot, staring up in awe at the immense, all-powerful, white foaming cascade above their heads. 'For a man is water's child,' wrote Thomas Mann, 'nine tenths of our body consists of it and at a certain stage the foetus possesses gills. For my part I freely admit that the sight of water in whatever form or shape is my most lively and immediate form of natural enjoyment; yes, I would even say that only on contemplation of it do I achieve true self forgetfulness and feel my own limited individuality merge into the universal.'

We climbed right up to the top, which was good fun, scrambling over wet rocks and under fallen trees and round crevices, but when we came down, we decided that the best view of all was from the bottom, where we'd begun. There's a spot between the bottom trees where you can stand back and have an uninterrupted view of all the tumbling cataracts above.

Back in Keswick, I went to see Crosthwaite church, parish church of the town. It now has an awful ring road whizzing behind it which I am sure Canon Rawnsley would have stopped.

It's a very confusing ring road and I kept on ending up on it, thinking I was heading the other way. However the church is beautiful, prettier on the outside than Grasmere, though Wordsworthians will no doubt disagree, and inside it has an affluent, rather lush feeling. I caught a glimpse of an orange anorak the minute I stepped inside and I thought not again, I've been following them all day, but this one was at rest in a back pew, sitting in his thick stockings, his climbing boots and ropes at rest beside him, quietly working on a sketch pad on his knee, doing a most elaborate and detailed charcoal drawing of the chancel.

The church's founder was St Kentigern, or St Mungo as he is known in Scotland, the sixth-century bishop of Glasgow. He was in Carlisle when he heard about the awful paganism of the folks in the mountain region so he made his way South, establishing churches on his way, churches which to this day bear his name, as at Caldbeck, where the parish church is called St Kentigern, Mungrisdale (Mungo's Dale), and Crosthwaite. He planted his cross in a suitable clearing in the vale between the two lakes, Derwent Water and Bassenthwaite, which is where the name comes from – Crosthwaite. (Thwaite is Norse for clearing.)

I looked to see if the present vicar showed any traces in his parish magazine of his illustrious literary predecessor. His signature looked bold and promising – Sam Doubtfire – but the contents were more religious than literary, though he had made space in his magazine for a joke. It was under the heading, 'To make you smile', and it was about three little boys. The first boy says his daddy earns most because he's a train driver. The second one says his father's a pilot and he earns most. The third boy says his dad's the Vicar and he only works on Sunday, but it takes six men to carry his pay.

The Southey connection is the main attraction for visitors to Crosthwaite church, though the attraction is modest, compared with Wordsworth and Grasmere. There's a marble effigy of him, with a long and rather dreary inscription composed by Wordsworth, and arrows outside saying 'Poet Southey's Grave' to guide you to the grave stone. The use of the word poet is somehow indicative, as if no one would know otherwise. Beside the grave a little plaque says, 'Restored by the generosity of the Brazilian Government, 1961'. We know why they are grateful.

Finally in Keswick, I went to visit Greta Hall. It passed through a variety of tenants after Southey's death in 1843, before being purchased in 1909, wait for it, by Canon Rawnsley and then rented to Keswick School. In 1921 the Governors of Keswick School bought the house and it's been used ever since as part of the school. It's a simple but rather handsome three-storey Georgian building. Two plaques record that Coleridge lived there from 1800–1803 and Southey from 1803–43. 'I question if there could be a room in England which commands a view of Mountains and Lakes and Woods and Vales superior to that in which I am now sitting,' wrote Coleridge in 1800, just after he had moved in. The views these days have the added attraction of the Cumberland Pencil Factory which is next door to the school.

Greta Hall still has a homely, family atmosphere, which was nice, with prints on the walls in the entrance hall, plus a letter from Southey and some visiting cards. The rooms are named after the original occupants, such as Southey's study or Mrs Coleridge's bedroom. Today, there are thirty-four girls sleeping there, first-year girls aged eleven and twelve. Only the five monitors can use the front door. The rest go round the side. The chatter of their conversations echoes down the staircases, much the same as when all those Coleridge and Southey girls lived there, all of them equally busy at their school work.

The matron, Mrs Whitfield, who took me round, said there had been talk in the past of the ghost of Mrs Southey haunting one of the rooms, but she had never seen it, nor had the girls. They still called a store room the apple room, as that's what the Southeys used it for, and a corridor outside Southey's study was always referred to as the duck board, a name handed down from the days in which it has been completely lined with Southey's books, the ones which Shelley had admired, and you had to duck down to get past them. In the summer holidays she regularly gets Japanese visitors arriving, all of them terribly knowledgeable, and she lets them see round the building, but doesn't encourage it during the school term, not when the girls are in residence.

I went into their bedrooms, when they were in class of course, and the high-ceilinged rooms and the windows are much as they were, but the decorations on the walls are a bit different. In Southey's study, where seven girls now sleep, the walls were covered with photographs of the Fonz, King Kong, Snoopy, Charlie's Angels and Star Wars. Not very literary but highly popular with young girls, back in 1978.

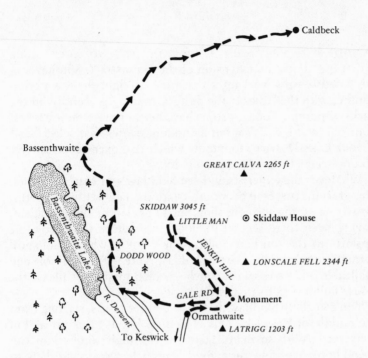

17
SKIDDAW

A misty day on Skiddaw. On meeting a ferret
by Bassenthwaite Lake. A short climb
with Mr Bonington.

SKIDDAW IS KESWICK'S MOUNTAIN. IT'S SO ACCESSIBLE that it's almost an extension of the main street. Southey and the Wordsworths went up it that time, to light their Waterloo bonfire, with the ladies in the party ascending gracefully on the backs of ponies. Today, people have been up it on motor bikes. Poor old Skiddaw. It's a big mountain, one of that select band of four Lake District mountains which rise over 3000 feet, yet no one seems to treat it with dignity.

Whatever the experts say, I see Skiddaw's virtues as virtues. Her graceful curves and smooth contours, her well-worn paths, are so re-assuring and consoling. She's Lakeland's oldest resident, having been there several million years before those volcanic upstarts in the southern Lakes. She's got a whole geological formation named after her – Skiddaw Slate – which is soft and malleable and gives to the touch – which might not please the house builders but satisfies the strollers.

You can climb Skiddaw and back in three hours, starting from the middle of Keswick. This is again a big asset as far as I'm concerned. With so many Lake District high climbs you can spend hours working out a good approach, wondering there to start from, where to park, how to return. With Skiddaw, you just go to Keswick and follow the crowds. No, that's a slight exaggeration. It's not *that* bad, though it would be interesting to know the annual figures.

Skiddaw is 3054 feet high, only 152 feet lower than Scafell Pike itself, so all this talk about it being easy is relative. The going might be un-treacherous and un-dangerous, but you still have to push the legs, bend the back and use a little bit of puff to get you up there.

I had the whole family with me, so I didn't subject them to walking through the streets of Keswick and having to cross that noisy ring road, though it was a shame to miss the walk round Latrigg fell. We drove instead up to Ormathwaite and along Gale Road to a rough road which leads to a car park, the beginning of the most popular way up Skiddaw. Even early in the morning there was a cluster of cars, spilling out enough stuff to open an Army and Navy stores. I didn't actually see any babes in arms (another of the anti-Skiddaw jokes) but a lot did look like senior citizens. An old man beside us was busy opening tins which I thought at first must be emergency rations but they turned out to be boot polish, his and hers. He and his wife then solemnly got out lovely yellow cloths and brushes and started applying polish to their already spotless boots. When at last they were ready, they set off *down* the hill, to my amazement, not up towards Skiddaw. Shoe fetishists? Off to the Keswick Boot Convention?

We all raced through a gate, round a little mound, and came to the monument, the first landmark on the foothills of Skiddaw. It's much smaller than you think it's going to be from the map, but then most things are – unless of course they turn out to be much bigger. (I think that covers everything.) It's a humble little cross to the memory of three shepherds, members of the Hawell family, with a humble little verse.

> Great Shepherd of Thy heavenly flock
> These men have left our hill
> Their feet were on the living rock
> Oh guide and bless them still.

Ahead, we could see the main path, stretching invitingly up the straight and steep slopes of Jenkin Hill. It follows a neat fence and might easily have been transplanted from a suburban park, but it's surprisingly steep all the same. We could see the usual orange blobs all the way up the path, as if suspended in mid-air. This first steep bit is actually the hardest part of the whole ascent of Skiddaw, as I kept telling the kids, though there was no need to, they'd raced well ahead. On some guide maps they boast about the Skiddaw hut, a refreshment place, which used to be on this slope, but it's long since gone. Just as well. It's one thing to defend the easiness of Skiddaw but Coca Cola as you climb would be definitely degrading. We had our picnics with us and felt almost professional for once, carrying little rucksacks. The weather was dull so naturally we were all wellie-wearers. Not even polished wellies either.

I forced them all to keep stopping, to turn back and soak up the incredible views of Derwent Water, a living relief map. New views and perspectives appeared so quickly it was almost like being in a lift, then, alas, we started to hit pockets of mist, which was a great shame. We all got to the top of the steep stuff with ease, and strolled gently along the wide and ample path towards Skiddaw Little Man, but the mist was thickening and our view was disappearing fast so the girls decided to have their picnic in the sun and light and not go any further. Skiddaw is not dangerous in the mist – it must be the only mountain even I couldn't get lost on, at least going up this route – but it's not much fun. Jake and I, going for our Duke of Edinburgh's award, decided to press on alone. Our only worry was colliding with other walkers, staggering down in the mist.

The path was about twelve feet wide and the going no harder than walking up Parliament Hill on Hampstead Heath. It was just a shame we could only see thirty yards or so in front of us. With the mist, came the cold, so we sang silly football songs to keep us warm. We went through all those inane chants they sing on the terraces, but instead of Tottenham and Arsenal, Liverpool and Manchester United, we substituted Lakeland names. 'We all a-gree, Skid-daw is ma-gic. If you hate Helvellyn, clap your hands. Nice one Keswick, nice one son. Caldbeck, Caldbeck, here we come. We hate Grizedale forest, we hate Scafell too; we hate Coniston Old Man, but Skiddaw we love you.' Well, it kept us amused.

We were singing so loudly that we almost knocked over an old man and his dog, coming out of the mist in front of us, fresh from the top of Skiddaw, judging by the mass of shining droplets clinging to his bushy eyebrows. You could tell he was a local, a real countryman, from the lack of anorak, boots or walking clothes. He wore an old suit jacket, in faded dark-blue stripes, grey unmatching trousers and a shapeless pullover. He did have a walking stick, a home-made one, which could be read either way – real shepherds have them, but so do phoney walkers, the sort with compasses fixed to the dash-board of their Cortinas. He turned out not to be a shepherd but a retired Cumbrian County Council storeman from Keswick who walked up Skiddaw at least three times a week with his dog. It made Skiddaw sound even more suburban.

During the war, he said, they really did have vehicles driving up Skiddaw when the army used it as a training area for jeeps. Only one ever got lost. He'd never actually seen an ordinary car go up Skiddaw, but plenty of motor bikes. In the old days, shepherds used to live out for several days at a time in Skiddaw House, an isolated building stuck out in the wild fells over the top of Skiddaw. Wainwright in his 1962 *Northern Fells* guide names the shepherd who was then using it, but our friend said today's shepherds have cars and tractors and can get home of an evening. It was now owned by a North-Eastern education authority who used it for school camps, as far as he knew. As we bid him farewell, we asked him, when he came to a little girl of five in a blue waterproof jacket who would be sitting on Jenkin Hill guzzling choccy bikkies, to walk up to her and say 'Hello Flora'.

He called his dog and strode off, smiling at the trick he was going to play, while we made a last surge for Everest, I mean Skiddaw. The jokes rather receded when we reached the final assault. There was thick snow all over the path, the mist was like freezing fog and the grass suddenly gave way to slippery scree and bits of slatey rocks and the going was surprisingly steep. We were furious, not amused, to look down and find fresh motor bike tracks at our feet. They just suddenly appeared. We hadn't seen them lower down. Was there a mad cyclist around, who had landed by helicopter? Then we were overtaken by a weird-looking bloke in shorts and running shoes, who belted past us and, almost as quickly, belted back again, going the other way. I half expected to see the Skiddaw Hermit, a gentleman called George Dodd who left Banff to live in a cave on Skiddaw, using a boulder for a table and hay for a bed, earning odd pennies by painting people's pictures, except that he would be 150 years old by now as it was in 1875 that he was last seen.

We reached the final ridge at last where we were chilled to the marrow by the most appalling blast of wild, freezing wind that took our breath away. We couldn't speak for fear of freezing our intestines. The blast felt as if it had come straight across Scotland from the North Pole. We staggered along the ridge, trying to decide which pile of cairns was the top, then turned round and rushed back, desperate to get out of the wind. We'd had visions of a jolly picnic on the top, despite the mist, sitting like Captain Scott, our hair matted with misty droplets, but we hadn't reckoned on the cold. No wonder they categorise the mountain tops as sub-arctic.

We didn't stop till we reached an iron gate, much lower down, where we crouched and quickly gulped our coffee and sand-wiches. That's another suburban touch – there are three gates and two stiles to go through on this route up Skiddaw. We were dried out by the time we reached the girls, with no signs of our ordeal against the elements. They'd been sunbathing all afternoon and didn't believe our terrifying tales about motor cycling yettis, thick snow, arctic winds and sub-zero temperatures, though they had been accosted by a strange old man and a dog who'd asked my wife if she was called Laura ...

Back O'Skiddaw is what the locals call, unsurprisingly, everything to the back of Skiddaw, but Back O'Skiddaw is a country in itself, a clearly defined area, a little region with exact boundaries. Behind its two dominant peaks, Skiddaw and Saddleback, are hidden away the Caldbeck fells, remote, lonely, silent fells, almost as unknown today as they've ever been. Many guide books miss them out completely, which is nice. It's as if there's an unseen sign: Kendal Mint Cake stops here.

Bassenthwaite Lake is the moat which acts as the western boundary. Its claim to fame is that it is the only lake in the Lake District. Short pause while this astounding fact sinks in. It's the sort of riddle you get in a Christmas cracker. The explanation is that every other stretch of water in the Lake District has either mere or water in its title and so doesn't require the word lake. On all good maps, only Bassenthwaite is called a lake. Correctly speaking, and correctly writing, you should never refer to Lake Windermere or Lake Derwent Water. Such mistakes don't upset me, though I noticed that in one of his Lakeland books, Norman Nicholson gets very annoyed by such tautology – saying that if people will insist on Lake Windermere, instead of just Windermere, they might at least say Windermere Lake and follow the Cumbrian tradition and put the topographical term second.

You can see the problem, of course, as there's usually a village with the same name as the adjacent stretch of water. You have to make it clear somehow that you want to know the way to the lake called Windermere/Coniston/Buttermere/Grasmere/Rydal/Loweswater and not the village called Windermere/Coniston/Grasmere/Rydal/Buttermere/Loweswater. Lucky old Ullswater and Derwent Water lakes. They've at least got their names to themselves.

Bassenthwaite Lake has its Bassenthwaite village and, despite the existence of the correct terminology, you still have to make it clear which one you're describing. On the road to Bassenthwaite (village), not far from Bassenthwaite (lake), I met a lady taking a ferret for a walk. It was brown and creamy and she picked it up, giving it a few secret cuddles, so I could peer at it more properly and see that indeed it was a real ferret, a Pole Cat ferret, she said. She had it on a very long lead and took it out for walkies every day. She only let it off the lead when she got inside her own garden. He was called Nicky and she'd had him seven years. He didn't make any noises, apart from an occasional tut tut tut, and he didn't really bite, except the odd glove, though she wouldn't want to trust him with a stranger, just in case he did try out his little sharp teeth. He was a lovely pet, she said, and she obviously loved him dearly. No, he'd never done any ferreting, never been sent down holes to chase rabbits. 'He wouldn't know a rabbit hole from a hole in the head, would you Nicky,' she said, giving him a squeeze. 'He does investigate mouseholes, but that's about all.' There was only one problem about having a ferret for a pet, which probably explains why few people have them. 'He smells a bit like a skunk,' she said, opening the gate of her garden and disappearing inside.

Bassenthwaite is a great sailing lake and I began to get fine views of the yachts as I climbed high along the road to Orthwaite. Derwent Water, the rival lake, is a bit rough, with fiendish cross winds, so sailors prefer Bassenthwaite. It was here that Tennyson was inspired by thoughts of King Arthur, and the throwing of Excalibur into the lake. He was staying with his friend James Spedding at Mire House on the shores of Bassenthwaite and it was after his lakeside walks that he wrote the description of the death of Arthur in 'Idylls of the King'. I wonder how many modern yachtsmen think they see ghostly hands in the water when they sail on Bassenthwaite.

Once Bassenthwaite is left behind, and the last vestiges of tourism, the roads become much quieter and emptier, even in the height of the summer. Towards Uldale you come into open moorland, with the little roads unfenced. This is still the Lake District, still well inside the National Park boundaries, but it's a different sort of Lake District. For a start, there aren't any lakes, not once you leave Bassenthwaite, except for Over Water which is really a large tarn. The fells are low and rounded, rough with heather and bracken, with very little arable land around. It's all sheep with a few cattle on the better meadows, plus the distinctive dark Fell ponies which are allowed to roam free all over the Caldbeck fells.

Coleridge came this way on his early walks. Being a man of taste, he soon realised that there were hidden delights the other side of Skiddaw, far from the madding hordes on their Picturesque tours. He even talked Southey into coming with him to Caldbeck, back in 1803 when Southey had just arrived in the Lake District. Coleridge had been going on in his letters about the terrific walks and he planned out a four-day tramp for the two of them. They got over Saddleback easily enough and eventually reached Caldbeck where they booked into an inn, but then Southey started moaning. He'd been a bit of a drag all day, complaining about being tired, wanting stops for refreshments, worrying about the weather, feeling very homesick. No wonder Coleridge really preferred to be on his own when he did his marathon walks. Anyway, after one night in Caldbeck, Coleridge agreed to cut the holiday short and they returned to Keswick, after just thirty-six hours on the fells.

Chris Bonington is Caldbeck's best-known resident today and he's not the sort of person to turn back, at least not on the Lakeland fells. He and his wife and two children live in a cottage amongst a huddle of four or five other cottages about a mile from Caldbeck. They have a perfect situation – off the beaten track, yet not isolated. Best of all, if you like fell walking, they can come straight out of their cottage and on to the open fell. The fell in question is one of the nicest in the whole of the Lakes, yet one of the least known – High Pike.

When I first went to see him I hit one of those perfect winter days that, looking back, seem almost unreal. It had been rainy and miserable and misty when we left Carlisle and I feared we'd be stuck chatting inside his cottage all afternoon, but as we approached the Caldbeck fells we could see snow on the top and the weather got suddenly sharper and clearer and a blue sky started to appear. It all happened in the space of ten miles, yet it was like crossing some climatic date line as we went up Warnell. One moment we were on a wet grey road – the next the whole landscape was virgin snow. You could actually see the line where it began. The snow had obviously fallen earlier that morning, soft and crisp and honest with no ice hidden beneath, no slush or puddles.

When we got to the Bonington cottage, his two boys, Daniel and Rupert, were on their skis, tearing down the slopes beside their house. They gave Jake a sledge – and I never saw them again till nightfall. Chris and I decided to go up High Pike at once, before anyone played a nasty trick and waved a wand to make it all vanish.

The snow was so gentle and comfortable and beautiful to walk in, not deep enough to drag you back, not hard enough to be dangerous. A walk in new snow in the Lakes has a dream-like quality. All the clichés come true. It's a magic blanket, a sensual covering, which deepens every familiar perspective, bringing out new lines and shapes, making white appear to have as many shades as a rainbow.

High Pike is a surprisingly big fell, occupying a complete corner of the north-east plateau of the northern fells. You sweep up and along its vast shoulders, climbing all the time, yet with nothing ever obscured, no tricks being played to make you think you'll never get there, no pretend summits to make you lose heart.

On top there is a seat, an ordinary garden seat, which somehow doesn't make it look suburban, just a pleasant treat after a pleasant, un-arduous walk. You could probably carry up a summer house, if you had the time. To the south, I could see a line-up of famous Lake District peaks, all clothed in white, majestic against the blue sky. The most prominent of course is Skiddaw, though I can never tell one peak from another, not when they all overlap and compete for position. I can't even follow the expert's directions when they point confidently and say that one is obviously Gable. Bonington knew them all, or at least convinced me he did.

As we stood in amazement, taking it all in, hardly daring to speak, a lone figure could be seen coming across the high plateau from the direction of Skiddaw. We'd previously seen ski marks so we wondered if this would be the lone skier. He was a climber, dressed in the real stuff, with ropes, ice axe, huge boots, very expensive anorak, and two pairs of thick coloured socks, one of them rolled up and one rolled down, as if done with set squares. He had a compass fixed very professionally to his plastic-coated map which hung from his belt. I think he recognised Bonington, the best-known face in British climbing, but made no personal comments. Bonington and I were both wearing wellies for our stroll, and denim jeans. That's another thing the guide books say. Jeans should never be worn, especially not in winter time or in snow. The solitary climber looked as if he, not Bonington, was the Everest expert, with all his high-class gear. I could see him eyeing our wellies, rather puzzled, as we stood and chatted. He and Bonington tested each other on the views, scoring house points each time one named a peak the other couldn't see. I kept out of it, except when we turned north and I pointed out the lights of Carlisle. No house points for that of course. A city of 70,000 putting its lights on isn't all that hard to identify.

The climber went off the way he'd come and we stood in silence, watching the sun going down. The blue turned to red and the peaks in the west went technicolour as the sun finally sank. We went down in a trance. The next day was wet and miserable and misty and the snow completely disappeared. It was as if we'd dreamt it.

It's not hard to see why Bonington loves the Lakes, but it's hard to see how he manages to live up here, to support a wife and family, living in the back of beyond, just by being a professional climber.

He's forty-three and was born in Hampstead and went to University College School, though his early school days were rather disturbed as his father, a journalist, and his mother, a copy writer, separated when he was only one. He had a provisional place at London University but failed his English A levels, his best subject. He thinks it was nervousness that caused it. He went to Cranwell, but failed there to pass as a pilot, and went on instead to Sandhurst where he did get through and became an army officer for five years. He started climbing at sixteen, after a relation had given him a book of photographs of Scottish mountains, and he kept it up in spare time in the army. After the army, he joined Unilever as a management trainee and became a margarine salesman, but gave that up after nine months. In 1962 he decided to go it alone and try to live as a climber. By then he had discovered that climbing was what he liked most in life.

He first hit the headlines in 1962 when he and Ian Clough were the first Britons to ascend the North Face of the Eiger. Since then he's become an expedition leader and his best-known trips have been Annapurna in 1970, Everest in 1972 (which failed to get up), Everest in 1975 (a success). He was also on the Old Man of Hoy climb which thrilled the nation watching on TV, hoping no doubt that one of the climbers would kill himself.

'I woke up a few times in black despair in those early years. People were always asking me "What will you do when you can't climb?" I said I haven't a clue. Still haven't a clue.'

Bonington has always been good at rallying support, getting money out of people, seeing chances others have missed, very professional in presenting himself. But he says he's never climbed for the money. He climbs simply because he loves climbing. In order to climb, especially on the face of Everest, which took a party of eighty in all, including porters, and cost £130,000, he had to get the team financed. And in order for him and his family to live when he's not up a mountain, he has to come back and talk or write about being up mountains. He's written two best-selling books about his climbs and done a lot of photo-journalism, especially for the *Telegraph* Magazine. He does radio and TV programmes when asked. But his main income comes from lecturing. He does three-week tours, several times a year, complete with audio-visual and electronics devices.

He bought the Caldbeck cottage in 1971, using it at first as a weekend cottage. Wendy, his wife, hated the thought of living in London, though she is also a southerner, from Buckinghamshire, so they compromised on Manchester where they lived, near a group of other young climbers, for five years. Wendy wasn't so keen on that either. In 1974 they moved full-time up to Caldbeck. Both of them say that they will never move again.

'This is the first home I've had with a real feeling of home,' she says. 'I can't explain the total freedom I feel here. I'm not a great walker. Little walks do me. I felt claustrophobic living in a town, surrounded by other houses. Here I can live by just look-ing at the sky and the fields and the hills. There's as much social life as I want, more really than I can cope with. The only problem is having to be a chauffeur, driving the boys everywhere, but even that is bearable. The drive into Carlisle is beautiful. Every time I see something breathtaking. The boys are so free. In the suburbs of Manchester I was always on their backs, keeping an eye on them, accepting all the rat-race pressures. Today, for example, they just got up and went out first thing and played in the snow. I never saw them again. Look at their cheeks now, all aglow. It happens all the year round. They are out doing physical things.'

Wendy used to be an illustrator of children's books, when Chris first met her at a party in Hampstead, but now she is turning to pottery and does three days a week at Carlisle Art College. She's building a kiln in their garden – something they couldn't do in the suburbs of Manchester.

'Friendships unfold round here,' Chris says. 'It's a gentle, un-forced process, and then it's full of pleasant surprises. This is a purely rural area – unaffected by any industry, as it is on the west coast, or over-run by tourists, as it is in south Lakeland. This is a *real* village, with a very strong life of its own.'

Bonington climbs High Pike almost every day he is at home. In the summer, he rings climbing friends, in either Carlisle or Keswick, and they arrange to meet on Great Gable in an hour. He can do a day's climbing in an evening, as the nights are so light in summer, after he's done all his other work.

'I get as much pleasure out of the Lakes as the Himalayas. It's a familiar beauty, and yet it is always refreshing. The very familiarity adds to the beauty. I could walk round the northern fells for ever.

'The Lakes are nicer than climbing in Scotland. The Scottish mountains are bigger and grander, but they have less humanity. Man is more intrusive in Scotland. The quality of the rural architecture is not as good. Man doesn't blend in Scotland. The basic designs are poor.'

He was busy, when we met, on another expedition, a British assault on K2, the second-highest mountain in the world, 28,740 feet high in north Pakistan. They were going up the West Ridge which had never been attempted before. Instead of a huge team of eighty climbers and porters, as on Everest, they were going with a simple team of only eight, all Britons. From the base camp onwards, which would be at 18,000 feet, they would be on their own. It was going to cost £64,000. The book rights had been sold – though he himself wasn't going to write the expedition's book this time. 'I don't want to write another expedition book – I've already done three.' In the end, though, Bonington's K2 expedition in 1978 had to be abandoned, after the death of one climber.

Their life is simple in their little cottage, but not austere. They run two Volvos, one old and one new, and he has enough work and money coming in to keep a secretary employed. He very much likes his home comforts, which might seem surprising, considering he goes off voluntarily climbing mountains for ten weeks at a time, carrying huge packs in arctic conditions. He says it's not as terrifying as it might look, perched in a tent on a little rock ledge, 20,000 feet up in sub-zero conditions, even when forced to wait for a blizzard to blow out. In this case he just sits tight for two days, snug in his sleeping bag, and reads books. 'If you have the right gear, and modern gear is very good, you can be surprisingly comfortable. I rather like it. Life is very simple. You're insulated from all the normal home problems and worries and insulated from the weather. You only have one thought in your mind – to get to the top.'

Although he's bored by writing about climbing, his love of climbing is no less strong. 'Basically, it's just tremendous fun, giving aesthetic and physical pleasure. There's an exhilaration about a long hard climb. I also like the organising process. Most of all, I like being in mountains. That's why I could never live anywhere else but here.'

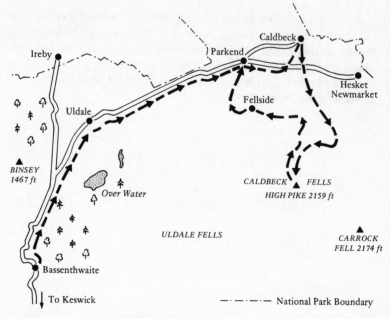

CALDBECK IS ALSO JOHN PEEL COUNTRY, THOUGH YOU could pass through it and never be aware that John Peel lived and hunted and died in this area. Hunting dominates so much of Lakeland life, but native life, not the life the tourists see. Peel's name, and the song written about him, are known wherever hunting takes place, which means almost the whole world. Tullie House Library, Carlisle, even has a copy of the song in Swahili. Most English-speaking people could manage at least two lines of 'D'ye Ken John Peel' as easily as they could manage two lines of 'Daffodils', yet there are no pilgrimages to Peel's birthplace, no tourist trade has grown up around him.

His grave is there in Caldbeck churchyard for all to see and several hundred do look at it every year, almost with surprise at finding it there. In the same grave yard, attracting even less attention, is the grave of Mary of Buttermere, the Beauty, who later married (becoming Mary Harrison) and settled in Caldbeck. And just to finish the grave spotting, look out for the parents of John Dalton, originator of the atomic theory.

John Peel's grave made the headlines for a brief moment in 1977 when it was desecrated by some hunt saboteurs, protesting against blood sports, but now all is peace and quiet. Little attention is drawn to it, nor to the Caldbeck pub where the song was first sung, The Oddfellows Arms, or the farm house in nearby Ruthwaite where John Peel died.

This farm house was empty when I went to look at it in early 1978. I had been looking for a little place in the Lakes all year, like so many exiled northerners, and had seen several on my travels, but all of them too expensive or in the tourist part of the Lakes. Now that I was in real fell country, I rushed to Ruthwaite when I heard that Peel's house was for sale. It's a handsome cottage, with stone flags, stone stairs, interesting rooms and alcoves and was only £11,000. Alas, it was all hemmed in, with no aspect, and was in a terrible state of repair. It was still for sale, months later, but no doubt somebody by now will have considered it a bargain. (Instead, I bought a smaller, less imposing cottage at Parkend, near Caldbeck, which turned out to have its own John Peel connections, though I didn't know it when I bought it. Imagine a southern estate agent missing such a trick.)

John Peel lived from 1776 to 1854, almost the identical lifespan of Wordsworth. He lived a life that was typical of the period, but one vastly different from Wordsworth's and I'm sure they never met or even heard of each other, though Coleridge and Southey, during their stay in Caldbeck and their tramp across the Caldbeck fells, might well have seen him on the horizon, blowing his horn, wakening everyone from the dead, or heard him talked about in the pub in the evening. In his lifetime, Peel was indeed a legend, if only a local one. He died without ever being known outside the immediate area – long before the tune we know today was even composed.

His parents, William and Lettice Peel, were living at Parkend, Caldbeck when he was born, the site now of a very good restaurant. They soon moved into an adjacent farm at Greenrigg of some twenty-five acres (part of which I now own) which was where John was brought up. His father specialised in horses, breeding and selling them, the sort of Fell ponies still seen in the area. John Peel's own favourite pony, which he used to ride when hunting, was called Binsey, after the gentle solitary fell above Ireby.

John Peel ran away to Gretna Green in 1797 with a local girl, the daughter of a fairly prosperous farmer at Uldale who didn't fancy John as a son-in-law, but they were later forgiven and were officially married in Caldbeck church. They eventually moved into a small farm at Ruthwaite, which his wife's parents gave them. Peel himself was one of thirteen children and he and his wife also had thirteen children – so there are lots of Peels still in the area – but he wasn't there for all the births. He lived only for hunting, closely followed by boozing and carousing in the local pubs after the hunt was over. In 1954, when some centenary celebrations were held in Caldbeck, the then rector of Caldbeck described him as one of Caldbeck's least worthy sons. 'Why make such a hero of one who neglected his farm and impoverished his family by his unrestrained pursuit of hunting?'

Peel had his own pack of hounds, getting friends and local farmers to feed and lodge those he couldn't afford to maintain himself, and he hunted the fox every possible day. When it was impossible, he and his hounds chased hares. He was by all accounts a brilliant huntsman and the sound of his horn, when he and his hounds had got the scent of a fox, would drag farm hands from their work, disrupt weddings and upset funerals as people all chased off to take part in the excitement of the kill.

Many contemporary accounts of his hunts appeared in local papers, such as the *Carlisle Journal*, and the local quality, like

Sir Wilfred Lawson, as well as the humblest farm hand, all joined in. A hunt could cover sixty to seventy miles, going on foot on the high ground or on horse on the slopes, and could last all day and night, with celebrations afterwards going on for as long again. Canon Rawnsley, that inexhaustible collector of titbits on all aspects of Cumbrian life, interviewed several locals who had known him personally. 'He wad drink, wad John Peel, till he couldn't stand; and then they would just clap him on't pony and away he wad gang as reet as a fiddle.'

He was six feet tall, weighed over thirteen stone and had a big nose (very Wordsworthian) and was probably a fairly disreputable character, without actually being downright wicked. His poor wife must have had a hard life with him. He was probably illiterate, apart from being able to write his name, but he was a character whose company all hunting and sporting men greatly enjoyed. He wore a grey coat – not a coat so gay as some versions of the song have it – knee breeches, a tall boxer hat and carried a whip and horn. The grey coat was the traditional coat of local farmers, made from the wool clipped from the local Herdwick sheep and woven in the Caldbeck area. Hodden grey, it was called, or Skiddaw grey. The wool was undyed and still retained traces of the rancid butter which shepherds often plastered on the sheep in winter. Peel wore his like a blanket and hardly ever took it off. Those twee table mats and beer mats in pretty hunting pink which many northern hotels love, purporting to be John Peel's image, bear little relation to the rather smelly, scruffy original.

The words of the song were written in 1829, when Peel was fifty-three, by John Woodwock Graves, a hunting friend of Peel's who ran a wool factory in Caldbeck, the sort which turned out grey coats made of Herdwick wool. He made up the John Peel verses on the spur of the moment, so he said in later life, when his young son asked him for the words of a tune his Granny was humming. The tune was an old Scottish Border rant called 'Bonnie Annie'. Peel is supposed to have had tears in his eyes when Graves first sang the words to him in the local pub.

Graves was a rather impetuous though clever young man, born in Wigton. Not long after writing the song, he had a row with the manager of the mill, whom he's supposed to have struck, got involved in a court case, left his wife and emigrated to Tasmania where he hunted kangaroos instead of foxes and died in 1886.

The song became quite well known locally amongst the hunting people, still being sung to the tune of 'Bonnie Annie', but it didn't appear in printed form for almost forty years, long after Peel was dead. A Carlisle bookseller carried out an involved correspondence with old Graves in Tasmania and acquired his permission to publish it in a book of Cumberland ballads. The song was read by William Metcalfe, choir master at Carlisle cathedral, who rearranged it to new music (he told Canon Rawnsley that he used only the 'germ' of the original rant) and in 1869 he sang it in public with great success, first in Carlisle and then in London. He'd been refused permission by the Dean of Carlisle to go to London to sing at a Cumberland evening, but had gone all the same and sold a hundred copies of the song to the London dancers. Later he was invited to sing it before the Prince of Wales.

The Border Regiment made it their regimental song and took it around the world. It was first heard being sung at the Relief of Lucknow. During the Boer War it appeared with some slightly new words:

> For the shouts of our men brought us from our bed
> They faced mauser and ofte times bled
> The Border 'Charge' would arouse, rouse the blood
> Or the Boer on his kopje in the morning.

It's a neat tune, instantly identifiable, easy to sing or whistle, adaptable as a quick march or a dirge and can bring tears to exiled Cumbrians in the far corners of the world. Such a pity John Peel never heard it. At his funeral in Caldbeck in 1854, however, fifteen years before the song was first sung in its present version, over 3000 locals turned out to mourn the great huntsman. The *Carlisle Journal*, no doubt with a bit of journalistic licence, reported that when the procession passed the kennels containing Peel's hounds 'they raised a deep-mouthed cry'. (I once worked on the *Carlisle Journal*, as a holiday job, and such flights of fancy were always subbed out of my copy. The paper, alas, is now deceased.)

To the Cumbrians, it's his memory as a huntsman that is kept alive, though he is no more than one of several great hunting characters in the last 200 years. Others, completely unknown outside the area, have had whole books written about their exploits, such as Joe Bowman, huntsman of the Ullswater hunt. It's on sentimental occasions, when Cumbrians are searching for

an identity, that John Peel usually comes out, such as in 1974–
1975, that great season when Carlisle United had their one and
only year of glory in the First Division. The symbol of the club
is a fox and their little handful of supporters was heard, rather
hesitantly if defiantly at foreign grounds, singing the words of
'D'ye Ken John Peel'.

Caldbeck today has 700 inhabitants, a third of the population
of John Peel's time, but is a very thriving and lively farming
community, off the main tourist track and therefore not dependent on visitors for a living. Only one of the thirteen pubs now
survives, though they have got a village clog maker. The old
woollen industries have all gone, the bobbin and other mills are
now romantic ruins. In a ravine beside the village, known locally
as the Howk, was once a waterwheel forty-two feet in diameter,
said at one time to be the largest in the country. Exploring its
remains, hidden away in the depths of the gorge, is like discovering Atlantis. I'd passed through Caldbeck for thirty years without
ever knowing it was there.

As for the hunting, that's as strong and peculiarly Cumbrian
as it ever was in Peel's day. The foxes are said to be smaller
than in the old days, but there seem to be more of them, judging
by the figures which each hunt proudly produces at the end of a
season. There are certainly more followers, though many these
days are in cars. Three hunts converge at Caldbeck – the Cumberland, and the Cumberland Farmers, which are both mounted,
and the Blencathra which hunt on foot.

It's the hunting on foot which is very Cumbrian. There are
six fell packs in all which carve up Lakeland between them –
Blencathra, Coniston, Ullswater, Eskdale and Ennerdale, Lunes-
dale and Melbreak. All of them hunt on foot. A horse couldn't
manage it, not on the high crags.

In Peel's day, a pack would depend very much on the personality of the man who organised it, a local farmer who called
out other farmers with his horn. Most farmers kept a hound or
two all the year round and joined in when they felt like it,
especially when their own stock was in danger, or simply because
they loved the hunt, as Peel did. Today, it's professionally
organised. Each of the six fell packs has a full-time huntsman
(who wears red, not grey, when hunting) and is in charge of the
twenty or so couples of hounds which each hunt maintains. He
gets about £1500 a year, not a great salary admittedly. It costs

each hunt between £2000 and £3000 a year to maintain their huntsman and hounds, which the locals and followers think a reasonable price to keep down the foxes and provide sport.

The areas are rigidly demarked and each little village has collectors who work for the local pack, organising socials and collecting subscriptions. You can subscribe to each hunt for a small charge – though they don't discourage you from watching and following whether you're a member or not – and in return you get the annual report and a fixture card. It's a most exciting sight to come across the hounds in full cry.

I first heard them one day in the Langdales when I was near Blea Tarn. (It must have been the Coniston hunt, now I look at the hunting map, though three packs overlap in that area.) I heard this yelping high up on the topmost crags, then I heard the echoes, and the more I tried to pick out the crags in question the more it seemed to be everywhere. I gave up searching and just sat and listened to their ghostly, eerie crying. Eventually, I caught a flash of red and followed with my eye the direction of the scampering huntsman and there, on some high ledges, well above the sheep line, I saw the hounds, tearing up and down, very excited, while miles below, the other hunt followers with some stray hounds were marooned in the valley. The huntsman covers enormous distances and he can tell the individual cry of each hound and knows where they are and how close they are to the kill.

The Blencathra covers John Peel's old stamping ground and both it and the Ullswater pack pride themselves on having hounds bred from his original hounds. Each hunt has a Master but the position has little of the social importance of the mounted hunts in the South. It's a completely classless sport, which they boast about in their local hunting songs.

> The brave pack o'Blencathra
> Is free alike to all;
> The peasant from the cottage,
> The lordling from the hall.

In another local song, 'The Mardale Hunt', they also boast about their lack of horses.

> Who'd hunt the fox with spur and reign?
> Away, away!
> To have a mount we'd all disdain,
> Away, my lads, away!

The season begins around mid-September and ends in April, with May and June being kept free for specific calls from local farmers if their lambs are being worried. The official meets are always listed in the local papers and start at nine in the morning, usually four times a week, meeting at a local pub, farm or cross-roads. A pack will often hunt one area for a week, with local farmers helping out with the billeting of the hounds. It's advisable to bring binoculars and an Ordnance Survey map.

In the close season, the hounds are boarded out in local farms in the care of Walkers, who are jealous of their position. The stars in each pack have names that go back for centuries, with certain farms always being allowed to walk the same-named hound, often a descendant of the original. The names are always two syllables, to make shouting easier, and John Peel's hounds' names still occur – Ruby, Ranter, Royal and Bellman. In the close season they appear at Lakeland shows where the hound and terrier competitions attract a lot of interest. (The main show for hounds is reckoned to be at Rydal in mid-August.)

The fell-hunting hound is smaller and lighter coloured than the foxhounds of the Shires, though they are part of the same original breed. The fell hound has a hare-foot, as opposed to a cat-foot grip, which helps it up steep rocks. It is kept light in weight so it does less damage to itself when jumping from high crags. It can catch a fox over level ground but the fox has the advantage on the rough ground when they can leave hounds marooned on isolated crags, often causing them to fall to their death. The fox understands the scent it leaves and will deliberately cross water or run along walls to throw off the hounds. It uses its brush as an extra leg, balancing on it when descending steeply.

The main point of hunting is the sport, whatever the apologists say about it being a necessary way of ridding the countryside of vermin. In talking to hunting people, or farmers in general, there's no sign of them *hating* the fox. They admire his skills if anything, calling him reynard (which they do in normal conversations), almost with affection.

I can't personally get worked up about the cruelty aspect. I think moles have a worse death – poisoned or garrotted then strung up. Life in the country is bloody and cruel anyway, with every animal, including humans, preying on others, but I'd be interested to see a *scientific* defence of the necessity of killing all foxes. There are figures which indicate that foxes are in fact a minor danger to lambs, and that the farmers' own domestic dogs kill more than the foxes, though you'd have a hard time to get a farmer to admit it. I've tried, and they just smile.

The biggest percentage of deaths (seventeen per cent, according to some Scottish figures) happen at birth or soon afterwards. After that, disease is the main cause of death. Mr Tod is very often the scapegoat for poor husbandry. (Tod is an old word for fox and it's interesting to notice how common the name Todhunter is in the Caldbeck area – the village carpenter, for example, is called Mr Todhunter.)

Some naturalists argue that the fox is actually a friend of the shepherd, eating up the dead lambs and mothers which litter so many fields in the early summer. It's when the fox is hunted, when one of a pair is killed, that in desperation they will attack lambs. During cub time in April, the dog fox does all the hunting for food, handing over his spoils to the vixen some distance from the den. If the dog fox gets killed, the vixen has then to hunt for food, as well as suckle and protect her young. She can't manage to kill enough voles on her own, so she goes for bigger stuff, such as lambs, especially the more weakly, dozy ones.

However, try telling all this to farmers, especially the hunting ones. Foxes do kill some lambs, for whatever reason, and will no doubt go on doing so for ever. And so will fox hunting. If you destroy the natural ecology of the fells by killing foxes, goodness knows what damage you might do by killing off the centuries-old sport of fox hunting. What would all the modern John Peels do for sport, take it out on their wives? Start chasing other people's wives?

Charles Norman de Courcy Parry has been hunting for over seventy years. You might know his name, or at least his pseudonym 'Dalesman', that's if you're a hunting type. As Dalesman, he has contributed a column to the magazine *Horse and Hound* for fifty-three years, from 1925 to 1978. He's still writing about hunting, at the age of seventy-eight, and has recently come back to live in Caldbeck, his native hunting ground.

Writers on country matters go on for a long time, holding down their columns far longer than normal journalists, but fifty years did seem like a world record to me. Mr de Courcy Parry – Bay to his friends – thought for a while then said that the late Major Fairfax-Blakeborough (don't they all have great names) probably did even better, writing his country notes until he was ninety. 'He once told me that the public's memory is only five years, so never throw away old copy. After five years, you can start to repeat it. Of course I've used my old stories. I couldn't have lasted otherwise.'

He'd done two articles already on the day I went to see him at his little farm house in Caldbeck. 'I've never had a wrong word with *Horse and Hound* in over fifty years. They always backed me in any row. I once wrote for a Welsh paper that went to press on a Thursday. The show I was covering was also on a Thursday so I did my article before hand, saying how good Mrs So and So's horse was looking, but the show was cancelled at the last minute. What a stink there was when my article appeared!'

His father was Chief Constable of Cumberland and Westmorland and he was brought up in Penrith. He went to Repton and then served in the First World War with the Seaforth Highlanders. 'I'm rather proud to have served in both wars. I joined each time as a private and then got commissioned in the field. I never had the intelligence to take the officers' exams. The Second World War? Oh, that one. I ran like hell at Dunkirk, I'm ashamed to say.'

As a young man he went round the world, working his passage on a boat, which he wouldn't do again, not for £10,000, much though he could do with the money. 'I was kicked all round the world by the mate. By God, I was sorry I ever went to sea.'

He's hunted all his life and first worked in hunt service in the early 1920s with the famous Joe Bowman and the Ullswater hunt. He's been a Master of Hounds for forty-five years, kept several horses and rode every possible day. He came back to Caldbeck a year ago from Ireland. 'It became too expensive any more to keep horses.' Now he's back amongst the foot hunters, he can afford to follow one of the local hunts two days a week.

He's very pleased to see the packs thriving. 'It's really booming. I think it's the only hunting in Britain not in the red. The fell men are dead keen. You should see the little local parish collectors doing their rounds. Everybody is involved. Socially, it's the same as it always was. If a Master says anything, they think he's interfering and just ignore him. Until you've walked the fells for fifty years, you're thought to ken nowt.

'The crowds are often enormous. On Boxing Day in Keswick the Blencathra had over 1000 followers, with 200 cars. I suppose the Blencathra is the best hunt socially at the moment, while

Eskdale and Ennerdale might have the best disciplined hounds, though I daren't say that round here. They're all in great shape. Each pack accounts for about a hundred foxes in a season. Perhaps I regret the large crowds in a way. People roar up the M6 and turn the hunt into a great picnic. Fell packs must kill foxes. The farmers really do want to be rid of them. I have never seen anything hurtful in hunting, nor cruelty in it. God save us, anything can be *made* cruel and a lot of life certainly is, but hunting is fair and honourable.'

One regret he does have dates back twenty years ago to his more prosperous, landed days. His father left him quite a lot of property and money, which he's since spent.

'I was drinking in a pub in Wales and somebody at the bar was saying that their ambition in life was to own a lake in the Lake District. Now, how often do you expect someone in a bar to say, actually, I've got a lake to sell. I wish to God I hadn't. I regretted it the next morning when I woke up, but it was too late. I'd agreed to sell, to this stranger, Over Water, which I then owned, for £500. I could do with owning a lake in the Lake District today. It was sheer bravado.'

19

WORDSWORTH AT RYDAL

Mr Wordsworth courts an earl and obtains an important job.Many tourists come to see him.

WORDSWORTH NEVER OWNED A LAKE IN THE LAKE district, nor even his own home. When he moved into Rydal Mount, in the spring of 1813, he was moving into yet another rented property. It was just a little journey, no more than two miles down the road from Grasmere, but it was a move into another life, another setting.

They had been thirteen years at Grasmere and William himself was rather loath to leave, but the women of the household were fed up. The Parsonage was damp and horrid and the fires smoked and the only comfortable room was William's little working parlour. Most of all, they were reminded each day by the graves opposite, in Grasmere churchyard, of their two young children. Thomas had died just a few months previously and they were all very glad to get away. 'The house only reminded me of desolation, gloom, emptiness and cheerless silence,' wrote Dorothy.

They moved into Rydal Mount without having seen inside, such was their excitement to start afresh. The previous owners, the Norths, a family from Liverpool, refused to give up the key as they hadn't yet moved their wine from the cellar. Fred North had bought the house in 1803 for £2500, a large sum, one which gives a clue to its desirability. The house dated back to 1574, when it had been a cottage, but it had been extended and improved over the years, the final seal of smartness being given by Fred when he'd added the word Mount to its name. The new owner was Lady Diana le Fleming who lived in the big house nearby, Rydal Hall.

So, it was a posh house with posh neighbours and the Wordsworths all got very excited at the thought of furnishing it accordingly. They knew that the gentry in Ambleside of the 'calling' type would soon be popping in and they wanted to look the part. Ambleside, socially, was more elevated than Grasmere. 'We are going to have Turkey!!! carpet in the dining room and a Brussels in William's study,' wrote Dorothy to a friend. 'You stare, and the simplicity of the dear Town End cottage comes before your eyes and you are tempted to say "Are they changed, are they setting up for Fine Folks? For making parties, giving Dinners, etc. etc.?"' They hung up prints by their smart friends, like Sir George Beaumont, and even William took an interest in the furnishings and bought some curtain material at a sale.

William himself didn't change his normal appearance, never being a one for smart clothes, and most days, wandering the countryside, he looked rather like a seedy country schoolmaster or a poor curate, but their domestic life from now on was much more genteel and he did make an effort if he was visiting the local nobs. They entertained much more and often gave smart parties in their drawing room. During most of their long years at Rydal, they employed two maids and a gardener.

The local nob William was most keen to impress was Lord Lonsdale. He attended dinners in Kendal, at which Lord Lonsdale was in the chair. Eventually, he got on to visiting terms, spending a few days every autumn as a guest at Lowther Castle where he met 'heaps of fine folk'. In a letter he wrote to a Cockermouth friend, apologising for not having called on him, he added 'but as you would learn I was in the carriage of the Earl of Lonsdale when I passed through Cockermouth'.

Wordsworth had now become an ardent Tory and he supported the Lowther family's Tory nominees at election times. He had good reason to be grateful to Lord Lonsdale because it was thanks to him that he had become financially secure in 1813, just two months before he moved into Rydal Mount. It was partly due to this bit of luck that he was able to afford a rather grander life style when he moved to Rydal Mount.

He had been writing begging letters to Lord Lonsdale, going on about how he'd been unable to provide properly for his family, how the sort of literature he'd devoted his life to didn't sell, not being suited 'to the tastes of the times'. It's strange that Wordsworth should have wanted to get mixed up with the Lowthers again, as his father's connection with them had proved so disastrous, but the present earl was now a friend and had long since paid off all the old debts. He said he had no jobs he could arrange for Wordsworth at the moment, but offered him £100 a year. Wordsworth decided to wait till a proper job came up which it did in 1813. William was made Distributor of Stamps for Westmorland and the whole Wordsworth household naturally rejoiced.

A Distributor of Stamps was in effect a sort of local tax man. All legal documents in those days, such as wills and licences, as well as insurance documents and pamphlets, had to bear stamp duty and you bought the stamps locally from sub-distributors, usually local shop keepers.

The Distributor had to look after all his local subs, tour the outlets, make sure the books were in order, take in the proceeds and give out new stamps. Wordsworth thought he would make £400 a year from the job when he took over, on what Lord Lonsdale had told him, but in the event he rarely cleared more than £200 a year. It was a good income, but it was by no means a complete sinecure. He'd never done any accountancy work in his life and so had to hire an assistant, who also turned his hand to gardening and general secretarial work. The women folk were always on edge whenever William was away, worried about being in charge of the stamps and stamp money. All the money was sent each quarter to the Board of Stamps in London.

Wordsworth had become the latest in a long and distinguished line of English poets who became servants of the Government. Chaucer had been clerk of works to Edward III; Spenser was secretary to Lord Grey in Ireland; Milton had been secretary to Oliver Cromwell. His close friends were pleased, knowing it would relieve the women of a lot of domestic hardship (though they'd never complained), and would allow Wordsworth to devote more time to poetry, but he was looked upon as a sell-out by many of the younger writers and poets, many of whom had earlier admired him.

Keats was very disappointed that he'd become a Government man. When he met Wordsworth in London, calling on him one day, he was shocked to discover him all dressed up in knee breeches and silk stockings, just because he was to meet his Government superior, the Comptroller of Stamps. Keats, ever the romantic, thought this was really creepy and was still talking about the incident three months later. Leigh Hunt was also upset. 'Mr. Southey and even Mr. Wordsworth have both accepted offices under the Government of such a nature as absolutely ties up their independence.'

Wordsworth had become more a Lowther man than a Government man. He turned down an even more lucrative Government job, as Collector of Customs at Whitehaven, which would have meant moving, but, as Sarah Hutchinson ruefully remarked, the London papers were less ready to publicise his refusal, compared with the fuss they had made over taking the stamp job.

It's hard to realise today what enormous power one family, the Lowthers, could have over such a large area as Cumberland and Westmorland. In Wordsworth's defence it has to be said that someone without private means needed such wealthy patronage, if they wanted to pursue a literary career. There weren't many

Walter Scotts around. Wordsworth, Coleridge and Southey were all desperate at many times in their life for private patrons to keep them going. There was no Arts Council handing out cash, no free-loading jobs at universities, no writers-in-residence. All the same, Wordsworth did rather toady to the Lowthers.

The Lowthers had been running Cumbria for centuries and had been based at Lowther, near Penrith, for almost 1000 years, probably from the time of the Norse settlements. The Lowther who put the family into the millionaire class was Sir James Lowther who became the first Earl of Lonsdale in 1784 – the miserly one who employed Wordsworth's father, yet never paid him the money. He might have been rotten to the Wordsworth family but he absolutely transformed the area, bringing the industrial revolution to west Cumberland.

Life for almost everyone in Cumbria throughout the nineteenth century was in some way influenced by the Lowthers. No wonder Wordsworth thought he'd made it when he started week-ending at Lowther and riding in the next earl's private coach. He used to work in references to the Lowthers in his poetry, and even wrote poems to them. The worst (even by Wordsworth's worst standards) is a sonnet to Lowther Castle which begins:

> Lowther! in the majestic Pile are seen
> Cathedral pomp and grace, in apt accord
> With the baronial castle's sterner mien.

He wrote a poem to the earl after he had successfully prosecuted some newspaper for libel, and another to the Countess, then an old lady, in which he described her 'nymph-like form'. Hartley Coleridge, Coleridge's son, read these poems when they were included in a new collection in 1835 and was saddened rather than amused. 'I do wish there had been a little less of Lowther Castle and that he had not called poor old Lady Lonsdale a Nymph.' Well, if you have a patron you've got to perform for him now and again. With a big house and a large household to support, and a smarter living style, Wordsworth needed Lonsdale, if only to secure him his stamp job. Joseph Hume, the Radical MP, ridiculed Wordsworth in the House of Commons for having the job and called him 'an idle poet', but in the end, thanks to Lonsdale's backing, Wordsworth retained and in fact increased the job, becoming Distributor for Cumberland as well as for Westmorland. In turn, he managed to fix a job for his younger son Willy, not the most talented of children, who became sub-distributor of stamps in Carlisle. All along, Wordsworth's defence was that he had to provide for his large family and retainers.

The household, when he moved into Rydal, consisted of his wife Mary, his sister Dorothy, sister-in-law Sarah and his three surviving children, John, Dora and William. None of them was very strong and Wordsworth was always fretting about their health, which was understandable, having lost two already. None was very clever at school work or displayed any specialist talents. Dora was perhaps the brightest but she was lazy, showing none of the devotion to her books that Sara Coleridge was displaying over in Keswick. In the Wordsworth household, they were all slightly in awe of the Coleridge children, but maintained that it wasn't good for them, all the studying. It made them rather conceited, so Dorothy once remarked about Sara.

William's own brother, Christopher, had turned out to be the cleverest, academically, in his generation. In 1820 he was appointed Master of Trinity College, Cambridge. He in turn was producing clever children who were doing brilliantly at school.

Wordsworth, however, had his own strong views on education, rather modern ones in fact. He was all for the mind and imagination being fed, being allowed to grow and develop, and was against encyclopaedia cramming. He was a great admirer of an educationalist of the time called Dr Bell and tried to get his eldest son John into Charterhouse, a school which practised his principles, but failed. John had gone first of all to a school at Ambleside, where Hartley and Derwent Coleridge were scholars. At fifteen, they managed to get John into the grammar school at Sedbergh where he made steady if unspectacular progress. He went to Oxford, thanks to a tutor at New College who happened to be an admirer of Wordsworth, but he got a poor degree. Wordsworth had hoped he might have become a Fellow. John himself fancied the army but Wordsworth was definitely against that, saying he couldn't afford the commission. Instead John became a curate – the one who officiated at Sara Coleridge's wedding ceremony.

Dora was Wordsworth's favourite. He fussed most of all over her and she was indeed always ill – it now looks that from as early as the age of eighteen she was showing signs of tuberculosis. She went to a local school at Ambleside for a while, in between spells at home when she was taught by Dorothy. 'She is a complete air gauge,' wrote her mother in 1827. 'As soon as damp is felt the trouble in her throat returns.' Wordsworth often had dreams about her and referred to her many times in his poetry. They were devoted to each other and enjoyed similar pleasures, like nature and walking, and she was his companion on many trips. When she finally left school, she became a full-time part of the Wordsworth ménage, the fourth woman of the family to be his doting secretary, companion and friend. She was able to tease her father and make fun of him and certainly didn't treat him with any awe, not in the way the others often did. They went on tip-toes whenever the muse was on him, dropping everything to be his willing slave, but Dora loved him nonetheless. 'I have my suspicions,' wrote Hartley Coleridge in 1830, 'that she would be a healthier matron than she is a virgin, but strong indeed must be the love that would induce her to leave her father, whom she adores, and who quite dotes upon her.' Dora was by then twenty-six. She remained at home, unmarried, and no doubt a virgin, for another ten years.

Then there was Willy. He was near in age to the two who had died and Wordsworth naturally worried about every cough, every touch of paleness. 'Really, his Father fondles over him,' wrote Dorothy when Willy was eight, 'and talks to him as if he were but a year old.' He too went first to school at Ambleside and then away to London, to the Central School. It looks as if the women folk had a part in this, knowing that he needed to be out of the house to stop William clucking over him. Neither of his sons went to his old school, Hawkshead Grammar, which William would have liked but he didn't approve of the new headmaster. After London, Willy moved on to Charterhouse but left after just under a year, thanks to a mixture of idleness and illness. After that, from the age of fifteen, he stayed at home where Wordsworth spoiled him, though he did have a bit more schooling at the local school for a time, being taught by Hartley Coleridge who was not impressed. 'Little Will is a bore.'

Dora wrote a nice mock-advertisement for Willy in a home-made newspaper which she and a friend wrote when they were on holiday. 'William Wordsworth: Wants a situation. A youth of about 15 years of age. He is able to do any kind of work, but prefers sitting to standing, riding to walking and lying in bed to anything in the world.'

At eighteen, unbeknown to his parents, Willy applied to join the army, but he was rejected, much to their pleasure. He was then sent off for a spell in Germany, hoping he'd pick up the language, or pick up something useful, and then they might get him a job in some business, perhaps in a counting house or, failing that, a government job. Families, families. Nothing much changes, does it?

Wordsworth tried pulling as many string as possible, soliciting friends and contacts when he was down in London, but in the end Willy had to be content with being his father's sub-distributor of stamps in Carlisle. You can see how important, therefore, it was to keep in with the Lowthers. Lord Lonsdale even arranged for son John to secure a living up in the Lake District, one that was in his gift.

John Wordsworth at least had a respectable job and he married that good local girl, Isabella Curwen, daughter of the Curwen family who owned Belle Isle in Windermere. Her father settled some money on them, which was useful, as John's clerical stipend was small. Wordsworth naturally was pleased by the marriage but he was never close to either of them, finding them too lifeless for his liking. 'Still and quiet as trees, whose branches *may* have been light and flexible, but are now less so than one of my disposition could wish.'

Wordsworth was by now disposing himself, his works and his personality, all over the place. He enjoyed much better health than any of his children and lived a very active life at Rydal. He now had a position of some national eminence, which gave him pleasure, though, as Southey observed, he would probably have denied it.

Today's experts, the literary critics and academics, consider that Wordsworth had written all his best stuff by the time he came to Rydal, but not many were aware of it at the time, least of all William who was turning it out in enormous quantities. His first long poem, 'The Excursion', was published in 1814 (and dedicated to Lord Lonsdale). It cost two guineas, an enormous sum for those days. When Wordsworth gave a free copy to an influential friend or likely patron, he always instructed them not to lend it around. He himself refused to lend a copy to a lady – 'a widow with £1,500 per annum, a blue stocking Dame, who considered two guineas an outrageous price'. It sold only 300 copies in the first year, out of a first print of 500, but it was treated as an event by the reviewers and readers. He got a good review from Lamb ('the noblest conversational poem I have ever read,'), a reasonable one from Hazlitt but a stinker in the *Edinburgh Review* which upset him.

Another volume of his poems came out the next year, including three by a 'Female Friend' which was Dorothy, and then came another very slim volume, *The White Doe*, which cost one guinea and was again criticised for its price. The contents weren't much liked by the critics either. Dorothy tried to comfort William. 'His writings will live,' so she wrote to a friend, 'will comfort the afflicted and animate the happy to purer happiness when we and our little cares are all forgotten.'

The initial excitement amongst the young poets and reviewers, caused by the publication of *Lyrical Ballads* and his earlier poems, now some twenty years previously, had begun to fade, but his work was reaching a wider public and when in London he was invited to all the best houses. The critics were extremely tough in those days, much more savage, and at much more length, than today, and most writers took a hammering at one time. Tennyson, after a mauling by the *Quarterly Review*, hardly published anything for ten years afterwards.

They had it in for Wordsworth, partly because of his reactionary views and his support of High Tories like the Lowthers, and of course for some bad poetry, which has always been an essential part of Wordsworth's output. He himself never knew what was good or bad. He felt the muse coming on, and out it all came, regardless of the quality. When the young poets, such as Keats, met him in London at social occasions, they were disturbed by his overbearing personality. They still admired his earlier poems – and Keats's private letters contain many lines from 'Ode to Immortality' – but didn't care for him personally and made their dislike fairly obvious. 'For the sake of a few fine imaginative or domestic passages are we to be bullied into a certain Philosophy engendered in the whims of an Egotist,' wrote Keats in 1818. 'I am afraid Wordsworth went rather huffed out of Town – I am sorry for it. He cannot expect his fireside Divan to be infallible.'

Keats and his friends played a rotten trick on Wordsworth in 1819. They saw advertised a forthcoming poem by Wordsworth, 'Peter Bell, A Tale in Verse' and before it was published, and before reading it, they produced a skit on it, using the same title.

Keats's publisher even got it out on the streets *before* the original. Coleridge wrote to the publisher to protest, saying it was unfair, but was told as their author had never read a word of the original, it could not be called a breach of trust. In the end, Coleridge was quite amused by the skit, though he called it 'buffoonery, not satire'. In the fake 'Peter Bell', which is in the style of a previous Wordsworth poem, 'The Idiot', they dragged in all Wordsworth's well-known rustic obsessions and language, having Peter as a leech gatherer who goes around 'poring and prosing' over the graves of other *Lyrical Ballads* characters. He ends up over a very strange grave – which turns out to be the grave of Wordsworth himself.

Keats did a review of it for Leigh Hunt's *Examiner*, not revealing he was a friend of the author. He criticised its publication, all very tongue-in-cheek, calling it 'false, hurried from the press, and obtruded into public notice while for ought we know the real one may still be wandering about the woods and mountains ...'. This review was reprinted in the *Kendal Chronicle*, the local Whig paper which was against Lowther and his Tory friends, such as Wordsworth.

It was all a clever bit of teasing, unless of course you happened to be Wordsworth, and it led to other wits of the day producing a spate of skits, all at the expense of Wordsworth. Thackeray, then a student, was one of the bright young things who always called him Daddy Wordsworth. Thackeray's first published work, in a Cambridge magazine, was in fact a Wordsworth parody. Oh what fun they all had. But Wordsworth had the last laugh, at least with 'Peter Bell'. Thanks to all the publicity, the real 'Peter Bell' went into a second edition after only two weeks and became one of his better-selling poems.

Shelley did his own skit on 'Peter Bell', but a much more serious and savage one, writing it after he'd actually read the real one. He wasn't just upset by what Wordsworth was now writing – Mary Shelley said that some of the lines used to send him into fits of 'almost uncontrollable laughter' – but by what he thought Wordsworth now stood for, the English Tory Establishment who were keeping the poor in its place, allowing terrible social conditions in the new towns and factories and depriving people of their rights. He sent it to Leigh Hunt for his magazine, but he didn't use it, probably realising that Shelley's reputation would have been damaged by such a violent outburst. Almost thirty years earlier, Wordsworth himself had done much the same, writing a highly emotional and political attack on a bishop's reactionary views, a pamphlet which was never published, for much the same reason. His friends thought it would harm his reputation.

Surrounded by all his doting women folk up in Rydal, Wordsworth of course could easily ignore – if not forgive – the attacks on him. De Quincey felt that Wordsworth himself was probably unaware of the irritation and disgust which the younger writers now had for him. After all, the great of the day, the other established figures, were rushing up to the Lakes to see him and Southey, often taking them both in on the same tour. Sir Walter Scott was a particularly frequent visitor and on one occasion Wordsworth took him on a trip to Lowther Castle, to see the nobs. Wordsworth later spent three days as a guest of Scott's at Abbotsford, with Dora as his companion.

Other eminent visitors included William Wilberforce who arrived at Rydal with a huge party of family and servants, taking over two houses at the foot of Wordsworth's lane. Dorothy, who had to make all the arrangements for them, was driven mad by an advance guard of seven servants and five horses who arrived on a wet day and filled the whole house, with the cook criticising the size of the Wordsworth kitchen and the others moaning about the inconvenience of it all.

Wordsworth made regular tours abroad, as well as an annual trip to London. In 1820, during a four-month tour of the Continent with Dorothy and Mary, plus an old friend, Crabb Robinson, he visited Annette, their first meeting since that separation on Calais sands some eighteen years previously. By this time, his daughter Caroline had got married. Dorothy had planned to go to the wedding, but Napoleon escaped from Elba and mucked up her plans. Caroline now had two young girls of her own, Wordsworth's first grandchildren. One of them was called Louise Dorothée, after Dorothy, who had kept in close contact by letter with Annette and still referred to her as her sister. On the child's birth certificate, Wordsworth ('Mr. Williams Wordsworth, proprietaire, Rydalmount Kindal, Westmoreland') was officially described as the child's maternal grandfather.

The Wordsworth party spent four weeks in Paris and the initial meeting with Annette took place in the Louvre where for the first time Mary met her husband's former lover. It turned out to be a terribly civilised meeting. Wordsworth gave them a pencil portrait of himself and two volumes of his poetry, despite the fact that none of them could speak English. (There are direct descendants of Wordsworth living in France today and one of the families still has one of these volumes.)

Crabb Robinson thought it was all a bit too civilised and in his notebook recorded that he considered it was a bit indelicate of Caroline to keep calling Wordsworth 'father'.

In 1837 Wordsworth visited Caroline for the last time, again with Crabb Robinson, but this time without any of his usual female companions. (He missed them terribly and vowed never to do it again.) Ever since Caroline's marriage, Wordsworth had been sending her £30 a year, a generous sum, considering his English family commitments, but of course coming into the Directorship of Stamps had eased his burdens. In 1835 he brought the arrangement to a conclusion by settling a lump sum on her of £400.

Wordsworth was never ashamed of his French family. His close friends all knew, and he even let Southey become involved. On a visit to Paris in 1817, Southey was asked to pop in and see Caroline, though Wordsworth hadn't explained properly to Southey who she was. Wordsworth, so Southey said, had told him that 'it would not be necessary nor pleasant to myself to be acquainted with the story of Caroline's birth'. As soon as Caroline herself realised that Southey knew Mr Wordsworth she blurted out at once that he was her father – and the whole story came out. They had a tête-à-tête of about an hour, with Caroline having a good weep. Next day Southey had breakfast with her and met her mother Annette. He was impressed by their love for Wordsworth and lack of resentment.

Considering how many people knew, it's a wonder the story never became public. Several magazines and papers of the day specialised in such gossip, and had already carried nasty tales about Wordsworth, usually about his creeping to the Lowthers or being mean with hospitality, unless he was entertaining the quality. They would have gone to town on any real scandal, or even just a hint of it, especially now that Wordsworth had become such an establishment, moralistic figure, attracting hordes of pilgrims to worship at his Rydal home.

As early as 1816, after the publication of 'The Excursion', Sarah Hutchinson in a letter talks about a party of fourteen

Cambridge students who were on a walking and reading tour of the Lakes. 'I suppose most of them will find means to get a sight of the Poet before the summer is past.'

After that, it became a regular, almost round-the-year sight, to see handfuls of admirers arriving at Rydal, hanging around the gardens, hoping for a glimpse of the great man. In July 1840 Wordsworth at last got a royal visitor to Rydal – not Victoria herself but Queen Adelaide, widow of William IV. He recorded later how she was much taken by the beauty of the scenery. 'I led the Queen to the principal points in our little domain ... she took her leave, cordially shaking Mrs. Wordsworth by the hand as a friend of her own rank might have done. She had also inquired for Dora, who was introduced to her.'

It wasn't until 1845, by which time he had become Poet Laureate, that he was invited to meet Queen Victoria. He made a special trip to London for the Queen's Fancy Ball and was presented to the Queen, putting on the full court dress, with sword and cocked hat.

In 1838 he got his first honorary degree, from Durham University (Oxford followed a year later) and in writing about it to his friend Crabb Robinson he makes one of his very few recorded jokes. 'I forgot to mention that the University of Durham the other day by special convocation conferred upon me the honorary degree of L.L.D. Therefore you will not scruple when a difficult point of law occurs to consult me.'

Well, it's a sort of joke. Wordsworth was never known for his wit. But as a Grand Old Man, people no doubt smiled broadly at any hint of humour. He was indeed a rather grand figure by now, certainly amongst the poets. Southey had of course died, and so had Coleridge and Scott, three of his eminent contemporaries. By one of those tragic coincidences of history, all the young poets, the generation poised to take over, had each died young – Keats, Shelley and Byron. Wordsworth was virtually left on his own.

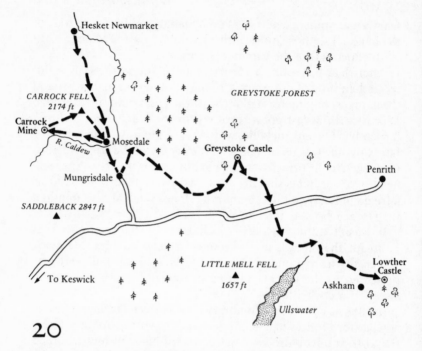

20

LOWTHER

Mr Stafford Howard of Greystoke and the wonderful work of the National Trust. The Earl of Lonsdale and the wonderful world of the Lowthers.

I SET OFF FROM CALDBECK, HEADING SOUTH FOR LOWTHER country, and came first to Hesket Newmarket, a one-street village and one too easy to rush through. On closer observation, you realise that the one street is actually a village green and that lined up on either side are some attractive cottages, not flash or twee in a Cotswold way, calling attention to themselves. You have to stand and stare to realise they're there.

Charles Dickens stayed here with Wilkie Collins in 1857 and wrote up his tour in *Household Words* in an article called 'The Lazy Tour of Two Idle Apprentices'. They couldn't have been all that idle because they climbed Carrock Fell. I decided to do the same. As High Pike dominates the top end of the northern Fells so Carrock Fell, just seventeen feet higher at 2174, stands guard on the eastern slopes, looking over to Penrith and the Eden Valley.

It was a very hot day and I decided to climb it the easy way, if the longest. The eastern slopes are surprisingly rocky, but then Carrock Fell is an anomaly in the northern Fells, having outcrops of volcanic rock, like the Langdales to the south. High Pike is beautifully smooth by comparison. I headed inland from Mosedale, following the Caldew River, aiming to attack Carrock Fell from the rear slopes. I'd never been up this valley before. The entrance is half hidden and I expected the little road to peter out and to have the valley to myself, even though it was the school holidays. But I was passed on the road by several cars full of people, all going nowhere as the valley is a dead end.

I eventually discovered them all parked at the end of the road, swimming in a little pool made by the Caldew, a secret swimming place; well, secret to the several dozen families who knew about it. They were obviously regulars, people who rushed out of Carlisle or Penrith on a hot day, taking with them rubber boats and lilos.

The Caldew is just a little river, but it makes a big impact, carving its way arrogantly through the high fells, a little trickle that pushes all the big bullies aside. It provides an easy walking path along its banks almost all the way to Skiddaw itself. Such presumption. I headed the other way, up the slopes of Carrock Fell, making sure I didn't put my feet in any nasty holes. This was mining country at one time. Carrock mine, the main one, had been closed for decades, according to Wainwright's guide, so I was half prepared to miss it completely, till I almost stumbled into one of its gushing water pits. It was back in full production. The market price of tungsten must have risen again.

I passed a very nice sheep pen on the way up, a three-room stone arrangement with walls about five foot high which would make an excellent shelter for any human in a storm. As I neared the top, I came to large outcrops of rocks, slabs of it lying in large piles, easy to bound over, in my ever-present Dunlop Green Flash plimsoles, and even easier for foxes to hide under. No wonder the Blencathra often call it off, when old reynard goes to ground up here.

The cairn on top of Carrock Fell came to a fine point, a perfect pyramid, which proved what good weather we'd been having. In normal conditions, the small pieces on top must all get blown away. At the base is a large mound of stone slabs which is supposed to be the remains of an ancient British hill fort. In a crevice in the cairn I spotted a flash of red which I thought for a moment was a disappearing reynard, giving me the brush off, but it was a small woollen knitted glove. I pulled it out and the name tape said Keith Farnham. I put it back. So Keith Farnham, you know where it is.

I came down like Coleridge, not following any path, and immediately tore my bare legs to shreds in some very thick bracken. On the top slopes there had been acres of beautiful, bright green verdant bilberry shoots, so gentle to walk through, but on the scree sides it turned into heavy, wiry bracken. I promised myself a good long drink at the Mill Inn in Mungrisdale but when I got there they'd run out of draught beer. The weekend had been so hot they'd exhausted their stock of bitter. Could this really be the Lake District?

My next stop was Greystoke Castle, but I changed before I got there, wanting to look respectable. Today's quality, of the sort Wordsworth enjoyed so much in his later years, tend to live on the flanks of the Lake District, either to the south or on the eastern slopes, towards the Eden Valley. Central Lakeland, especially the fells and the little dales, has always been the preserve of the states-man, small-time yeoman farmers, a proudly independent breed who somehow over the centuries have managed to make a living out of owning only thirty to forty acres in the narrow valleys, plus the use of the common lands up on the high fells for their sheep. The big boys, such as the Lowthers, have based themselves on easier ground, building their castles in the plains, keeping their mountains safely on the horizon, surrounding themselves in the foreground with a thousand or so of the lusher pastures.

Greystoke Castle is the home of Stafford Howard, a member of a family long famous in English history. Howards seem to have stately homes and castles all over England, and most of them are related to the little family of pig farmers – hog wards, as they were called, hence howard – who lived in Norfolk about 500 years ago, and went on to produce three earls and, of course, the Duke of Norfolk. Howards came to the border lands about 400 years ago when the king needed someone to sort out the Scots. They got land and castles in return – and even more land by some judicious marrying. There's a branch of the Howard family at Naworth Castle (the Earl of Carlisle) some twenty-five miles to the north and another branch in Yorkshire at Castle Howard.

Two Dukes of Norfolk have lived in Greystoke Castle and in the nineteenth century one of them was responsible for tarting up the basic peel tower (which dates back to 1120) with an ornate Victorian, mock-Tudor front. Stafford Howard (a third cousin of the present Duke) inherited the Castle, ten Lordships of the Manor, and some 6000 acres – almost by chance, at least there were two people between him and his inheritance and it was only on the death of a half brother, forty years his senior, that he became the owner.

He arrived at Greystoke in 1950, after Eton, Oxford and the Guards ('I'm an absolute stereotype, I'm afraid') to find the Castle in a very bad state, with the army in residence and Nissen huts in the courtyards. 'They did more damage than Cromwell.' Since then, he's devoted his life and money to restoring the Castle and grounds. Before the war, the Castle had twenty-five living-in servants. Now they have none, managing with a couple of dailies. He farms 3000 acres himself, the other half being owned by his elder son. They also own 6000 acres of common land, mainly in Mungrisdale and the slopes of Skiddaw. Neither of his two sons is a farmer, one being in the Foreign Office and the other in the army, and he has little hope that either will be able to take over the Castle. 'I don't expect *anyone* to live here after I've gone. I don't know what will happen to it. I only hope it's nothing too awful. I was born and brought up in Wales, so I don't feel as sad as I would if I'd always lived here, but it would be nice to see it lived in by someone, after all my wife and I have done to it. Someone has said that the future of the English country house lies firmly in the hands of the daughter-in-law. It's perfectly true. I wouldn't wish this Castle on anyone, if they didn't want to live here. My wife is American and when she married me she came from a comfortable apartment on Fifth Avenue to a draughty old castle in Cumberland.'

He and his wife are very active in local charities. He's always been connected with the Outward Bound Trust, taking over a family connection from his uncle, Lord Howard of Penrith. He had twenty years in local government and in 1979–80 he will be High Sheriff of Cumbria for a year. But Mr Howard's main claim to Cumbrian fame is as chairman of the National Trust in the North-West (which means Cumbria and Lancashire), a position he has held for six years.

Everywhere you go in the Lakes you meet the National Trust, which isn't surprising as they're the biggest single landowner in the Lakes. The National Park has got legal powers, being a planning authority, but it doesn't actually own very much. There are many other bodies, like the Friends of the Lake District, the Forestry Commission, Cumbria Tourist Board, the North-West Water Authority, the local councils and countless conservation groups, in fact so many it's a wonder anything ever gets decided in the Lake District, but, of them all, the National Trust is probably the most important single organisation.

The National Trust is not a Government body, despite its name, but an independent charity with membership open to everyone. It's the greatest and biggest conservation society in Britain, set up at a time when only a few rather eccentric souls cared anything for preservation and the countryside. The Lake District has strong connections with its foundation as Canon Rawnsley was one of its three founders – the others being Octavia Hill and Sir Robert Hunter.

There had been cries for conserving the countryside throughout the nineteenth century. Wordsworth on several occasions talked and wrote about the need for somebody to protect the Lakes – as later did John Ruskin. It was left to Canon Rawnsley, the ultimate agitator for nature, to get things moving.

In 1893 he and Hunter and Miss Hill met at the Duke of Westminster's London house and it was from this meeting that the National Trust was formed, with Canon Rawnsley as its first secretary, a position he held till his death. The first property in the Lakes they bought was on the shores of Derwent Water in 1902.

Today the National Trust owns over 90,000 acres in the Lakes, plus the care of a further 14,000. It owns 280 cottages, seventy-one hill farms, eleven lowland farms and 17,500 sheep. It owns Buttermere, Crummock Water, Loweswater and large sections of Derwent Water, Ullswater and Rydal; mountains like Scafell Pike and Great Gable and the Langdale Pikes; famous houses like Hill Top, Sizergh Castle and Wordsworth's Cockermouth home.

There's a rush whenever any of their cottages fall free and between forty and fifty people apply. They don't keep a short list. You just have to watch the local papers and rush. Unlike normal landlords, they want a tenant in for life. Normal landlords dread the thought of tenants getting a grip on their properties, which is why today there are so few properties to let.

The National Trust in the Lakes is a little industry. Their headquarters is a large house called Broadlands, just outside Ambleside, and they employ a full time staff of sixty – going up to a hundred in the season. One of their current enterprises is to save the *Gondola*, the eighty-five-feet-long steam yacht which used to be the pride of Coniston, steaming up and down in great elegance between 1860 and 1940. She operated in very shallow water which is why she was built like a gondola, with a distinctive long, curved prow. At the stern end, she needed only twelve inches of water, yet carried up to 225 passengers on a one-and-a-half hour cruise round the lake at ten knots, using only one bag of coke. She was ornately decorated and furnished and was greatly loved by the public. Arthur Ransome, John Ruskin and Thomas Carlyle are amongst those who wrote about her with affection.

She ceased service at the outbreak of the Second World War and was dismantled, becoming a houseboat for a while, until a stormy night in 1963 when she was washed ashore and was condemned to be broken up. She was saved from the scrap merchant by a Mr Arthur Hatton who half submerged the hull to preserve her, but he was unable to finance the renovations. The National Trust came to the rescue and bought her in 1977, refloated her and brought her ashore at Coniston Hall. Now they have launched an appeal for £95,000 to completely refit and refurbish her in the original style, complete with steam engine. They are confident that by 1980 she will be plying for passengers once more on Coniston. (This will mean that, as in the old days, four lakes will have passenger steamers – Windermere, Derwent Water, Ullswater and Coniston.) Mr Howard is confident that, eventually, the *Gondola* will bring the Trust an income of around £8000 a year.

On a slightly smaller scale, another current National Trust campaign has been to change the colour of tents. 'Bright orange tents are so awful,' says Christopher Hanson-Smith, their Information Officer. How much nicer, they all thought, if campers would chose rather more subdued colours, such as a nice dark green or dark brown, and fit in better with the natural landscape. Their first move was to take a stall at camping shows and badger camping manufacturers about the error of their ways. Several people told them to get lost and mind their own business, but one big tent manufacturer, Bukta, thought it was a good idea – and could see some sales potential. They produced a line of tents in suitably discreet colours and the National Trust slapped on their labels, saying the tent was a National Trust approved conservation colour. At the same time, to encourage the use of conservationally coloured tents, the Trust gave free camping on their camping sites in the Lake District to anyone with the right coloured tents. This special offer ran for three years, but has now finished. They say it was a success, but some camp site wardens weren't exactly thrilled, especially those who were slightly colour blind. They got involved in hassles with campers who swore their tents were dark green, not light green. There was discontent amongst campers who had to pay – and a bit of fiddling. Some campers were spraying their tents overnight, and demanding rebates.

The National Trust can also think vertically, as is shown by their campaign to help the Herdwick. First of all they went into the wool-spinning business – buying raw wool at auction and getting it spun. Mr Hanson-Smith himself went round Lake District shops with samples of National Trust Herdwick wool and took lots of orders. They have built up a thriving mail order wool business as well as selling to the retail shops.

Now, they've moved on even further and publish National Trust knitting patterns (price 20p from NT outlets). Special Herdwick and Swaledale patterns have been created for them, for sweaters, hats and socks, designed to make the most of the natural, undyed, local wool. The knitting patterns have already had the desired effect and put up sales of local wool.

Mr Howard, being only a voluntary official, doesn't take part in the day-to-day business enterprises, but he's particularly pleased about all the efforts to help the hill farmers who live on National Trust property. 'In the old days, the Trust was simply concerned with preservation, which was rather negative. If all you're doing is preserving, you could end up with dead villages and dead communities. We're now concerned with people as much as buildings.

'The most important thing I shall have done as chairman is to encourage a co-operative movement among some hill farmers. They don't fatten their own sheep, as they haven't the pasture, and most have to sell their lambs to be fattened by others. As they sell at the same time each autumn, it means the prices go down. We've now got ten of our farmers in the Langdales to work together as a co-op, renting their own lowland pasture and fattening their own sheep. They can therefore choose the time to sell, and get the best prices. We'd found them the land, at Netherby the other side of Carlisle, and the co-op has hired a local shepherd to look after the fattening. The first stage has been hard, getting the farmers to work together. Lakeland farmers are not used to co-operating. They often do the reverse. We don't know if in the end it will work, but I hope so. It's a most exciting prospect.'

I went on a little tour of his own Greystoke estate before leaving, including a visit to his stables, scenes of great excitement just a few months previously. He rents the stables to Gordon Richards, trainer of Lucius, winner of the 1978 Grand National. The whole village of Greystoke naturally had money on its local horse, though Mr Howard didn't. 'Win or lose, I still get the rent.' Mr Richards has fifty horses training at Greystoke and has built up a mini-Newmarket. 'We now have an Irish community living in the village. Thanks to the National Health, English boys are too big to be jockeys.'

Lowther land begins just a few miles south of Greystoke and, in Cumbrian terms, the Lowthers have always been top of the bill. Anyone these days who owns a thousand acres is, on paper, in the millionaire class, with local land fetching £1000–£2000 an acre, but the Lowthers at one time seemed to own everything.

Lowther Castle, the building so lovingly but so badly acclaimed in a sonnet by Wordsworth, is still there. So are the Lowthers, the family which so governed Wordsworth's life. The

Castle is a truly magnificent sight, especially from the distance, all rounded turrets, fairy-tale battlements, the sort so loved by romantic Victorians. But don't get too close. It's just a shell, the sort of ruin *particularly* loved by romantic Victorians.

The Lowthers continued to increase and multiply their great wealth after Wordsworth's day and when the fifth Earl of Lonsdale took over in 1880 he was regarded as one of the richest men in the whole of England. Nobody in Cumbria can be unaware of the family's influence. As a boy in Carlisle, I walked to school every day down Lowther Street and on Saturday morning went to the children's matinée at Carlisle's smartest cinema, The Lonsdale. Almost every town and village in Cumbria has similar connections, showing where the family has been and bought and conquered.

The fifth Earl had a long run, holding the title from 1880 to 1944 – and what fun he had ruining the family. Wordsworth would have been appalled to see the collapse of a once all-powerful feudal estate. The Yellow Earl, as he was called, is still talked of in Cumbria today. His extravagances improve with the telling, especially in an age when the aristocracy provide such little fun for the rest of us. He loved yellow, the family colour, and painted his carriages yellow, later his motor cars, and had all his servants in yellow livery. He had an enormous number of servants. When the Kaiser came to stay with him, one of many Royal visitors, he had on duty in Lowther Castle over sixty *indoor* staff.

He was a great car man and was the first President of the Automobile Association. (Their colour today is yellow, thanks to the Yellow Earl.) In Cumbria, the Tory party's colour is still yellow, despite the fact that in the rest of the nation the Tories always sport true blue. (This dates back to Wordsworth's day when the Lowthers controlled most of the Cumbrian constituencies.) He was a great sporting Earl, loved races and games of all sort, and was always organising sports for his tenants and employees, such as on Burgh Marsh when the whole area had a feast day. His name today is probably only known nationally through boxing and the Lonsdale belts which he bequeathed.

By 1910 he was spending at the rate of £180,000 a year which, even for the Lowther coffers, couldn't go on. He lived on the mineral royalties, but put none of it back, the worst sin in any landed family. When the 1930s depression came, and it hit west Cumberland so hard it has today hardly recovered, his income dried up overnight. By 1935 his disposable income had fallen dramatically to £6000 a year. On his death in 1944, £1.7 million had to be paid in tax.

That was the end, or so it seemed, of Lowther power, of 1000 years of almost continuous feudal control of a vast chunk of north-west England. The next Earl was an old man of seventy-six when he took over. Then on the scene comes his grandson, young James Lowther, who, in 1949, at the age of twenty-seven, was brought across from Newcastle, where he was working as a business man, to manage the estates. He'd gone straight into the war from Eton with hardly a thought that one day he might inherit the estates, but his father, Lord Lowther, had suddenly died and in 1953, on the death of his grandfather, he became the seventh Earl.

'It had been a traumatic time for the family,' says the present Earl. 'They felt that the end had come and that it was all over. In the late thirties they had despaired and given up any form of intelligent management or intelligent thinking at all. I suppose the final blow to their morale was the requisitioning of 10,000 acres as an army training ground at the beginning of the war.' Even worse, Lowther Castle, the family seat, had fallen into disrepair. There was no money to keep it going so in 1958 it was partially demolished and became the semi-ruin it is today.

There was yet another set of enormous death duties to be faced, with the death of the sixth Earl, and once again no attempts had been made to prepare for them by forming trusts. But in eight years, by massive rationalisation, judiciously selling outlying portions of the estates, the present Earl had discharged unpaid liabilities of £2.1 million.

In 1953, when he became Earl, the estate was turning over about £100,000 a year and employed seventy people. In 1978, the turnover was six million pounds and the employees numbered 307. The estates, as a whole, are probably worth today 25 million pounds.

The Lowther Estates are now run as a corporate body with seven different trusts and twenty different shareholders owning different sections, just like any other modern business organisation. It's been a team effort and the young land agents he brought in with him, such as Derek Pattinson, have stayed to build up the estates in the last thirty years, but the driving force has come from the Earl himself. It's been lucky for the family that he has shown the business acumen and energy of the first James Lowther, the one who built up the family fortunes in the first place. He's diversified into things like a Wildlife Park, a caravan site and property companies. Their own management business is now so successful that it manages thirty other big estates in and around Cumbria.

The most profitable single division is their saw mills. The Lowthers, over the centuries, had always planted oak, as a good landed family should, in fact as only landed families can do, being in the position to wait 120 years for any return. The oak went for ships in the Napoleonic wars, then for railway waggons during Victorian days. Those markets had obviously gone by the time the present Earl took over but by careful research he found a new one – oak for fencing the new motorways. He produced £750,000 from motorway contracts and the saw mills which he opened to process the wood have gone on to become a thriving business in their own right. The Lowther revival has not only assured the family fortunes but brought new money and jobs and opportunities to Cumbria as a whole. The day I saw him, he had been lunching with representatives from a London merchant bank, who were discussing pumping in half a million on some new Lowther scheme. It's been an unsung revival, unseen by the general public, and hasn't even made the business pages of the newspapers, but it's been a remarkable one nonetheless.

It could be argued that he had many advantages, inheriting all those thousands of acres, but he has been the first head of the family for a hundred years to put them to any use. It also shows that death duties needn't necessarily be the death of a family. So much for those who bleat about today's high taxes ruining families and killing off stately homes, putting all the blame on the Labour Government. It does, of course, take a lot of energy and enterprise. Those born with a silver spoon can't sit back and do nothing and hope to pass it on intact, as they used to do for centuries. The Labour Party has in one way done the aristocracy a good turn. It has revealed the run-down families, the dead wood, the ones incapable of finding new blood. Whatever you think of inherited wealth, it's surely better when the lucky few have to *work* to keep it going.

Lord Lonsdale has shown great energy in other directions. He's now married for the fourth time and has eight children, ranging from thirty years to three months, (girl boy, girl boy, girl boy, girl boy – how's that for neat accountancy) and has been actively involved in almost every important local organisation, from the Northern Region Economic Planning Council, Sports Council, Tourist Board, to Forestry Commission and British Legion. He's a director of Border TV and several other commercial companies.

The Lowther estates are the biggest private land owners in the Lakes (coming third in the overall league table after the National Trust and the Forestry Commission) and they own the freehold of 27,000 acres in Cumbria and manorial rights over a further 45,000 acres of common land. He knows there's still untold mineral wealth waiting to be secured, and maintains that landscaping could be done afterwards to hide the scars, but, as a member of all the right conservation bodies, he knows full well the uproar it would cause. This is the main reason why he's let the National Trust have 15,000 acres of Lake District fells, and 1500 acres along the Solway, for five pence a year until the year 2000. 'My successors can then decide what to do with it.'

He looks upon the Lowther success as part of the fifties and sixties Cumbrian revival, a piece of private enterprise comparable with the emigrés to west Cumberland who began the new chemical, textile and other industries, but he's saddened by all the firms who've disappeared over the same period. 'Almost every old family business in Cumbria seems to have sold out in the last thirty years – many becoming part of bigger international combines. It means there's a management, not an entrepreneur class coming into the area. But I've noticed a new development in the seventies. Many of those huge Windermere sort of houses, which the cotton magnates built during the Victorian era, are now being bought up by a completely new wave of self-made property tycoons, men with their own holding companies, who buy a castle in the Lakes area for themselves and their families, though they officially call them management training centres. They move in computers and make it the centre of their operations, but it's also their home. These sort of people do have cultural leanings and are very keen to improve life generally in the Lake District.'

The future management of his company was in his mind the day I passed through. From the way he was speaking, it looked as if there might not be a suitable Lowther around, at least not for a decade or two. His chief assistant, Derek Pattinson, is approaching sixty and he himself was making plans to retire in 1982, when he would be sixty. 'I want to take six months' holiday a year and travel round the world. I want to go to Greece, Italy and Israel and look at the archaeological sites.'

He couldn't work up much real interest in the current Lakeland squabble over Ennerdale Water, leaving that to the younger activists. He found the 1962 Ullswater battle tiring enough. Lord Birkett got most credit for that win, deservedly enough, but it was Lord Lonsdale behind the scenes who ran the campaign to save Ullswater from Manchester Corporation and their reservoir scheme. It was a battle against the then Tory Government who were steering the bill through – and Lord Lonsdale, like his forebears, is a good Tory, though a rather liberal, self-willed Tory. 'I moved down to London with my secretary and for six weeks solid we did nothing but contact people and lobby them. I got in the end 230 Lords upon whom I could make some sort of claim – through my National Trust work, British Legion, Forestry, family, old school, any connection I could think of – six bloody weeks. Lord Hill took me aside to say I was rocking the Tory boat, but I told him what he could do.

'We all went for a drink the night the vote came through in our favour – and I realised that everyone was there, except Lord Birkett. He didn't drink, but my brother and I went down into the chamber where he was still sitting, packing up his papers after his great speech. He declined to have a drink with us and just wanted to be put in a cab, which we did. That was the last I saw of him. He died two days afterwards.'

Lord Lonsdale prefers to work by stealth, behind the scenes, keeping out of the limelight. I had half expected, when I first met him, that he might be a chinless wonder, someone tall and floppy, but he's more in the self-made aggressive businessman mould. He's not very tall but carries himself well, like a bantam cock, and wears rather heavy spectacles through which he glares at strangers rather suspiciously. He pauses suddenly, summing you up, as if waiting for a reaction, then he starts again, without waiting. When he does stop, he has a habit of repeating his last sentence, word for word, and you think at first that all those centuries of high breeding have taken their toll, but then he's away, rattling off amazing lists, facts and figures and legal intricacies. He gave the genealogical table of almost every person who came into his conversation – and there are families who date from Wordsworth's day who still work for the Lowther estates.

He has no literary pretensions but is obviously proud of the

Wordsworth connection. As well as employing Wordsworth's father, he maintains that his family in effect employed Wordsworth himself, paying him for all the political work he did on their behalf. His evidence is 132 letters written by Wordsworth to the Earl of Lonsdale, mostly full of political intelligence. They are at Carlisle Castle, on loan to the county archives, but he is contemplating selling them. His financial brain was working out a scheme whereby he could let the Government 'buy' them from him in lieu of tax, then the Government would hand them over as a gift to Dove Cottage. That way, they'd go to a worthy home in the Lakes, and not abroad, but at the same time he'd realise their worth. He'd done this, apparently, some years previously with some Royal silverware.

In conversation, he referred to the first Earl, James Lowther, the one who mucked up the Wordsworth family for so long, as Wicked Jimmy and the next one as William the Good, which was a nice way of making them clear, but he picked me up when I presumed to lump *him* with those who agree that Wicked Jimmy really was wicked. He was simply making the distinctions clear.

'It depends on your point of view, where you stand, if you think he was wicked. The Wordsworth family certainly thought so. But if he was wicked, so am I wicked. He was simply a brilliant businessman. What I consider *wicked* is what happened in the 1930s, when the family fortune was thrown away and nothing at all was ploughed back in, yet unemployment in west Cumberland was seventy per cent.'

Lord Lonsdale lives near the famous Castle, just a couple of miles away at Askham Hall. He has several other bits of Wordsworth memorabilia around, such as a portrait of Wordsworth's grandfather and three poems in the poet's hand, written in the visitors' book after he had stayed the weekend at Lowther Castle, no doubt having enjoyed himself with all the quality in the palatial banqueting halls.

I had a last look at Lowther Castle before I headed for Ullswater. It really is a most remarkable building. I've seen old photographs of it with rows and rows of carriages lined up outside, and the ladies and gentlemen in all their finery. The north face of the building is 420 feet long, so you can see why all those indoor servants were needed.

'What pain must it be to the owners to live so near this memorial of past glories,' observes Nikolaus Pevsner in his series on the buildings of England. 'The county can ill afford to lose so spectacular a ruin.'

The Castle is bolted and barricaded and the public aren't allowed inside, for fear of falling masonry, but I went round the back and discovered a strong smell of hens. The back gardens have now been taken over by the ever-enterprising Lowther Estates and are covered with huts for battery chickens. Such is progress.

21
ULLSWATER

A tale of two hotels.

ONE OF THE MOST AMAZING CHANGES IN THE LAKE DIS-trict in recent years has been the food. The vast majority of it is still awful tourist fare, the sort which the vast majority of tourists seem perfectly happy with. You just have to walk round the streets early in the morning in Bowness, Windermere or Keswick to smell the fry-ups. The lunches are frozen peas and frozen fish and very often frozen chips. If it's not frozen, it comes out of a tin or a packet. It's all perfectly clean, relatively friendly, mostly harmless and all of it with as much flair as motorway caffs. You might be anywhere.

I wonder where Wordsworth and company went for a meal? There are records by De Quincey of them dining well at private houses on things like pheasant – but not much about restaurants. Perhaps there weren't any, as such. They often stayed at inns and took pot luck on the evening meal, but there aren't many details. (They were too busy ogling Mary of Buttermere when they went to her inn to describe the menu.) One would have expected De Quincey to have written about any smart eating place, if one had been well known enough to have attracted the quality. Wordsworth, of course, wouldn't have noticed. He was above such things. He and Dorothy spent a night at an inn at Rosthwaite in Borrowdale in 1812, on the way to visit Southey, and Wordsworth was obliged to share a bed with a Scottish pedlar. The Southey household, when they heard, were appalled, but Wordsworth did not seem to have minded. When the Wordsworths left, they all discussed it endlessly. Southey himself said that he 'would rather not lie in bed the next forty years than sleep with a Scotch pedlar'.

Travellers in the Lakes over the next 150 years or so have usually managed to avoid sharing beds with tramps, but in the main their needs and their expectations have been modest. They've come for the simple pleasure of the great outdoors, to taste the wild hills, not expecting to sink into interior-sprung luxury or taste gastronomic delights. The Victorians built some solid lakeside hotels, which have catered solidly for family holidays, but they've not exactly been known for their food.

Fifteen years ago, when I used to go home to Carlisle, flashing my first pay packets, I was always looking for a good place to treat the relations, but there was nowhere to go. I'd end up in a mausoleum culled from the AA book, served by waiters of ninety-five with uniforms just as old, heavily stained and smelling of boiled cabbage. Today, I rarely eat out in London. It's not the expense, which is frightening, or the parking, which is hell, or the staff, who don't care, or the other guests, who are all American tourists, but the food which isn't worth the effort. Today, I do all my guzzling in the Lakes. No wonder my spirits soared as I approached Ullswater.

The hotel which started the transformation in the Lakes is called Sharrow Bay and it's right on the banks of Ullswater. I first went there ten years ago and was astounded to find that the man at the next table had come up that day from London – 600 miles return journey – just to have lunch. I couldn't believe it. The South Coast and the Home Counties and even the Cotswolds have always had hotels which people would go to, simply to have a meal there. But not the Lakes. One thought Northerners would not encourage such nonsense.

Today, there are two hotels in the Lakes which regularly win the top awards from the experts and are always being described as the best place to stay in England, Western Europe, the World, the Universe. All food books these days are obsessed by ratings and stars and funny symbols and smart remarks – must try harder, see me – and naturally there are backlashes, as even smarter guide books look for something to criticise, even if it's just the excesses of the prose used by previous writers, but there can't be a current eating guide to the UK that doesn't have Sharrow Bay and Miller Howe in their all-time greats.

There are now about five or six other hotels in the Lakes with similar pretensions, who also feature in the best food guides, but the Sharrow Bay–Miller Howe methods are very hard, and very expensive, to follow.

Their style positively drips good taste. You get nothing so vulgar as a reception desk, a bar or any hotel-like notices. You're meant to think you're in an exquisite country house. These two hotels can be intimidating at first experience, if you don't know the unspoken rules and unwritten routines, and they can also sicken, if you don't care for such ultra-rich eating and equally rich decor and presentation. It's all such a performance that at times they can be parodies of themselves. At Sharrow Bay they can garland a simple dish of vegetables with so many flowers you think you're in Kew Gardens. At Miller Howe they dim lights, turn on the effects and present the meal like a five-act play at the National Theatre. But whether you approve or not, they've set themselves enormously high standards in food, surroundings and service. The excitement in each of them, amongst the staff and guests, before dinner every evening is unbelievable. It must be all terribly exhausting to work there.

They hate being lumped together and will scream at any suggestion of connection and in fact there is little love between them at the present time. Sharrow Bay was first and Miller Howe, so they suspect, copied them, which naturally they deny at Miller Howe.

Francis Coulson first opened Sharrow Bay in 1948, having travelled up from Euston with his cooking pans hanging from the haversack on his back. His partner, Brian Sack, who later joined him, was formerly a surveyor. Coulson had been in the theatre. They were both very much amateurs, starting with very little money and little experience, building it all up painfully slowly. Sharrow Bay is an isolated country house on the shores of Ullswater, a sensational situation as far as views are concerned, with the dining room looking straight up the lake, but it's on the remote side of Ullswater, the Howtown side, away from civilisation. Getting staff and supplies was a terrible problem in the early days. When you have such standards as they have, the slightest breakdown can become high drama. They're both bachelors and Sharrow Bay is their love and their life. Francis is still the chef and Brian is the one in the neat suit who supervises the tables.

Miller Howe has equally good views, this time over Windermere, though it's on the busy side which has, no doubt, been good for getting staff but not so quiet for guests. Like Sharrow Bay, the building itself is basically rather ordinary, of little architectural interest, just one of the many Edwardian summer houses which litter the lakesides. It's the internal transformation that has made them seem so rich and gilded, bursting with antiques, precious knick-knacks, and the heaviest of soft furnishings.

The bedrooms have individual names, not numbers. At Sharrow Bay they're named after Victorian girls, like Prudence and Patience. Miller Howe has local place names, like Troutbeck. I think Sharrow Bay has the edge on antiques, but then they've had more years in the making. One or two items of bedroom furniture at Miller Howe are, dare I say it, a bit modern, even flash, such as the bed heads. However, in this age of standardised hotel furniture, where every hotel room in the world looks the same, each is a pleasure to inspect.

I've stayed at Sharrow Bay many times, always with enormous pleasure, so this time I booked into Miller Howe, never having spent a night there before. There was no glass of sherry in the bedroom, as there always is at Sharrow Bay, but I found binoculars, hair dryer, electric trouser press, Scrabble, dictionary, one puzzle, two very large bath robes, two shampoos, two foam baths, two unopened packets of Riley's skin soap, one magazine (*House and Garden*) and seven books, including Derek Cooper's *Skye*, Margaret Costa's *Four Seasons Cookery Book*, the collected *Punch* for 1905 (original volume) and something called *The Springs of Jewish Wisdom*.

There was a terrific view, when I opened the French windows and stepped on to my private balcony, which was why someone had thought ahead and provided binoculars. I didn't actually feel like some Jewish Wisdom during my stay but it was nice to know it was there. I won't bother listing the items of furniture. I gave up anyway after counting twenty-nine pieces of decorated china or glass ware. Nothing gets stolen, so I was told, though it would be so easy. In the early days, when they had far less clutter, sorry, I mean objets d'art, an occasional item did disappear. Now, with so much, people must become overawed by it all.

I hadn't got a tie for dinner as I wasn't expecting to get in. (In each hotel, you practically have to book in at birth.) Wolfgang, the head waiter (I knew it was Wolfgang because his portrait appears on a hotel leaflet), said it didn't matter. I found myself in a huge leather chair in a large, rather formal, lounge wondering if by chance I'd wandered into the Harvard Club in New York. I was surrounded completely by Americans, the sort who are more tweedy and more gentlemanly and more English than the English. That evening, by my estimate, ninety per cent of the guests were Americans.

The couple nearest me were discussing what he was going to buy at Christie's wine sale. He had apparently come all the way to England for two things – to buy wine in London and stay at Miller Howe. All around I could hear people quoting comments from the *New York Times*, or *Gourmet*, either boasting about how many times they'd been here, or humbly admitting it was their first, but they had been to Sharrow Bay and boy, was that a truly wonderful experience.

Waiters, in lovely uniforms of green blazer and fawn slacks, appeared from nowhere and took orders. As at Sharrow Bay, nothing is ever written down, no list is shown, no prices are mentioned, no names or rooms are asked for, and when the desired drinks arrive, just as quietly and unobtrusively, no money is ever requested. No private country house could ever have been so exquisite. How do they remember? Is it done by Pelmanism?

I had a seat in the dining room next to the main window, giving me a panoramic view of the lake and a close-up view of two cupid figures outside, sitting cuddling on a fountain which sprinkled and sparkled and changed colours. There seemed to be an awful lot of water on the ground for a dry summer's evening. Perhaps the cupid figures' aim was off-target with all that cuddling.

At the next table, a young American about seven feet tall was telling his partner, very slowly, the plot of Beatrix Potter's *The Tailor of Gloucester*. I could tell she wasn't listening, though smiling and nodding hard and obviously pleased that her partner should appear to be so loquacious in front of all the other Americans, but I was following every word. The waiters hovered, charming for England, and I noticed how well pressed their smiles were, as neat as the creases in their slacks. Their lovely badges, on close inspection, had the name Miller Howe and a Mortar and Pestle symbol embroidered on them.

The first course was Miller Howe Onion Tart with a Spinach, Mushroom and Bacon Salad. The tart was delicious. The little salad came at the side and was very interesting. I'd never had cold fried bacon in a salad before. Then it was back to *The Tailor of Gloucester*. He had obviously researched Beatrix Potter with great care. If he had chosen *Peter Rabbit*, he could have told the plot in ten seconds, but he was well set to make a meal of it. He'd started on sexual symbolism and the moral significance of the poor tailor's dilemma, without even having gotten halfway through the plot.

Next course was Duck and Marsala Soup with Chopped Chives which again was a taste thrill. I only seemed to have been served with one spoonful, which I thought at first was a bit mean, but I looked at the menu with all the goodies to come and thought how wise. With the soup, the waiter brought round a dish of Cream Choux Puff – so it said in the menu. They were little balls of pastry with what looked like chocolate sauce on top and I thought I'm not having them, not with my soup. I didn't want the tangy flavour of the soup ruined by something sweet and creamy. While I waited for the next course, I learned how Beatrix Potter had pinched the plot from an existing story current in Gloucester at the time.

The fish course was Cod Baked on Pear Slice with Provençal Sauce, which rather worried me, hating as I do things like pears or peaches mixed up with fish or meat. It turned out to be another triumph. It all went together remarkably well and I licked the plate, half hoping the Beatrix Potter freak would be disgusted and give us all a break, but he was scraping his dish as well, and still talking.

Then it was top of the bill, the big attraction, the main course, and I could swear the lights outside dimmed specially. It looked simple enough on the menu, Spiced Loin of Pork served with Sweet and Sour Sauce, but it was the line-up of vegetables in the supporting cast that had everyone anticipating and even put B. Potter into second place for a few moments.

Seven vegetables were listed in the *dramatis personae*: Salsify in Cream Sauce, Purée of Parsnips with Toasted Pine Kernels, Glazed Carrots, Fried Cauliflower, Diced Turnip in Honey, Baked Cabbage with Garlic and Juniper and Savoury Potatoes. It all came together, on one plate, which normally I don't like, but it was piping hot and delicious. I'd feared that such lovely common or garden vegetables might be ruined by all that tarting up, but they were enhanced if anything, apart from the Parsnips. They're my favourite vegetable (especially roasted) but they'd been made into a rather sickly purée. However, I could hear little screams of delight and discovery all round, then a pause while the comparisons started, the references to similar dishes in Venice, or was it Paris, or San Francisco, or Sharrow Bay.

We were given some time to let it all sink in and then the lights brightened and in bounced the man of the match, star of the show, creator of the words and the music, John Tovey. He was in his white kitchen clothes, complete with white wooden clogs, and he went round each table in turn, either smiling and joking and going thank you, thank you, thank you, like Mrs Tittlemouse, or being very serious and explaining some finer point of a recipe. When he came to my table I asked if anyone ever complained or criticised. 'Oh, I get sloshed some time. I've just been told you don't make clam chowder with tomatoes. It wasn't clam chowder.' Then he was off to the next table where my Beatrix Potter friend said it had been a truly wonderful experience.

The list of the puddings was as impressive as the vegetables. I don't know how on earth he manages to produce so many different and complicated and delicate dishes every day. There was Chocolate Orange Cream in Butterscotch, Shortbread Tartlet, Port and Claret Jelly with Shortbread, Hazelnut Meringue Slice with Fresh Guavas, Pineapple and Passion Fruit Cream Pavlova, Lemon Curd Galette Slice, Black Cherry Rum Farmhouse Pie, Strawberry Cheesecake, Calvados Apple Chocolate Crunch.

I'm sending my copy of the menu to the Victoria and Albert Museum. The art work alone, which is as decorated as the puddings, should be an interesting example of what was considered high taste back in good old debauched 1978.

I arranged to speak to Mr Tovey afterwards and I went with him for coffee at his own home, a brand new, architect-designed building about a mile away along the lakeside, equally dripping with precious objects, but about as lived-in as a window at Heal's. He's a bachelor and was living alone, much to his displeasure, as he's a great extrovert and likes someone to share his life and triumphs with him, especially winding down after his evening performance.

He's a local lad and comes from Barrow, an industrial town in south Cumbria, not normally noted for sophistication. (Bang go sales of this book in Barrow.) He's 45, so he says, and his first job was at sixteen when he went abroad as a clerk with the old Colonial Service in Central Africa, till he got the sack in 1959 and came home to Barrow. He did explain how he got the sack but I didn't quite follow it as he had insisted we sit in the garden in the dark and I'd begun to shiver. When we got inside, to the hot coffee and more wine, he was on to his theatrical days.

'I'd fallen in love with a theatre director which was why I bought Her Majesty's Theatre in Barrow. I'd realised the sort of person I was for the first time. I managed the theatre and he directed the weekly rep. and we were very happy. It was halycon days.'

Then the money ran out, the friendship finished, and he had to find a job and went as secretary to the boss of a hotel on Windermere. He moved on to waiting and cooking to becoming a manager. In 1970 he worked for six weeks at Sharrow Bay. He gets very insistent that it was only six weeks.

'I'll show you my insurance stamps. Go and see my bank manager. Ask anyone. I've heard people say I took their ideas and even pinched their customers, but it's all untrue. The biggest influence in my life has been Margaret Costa. I followed her recipes and I took her contacts – it was she who sent up journalists, once she discovered what I was doing here, and they all wrote about me. My first break-through was when she wrote about me in the *Sunday Times* Magazine in 1974. Getting there was easy. The hard thing is *staying* there.'

Miller Howe began on 26 May 1971 when he bought the house for £26,500. He put up half the money and a sleeping partner put up the rest. Seven years later, he thinks the business, if he were to sell it, would be worth £280,000. He expects to be a hundred per cent full from June until the end of October. April and May had been only 99.9% full. You need to book at least six days ahead to get a meal and six weeks ahead to get a bed.

'You'll never believe what I went through. I slept in the cellar for two years, next to the boiler. I scratched and schemed and spent when I didn't have any money and now it's a great bloody big tarantella which is my family, my children, my life.'

There are thirteen bedrooms, seating for seventy and he has a staff of fourteen, eight of whom have been with him for six years. He keeps them on all year and when the hotel is closed, from January to April, he still has to pay them £3000 a month, despite the fact he then has no income. He gets them painting and decorating and when that's done, he's off round the world, taking his staff with him. He's a great lad for publicity and promotion and during the last close season he took them on a whistle-stop tour of the States, going coast to coast giving one-night stands, demonstrating to large audiences the art of English Country House Cooking. The British Tourist Authority and British Airways now back him, realising what a crowd-puller he has become. No wonder his hotel is so full of Americans. Many have eaten his meals out there, or seen him on their local television. He's also done tours of Egypt and South Africa, and performances in Torquay and London. One could easily think he was still in show business. 'It *is* like producing a play every night. Eating out has got to be fun.'

I said my meal had been great fun but I hadn't fancied chocolate puff balls with my soup. 'You fool! It wasn't chocolate on top. It was essence of beef. I'd spent five days producing it.

It goes beautifully with the soup.' He agreed the parsnips were perhaps a little elaborate. 'But have you looked at parsnips just now? They're terrible. It's not the season. You have to do *something* with them.'

Before breakfast the next morning, as all the guests came down the stairs, he was standing in the hall, as bouncy as ever, handing out glasses of Buck's Fizz to everyone. As you well know, this is a mixture of champagne and fresh orange juice, just the thing to perk you up for another hard day's eating. It wasn't on the literature, nor was it charged for as an extra, but he had decided that as he liked it so much, all his guests should enjoy it every morning as well. Over to you, Sharrow Bay.

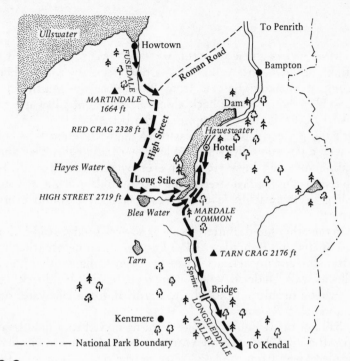

22

HAWESWATER

A walk along the High Street. Some reservations about reservoirs.

I THINK ULLSWATER IS STILL MY FAVOURITE LAKE. AND I
think my favourite walk, one I've done so many times while
staying at Sharrow Bay, is from Howtown, up Martindale,
round Place Fell, coming back along the shores of Ullswater to
Howtown. Or is the reverse order even better?

It's the perfect round walk, with so many different types of
scenery, dales and fells, wild and lush, hard and easy, cosy and
bleak, empty and busy yet never ever overcrowded for all its
popularity. On the last stretch, the lake unfolds in front of you,
peeling itself away in layers, a new perspective round every
corner.

On the other hand, Buttermere was so very pretty. And as for
Wast Water and Ennerdale, lakes I'd never seen before, they're
so dramatic and mysterious. There has been so many other good
walks as well. Duddon Valley, Langdale, Scafell, Caldbeck ...
Oh, what a problem, I thought, as I cruised down Ullswater on
the good ship *Raven*.

I had got on at Pooley Bridge, treating myself to a final boat
trip. After all, I'd started my year on a boat. At Howtown pier,
I headed away from the lake, resisting the temptation to walk
yet again round Place Fell. I was aiming to get to Kendal, or as
near as possible, all in one day, the last long, overland stretch of
my journey.

Hidden behind the Howtown Hotel is a little valley called
Fusedale, one I had never even known existed, which was worrying. The more I got to know the lakes the more I got to know
about places I still didn't know anything about. More problems.
More choices.

I'd chosen Fusedale on the map, where it had been lying quietly,
keeping a low profile, as it looked a quick way up to High Street.
In under fifteen minutes, since leaving the other hikers at Howtown pier, I was halfway up the valley, walking in complete
isolation, the day and the world all to myself. I followed the
beck through several little gorges, each with a couple of rowan
trees where nature had perfectly planted them. Rowan is my
favourite tree. Beeches are very nice, though. And birch. And as
for oak, they can be very grand. I'm giving up favourites.

I stopped at a ruined cottage which was where Wainwright
in his fell guide had said it would be, amazed by the initials
BR painted in such bold white on black paint at the doorway.
It looked so recent, and so professionally painted. Who had

brought paint and brushes all the way up the valley. More mysteries.

At first, looking back down the valley, I could see one chunk of Ullswater, but, getting higher, two slices appeared. Then they merged and then, as I reached the top, they disappeared. The sheep began to disappear as well. I'd been coming across them all the way up the valley, but I pretended to look the other way, averting my gaze from their nakedness. I could tell they hated being stared at, and no wonder. If you'd just had your hair shaved off, stripped naked and dumped back on the fell, you'd be a bit embarrassed. I could see why Herdwicks (now that they'd been newly shorn) don't bring fortunes to the hill farmers. There's hardly anything there. Underneath all that shaggy exterior is a scraggy body, trying hard not to get out. Their necks seemed enormous which is never apparent when they have their clothes on. They'd never get very far on a casting director's couch.

The landscape went blank, once I climbed out of the valley and reached the first stages of the high ground. Miles of empty, tree-less, rough grass, stretching forever in the distance, the only break in the grey-green monotone being some patches of peat hags which looked from afar like giant brown earthworms, crawling over the hillside.

I rested at a second ruined cottage where I heard some heavy breathing. I didn't really want to look, in case it was another naked body, sheep or otherwise, but it was a couple in blue anoraks, sitting behind the wall, who jumped up when they saw me and walked with me for a while. The man had been doing the heavy breathing, a gentleman of about fifty, rather over-weight, who said it was his first ever visit to the Lakes and this was his first walk. They had booked in the day before into a farm-house in Martindale and had planned themselves a six-hour walk up and round High Street. By the look and sound of him, he was never going to make it. He said he was from Hertfordshire and spent most of his working life driving a motor car.

Having poured scorn earlier on the mountain rescue people, for ever giving out lists of common-sense instructions, I could now see that even normally sensible people do silly things. I consider myself fit but I wouldn't attempt a six-hour climb on the first day on my hols, especially if I wasn't used to fell walking. No wonder exhaustion is such a prime cause of acci-dents. He was getting slower and slower, and breathing so heavily, that he eventually sat down, calling back his wife to sit with him, telling me not to wait. I kept looking back for the next hour or so, catching glimpses of their little blue dots in the distance. He was at least still on his feet when I last saw them.

High Street is the name of the highest point on the ridge, some 2719 feet high, but the ridge itself is also known as High Street, which can be confusing except that, when you walk it, there's no confusion. It's the most clearly defined fell walk in the whole of the Lake District, a high-altitude path that cuts a clear swath right across the eastern flanks. Once you're on the top, it soars for over ten miles, up and down, taking everything in its stride. The Romans walked this way, using it as part of their main route from Penrith across to Windermere, a brilliant patrolling system, looking down on all the world.

On the very top, a strongly built stone wall follows the path for several miles. It reminded me very much of Hadrian's Wall in the way it followed the slopes of the dominant ridge, commanding the heights, sticking to the winsills. In ancient days, the valleys and fell sides were all forested. This path, as the Romans found, was not just the best but almost the only way into the Lakes. Over the centuries, it's been trodden by marching soldiers, raiding Vikings, government inspectors, celebrating shepherds. It was once used, not so many decades ago, as a sports arena where shepherds wrestled and ran fell races. I can imagine it as a good meeting point, and a good playing ground as the ridge is smooth and level, but I can't believe that many spectators trailed up, just to watch some shepherds playing games.

The Romans have left few traces in the Lakes but then there wasn't much here for them. They concentrated their energies some thirty miles to the north, on Hadrian's Wall, and down the Cumbrian coast, where it now looks as if they had a complete string of forts, perhaps even an extension of the Wall, guarding themselves from a seaborne attack. In central Lakeland, they had only a few little forts, as at Ambleside, Hardknott and Ravenglass, but not much else.

There's a surprising amount of evidence of the Celtic people who were here when the Romans arrived. The Celtic people in Lakeland were related to those in Wales, both calling themselves Cymry, which is where Cumbria comes from. The prefixes Pen, Glyn, Caer and Blaen as in Penrith, Glenridding, Carlisle and Blencathra are all part of the Celtic–Welsh connection. Many

Cumbrian shepherds still use the old Celtic form when counting their sheep – yan, tan, tether. Yan, meaning one, is common usage throughout Cumbria. Helvellyn, that must be Celtic.

The people who had the biggest influence on the Lake District were the Norsemen. They didn't come direct from Scandinavia but raided the Cumbrian coast from Ireland and the Isle of Man. They settled here, unlike the Romans who saw us as a colony not their home. They cleared space in the forests and left their mark on countless place names. Thwaite, meaning clearing, appears in so many place names, and in surnames. Then there's beck, fell, pike, dale, force (meaning waterfall), gill (meaning cleft or ravine), hause (pass between hills), holme (island in a lake), how (hill), rigg (ridge), scale (hut), ness (promontory) and wath (ford) – all of which have Norse origins.

Ullswater gets its name from Ulf, a Norse lordling. Windermere comes from another early settler, Vinand; Thirlmere from Thorhall and Coniston used to be called Thurston Water, after someone called Thursteinn. Without the Norse, Cumbrian dialect and names would lose a lot of their distinctive flavour.

I left the High Street, and the paths of history, at the top of High Street itself where I turned left, heading for Haweswater. I didn't spend long on top, as there's so little to see. A young couple were sitting by the trig. point when I arrived. 'Wasn't worth it, was it,' he grunted, getting out his Thermos.

The immediate views are boring but once off the rough, tufty plateau, there's a dramatic and rather frightening fall down towards Blea Water (blea is Norse for blue). I was heading for Long Stile and I was glad I didn't miss it. It's a narrow route down a razor's edge of jagged rocks and steep scree. I wouldn't dare have tried to descend that way in mist.

I could see a glimpse of Haweswater as I came down the valley and what a strange sight it is. Around the entire lake is an enormous white kerb about fifty feet wide, a strip of bleached stones and rocks framing the entire lake. It's not ugly, nor is it attractive. It's weird, making you do a visual double-take. Something's gone wrong but you can't at first work out what has happened. It's as if the Ice Age has just left, scouring out the valley and leaving strange formations. I could see a little island with its own bleached tide marks all round it, beautifully measured whorls like a giant pebble.

From a distance it was hard to decide what was natural and

what was man-made. The bleached edges, for example, were they caused by gravel being dredged out of the middle of the lake and dumped on the side, or has the water itself done it, rising up and down and carrying away the soil? Or could it all be concrete? From a distance, you can't tell.

I walked down to the water's edge and found that they were real stones, not concrete or hard core. I could feel that it was soft not far beneath my feet which made the stones strangely springy. The water level was very low and out in the lake I could clearly see lines of stone walls marking old fields and buildings. It was as if there had been a high flood quite recently and the farmers had abandoned the land and their buildings, but would be back soon. They won't, of course. A whole village has gone, including a church and a pub, the Dunn Bull, never to return. A community which only a hundred years ago sent 3000 pounds of butter every week by rail to Manchester will never live again.

Haweswater is a reservoir. Manchester Corporation flooded the valley and the village of Mardale just before the last war. The huge dam at the far end, which is 1550 feet long and ninety feet high, was completed in 1940. There was originally a little lake called Haweswater but they raised the level to ninety-six feet, flooded the valley right up to the dale end and increased its size by roughly threefold. It was another battle which the preservationists failed to win.

There are two lakes in the Lake District which are wholly reservoirs, Thirlmere and Haweswater, with others like Ennerdale, Windermere and Ullswater being part-used, but not yet captured and killed and left for dead. Thirlmere was lost first, though after a great struggle. Manchester had its eye on Thirlmere from the 1870s, when it sent men up on horseback to look for water, and there was a national outcry when their plans were made public.

Letters to *The Times* said that the preservers were just 'poets, artists, bishops and sentimentalists' while the preservers said they weren't sentimental, they just wanted to keep all the lakes as 'playgrounds for the jaded industrial populations of the future'. The water people pointed out that Manchester's demand for water had tripled between 1850 and 1860. Pollution in their local rivers meant they couldn't use them any more. Something had to be done. Canon Rawnsley was there fighting for Thirlmere, aided by Octavia Hill, but they lost and in 1894 the work of flooding and damming and building the aqueduct to Manchester was completed.

Thirlmere, today, isn't ugly either, unless you object to the conifers which now dominate almost every side. They've even got nature trails. It's just south of Keswick and so ruined by the main road which runs right along it, down to Windermere, that even if it had never become a reservoir, the traffic would have killed most of its natural beauty.

In a hundred years, the arguments for and against the need for water supplies from the Lakes have hardly changed. No doubt we're going to have them all trotted out again for Ennerdale. The sooner they can get fresh water from the sea the better.

Ullswater, in 1962, has been the only big victory for the anti-Water Board people. In that case they reached a reasonable compromise, deciding to pump spare water from Ullswater underground, taking it across to Haweswater, the real reservoir. They keep the Ullswater pumping station very quiet. It's not on any map and there are no Water Board signposts to be seen. They presumably feel that Ullswater lovers might still come and blow it up.

The trouble with a reservoir is not just the loss of a valley, farmland and perhaps a village, but that you lose a lake. It needn't necessarily look horrible, if they spend enough money on landscaping, but you can't use it any more for swimming or boating or anything very much. They even stop you throwing stones in, if they catch you. The sides are mostly out of bounds and picnickers have to go elsewhere, though in recent years the Water Board have relented a bit and there's now a walkers' path along the other side of Haweswater.

The nicest part of Haweswater is the dale end. It comes as a surprise, if you've been following the road and the concrete-looking sides of the lake, when the road comes to a dead end and there in front of you are the magnificent crags and soaring heights of the High Street range. There are no buildings in sight and not really all that many walkers, considering the richness of the views. Perhaps the Water Board have done the valley a good turn, keeping down the crowds. This is the area, so they say, where the eagles have returned. I hadn't seen any on the way down, nor did I see any as I worked my way over to the head of Longsleddale.

There are two very long, very interesting valleys which lead down from the High Street range to Kendal and both of them tend to get overlooked by most tourists to the Lakes, yet they are the most accessible valleys for people arriving from the South. I have a friend with a cottage in one of them, Kentmere, and he can come up the M6 from London in three hours, so he boasts, nipping almost straight off the motorway into complete seclusion, turning right just after Kendal while most motorists trudge on into the heartland, thinking they haven't reached the good stuff yet. That was something Wordsworth never imagined – weekenders from London.

I practised trying to say Longsleddale as I came down over the rough, wild fell tops. Could it be Longs-le-Dale, or perhaps Long-Sled-dale or possibly they shorten it altogether and pronounce it Longs'dale, almost like Lonsdale as in Lord. I got frightened in my reveries by two huge birds with gigantic wings which I almost fell over. They rose like vertical take-off aeroplanes, whirling their jet-black wings, glaring at me, wondering whether to attack me and carry me off to their eyries. They weren't eagles but ravens, or possibly buzzards. All around were stunted trees and dangerous craggy enclaves and dried-out tarns. Even the stone walls looked frightened, hunched and beaten.

When I reached the valley, the stone walls were their usual selves, bold and strong, soaring up impossible heights, disappearing over the tops, marking one chunk of apparent wildness from another chunk of wildness, demarcation lines that only eccentric millionaires would now build. The dry stone walls are everywhere a great feature of the Lakes, but they're not really all that old, mostly being built in the early nineteenth century, at the time of the enclosure movement. Since 1850, they've hardly been touched. Nobody could afford to build them now. At that time, you could get seven yards built for eight shillings (about 40p). Today, it would cost you about £400, if you could find anyone skilled enough to do it. I've tried it myself, at Caldbeck, and it's far harder than it looks.

The secret is to have a wide base to give stability, two layers with rubble in between, regular through stones binding the wall together, and not to balance one stone straight on top of another but to cover gaps, making T-joints the way a bricklayer does. Well, I was told those were the secrets, but my walls still fall down. The cam stones on top are supposed to point downhill, to let the water drain off, and individual wallers left their own mark by the way they laid the cam stones. Good wallers also built hogg holes, to let young sheep pass through, but I haven't tried that yet.

On the high fells many have been allowed to crumble these days but, in the valleys, they are kept in good repair, often topped with a wire fence. Sheep, stupid though they may be, are incredible at jumping and scrambling. Dry stone walls also have an extra quality I had never imagined till a farmer in Caldbeck, Tommy Pearson, told me how he'd lost six sheep in a snow storm once for four weeks. He fell through a drift one day in a corner of a field and found them beneath the snow, huddled against the wall. They were still alive, though they'd eaten most of their wool away. Thanks to it being a dry stone wall, they'd been able to breathe *through* the wall.

I scrambled down into Longsleddale valley and soon hit the road beside the little river, the River Sprint, which is a nice neat name. There was an old shepherd standing with his dog beside a bridge so I stopped and chatted to him, hoping he would pronounce Longsleddale the correct way, so I could hide my ignorance. I said how pretty the valley was.

'You think so,' he said, laughing to himself, almost derisory. And the lovely stream, I added, what a perfect situation for a cottage.

'You think so,' he said. 'Give it another month. You'll need a boat to get across. They get no sun that side of the valley. It's like a bog.'

Further up the valley I'd seen a cottage for sale, so I asked him if he knew the price.

'I might do,' he said, pausing. 'What do you think?'

I suggested twenty thousand pounds. 'Add another ten thousand, then you might be near it.'

He said it was the planning people's fault that house prices were now so high. They won't allow any new buildings, so the old ones cost a fortune and no locals can buy them.

'Them planning folk want shotten. They don't live here. They don't own a blade of grass, but they tell us what to do. They tell us we don't want new people and new houses. Who says we don't? You need permission for everything. I could tell you some stories about caravans nobody knows about. The money they take in. They never declare it, you know. But good luck to them.'

It was a rather elliptical conversation, and I wasn't quite clear at the end whose side he was on, but in passing he had mentioned the name of the valley, pronouncing it Long-sledle. So now I know.

At the end of the valley, on the main road to Kendal, I felt very tired and decided to look for a lift. Who should stop but a Water Board landrover. They're quite human after all, these desecrators of our countryside. 'Yes, people moan about us, but they'd moan even more if they had no water out of their taps.'

The Board is simply called North-West Water these days, with their head office in Warrington, but most of the water still goes to Manchester and district. Up to 140 million gallons a day is taken from Thirlmere and Haweswater reservoirs and flows by gravity down to underground aqueducts some ninety miles to Manchester. (Ennerdale supplies purely Cumbrian needs, mainly Whitehaven, while Crummock Water supplies Workington and Hayes Water supplies Penrith.)

He explained that the bleached effect round Haweswater was caused purely by the rise and fall of the water level. It just shows how thin the soil level must be, if it can be swept away so easily to reveal bare stones. I hope that never happens at Ennerdale.

He was proud to work for the Water Board and said what a good job they did with landscaping. It was all so cheap to run, thanks to all of it falling by gravity down to Lancashire. It was the Ullswater pumping station that was so expensive. That had to go up hill, and then down to Haweswater. And when the water was low, they couldn't take much out anyway. I asked him where the pumping station was, and he told me. He was just a workman and I suppose he shouldn't, but he was so pleased that no one could ever find it. It was behind a public caravan site whose name I will not reveal, down a track which disappears underground. If any fish are ever pumped out by mistake, they have a special system for putting them back. Very considerate, these Water Board men.

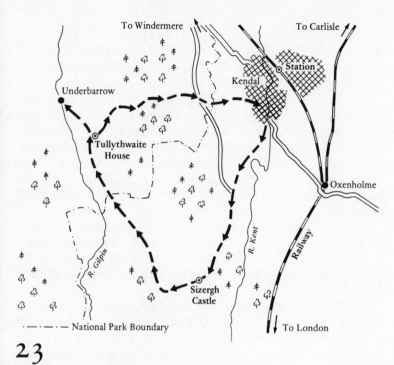

23
KENDAL

The incomparable Mr Wainwright. A nice tea and a visit to a newspaper.

THE MAN I MOST WANTED TO MEET DURING MY WALK around the Lakes was Wainwright. It would have been nice to have met Wordsworth but I fear in the flesh, especially in his old age, he might have been rather hard going, though on his arrival back in the Lakes, settling down at Dove Cottage, he would then have been very exciting to meet. Coleridge, so people said, was probably nicer, if you found him not too depressed or too ill. Southey sounds charming but boring. Most entertaining to meet of that circle was probably De Quincey. What gossip he could have provided – and we could have provided for him, telling him about the skeleton in old Wordsworth's cupboard.

Beatrix Potter only wanted to talk about sheep but John Ruskin, until he went dotty, had many interests. Canon Rawnsley might have been the liveliest of all, at least for all lovers of the Lakes, but I was a bit late for him. He died in 1920.

Of the present-day greats Wainwright has few equals. I can't think of any prose writer on the Lakes who has ever been read in greater numbers. He's certainly beaten Wordsworth's *Guide to the Lakes*. When you consider his little Lakeland guides have sold half a million, all in hardback, then it's hard to think of many living non-fiction writers who do better with their British sales. Book Four of his *Pictorial Guide to the Lakeland Fells*, the one on the southern fells, came out in 1960 and is now in its eightieth impression. They will doubtless last for ever, partly because it's unlikely that anyone again will ever have the energy to climb and describe every fell in the Lake District; partly because they are already collectors' items; and, most of all, because they are a joy to read.

Yet he's completely unknown to the general public. Even those half a million or so who have bought his books have little idea who he is or whether he's still alive. I consulted his fell guides all year, read them all with enormous pleasure, never attempted one fell without looking at my Wainwright first, yet I learned no details about the writer himself. You see them everywhere, a status symbol for all Lakers who spread them out in the back of their cars or clutch them on cairns. Many people I spoke to thought he must have lived about a hundred years ago.

It's not just the contents but his individual style of presentation which is so unique and such a delight. Each book contains no line of printer's type. It's all in his own handwriting, from the covers and headlines and numbers to all the words, which is why it looks at first sight like the facsimile of some nineteenth-century gentleman's commonplace book. In many ways it is. He did it for himself – and to everyone's amazement, the public flocked to buy them. The books are full of his quirky personality. He admits in them that his drawings are often just 'to fill up awkward spaces' and that 'the hills don't really look as good as this'. He tells readers to 'be quick, turn over' and has his own little jokes and personal hints and impressions. Out of context they can sound a bit weak perhaps, but they are a vital part of the personality of all his books which is what people love so much.

He doesn't like interviews and has never appeared on TV, despite constant requests, ranging from the BBC in London to Border TV in Carlisle. He never does signing sessions or appears in public. So much for those publicity and advertising men who are so important in publishing today, the sort who think you need to hire a train and do 200 signing sessions a day to be sure of success.

I rather tricked him into seeing me. He never answers the telephone which makes it hard, for a start, to get to him. But one day I got his wife on the phone and she was kind enough to say that Wainwright knew my book on Hadrian's Wall and she was sure he would see me. I said I just wanted to talk to him about his own experiences in the Lakes and hear any advice he might give me. He agreed, on condition that nothing ended up in any newspaper.

He's a very tall, well-built man of seventy-one with thick white hair and a soft Lancashire accent. He lives in a modern house in Kendal which is rather suburban at the front, facing other houses in a cul-de-sac, but at the back it has fine, open views of the fells. The interior is modest and chintzy, with no sign of affluent living. There are a lot of cats around. He doesn't appear to be a reader, as there were only a few books, many of them presentation copies of books by other Lakes writers (which he admitted he hadn't yet read). The telephone rang constantly during the four hours I was with him and he never answered it once. His wife was out. If her friends ring and there's no answer, they know she's out and soon hang up.

He was born in Blackburn and was christened Alfred, a name

he obviously dislikes. He always put 'A. Wainwright' or simply 'AW' when he's signing off at the end of another book. 'I never disclosed what the A stood for,' so he wrote in one of his books, *Fellwanderer*. 'It suited me to hide the truth of this affliction. But it isn't Aloysius, if that's what you're thinking.'

His father was a stone mason but unemployed for long periods. Alfred went to the local elementary school and left at thirteen to be an office boy in the Council offices for fifteen shillings a week. He started in the surveyor's department, then moved to accounts as a clerk where he was persuaded to take the professional exams to become a municipal accountant. 'I'd only been to board school and all the others had been to grammar school and they were given certain exemptions. The boss forced me to do it and it took me eight years of study at nights. I didn't want to do it but I made the best of it. I drew up a huge programme and filled sheets and sheets of graph paper with what I had to do. I enjoyed that bit, but I think those years of killing study killed any reading instinct I ever had. I've hardly picked up a book since. I hate any sort of research. But it did turn me into a hard worker, a habit I've never lost. If I'm not working, I think I'm wasting time. I still do ten hours a day, seven days a week. I have no social life, by choice.'

His boyhood and youth were spent in Blackburn, in an environment of dingy houses and shabby streets, gaunt mill chimneys, huge factory walls that shut out the sun, flickering gas lamps, hot potato carts, fish and chip shops, public houses. 'I was twenty-three before I could afford a holiday away from home. The Lake District was only sixty miles away but it was another world, distant, unattainable. I went there with a cousin for a week's walking. Well, I was utterly enslaved by it. I gazed in disbelief at the loveliness around me. I never knew there could be so much colour and charm in landscape. That was the first time I'd looked upon beauty, or even imagined the idea of beauty.'

After that, he took his holidays in the Lakes, when he could afford it, and in 1941 came to Kendal to work in the treasurer's office. In 1948 he was made Borough Treasurer of Kendal. He now spent all his spare time on the fells and in the winter, when it was too dark to climb, he sat by his own fireside doing pen and ink drawings of Great Gable and other places he'd climbed, re-climbing them in his mind.

In 1950 he moved into his present house, which was then new, and drew up for himself a five-year plan to knock the untouched garden into shape. He worked day and night, even digging with the aid of electric light, and had finished it in two years. He felt desolate without a plan of campaign to occupy himself. 'I read Westerns solidly for six months but all the time I felt I ought to be doing something.'

One day in November 1952 he decided to set himself a new task. He would climb all the fells and mountains in the Lake District and keep a note book and drawings of all the routes, just for his own enjoyment. He was by then forty-five, with a full-time job, and he calculated that doing the 200 or so climbs in his spare time would take him thirteen years, nearly up to his sixtieth birthday.

It was the publication of the Ordnance Survey's new two-and-a-half inch maps of the Lakes which triggered off the idea. He'd always felt disappointed by the one-inch maps because of the lack of detail. 'On a one-inch map a walker can frig about all day in an area represented by two square inches. With the larger scale map, you have the illusion of covering more ground more quickly. You can move from the top of the map to the bottom in a day's trek. I wanted to check out the new, bigger scale maps and fill in for myself details like fields and walls.

'I love maps. Maps have always been my favourite literature. I would always rather study a map than read a book, even a map of a place I have never been to and never will. Have you ever tried to draw a map? There's nothing like it for sheer fascination and concentration. I like to follow streams up from the valley to their source and if I cannot do it on the ground I like to do it on maps. I like to stand on a summit and see the valley below as on a map.

'Sometimes I think I should have taken up cartography as a career, instead of which I turned out to be an accountant, sitting in an office all day, with figures that passed in and out of the mind. The figures that stay there permanently are Scafell Pike 3206, Bowfell 2960, Pillar 2927.'

He didn't start off with the idea of publishing a book. He had never written anything in his life before. His professional work was with figures. He did it simply for the pleasure of doing it, something for when his fell walking days were over and he could relive all the memories. 'I thought they would be nice to read when I was an old man. Now I am an old man I never read them. I'm too busy.'

On the fells, as he went around making notes for himself, he was continually being asked by other walkers where paths led to, what was this and what was over there. He began to realise that other people might perhaps like some advice, but he never thought of submitting his notes to a publisher. 'I knew they wouldn't be interested in something handwritten.' So eventually he went to a local printer in Kendal, taking with him £30, and asked him if he could do him a few copies. The printer, Sandy Hewitson (now dead), said that he would have to print 2000 copies to make it economic – and that would cost £900. Wainwright didn't have that sort of money.

But Hewitson was so interested personally in the guides that he said he would print them at his own expense, and then wait for them to be sold before being paid. 'Over the next two years, I sent him nine cheques for £100 each as the books began to sell. During those two years, he never once reminded me of the debt.'

He was helped with the selling of the first book by the local librarian in Kendal, Henry Marshall. It was he who advised Wainwright not to have his name on the book as both author and publisher. Even though he was his own publisher (and remained so for the next four books), booksellers might think it smacked of amateurism. 'So I borrowed his name and put it on as the publisher. It had more dignity than mine. I especially liked the Henry.' Together they spent a day going round bookshops in the Lakes. They got orders of 250 and then sat back, waiting for repeats which at first came in very slowly. By the time they did, Wainwright was well on with the next book. 'Between finishing one book and starting the next, I paused only to fill my pipe.'

By being his own publisher, he was able to produce the books exactly as he wanted them. He wrote and drew every page by hand, using a steel nib and pen, laying out every word and drawing as he wanted it. He has a phobia about never breaking words, which regularly happens at the end of lines of printed type, so if you look carefully at his very neat, absolutely symmetrical handwriting you'll see him fiddling the spaces so that he can squeeze all the words in each line. It took him a long time to perfect his own style – in fact he scrapped the first hundred pages after six months and started again. He wanted it to look

ASCENT FROM WASDALE HEAD
via PIERS GILL

3,000 feet of ascent
3¾ miles
(from Wastwater Hotel)

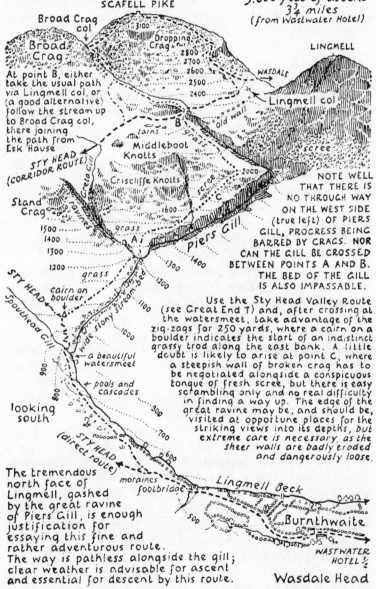

SCAFELL PIKE

Broad Crag col

Broad Crag

Dropping Crag

3100
2800
2700
2600
2500
2400

LINGMELL

WASDALE

Lingmell col

At point B, either take the usual path via Lingmell col, or (a good alternative) follow the stream up to Broad Crag col, there joining the path from Esk Hause

old wall

scree

STY HEAD (CORRIDOR ROUTE)

tarns

grass

Middleboot Knolts

Criscliffe Knolts

scree

2000

Greta Gill ravines

Stand Crag

1500
1400
1300

1200

grass

Piers Gill

1600

C

A i

1300

1400

grass

cairn on boulder

1200

1100

wide stony stream-bed

STY HEAD

Sprouthead Gill

1000

← a beautiful watersmeet

900

← pools and cascades

800

looking south

STY HEAD (direct route)

700

300

600

NOTE WELL THAT THERE IS NO THROUGH WAY ON THE WEST SIDE (true left) OF PIERS GILL, PROGRESS BEING BARRED BY CRAGS. NOR CAN THE GILL BE CROSSED BETWEEN POINTS A AND B. THE BED OF THE GILL IS ALSO IMPASSABLE.

Use the Sty Head Valley Route (see Great End 7) and, after crossing at the watersmeet, take advantage of the zig-zags for 250 yards, where a cairn on a boulder indicates the start of an indistinct grassy trod along the east bank. A little doubt is likely to arise at point C, where a steepish wall of broken crag has to be negotiated alongside a conspicuous tongue of fresh scree, but there is easy scrambling only and no real difficulty in finding a way up. The edge of the great ravine may be, and should be, visited at opportune places for the striking views into its depths, but extreme care is necessary, as the sheer walls are badly eroded and dangerously loose.

The tremendous north face of Lingmell, gashed by the great ravine of Piers Gill, is enough justification for essaying this fine and rather adventurous route. The way is pathless alongside the gill; clear weather is advisable for ascent and essential for descent by this route.

moraines footbridge

Lingmell Beck

500

Burnthwaite

WASTWATER HOTEL ½

Wasdale Head

A page from *A Pictorial Guide to the Lakeland Fells*, Book Four, by Alfred Wainwright.

as neat as printer's type – with straight alignments at both the right and the left-hand side.

Each page, exactly as he has drawn it, is then photographed so that the end result is like an engraving. 'I was determined that no printer should interfere with my lay-outs. I didn't want some clumsy publisher crowding my drawings.

'Naturally, I did it all in pen and ink because I've always been a pen and ink man. I was trained to believe that accountancy was an art and it seemed to my juvenile reasoning in those far-off days that accountants must therefore be artists. I remember being told that every page of my ledgers should be fit for framing. I never saw anything that came out of a machine that was. Machines are monsters and produce little horrors.'

But he does use one machine – a camera. He admits that the drawings are a bit of a cheat because he never does them on the spot. 'Not for me the day-long vigil on a tuft of grass waiting for the right conditions. Not for me all that carting up easel and equipment. Life was too short. It took enough effort to get myself up on the hills without burdening myself with impedimenta. No, a quick halt and a clear photograph were enough for me. I am a cheapjack at the drawing game but I'm sure fidelity to the scene has not suffered. I then drew the mountains later, not in a romantic and imaginative sense, but as they are, based on my photographs.'

He finished his self-imposed task in exactly thirteen years as planned, in 1965, with the completion of Book Seven in the series, the *Western Fells*. These fells were the furthest away from his home in Kendal and he saved them till the end, being the only ones he couldn't get at in a day. To finish them off he had to stay in digs for a week in Whitehaven.

'I was always careful at the end of each book to say that the series would be completed "all being well". I didn't anticipate a loss of interest or enthusiasm. What I had in mind was illness, accident, death. Failing eyesight or a tremble in the right hand were all possibilities I feared. I needn't have worried. I have never been ill. I never missed a minute at work in forty-six years' service. I have now reached an age when my non-walking, car-owning contemporaries are dropping like flies. Walking is almost the only exercise that a man can indulge without loss of facility from childhood to the grave. It's a natural function of the body to walk. It isn't to drive a car.'

However, looking back now at his fell guides, he often wonders how he managed to get round them all. To me it is astonishing. It's awkward enough when you can drive, getting back and forward to the places where you want to climb, but doing the entire Lake District *without* a car would seem impossibly perverse.

Wainwright himself did it all on local buses – which he couldn't do now, not with local buses being withdrawn almost every day. 'I started at 8.30 in the morning, getting the bus to Keswick. Then I changed for the Penrith bus, if I was doing the northern fells. I'd get off at Mungrisdale road end and walk the four miles to Mosedale and then get started on High Pike or wherever. I rarely got started walking later than 10.30.

'I never missed the bus home in the evening in the thirteen years. I was always at the road end twenty minutes before the bus was due, just in case my watch had gone wrong during the day. The slower the bus the better I liked it. There's nothing more restful than a stopping bus.'

As the series progressed, he began to be accosted on the fells and asked if he was Wainwright. At the end of each book, he'd always say which section he was next working on, so some fans were soon on the lookout for him, but he did everything he could to avoid them.

'If there's one thing I cannot stand,' so he wrote in *Fell-wanderer*, 'it's someone looking over my shoulder. If there's another, it's silly questions. If there's another, it's being pointed out. I suffer fools badly. So I had to be anonymous and what a furtive character I became. I like a fell to myself, particularly a summit. If a summit was already occupied, I had to hang about in the vicinity until it was vacated. If others were coming along my path I wandered off for a while, behind a boulder, to avoid conversation. I kept hearing stories of other solitary walkers, poor lads, who were having a rough time of it. "Mr Wainwright, I presume?" But I did pretty well myself. If challenged, my answer depended on the time and the sex of the questioner. Yes, I made the acquaintance of some nice ladies.

'There was one lady, however, I owe a profound apology to. It happened on the summit of High Stile on a glorious Sunday afternoon, July 26, 1964. She was seated by the cairn and accompanied by a small boy and had apparently come up from Buttermere. I was in a desperate hurry to catch a bus at Ennerdale

Bridge and there was no time to wait for her to depart. Conditions were ideal for two photographs I needed to complete my panorama of the summit. I sat down a few yards away and got my pictures. She said, "Are you Mr Wainwright." "No," I said. "Well," she said, "I know he's working in this area at present; I do so want to meet him." I was a bit sorry then. My chances with the ladies were few and far between, but there was that confounded bus. "No," I said again, "but I know who you mean." Then I went off. I'm sorry, lass, whoever you are. There were others to whom I said yes, others to whom I said no. People in parties always got a no. I adopted the name of A. Walker which I thought very clever. The A here can stand for Aloysius, if you want ...'

After the first four books in the series, which he himself published, the paper work of being the publisher was becoming very arduous, so when his printer was taken over by the local Kendal newspaper, the *Westmorland Gazette*, he decided to go with them and they became his publisher, which they still are.

After his final book in the fell guides was finished in 1965, he was straight into more books, producing guides and drawings on other parts of the Lakes, such as the coast, the limestone region and the lower fells (suitable for OAPs). He has also moved to other fell regions, such as the Yorkshire Dales and Scotland. All together, he has so far produced twenty-nine books.

Perhaps his best known book, after the Lakeland fell guides, is his guide to the Pennine Way. This came out in 1968 and in ten years has sold 100,000 copies. At the end of it, in one of his usual little personal pieces, he said that whoever did the whole walk and got to the end at Kirk Yeaton could have a drink on him. Every year, the publican of the Border Hotel sends him a bill for the free pints he's given to Pennine Way walkers. Last year, Wainwright had to fork out £400. 'It's quite shocking the price of beer now. Back in 1968 beer was only 1/6d a pint. Now it's four shillings! But I don't really regret the promise. If you've walked 270 miles, a free pint is a nice thing to have at the end.'

At the present time, he's working on two more books about the Dales and the final two in his series on Scottish mountains. Naturally, at the age of seventy-one, he's not managing person- ally to climb all the Scottish mountains – getting helpers to do the more awkward routes for him – but he's doing all the drawings himself. After Scotland, he plans a book on the Welsh mountains. The real deterrent so far is English as she is spoken in Wales. 'The voice of Clive Jenkins gives me the willies. But I wouldn't expect to find him holding forth on the Glyders.'

He's brought out several books of drawings and photographs, without any words, admitting very honestly each time that these are illustrations left over from previous books, but his readers still rush to buy them. He did a book of drawings in 1975 of local villages, called *Westmorland Heritage*, brought out to commemorate the end of Westmorland, which was then disappearing to become part of Cumbria. He thought the market would be very limited for it, as there aren't all that many Westmerians around, and decided to do only 1000 copies. The price had to be £11, for such a small print, but he decided to sign each one and make it a limited edition, never to be reprinted. Two years later, copies of the book were changing hands at £85 each.

The day I was with him he'd just brought out another book, drawings of nineteenth-century Kendal. He'd based them on old photographs which had recently been discovered, glass negatives which were too worn to reproduce as photographs. That afternoon his wife was busy hanging his hundred or so originals in Abbot Hall Art Gallery, getting ready for an exhibition the next day. I went along later to see her and bought three of them – and to my surprise found I had to sign the cheque to 'Animal Rescue Cumbria'.

In Book One of his fell guides he explains in his personal note at the end that he wasn't doing the book for material gain – just for his own pleasure, to bring the fells to his own fireplace. By Book Seven he has to admit in his final personal note that things have rather changed. 'Unexpectedly, it has been a profitable venture for me in terms of money, bringing me a small fortune through the continued support of the many kind readers who have both bought and recommended the books. It is money I have not spent and do not want. These books have been a labour of love. I have had full reward in a thousand happy days on the fells. One surely does not wish to be paid in cash for love-letters.'

He considers he has quite enough for his own personal needs, from his local government pension and his old-age pension, to look after himself and his charming wife Betty. Instead, he has devoted himself to helping animal charities. His biggest project is to acquire a farm in the Lakes somewhere which will have land and a full-time staff and be a sanctuary for stray or unwanted animals.

'I have more compassion for animals than people. I became disenchanted with the human race after the introduction of myxomatosis, battery farming and vivisection. I've never yet met an animal who was deceitful or dishonest but I've met too many humans like that.'

It is in a way fitting, as he points out in one of his books, that the proceeds from his fell guides should go back on to the fells. 'Every true fellwalker develops a liking and compassion for birds and animals, the solitary walkers especially for they are his only companions, and it seemed to be appropriate that the windfall should be used to provide a refuge in Lakeland where ailing and distressed creatures can be brought for care and attention.'

On the official writing paper of Animal Rescue Cumbria it has his name on as chairman – A. Wainwright, MBE, MA. He's a bit embarrassed about the MA, and wasn't very keen to talk about it.

He got the MA, an honorary one, in 1974 from Newcastle University, but didn't care for all the palaver and dressing up he had to go through. Later, Salford University offered him an MA which he refused and he also refused when Lancaster University did even better and offered him a D.Litt. He refused that when he heard that the biology department was conducting experiments on live animals.

Over the years, readers are continually writing for advice on walking. He made it clear in *Fellwanderer* that he considers such questions pretty potty. 'It amused me to see all the articles and treatises and even books written on the subject of walking on fells. Goodness me, if a person needs a manual of instruction on walking he should stay at home. Our mothers taught us, remember? In a city street it's a matter of staying balanced on the feet while moving forward, just as we were taught as children. On a fell it's a matter of staying balanced on the feet while moving forward, just as we were taught as children. What else is there to learn? Nothing.'

He rejects all notions of it being a dangerous sport. 'It is not a sport at all. It's a pleasure. Fellwalking isn't dicing with death. It is a glorious enjoyment of life. Accidents happen only to those who walk clumsily. A good walker moves silently and is a joy to behold. Clumsy walkers are often verbally noisy, a common characteristic of the inefficient, but it is their boots that cause most clatter. A good walker will climb Scafell Pike from Sty Head and hardly disturb a single stone. A bad walker will leave a trail of debris. Their respective journeys through life will be the same.'

The only serious bit of advice he will give, and even then he says it is common-sense, is to try to keep the feet pointing slightly upwards when coming downhill, taking advantage of any tufts or stones to act as a brake. If all else fails, don't be afraid to slide down. 'A walker's best asset can be a tough, rubbery bottom. The posterior is a valuable agent of friction, a sheet anchor with superb resistance to the pull of gravity.'

As for the conventional wisdom, put out in so much of the tourist literature, that you should not venture alone on the fells, he is dead against it. It's excellent advice for those who lack ordinary gumption or are plain daft. If such go on the fells at all, which they shouldn't, they can be further advised to keep themselves in the middle of a big party, hemmed in by the sweating flesh of others. At the end of the day they won't know where they've been and they won't have seen much.

'It is the man or woman who walks alone who enjoys the greatest rewards, and sees and feels and senses the mood of the hills. If a man cannot enjoy his own company, what effect does he think it has on others? I am least lonely when I am alone on the hills and free to indulge my imagination; most lonely in a crowd.'

Wainwright also has some good advice on clothing, with which I'm in complete agreement. His advice is to ignore all advice. 'Comfort is the thing. Wear shoes or sandals or go barefoot if these suit you better than boots. Comfort includes keeping warm and dry but ways of achieving it differ widely. The most ghastly apparitions appear on fells. If sheep didn't have such good manners they would laugh their heads off.

'You see hikers setting forth for a day on the hills burdened as though they were starting a six-month expedition to Antarctica. They are grim and anguished when they ought to be carefree and smiling. The fells are not monsters, but amiable giants. You can romp over them and pull the hairs on their chests and shout in their ears and treat them rough and they don't mind a bit. Go amongst them as you go amongst friends.'

Wainwright, as his readers know, has left instructions in his will for his remains to be scattered on Haystacks, by the side of Innominate Tarn. 'A quiet place, a lonely place. I shall go to it, for the last time, and be carried. Someone who knew me in life will take me and empty me out of a little box and leave me there alone. And if you, dear reader, should get a bit of grit in your boots as you are crossing Haystacks in the years to come, please treat it with respect. It might be me.'

I had a walk around Kendal afterwards, looking at Wainwright's drawings in Abbot Hall Art Gallery. Kendal is well off for galleries and museums, especially in the visual arts, a tradition which dates back to Romney's days. He was born in south Lakeland, at Dalton-in-Furness, but received some early training in Kendal, eventually returning to Kendal where he died in 1802. In his early days, the local quality in Cumberland and Westmorland rallied round and commissioned him, before he moved on to London and painted the stars of the day, such as Lady Hamilton. There are still several families in Cumbria today who have Romney portraits on their walls, particularly the Curwens of Belle Isle and the Howards of Greystoke Castle.

Kendal used to be a very important wool town, a trade that flourished for six centuries. Shakespeare refers to Kendal Green in *Henry IV*. It's a busy, honest, grey-stoned, independent little market town with a population of 21,000. It was the biggest town in Westmorland and still is an administrative centre for Cumbria County Council. It likes to call itself the Gateway to the Lakes, which it is, if you come from the South as most people do, but though it has its share of tourist shops, they're almost incidental to the town's well-being. One feels that Keswick, Windermere and Ambleside would collapse if the tourists decided one year not to come but Kendal would shrug its shoulders and carry on.

The town stands by the River Kent, a dark tough-looking river which always seems to be swollen by flood streams from Kentmere and Longsleddale. The second dominant feature is a one-way system which takes you round and round the river for ever, without actually dropping you where you want to be. At least the local taxi drivers are honest, advising you to walk across the town as it will be quicker. There's the remains of a castle, Kendal Castle, the birthplace of Katherine Parr, one of the wives of Henry VIII. The Parrs, along with the Bellinghams and Stricklands, were for centuries the three ruling families.

I went to visit Sizergh Castle, just south of Kendal, which has been the home of the Stricklands for 700 years. Like other castles in Cumbria, it started as a peel tower to repel the Scots, but its best features are the Tudor Great Hall and Tudor wings, decorated with some very fine early Elizabethan woodwork. The gardens and the castle have an attractive lived-in feeling and many rooms have bits of personal tat, such as old Coronation tickets, locks of people's hair, as well as valuable antiques. In one bedroom there were lots of recent photographs of the present Stricklands and their children, lined up on top of a chest of drawers. There were flowers in the vases and clocks ticking. The castle is owned by the National Trust but still used by some of the family, judging by that bedroom. I asked if any were in residence, but the guide said no. I did meet a real live Strickland once, the Hon. Mabel Strickland, a resolute old lady who lives in Malta. She took me into her garden, grabbed a hen, drew a mark in front of its eyes with a stick and proceeded to hypnotise it.

I went from Sizergh Castle to the little village of Underbarrow, not far away, where I met another formidable old lady who gave us the best tea I've ever had in the Lake District. And I've had more Lake District teas than I've had hot dinners. Mrs Johnstone, aged eighty, runs Tullythwaite House in her own personal country-house style. It's not at all camp, like Sharrow Bay or Miller Howe; just genuinely chintzy. Every old ornament gleams, the elderly furniture is so spick and span. We were led into what looked like her own front parlour. I had my family with me and I worried that she might get upset, in such a sedate setting, by our noisy kids, but she was very welcoming, in a no-nonsense sort of way. She turned other people away at the door as we sat waiting for our tea, though we were the only guests. She only does one sitting and if you're late, too bad. She likes to settle people down and attend to each of them properly and personally. 'We're all just treated like numbers outside today,' she said.

We had got the name out of a guide book, and it was just by luck that we turned up at the correct time. We sat with some trepidation, wondering what sort of tea it would be. She and her daughter-in-law started arriving in stages, building up such a table that our eyes ached at the very sight of it. There was white and brown buttered bread, plum jam, apple turnovers, currant bread, shortbread, coffee cake, hot bilberry pie, ice cream and the main dish, which was fresh salmon and salad. Everything was home-made, even the mayonnaise with the salmon and the ice cream with the bilberry pie. The total charge, for the five of us,

was £12.50. It was incredible. We staggered from the table, determined not to tell anyone, to keep it to ourselves and go back
every month, just to gorge. 'Oh,' she said, clearing the table.
'You haven't tried my cream.'

Back in Kendal itself, I went to get a copy of the *Westmorland
Gazette*, hot from the presses. It's a more contemporary-looking
paper than the *Keswick Reminder*, the Lake District's most
archaic-looking publication, but it still has an attractive old-
fashioned look, with none of those ego-tripping by-lines which
London papers throw over even the smallest story.

The *Westmorland Gazette*'s offices are right in the middle of
Kendal, in Stricklandgate, and you get to them through a
stationery shop. At the front, they're selling cards and envelopes
while at the back of the shop a lady writes down your classified
advertisements. Such a humble facade hides a very prosperous
printing and newspaper business. They publish all Wainwright's
guides, from their printing works behind the shop, which must
be a little gold mine, but the *Gazette* itself does very well, having
a circulation of 31,000.

It's one of the few newspapers in the country which doesn't
have a seasonal sales drop in July and August. It's all those
tourists, of course. They rush up the motorway from darkest
Lancashire, fall in love with the Lakes and make a grab for the
nearest local paper on the way home, which usually happens to
be the *Gazette*. They then sit at home, devouring it for the house
adverts, hoping for that little cottage, needs some improvement,
v. desirable, no mod. cons, a snip at £39,900 ...

The real reason I went to prowl round the *Gazette*'s offices was
all thanks to Wordsworth. You will remember that his young
friend De Quincey rather disgraced himself, knocking down the
moss hut at Dove Cottage, knocking up a local girl and getting
her pregnant, and that it led to the estrangement between them.
Well, Wordsworth didn't completely abandon De Quincey. In
1818 he got him a very nice little job, editor of the *Westmorland
Gazette*.

The paper had been created just two months earlier as a
deliberate political manoeuvre by the Lowther family and its
Tory supporters, including Wordsworth, who were fed up with
the *Kendal Chronicle*, the only other newspaper in Westmorland,
which always supported the rival Whig faction.

Wordsworth had been sent by the Lowthers to the editor of the

Kendal Chronicle to persuade him to deal fairly with the Tory case, but had failed, so the Lowthers decided the only thing to do was to start their own paper. The official purpose, so they said, was to 'counteract the vile effects upon the lower orders produced by the *Kendal Chronicle*'.

It looks as if Wordsworth himself was offered but declined the job as first editor. He tried hard with his London newspaper contacts, writing to them for any suggestions for a likely editor. The person who was initially brought up from London lasted only a couple of months and then De Quincey took over on a salary of a guinea per week, thanks to Wordsworth putting in a good, if slightly guarded, word. 'The editorship of the new Kendal paper has passed into the hands of a most able man, one of my particular friends, but whether he is fit (I mean on the score of punctuality) for such a service, remains to be proved.'

Judging by the early editions, which are still in their files in Kendal, De Quincey certainly had a streak of good yellow journalism in him, filling the pages with gruesome court cases, 'orrible crimes, all described in lurid terms. He did his own leaders at first, turning out such fire-eating political attacks on the opposition that even Lord Lowther began to get worried. 'I think our own Kendal paper is now getting too libellous. Last week's specimen is certainly a most blackguard production.'

After a quick initial burst, De Quincey displayed his bad habits of unpunctuality which Wordsworth had feared – even worse, he stopped turning up in the office and edited the paper from Dove Cottage in Grasmere. The paper's Minute Book of 29 June 1819 records how the proprietors reprimanded him – complaining that he wasn't in regular communication with the printer and was missing the latest London news. They warned him to 'prevent a recurrence of that inconvenience which they conceive has arisen from his residing at so great a distance from the office'.

In July, De Quincey announced in the columns of the paper that he had received a letter from one of the proprietors which he purposed 'to notice fully next week'. That would have been great fun to read but alas he never made it. As still often happens today, when there's a row between proprietor and bolshie editor, the proprietors have the last word. They got his resignation out of him before he could reply and by November he'd gone, after only fourteen months in charge, leaving the paper with a loss of £42 on its first year of trading.

'De Quincey was a dead loss from the beginning,' said Mr William Gardner, the *Gazette*'s present editor. They seem almost ashamed to have had him as their early editor. When the paper did its 150th anniversary edition, back in 1968, they referred to the 'dark mind of the opium eater'.

Drugs, you see. No one wants to be associated with them. Wordsworth had at least been kind, helping out an old friend. But then William Wordsworth was a kind man.

24
DEATH OF WORDSWORTH

Last days at Rydal.Dorothy and Dora.
Mr Wordsworth dies.Rydal today.

WORDSWORTH WAS SO VERY KIND TO STRANGERS THAT, by the 1840s, Rydal Mount had become something of a show place, part of the tourist trail. On show would be William Wordsworth, acting the part of William Wordsworth, Poet Laureate, and he was very good at it, ever willing to conduct parties, pointing out the sights which everyone had read about, such as Dorothy sitting in the garden, or the views described in his poetry, which everybody had learned at school.

There are many contemporary accounts by people who took in the Wordsworth home on their Lakes tour. A young girl, who visited the house in August 1845, recorded how she had been in the fifth party that morning, while two carriages still waited at the gate, 'filled with company come to pay the poet a visit'. Wordsworth wasn't interested in who the visitors were, their names or where they'd come from. He saw them as part of an ever-changing audience whom he could address. 'It was a sort of thinking aloud,' so another visitor described, 'a perpetual purring of satisfaction. It seems as natural to him to talk as to breathe. He is by nature audible as well as visible and goes on thus uttering his being just as a fountain continues to flow or a star to shine.'

Friends, or friends of friends, would get the number one tour, which meant a conducted monologue round the house, though very often he would mix the guests up, by not listening to the introductions. Harriet Martineau, an eminent literary lady who lived nearby in Ambleside, one of many literary types attracted to the Lakes by Wordsworth, sent round two of her friends one day who wanted specifically to hear his views on education. He gave them his outdoor, talking-to-strangers recital, ignoring all their questions. Later, when he heard that two educationalists were in the district, he sent for them, not realising he'd already met them.

It was estimated by Harriet Martineau that around 500 visitors a year were received by Wordsworth at Rydal Mount. If the poet happened to be out, the servants were trained to take them round. If anyone enquired where the poet's study was, hoping no doubt to get into the house, they would be told that the master 'studied in the fields'.

He was still as shabbily dressed as ever, but he'd taken to a shepherd's style of dressing, with rough plaid trousers and a black handkerchief as a neck tie. He'd allowed his hair to grow rather long at the back, so his appearance had now become quite distinctive, if rather eccentric.

On one occasion, a visitor who had travelled in the East managed to break into Wordsworth's usual flow, all about the joyous lakes and the foaming mountain streams, and had the daring to say that, personally, he preferred the solitude of the Arabian desert. 'My mountain blood was up,' so Wordsworth related later. 'I said "I'm sorry you don't like this, perhaps I can show you what will please you more." I strode away and led him from crag to crag, hill to vale, for about six hours, till I thought I should have to bring him home, he was so tired.'

In his own letters he records long fell walks until late into his seventies and in 1845, when he was seventy-five he described how one day he helped with the hay in his field from half past eight in the morning till one o'clock. This field, just beside his garden, was bought by him in 1826 when it looked as though the owners of Rydal Mount were going to evict him, wanting the house for their own family. Wordsworth threatened to build a brand new house in the field, right beside the house, and they relented. He later gave the field to Dora and they knew it as Dora's field, which is its name to this day.

On his seventy-fourth birthday, on 7 April 1844, there was a huge party given in the garden at Rydal Mount to which all the children in the neighbourhood were invited, some 300 of them, and they each got an orange, a piece of gingerbread and a hard-boiled pace egg. (Cumbrian children still get pace eggs at Easter time.) The treat was paid for by Miss Fenwick, yet another lady friend who was a Wordsworth devotee and close friend of the family in the later years. Wordsworth did his bit, though, joining in all the fun and romping with the children. Wordsworth to the end was a great lover of children, and all his contemporaries noted it, but was he still in touch with the ordinary people in his old age? Had he perhaps moved away from the rustic characters, the rural workers, he had written about so often in his early poetry?

One of the most interesting bits of journalism which the great and good Canon Rawnsley did was to go round, some thirty years after Wordsworth's death, and interview all the people he could find who ever knew or worked with the Wordsworths. This was his famous 'Reminiscences of Wordsworth among the Peasantry of Westmoreland' with which he delighted the members of Keswick Lecture Society and which he later published.

One of the people Canon Rawnsley went to see was a publican who in his youth had been the gardener's boy at Rydal.

'He was ter'ble thrang with visitors and folks, but if he could git awa fra them for a spell, he was out upon his gres walk; and then he would set his head a bit forrad and put his hands behint his back. And then he would start a bumming and it was bum, bum, bum, bum, stop; then bum, bum, bum, reet down till t'other end; and then he'd set down and git a bit o' paper out and write a bit; and then he git up, and goa on bumming. I suppose, ya kna, the bumming helped him out a bit. His lips was always goain' whoale time he was upon the gres walk.'

A butcher said that he had delivered meat to the Wordsworths' door four times a week as a lad, but he never spoke to him. 'He'd pass you, same as if yan was nobbut a stean.' A waller said much the same. 'He wozn't a man as said a deal to common fwoak, but he talked a deal to hiseen. I often seead his lips a ganin.'

The only workman who did get much chat out of him said he was either laying down the law on chimneys or complaining because he didn't want things altered. They all remember him for walking on roads and not the mountains. Another said that, as a boy, Wordsworth had asked him one day to clear the snow off the ice so he could go skating, but he didn't tip him anything. However, Wordsworth fell over as soon as he started skating, so the boy had a good laugh.

According to all their memories, it was the two women in the household, Mary and Dorothy, who appeared to be the really clever ones. They found Mrs Wordsworth, though plain and stiff, very good at accountancy and looking after the household. 'Miss Dorothy, she was a ter'ble clever woman. She did as much of his poetry as he did and went completely off it at the latter end, wi' studying it, I suppose.'

Although Canon Rawnsley had gone to talk to them about Wordsworth, almost every one brought the subject round to Hartley Coleridge, or Li'le Hartley as he was known. They all liked him so much better. 'Wudsworth was quite different fra li'le Hartley. Hartley allus hed a bit of a smile or a twinkle in his faace, but Wudsworth was not loveable i't faace by nea means.

'There's nea doot but what he was fond of quality, and quality was fond of him, but he niver exed fowk aboot their wark, nor noticed t' flocks or nowt; not but what he was kind man if fwoaks was sick or taen badly.'

None of them had ever read his poetry, or knew anything about it, though several said they liked poetry themselves, the sort with jokes in. 'You cud tell fra t' man's faace his potry wad nivver hev nea laugh in it. I don't mind he iver laugh in his life, but he'd smile times or two.'

Random memories, recalled later, aren't all that reliable of course, though I'm sure Rawnsley got honest replies from the peasants he met, such as they saw it. Cumbrians pride themselves on not dissembling. Professor Geoffrey Tillotson thinks the memories give a good account of Wordsworth in his middle and later years, living in a region but not fully of it, withdrawn from the sort of people who'd inspired poems like 'The Idiot Boy' and 'Goody Blake'.

From the evidence of his own letters, Wordsworth prided himself on being very concerned with anyone who was ill, and always gave to beggars, sometimes the same ones twice a day, but it was obvious that he really preferred the world as it had been, in its old class divisions. One should help the poor and deprived, of course, but they were still a different sort of people. He was completely against things like the Reform Bill or campaigns to give the working classes more power and freedom.

He was an old man by now, understandably missing the former days, upset as many were by the enormous social and industrial changes which had happened in such a short time. With old age, a certain melancholy crept into his spirit.

He went on a long trip down his beloved Duddon Valley in 1844 (his last expedition in that area) with Mary and some friends. They stayed the first night at an inn at Ulpha and the party was surprised to find that he was first up in the morning, already walking down the road. He hadn't slept well, so he told one of the party, because of the memories of the old days. 'When I thought of those who had passed away, Coleridge, Southey and many others, while I am left with my infirmities, if not sins, in full consciousness, how could I sleep?'

The first death in his own household was Sarah Hutchinson's in 1835. The whole house had been struck down with flu and Dora and Dorothy had looked the most seriously ill, then Sarah suddenly weakened and died very quickly of what looks like rheumatic fever. She'd made her home with them for thirty years and gave pleasure to all of them, and to the Coleridge and Southey households. She possessed a quality which Coleridge, her devoted but unsuccessful suitor, once called 'entertainingness'.

Dorothy physically recovered from the worst of her illness, but not mentally. From then on, for the next twenty years of her life, her mind and her memory had gone. She had long spells of crouching over the fire, both winter and summer, in unbearable heat. William thought at first it was the shock of Sarah's death which had deranged her, but it was probably a coincidence that it had happened around the same time. It seems to me, reading Dorothy's Journals, written all those years earlier, that she was never completely mentally stable. All those headaches and hysteria were caused by more than just a passion for her brother. Gradually, the household got over the shock and became used to her as an invalid. She eventually became confined to a wheelchair but was often left in the garden and introduced to visitors.

In 1837 Wordsworth's beloved daughter Dora was proposed to by a gentleman called Edward Quillinan. He was a retired Irish army captain who had formerly lived at Rydal with his wife and two daughters (one of them named Rotha, after the river). They'd become family friends of the Wordsworths but he had moved away after the death of his wife, living in the South of England or in Portugal, helping his brother with the family wine firm. He was a person of some charm but with no settled home, no visible means of support, no profession apart from a bit of poetry and some translations from the Portuguese. He came back occasionally to the Lakes, which was how he met Dora again, though he became rather suspect as there was talk of shady financial deals involving his dead wife's family money.

Dora was by now thirty-four. She had devoted her life so far to her father and the family and she very much wanted to marry Quillinan. Wordsworth was aghast and refused his consent to the engagement. The rows between him and Quillinan went on for four years, with Dora and other members of the family pleading with Wordsworth to change his mind. He maintained he wasn't being possessive, devoted though he was to his beloved daughter. He was thinking of her good. She'd always been delicate and marrying Quillinan would be giving his daughter up to 'a rough chance'. That was a phrase he actually used in a letter to Quillinan himself, which naturally led to more furious correspondence.

Dora was eventually married in 1841 in Bath, with brother John performing the marriage ceremony. Wordsworth had been talked into it by the family, and by Miss Fenwick, but was still very upset by it all. He went down for the marriage but at the last moment he couldn't face going to the church itself, exactly as Dorothy had done on William's own wedding day, thirty-nine years earlier. He bid Dora farewell, in an emotional scene, and then stayed indoors till it was over.

Once the marriage had taken place, Wordsworth stood by Quillinan, even when he ended up in court for fraud (of which he was cleared) and Quillinan himself proved a loyal son-in-law. But Dora's health was not improved by the wandering life Quillinan led her, though she did feel better during a spell in Portugal. They returned in 1846 to live in the Lakes, renting a house near Rydal, much to her father's relief. But in 1847 Dora caught a bad cold while staying in Carlisle, helping brother Willy to furnish a home for his bride. She never recovered and died several months later, after great suffering. Wordsworth was distraught, overwhelmed with grief for many months.

In 1849, Hartley Coleridge died at Nab Cottage, beside Rydal Water. The Wordsworths had always been fond of him and helped him in times of trouble. Wordsworth chose a site for him in Grasmere churchyard. 'Let him lie by us,' he said. 'He would have wished it.' He made the sexton measure out not only Hartley's grave but one for himself and for Mary, pointing to a spot beside Dora's grave.

Wordsworth made his last trip outside the Lake District in June 1849, when he and Mary went to visit relations in Great Malvern. They came back to Oxenholme on the express train from Birmingham, but at Oxenholme they had a two-hour delay for the Windermere train. Then when it came, it was absolutely crammed with holidaymakers, the sort Wordsworth had always dreaded. Many of them were coming to see the Lakes that Wordsworth had made famous, possibly hoping to catch a glimpse of the poet himself. Wordsworth was by now seventy-nine and such a journey proved very tiring.

The following March, after a walk from his home to White Moss Common, he caught pleurisy and never recovered. Mary came to his bedside to tell him he was dying. 'William,' she said, 'you are going to Dora.' He didn't die that night and the next day, when a niece came into the room, he woke up and said, 'Is that Dora?'

Wordsworth died on 23 April 1850, Shakespeare's and England's day. He had celebrated his eightieth birthday just a couple of weeks previously. Dorothy temporarily regained her sanity when Mary told her that William had gone to Dora. There was no outbreak of anger or distress. When she was wheeled in her chair to where he lay she quietly murmured, 'O death, where is thy sting? O grave, where is thy victory?' Dorothy lasted another five years, dying in 1855 at eighty-three; Mary lived until 1859, dying of old age at eighty-eight.

Mary's last literary task, on William's death, was to take his autobiographical poem from its resting place, where it had lain untouched for eleven years, and prepare it for the publisher. The dedication was to S. T. Coleridge, as it had been when he'd begun it some fifty years previously, but it had never been given a title by William. It was Mary who named it 'The Prelude'.

Rydal Water is just a little lake, a twin sister for Grasmere next door, nothing like big brother Windermere further along which can more than stand up for itself, despite the hordes. Wordsworth wrote a lot of verse about Rydal Water, all about it being soft as a cloud, tender green, dewy twilight, dazzling sheen, staid simplicity, all that sort of stuff. He even wrote one to the laurels on Rydal called 'Adieu, Rydalian Laurels!'

If only he could see it now, or even worse, hear it now. The most horrible road in the Lake District, the A591, takes the millions tearing right along the lakeside, from Windermere and Ambleside up to Keswick, the summer shuttle beloved by all day trippers.

Little Rydal seems somehow diminished, taken over, eaten up, dismissed in a flash by the road thundering by, yet you could still take photographs and make it look as pretty as ever. From the right position, avoiding the road, it does *look* very much the same as when Wordsworth saw it last, with very few buildings in sight, but if he had to come down the little lane from his house today, to sit awhile on his favourite seat by the lakeside, he'd get knocked over by a host of golden Cortinas, beside the lake, beneath the trees, roaring and charging in the carbon monoxide breeze.

I booked in for the night at Nab Cottage, a little guest house I had passed many times on my journeys and had always thought an attractive place – but what a noise they must have to put up with from that road. It's halfway along the banks of Rydal Water, a fantastic setting with beautiful views from all around. From the back of the cottage you rise steeply up to Nab Scar. Viewed from the other side of the lake, from Loughrigg Fell, it looks like a child's painting of the perfect cottage.

This cottage was De Quincey's wife's home and De Quincey himself lived here for a while. Hartley Coleridge lodged here during the last years of his life, dying in an upper room. It's a long, low cottage with church-like pointed windows and a plaque above the porch dated 1702.

I'd had a marvellous day in hot sun walking on White Moss Common, my copy of Dorothy's Journal in hand, looking for her favourite spots, watching her trying to describe that subtle blend of colour that you get on a hot day in the Lakes, a colour that in the end becomes no colour because it blends into one continuous hazy rainbow.

Tony Hunt and his wife Wendy and two children had recently come from Singapore, where he'd been teaching, and had just taken Nab Cottage on a long lease, their first experience of the guest house business. She was doing the cooking, breakfast and dinner only, and he was the waiter and general manager, though at the same time he was still teaching part-time, travelling down to Lancaster three days a week to take a drama class.

It was the cheapest place I stayed in all year, £7 for dinner, bed and breakfast. Naturally, the food wasn't Miller Howe or Sharrow Bay quality, but was simple and very homely. They don't have a licence, which keeps down one's bill, but most guests go up the road after dinner to have a drink at the Glen Rothay Hotel near Rydal Mount.

None of the guests I spoke to were aware of Nab Cottage's literary connections. Tony Hunt, being an English graduate from Leeds, was well informed, though he wasn't such a fan as I am of De Quincey's prose. He maintained that at one time De Quincey bought the cottage for £2500 which was news to me, but he couldn't remember where he got the information from.

Despite my worries, I had a perfect night's sleep. The traffic seemed to stop miraculously about seven in the evening and I heard nothing all night. Next morning, before breakfast, I walked round Rydal Water, a mystical walk in a dreamy dawn with mayflies wakening, cuckoos calling and little black slugs glistening on the paths. It was bluebell time and on Loughrigg Terrace they looked like an ethereal blanket that had dropped in the night, an unreal colour, more purple than blue. I thought once again how a modern colour photograph can never do the Lakes justice, except on a chocolate box.

My main object in visiting Rydal was to go and see Rydal Mount. There's not much else to see in the way of buildings as there's not really a village, just a church and a few houses, but the church is worth a visit as Wordsworth helped to choose the site for it. Behind the church is Dora's field which was left to the National Trust in 1933 by Gordon Wordsworth, the poet's grandson. In the spring, it's a mass of flowers, especially daffodils.

Rydal Mount is a lovely surprise. You can understand how pleased the Wordsworths were to move into it, after all the problems with their Grasmere houses, and why they stayed there for over thirty-seven years. It's rather elegant, in a restrained way. The rooms are light and airy, gracious and spacious. The drawing room is bigger than it was in Wordsworth's day, having been joined on to the library in 1968, but it's very easy to imagine the sort of entertaining which Wordsworth delighted in. 'In the room where I am dictating we had three days ago a dance, forty Beaus and Belles besides Matrons, Spinsters and Greybeards ... tomorrow in this same room we are to muster for a venison feast.'

Rydal Mount is one of the newest homes to open to the public. It's an upstart, really, in the Lakeland tourist stakes, compared with Dove Cottage which has been cramming them in for decades. Rydal Mount was in private hands until it was bought by Mary Henderson and opened to the public for the first time in April 1970, on the bi-centenary of the poet's birth. Mary Henderson is a direct descendant of Wordsworth (being his great-great-granddaughter) and lives in Winchelsea, Sussex, but she and her family spend many weeks there every year, using the house as their Lakes home. It's been her own private bit of initiative, opening up the house, though one day she would like to hand it all over to a trust.

One hopes that Rydal, Cockermouth and Dove Cottage will be all owned by the same trust one day, or at least supervised as one. It's silly that they should each be separately owned and organised and in some ways run in competition. Wordsworth scholars who come from all over the world to visit the Lakes and see his homes, and for that matter the passing tourists coming in out of the rain, would like to know about the other homes and have easy access. Behind each other's backs they mutter that at Dove Cottage they never direct people to Rydal, and at Rydal they say much the same. They could pool Wordsworth postcards, pamphlets, books, tickets and all the other Wordsworth memorabilia. Rydal Mount, for example, sells Wordsworth pencils (7p), ashtrays (55p) and mugs (60p). Think how bulk buying would bring the prices down. Anyway, this is a happy book so we won't go into little rows and rivalries.

The resident curators at Rydal Mount are a married couple, both called Pat Dane. (He is Patrick and she is Patricia.) Mr and Mrs Dane came to Rydal in 1975 after they had seen an advert for the job in *The Times*. He was formerly a Lt Commander, RN. They had been a running a small hotel in Cornwall. 'Oh heck,' said Mrs Dane, showing me round the house, 'I just got tired of cooking. We tried to work for the National Trust but there were no vacancies, then this came up. We thought we'd have a jolly good go at getting it, as it sounded so right for us, and we did. My husband now knows a lot about Wordsworth. He learns very quickly. I don't know a *great* deal.'

In the doorway of Rydal Mount are some tiles on the floor given to Wordsworth by his great friend, Henry Crabb Robinson. They spell the word – Salve – a smart greeting for all classically trained visitors. It's fading slightly and it looks a bit like Save, though Mrs Dane cares for it well. There's some fine furniture in the house and a surprising amount of Wordsworth belongings, considering they were late into the Wordsworth market, particularly some good portraits – of Wordsworth, Dorothy, Coleridge, Christopher Wordsworth, Queen Victoria and the Prince of Wales (presented to William by the Queen when he became Poet Laureate) and Robert Burns (presented to William by Burns's sons). The four-and-a-half-acre garden is kept very much as the Wordsworths had it.

Their yearly total of visitors is about 33,000, roughly half that of Dove Cottage, but they're the only Wordsworth home that lays on teas and coffees, a nice touch. 'I worry in the busy times if I've said the same thing to the same group, but I do try to vary my talk if I can. It's basically the same. I ask them first if they know much about Wordsworth. Some couldn't care less about him. Others are only interested in the house and furniture. Some have just come out of the train. Americans love it – they love the ground he trod. They ask if I get nervous living here, if I see any spooks. We had forty French students on the doorstep at 9.30 this morning. Then we had Indians, Africans, Japanese. We get a lot of Japanese. They've got a Wordsworth society out there. We do tell them about Dove Cottage. They're better known than us, but I don't think they recommend people to come here ...'

Dove Cottage, it has to be admitted, for all Rydal Mount's attractions, is the place that everyone associates with Wordsworth. It was, after all, where his greatest poetry was written. It's why Grasmere today is still the greatest pilgrimage centre for all the world's Wordsworth lovers.

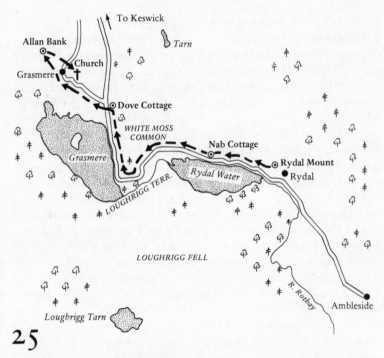

25
GRASMERE

*Dove Cottage today. A walk round
the graves and a talk with the rector.*

I ARRIVED AT DOVE COTTAGE EARLY IN THE MORNING, determined to see round it before the crowds arrived, so I was waiting at the door before ten. It's a small, white-washed cottage in a little lane with no view today of the lake. Some cottages opposite, which include a book store, all belong to Dove Cottage and their windows are framed in a rather official, orange colour which reminded me of Camden Council. I wondered about Wordsworth's cottage being white-washed, as he was always moaning about other people white-washing their cottages and spoiling the fell-side views, but no doubt the trustees have got it correctly painted, having taken such trouble to get everything else right.

A guide eventually opened up, rather bleary eyed, saying he was a bit tired as he'd been up late. Did I want taken round or would I walk round on my own? I said I wanted taken so we waited for some more visitors. Eventually a very dopey-looking young couple arrived on a motor bike and, hand in hand, carrying their helmets in their free hands, they joined me on the guided tour. It was terrific. I'd never met such a knowledgeable, fluent, amusing guide. I deliberately asked no questions, just to hear what his spiel was like, while the motor bike couple also stayed silent, more interested in holding hands. The guide even made jokes at Wordsworth's expense, poking fun at his lack of modesty, and he got in all the scandal, such as Annette and about Coleridge fancying Sarah Hutchinson. In the kitchen he pointed out where Dorothy made the family's two meals a day – 'both porridge' – and drew our attention to three chairs embroidered by the three poets' daughters – Dora Wordsworth, Sara Coleridge and Edith Southey, which for once made the motor bike girl unclutch herself from her friend and bend down to admire them. The guide only made one mistake – saying that Wordsworth met Annette in Paris (as opposed to Orleans). I made a date to talk to him after he'd finished work.

Dove Cottage is a pleasure to go round, not just because of the excellence of the guide, but because it's been so beautifully preserved and furnished that you can almost believe the family is still living there. It is so much bigger and richer than it looks from the outside, though of course the feeling of richness comes from it being a preserved, period cottage. In its day, it was relatively humble. You enter immediately into the kitchen-parlour which has stone flags, dark wooden panelling, a fireplace and a window seat, all as they were in Wordsworth's time.

I suppose the atmosphere is helped by the fact that so many detailed descriptions have been left to us about Dove Cottage, by Dorothy in her Journals, by De Quincey and by Wordsworth himself, that anyone who has done a little bit of background reading immediately recognises many of the objects and feels some of the memories. There's a little pair of balancing scales, perfectly ordinary in themselves, till you see they are marked 'T. de Q.' and you know who mixed his opium on them and caused such ruptures in the Wordsworth circle. There's a cuckoo clock on the stairs, made in Germany, a present to Wordsworth on his seventieth birthday, which soothed him on sleepless nights, inspired a poem and gave the children of the house endless entertainment. You can so easily imagine Walter Scott sitting by the big fireplace, and all the other famous visitors. The newspapers have been replaced on the walls of the Newspaper Room, the bedroom Dorothy papered to try and keep it warm, but they are all genuine, contemporary newspapers from Wordsworth's day.

The garden has been equally carefully tended with plants and paths and little bowers arranged as much as possible as Dorothy described them. If of course you'd never heard of Wordsworth, most of the details would be wasted. It would just be another nicely preserved little seventeenth-century cottage – hardly worth the entrance fee. Townend at Troutbeck, a yeoman farmer's house which is owned by the National Trust, dates from a similar period, and is a much more interesting traditional Cumbrian house. It so happens that no one today has heard of the family that once lived there – the Brownes – while the world and his wife have heard of Wordsworth, even if it's only 'Daffodils'.

Dove Cottage attracts scholars from all over the world – as distinct from Hill Top Farm, Beatrix Potter's house, which seems to attract mainly middle-class mums. Grasmere is always full of Wordsworth experts, students from Japan or America, writing yet another Wordsworth study or Ph.D, often on some justifiably neglected sonnet. Dove Cottage, as scholarship goes, is big business and the library and the museum nearby, which contains priceless Wordsworth manuscripts and should not be missed, are always humming with intellectual activity.

George Kirkby, the guide who took me round, was born in Grasmere, left school at fourteen and for twenty years worked for the then Manchester Corporation Waterworks, based at

Thirlmere. For fifteen years, George was one of their foresters, felling trees and doing other heavy jobs, till he hurt his back and was given lighter duties.

'They were working on an interesting theory when I joined them. The experts thought that conifers attracted moisture because it was noticed that the mists always hung in them and they were always wet, which is true. They thought if they planted the banks of Thirlmere with conifers it would help to keep up the water level on the lake. The opposite happened – the conifers took more water from the soil than they put back. They are useful of course as they do help to stop erosion.'

His light duties, for the next five years, consisted of walking the pipe line from Dunmail Raise to Troutbeck, a distance of some ten miles, doing the round trip three times a week, just to make sure there were no leaks and all would be all right for the heavy drinkers in Didsbury and Chorlton-cum-Hardy. 'There's a difference between being lonely and having solitude. I liked the job because of the solitude. I've never had anything against my own company. There's nothing wrong in talking to sheep – it's when they talk back you should worry.'

He saw a job advertised in 1969 at Dove Cottage, as an extra guide, and in 1970 he became Head Guide. He has two full-time assistant guides, plus two part-timers. There's also a curator in the museum, someone in the shop and a librarian.

He can't remember learning much about Wordsworth at school. It was war-time and his schoolday memories in Grasmere were of utter freedom. 'You could wander everywhere with no traffic and no one to attack you in the dark. My father liked Wordsworth, at least his early years. My father was a socialist.' Since coming to Dove Cottage he has made it his business to teach himself everything he can about Wordsworth. The previous Head Guide took him round, loaned him a few books, and he's gone on from there. 'The day I stop reading about Wordsworth is the day I stop this job.'

I had met many academic experts on Wordsworth over the year but I had to admit that few I talked to had more *breadth* of knowledge about Wordsworth's long life than George. George's conversation is full of quotations from Wordsworth poems, from all periods, and opinions from all the leading Wordsworth scholars, backed up with a few of his own personal views. He corrected me when I called Southey 'Suthy', saying it should be

'South-y', to rhyme with mouth. The clue to the correct pronunciation is in a Byron poem.

As he gets older, he finds his own views on Wordsworth changing – just as Wordsworth's did – and his chat when guiding visitors has changed accordingly. 'I arrived at Dove Cottage at the same age as William did. As I've got older, my view on politics has changed. I've become more mature, no, that's not the word. I've become what everyone becomes as they get older – more conservative. I'm more interested in the different stages in William's life than I was seven years ago.'

I asked him which poems he liked best, but he said it wasn't a matter of liking. 'Being moved is more the word. I agree with Margaret Drabble that at sixteen you would tend to laugh at "The Idiot Boy" but at thirty you feel more like crying. It takes time to get the full meaning. I was working in the Dove Cottage garden not long ago and I happened to stop and stretch my back for a few moments and I suddenly turned round and I saw the "hazel leaves sparkling in the gusty breeze". I'd read that line years ago but it took me till then to suddenly see it as Wordsworth saw it.

'Wordsworth very fascinated by Wordsworth, and he's easy to make fun of, but you have to be careful. He was a special person. He wasn't precocious, not like Keats, but he was special, and everyone knew it. Coleridge was talented but he lacked what Wordsworth had – application. Wordsworth went full circle in his life – he started as good middle class and ended as good middle class.

'It's wrong to talk of Wordsworth's women as his petticoats, as people have done. Dorothy and Sarah were highly intelligent women. They knew he was special. I'm glad he didn't marry Annette. It was the best thing that ever happened to him. I don't think she would have let him go on his travels just with Dorothy. There would have been fireworks. Not that Mary was completely passive. She just saw it as her duty to be his wife and stay at home with the children.

'I've read all Bateson and he hasn't a scrap of evidence to prove it was incest with Dorothy. His argument rests on a negative case – just because there are blanks in Dorothy's Journals. They might have meant anything. No one knows. Anyway, whatever the relationship, look at the marvellous poetry it inspired. All you can say with any confidence is that from Dorothy's point of view, the relationship was less than healthy.'

Like so many Wordsworth admirers, George tends to defend him on almost all counts. He points out that Annette, being the older person, was equally responsible for that relationship. He even refuted my suggestion that the vital element missing in Wordsworth as a person was a sense of humour.

'You must read *all* Wordsworth again,' said George. 'He has a dry, putting-down humour which you can miss at first glance. It has a cruel streak to it. Very Northern.' He admits, though, that Wordsworth did have sheep-like qualities and thinks those experts who dig out later, unknown poems and try to make out that they're good, are doing him a disservice.

George still tends the Dove Cottage garden, something else he would never like to give up. 'I was in the garden working one Sunday, when the cottage was closed, and I was talking to a lady and gentleman as I was planting a plum tree. The next day at opening time, I opened the door, and the same couple were there, waiting to be shown round. The woman was surprised to see me. "I do not wish to be told about Wordsworth by someone who digs holes in the garden," she said. And they both refused to come in.'

He dislikes those students who think they know it all and the clever-clogs who begin the tour by announcing loudly, 'I can never forgive Wordsworth for what he did to Dorothy and Annette.' Then there's the French whom he finds very difficult. He says they tend to be arrogant in their ignorance of Wordsworth and have been unkind to one of his guides who speaks French, endlessly correcting her accent. The Germans and Japanese he finds delightful, despite the language problems, and the Americans. School parties can be tough, especially the ones who haven't prepared the children first but at the last moment have come in to get out of the rain.

In the height of the summer, he and the two other guides show round 600 visitors a day, doing up to twenty tours between them. He tries to suit his spiel to his audience. 'You can weigh them up in the first two rooms. There's an interested silence and a not-interested silence. You can tell from little questions, or special attention they give to some things, that you should talk more about the fabric of the house, as that appears to be their interest, or play up De Quincey if that would suit them.'

He gets a bit hurt when people point out, as I did, that Beatrix Potter now beats Wordsworth into first place in the Lake District visitors' league, though he says he doesn't want to get into any numbers game. Dove Cottage, of course, doesn't open on Sundays. (He thinks this is due to the Rev. Brooke who helped to buy Dove Cottage for the nation in 1890. He wanted people at church on Sundays not visiting houses.) If they opened on Sundays, like Hill Top, he thinks they would notch up another 10,000 a year. However, like Hill Top, the problem is the same – over-popularity. They can't in all truth cope with many more visitors. The best would be to stagger them, not stimulate them. Out of their 53,000 visitors in 1977, 43,000 came in only fourteen weeks – the peak period being in July, August and September. It would be better to have more at the quiet times of the year. In 1978, they had to spend £48,000 on strengthening and renovating Dove Cottage, just to make up for all the tourists tramping through it.

He has a wife and two grown-up children, one at college and one in the navy, and they live in one of Dove Cottage's ten tied cottages. 'If it wasn't for the National Trust, the Council and Dove Cottage, Grasmere would lose its indigenous population. They wouldn't be able to afford a house otherwise. It's vital for local people to be able to stay. We're part of the continuity. I look around the fells and I look at the stone walls and I think of the lives that my forefathers put into building them. If the real locals go, Grasmere becomes a green desert.'

He particularly likes American visitors because they look upon him, and the other guides, as Wordsworthians. They aren't put off by their local, apparently uneducated accents – in fact Americans find them delightful. They simply accept the facts and the knowledge which George has and judge him by that, whereas he feels the British experts operate more of a closed shop. 'I think it's the public school system. They think you can't know much if you have a dialect.'

Grasmere is definitely a tourist village but it's tried hard, oh so terribly hard, to remain as refined as possible. The new settlers are very genteel and well heeled and very nice types of persons and do their best to make sure nothing horrid or squalid happens to alter their little paradise. The more strident shops and commercialism are kept at bay and even the one or two rather flash-looking new shops, such as something called The English Lakes Perfumery, has a discreet notice inside which says 'Sorry No Ice Cream allowed in the show room.'

The village was plastered with notices the day I arrived, with the headline, 'Is there no nook of English ground secure from rash assault?' This of course was Wordsworth, trying to stop the Kendal railway. Surely British Rail weren't trying to bring trains to Grasmere? It turned out to be a campaign to save the Rothay Hotel, the large eccentric-looking hotel which is next door to the churchyard. A Newcastle builder had bought the hotel and eleven-acre site in order to redevelop it, planning to put up new holiday flatlets. He'd got planning permission, much to the horror of the inhabitants, who'd organised a national appeal to buy it and preserve it – roping in such figures as Sir John Betjeman, the Poet Laureate, as a patron. Other patrons, so I noticed, included Chris Bonington, Joss Naylor and Melvyn Bragg. They needed £80,000 to buy it back. Meanwhile, the hotel had lain empty for seven years and had become a positive eyesore, derelict and vandalised.

The village is really in two chunks with Dove Cottage in the east and Allan Bank in the other, bigger part of the village. If I was living in Grasmere today – which I'd rather not, as it's so popular and overrun and always seems to me to have a claustrophobic feeling, overshadowed by the towering fells on all sides – then I'd prefer to be in Allan Bank, Wordsworth's second Grasmere home. It's a handsome house on high ground, on the slopes of Silver Howe. This is the one Mr Crump, the Liverpool lawyer, built for himself, and which Wordsworth so despised.

It was bought in 1915 by our old friend, Canon Rawnsley, who left it to the National Trust. It was empty when I wandered round and the National Trust was currently advertising for a new tenant. There were sheep on the lawns and nobody around except a painter working inside. It has recently been used by Ken Russell, the film director, who'd been making a TV film about Wordsworth. The painter was full of tales about the film people taking out TV aerials and central heating radiators, just to keep it authentic. As reparation, they were paying for the house to be repainted. It was almost finished and looked very grand.

I next went to visit the parish church, St Oswald's. At the gates there's a little cottage announcing 'Sarah Nelson, Original Celebrated Gingerbread'. I thought, oh ho, smart spot of modern commercialisation, almost on hallowed ground, but then I realised that gingerbread (of the original and celebrated variety) has a long history in Grasmere. The floor of the church was earthen until 1840 and every year for centuries, so the earliest records of the church show, there was a rushbearing ceremony in which rushes were brought from the lakeside and laid on the floors. Every year in August, the ceremony is repeated, this time by children, and as in the old days, they are rewarded with a piece of gingerbread. So I bought some. I still have it. Nobody in the family liked it, saying it was too hard to eat.

At the church I espied another notice, this time an archetypal church notice, one that seems to appear on rural church doors all over England. It announced that a gentleman called David English was going to give a talk and film show to the Women's Fellowship on the subject 'Through Patagonia with a Pack Horse'. What would the Church of England do without them.

The church from the outside is rather blank and boring, being rough-cast and featureless, and the famous gravestones of Wordsworth and company are equally blank – a case this time of plain living and plain dying. They lie in a corner of the churchyard, just beside the little River Rathay, in the spot which Wordsworth himself chose, near where he planted eight yew trees. The very simplicity of his stone and inscription, 'William Wordsworth 1850, Mary Wordsworth 1859' is in itself rather striking. Beside them is a veritable army of Wordsworths, almost the whole cast list of his life, and it provides good sport for anyone with a bit of Wordsworthian lore, working out who Edward Quillinan was (Dora's husband), or Catharine Wordsworth and Thomas Wordsworth (the two children who died young), or remembering that Hartley Coleridge's grave was personally chosen by Wordsworth. William Wordsworth junior and his family are also there. (On her gravestone, Sarah Hutchinson is spelled Sarah, though in letters it was often Sara.)

Inside, the church is much more attractive – and is a great surprise. It has beautifully white-washed arches and a most unusual roof of open wooden rafters, the upper timbers being supported by the lower timbers. They date back to 1562 when a bequest instructed the carpenters 'so that the Roofe be taken down and maide oop again'.

Wordsworth describes the interior very faithfully, very much as it is today, in Book 5 of 'The Excursion':

> Not raised in nice proportion was the pile,
> But large and massy; for duration built;
> With pillars crowded, and the roof upheld.

By naked rafters intricately crossed,
Like leafless underboughs in some thick wood,
All withered by the depth of shade above.

Wordsworth wasn't a great church goer in his young days, rebelling against compulsory chapel at Cambridge and flirting with William Godwin's philosophy of reason as a young poet in London and the West Country, but he came back to his roots with age and with his position as a solid local establishment worthy. During their Dove Cottage days, St Oswald's, Grasmere, was a sadly neglected church with an insane rector who never lived in the rectory. There was a curate in charge and he wasn't much better, being overfond of the bottle. Dorothy in her Journal describes attending a funeral one day, walking behind the mourners carrying a coffin past Dove Cottage, and at the church being met by the curate. 'He did not look as a man ought to on such an occasion – I had seen him half drunk the day before in a pot-house. Before we came with the corpse, one of the company observed he wondered what sort of cue our parson would be in. N.B. It was the day after the Fair.'

William himself had a fairly poor view of village vicars, thinking little of their education or their sermons, writing a letter once in which he ridiculed one vicar talking about 'hadversaries of Christianity and henemies of the Gospel', but in later years, especially when they moved to Rydal, he and his family walked to church most Sundays at Grasmere. The church is much as it was in Wordsworth's day, with the same bells, though stone slabs have now been laid on the bare earth. In his day, rushes were more than necessary on the bare floors as aisle burials were still allowed.

Wordsworth and his family spent two years living in Grasmere rectory, from 1811 to 1813, before moving to Rydal, though at the time it was known as the Parsonage, the rector living elsewhere. Wordsworth never retained happy memories of the Grasmere Parsonage, which wasn't surprising as two of his five children died while they were living there and the house was generally damp and unhealthy. They thought it was the damp that probably helped to cause Thomas's death. Luckily for the present inhabitants, the rectory is now a lot better to live in, having been completely renovated and raised five feet to avoid flooding.

I knocked at the rectory door, just as the postman was arriving, handing over a pile of books and letters. At the same moment, one of the church wardens, a retired brigadier, was emerging, having just handed in his latest rainfall figures. Dr Richard Bevan, the rector, faithfully prints Grasmere's monthly rainfall figures in his Parish Magazine. 'The Brigadier's very good on rainfall,' he explained. 'He was something to do with rain in India. He knew Sherpa Tensing.'

It was quite an interesting post that morning, but then it usually is, Grasmere rectory having become an unofficial clearing house for Wordsworth worshippers. A young woman from Illinois, USA, who said she had a Master's Degree in Romantic Literature and William Wordsworth, was wanting to know if she could get married in Grasmere Church in the last week of July. She'd been to study Wordsworth in Grasmere for the last two years and had worshipped in the church.

'Upon first seeing Grasmere,' so she wrote in the letter, 'I became convinced there was a heaven and Grasmere was its example on earth.' Dr Bevan was most impressed by the lady (a Miss Valerie Harlan Friedrich), but he wasn't quite sure, by her use of the words 'exchange of vows', if she wanted the full marriage ceremony or not. He was going to find out if an archbishop's special licence would be necessary. He doesn't usually agree to marry complete outsiders, always being wary of people trying to exploit Grasmere's fame for their own purpose. (All went well, though, and the wedding took place on 1 August 1978.)

Dr Bevan is a Welshman but has spent most of his career in Durham where he was a chaplain to several colleges and came to Grasmere in 1974. His large, rather untidy study (he said he was spring cleaning, as he bustled around, trying to find things) is covered with photographs and paintings of Durham Cathedral and Castle. Considering how many strangers must arrive to see him over the year, he was unfailingly generous with his time and attention. He sat throughout our chat with his coat on – despite the fact that he was in front of an electric fire with all its bars on. He uses a complicated combination in an attempt to heat the five-bedroom rectory – electric fires, coal fires, logs, calor gas, oil-fired stove, paraffin heaters and an oil-fired boiler with six radiators. All the same, it costs £600 a year to heat. Even raising the floor five feet and putting in a new drainage system hasn't made it much easier to heat than in Wordsworth's day. 'This part of the valley still gets totally flooded. One night last November we had six-and-a-half inches of rain – just in one night!' They all seemed obsessed by the weather in Grasmere, again as in Wordsworth's day. The normal greeting, when two locals meet, is, 'Managing to keep warm?'

All the same, Dr Bevan says he and his family enjoy living in the rectory and really, he can't believe that Wordsworth ever seriously *hated* it. 'Losing two children and having all that damp must have caused great sadness, but does that all add up to *hating* it? Hmm? It's such a lovely setting and Wordsworth so loved the church and the churchyard. Look at the trouble he took to pick his own burial place. I know he never settled in this house but I can't believe he *hated* it...'

Dr Bevan also doesn't believe that the rector in Wordsworth's day really was insane, as all the contemporary accounts allege. 'People had such a black and white distinction about madness in those days. I don't believe he was *insane*, not as we would call it today.'

So, having got those points cleared up, he moved on to the nice things about Grasmere, of which there are many. 'I do believe that certain spots on earth can be associated with certain visions, as that young lady from America believes. People do come to Grasmere for spiritual uplift, and they find it. It's remarkable. I see it so often in their faces.

'They come from all over the world. We have a Japanese professor who comes regularly. His speciality is the comparison between Wordsworth and Gerard Manley Hopkins. Can you imagine. Hopkins is almost indecipherable to English people! Last summer, when he was here, I happened to be in the church, about five o'clock one evening, and the church suddenly filled up with a party of Japanese tourists. I said to them, making conversation, that there was a Japanese professor already here, though I'm sure they wouldn't know him, Professor Tatsuma from Niigata. And d'you know, they were all from Niigata as well! So they all met up, here in Grasmere.'

One of the highlights of the Wordsworth year is a Wordsworth summer school which is held in the Tithe Barn, part of the rectory, and organised by Richard Wordsworth, one of the descendants. 'They swarm round the Wordsworth terrain, people from different cosmic backgrounds, drinking it all in. They talk and eat Wordsworth and it's the most incredible resurrection of the

Wordsworth spirit that you can imagine. You see that Wordsworth is a real force in the world, a spiritual power. Another nice thing is that the Wordsworth experts later send me copies of their Wordsworth books.'

The phone rang and Dr Bevan stopped rubbing his hands which he'd been doing not for warmth but out of enthusiasm. His other habit is to cross and recross his legs, shaking his shoulders and rubbing his hands, as each time he warms to his topic. He handed me two of the latest American books on Wordsworth as he talked on the phone to a parishioner. They were both on religious themes in Wordsworth, one published by the University of Yale and the other by the University of Princeton, both handsomely produced, both very learned.

One book was called *Wordsworth's Natural Methodism* and I studied the dust jacket:

Richard Brantley goes against a strong tradition in literary history by arguing that Wordsworth's distinctive symbology, structure, tone, irony, characterisation and narrative patterns throughout the body of his verse can best be understood in terms of his pervasive Evangelical idiom which emphasises such themes as conversation, reciprocal covenant between Man and the Holy Spirit, experimental faith, practical charity, man's striving towards spiritual perfection and his emblematic and typological 'reading' of the Book of Nature that surrounds him . . .

That was just one sentence at random. It was like reading a foreign language and I felt very ignorant.

Dr Bevan has four children, three grown-up sons aged twenty-seven, twenty-four and twenty-two and a daughter of nine, 'A shock, yes, but a wonderful shock.' He is very active in all aspects of Grasmere life. As president of the Grasmere Village Society, he was playing a leading part in trying to save Rothay Hotel. 'In fact I was one of the first people to spot what was happening. Property developers do have a habit of working very quietly. We just have got to stop such new building work. This is a Wordsworth shrine. People come to drink it in and we must preserve it. Wordsworth himself was against the encroachment of man on Nature. It's part of my special theological interest – upholding nature against the artificial environment of science and technology.'

The day I saw Dr Bevan the appeal had got only £26,000 of

the £80,000 needed and the time was almost up, but a week later a large anonymous donation arrived and they secured the hotel at last.

Dr Bevan goes almost every day to look at Wordsworth's grave and thinks he can feel his presence everywhere around him. 'I've looked at his picture so many times that I feel I know his features. His face is so vivid to me, as if I really have met him. I would love to have done, but it would have been difficult. He had little small talk and he didn't suffer fools and he did have an eccentric manner, but, like him, I see spiritual reality from natural objects and I know I would gain insights from talking to him.'

Dr Bevan forgives him entirely for the Annette incident. 'That was the sort of personal involvement which all men can get into at some time. It had no moral effect on him. After all St Augustine, one of the greatest of the saints, had associations with concubines in his youth.'

He also thinks there was no incestuous relationship with Dorothy. 'Visiting the graves so regularly, seeing Dorothy lying so close beside him, did make me wonder at one time about their in-breeding type of relationship. But I think not. Dorothy was his tangible link with familiar things – she was his electricity.

'Wordsworth was a genius which was why he had so many people around him. Christ had people hanging around him, touching the hem of his garment. We scoff at notions of genius today although we do treat pop stars with idolatry. But Wordsworth was a genius and his attraction was very potent, as Dorothy well understood.'

26

GRASMERE AND SPORTS

Some cock and bull stories. Hounds and wrestlers. A meeting with a world champion.

GRASMERE IS MORE THAN WORDSWORTH. THE BIGGEST single event in Grasmere's year, in fact the biggest single event of its kind in Lakeland's year, is the Grasmere Sports. Over 10,000 people turn up in a good year to watch the fun and games which must make it the most popular old English sports day in the whole country. It's very much a rural occasion, like an overgrown village fete, with races for boys and girls as well as traditional sports which are peculiar to the Lake District. It's always held on the third Thursday after the first Monday in August, if you can work that out, and if you can, make sure you're there early.

I'd waited all year for it, like most of Cumbria, and Grasmere as usual was completely taken over. It's hard to believe that one small village, with a population of only 1000, can grow so huge in a single day. You realise then why the bowl shape of Grasmere Vale, which can seem forbidding and claustrophobic on a dull day, is so perfect for open-air sports. It's one of nature's amphitheatres. They could hold the Olympics in that lush, central field, just as long as they moved things like the village church back half a mile or so.

There are sports all over Lakeland, from June to September, and some people, having once been to Grasmere, prefer the little, out-of-the-way sports, where you can park and wander and actually see everything that's going on. Each one is always on the same, if complicated, annual day – such as the Thursday before the first Monday in August for Ambleside Sports, the third Saturday in September for Egremont Crab Fair, and the last Wednesday in August for the Ennerdale Show. You can plan to watch them well ahead, though if you forget the local papers will always remind you.

It's the Norse blood which is supposed to have had such a big influence on the Cumbrians' passion for outdoor sports. Ever since local records have been kept, some sort of annual running and jumping, hunting and chasing, pushing and shoving, with or without the use of animals, has been a great feature of the Cumbrian year. Wordsworth's favourite sport, apart from walking, was skating, but he also used to go and watch the wrestling, the fell running and the sailing. Cumbrian sports have always been very democratic, with the lordlings being as passionate as the shepheds. There was Sir Wilfred Lawson, who followed scruffy old John Peel, and the

286

Yellow Earl of Lonsdale who lived for all sports. The present Earl of Lonsdale is a patron or president of many Lakeland sports.

Perhaps the most notable sportsman from the non-farming class was John Wilson, who became Professor of Moral Philosophy at Edinburgh and wrote for *Blackwood's Magazine* under the name of Christopher North. Like De Quincey, he was attracted to Wordsworth's poetry as a young man, while at Glasgow University and then Oxford, and came specially to live in the Lakes, near Windermere. He was wealthy and generous, big and strong, and cared passionately for the moral well-being of youth – and engaged in great philosophical discussions with Wordsworth – but he also cared about their physical well being. He took Wordsworth on a fishing expedition in 1809, in a party of thirty-two, ten of whom were servants, and they spent a week camping at Wast Water. Sir Walter Scott came to stay with him, and he organised yachting parties. But his biggest sporting interest was in wrestling and he revived and organised many village sports which are still going to this day. He saw the Lakes as one huge gymnasium and he himself took part in all sports, particularly wrestling, taking off his jacket to grapple with the brawny shepherds.

Over the years, several sports have died out. I used to hear tales as a boy that they were still practising cock fighting in secret meetings out at Dalston, but I don't believe it. Cock fighting was legally outlawed in 1849 and it was a pretty savage, though very ancient sport. Silver spurs used to be tied on the cocks and they would fight each other to the death, with each being completely covered in the other's blood. Bull baiting, prohibited by law in 1835, was also very popular. A bull would be tied by a chain and a pack of hungry dogs was then set to attack it. The bull would chase round and round, tossing and killing a few dogs, till it eventually dropped dead from exhaustion. Bull baiters used to defend the sport by saying that it made the meat more tender, but there are always those who have a justification for almost any cruelty.

Gurning has continued over the centuries, though that's not exactly cruel. Gurning is a speciality of Egremont Crab Fair, a fair which dates back to 1267, and consists of trying to pull the most awful or funniest face. You put your head through a horse collar and grin, or gurn. It's much loved by Americans and by

TV news programmes, hard up for a daft item to finish off their evening bulletin.

The thing about Grasmere Sports, which has been held since 1852, is that they have the best of the truly Cumbrian sports, the sort which locals and strangers can get a great deal of pleasure out of watching. It's been greatly commercialised, not particularly by the organisers, as they do it for the love of the sport, but by the bookies who are there by the score, all shouting the odds. The competitors are professional as well, in that there are money prizes, though you could never get rich on them and they all have other jobs. But it means that true amateurs, like Joss Naylor, the best fell runner of all, have never taken part in Grasmere's fell race, or the Guides' Race, as they call it. This merits the best prize of the day, usually about £75 for the winner, and as with the flat races, the competitors come from all over the North of England and Scotland. It's a grand sight, as they all surge out of the field and up the hill opposite. You can see how steep it is, yet the best ones dash up and down in under fifteen minutes.

The other two big events, both even more Cumbrian, are a bit harder for the outsider to really appreciate, at least to understand the finer points, but they are nonetheless very exciting.

Tony Bragg had come to Grasmere for only one thing, the hound trailing. He's a driver from Skelwith Bridge and I had met him earlier in the year, exercising his dog while I was walking in the Langdales. Last year he won third prize at Grasmere with his hound Screamer. The prize was only £12.50, not much for his best prize of the year, not when he can spend £6 a week on food for Screamer. His wife feels like screaming herself, especially when she finds out that he's sneaked yet another bottle of sherry into the house, just to feed his hound.

In the days of cock fighting they used to feed the fighting cocks on what was called cock loaf. When the cocks killed each other, as they inevitably did, their carcasses were then thrown to the trail hounds, who therefore got double grub, cocks and the loaves inside them. All hound trail enthusiasts in Cumbria have their own secret cock loaf mix which they give to their dogs.

'I usually bake mine when the wife's out. It weighs only 2 lb, but it costs me £1.40. It's a sort of fruit loaf, made with wholemeal flour, plus sherry or port. I've used up three bottles of sherry in the last seven weeks. I put a bottle under me coat so the wife can't see it. You bake it till it's really hard.'

He was a bit worried about Screamer's chances at Grasmere. He had broken his toe the previous season while running in a trail and it hadn't healed properly. Tony had just run him at Uldale, in the northern fells, where he'd come fifteenth out of ninety-eight, which was quite good. Uldale is a fast course, on fairly smooth going, which Screamer doesn't like. He prefers rough going, up over bracken and rocky fellside, as at Grasmere.

The hounds follow a scent over a circular course, starting and finishing in the same place. The scent, or trail, is laid with a mixture of aniseed and paraffin, which the dogs appear to love. Two men, called trailers, who know the local area and conditions, lay the trail with a rag soaked in the mixture, dragging it round the course, over fences and walls and up hillsides. The trails for dogs over two years are about six–eight miles in length (shorter than they were in the old days) and about half that for puppies.

It's been a very popular sport in Cumbria for well over a century and is presumed to have started when huntsmen laid down trails, dragging fox skins, in order to teach young hounds how to follow a scent. Local associations of hound trailers joined themselves together in 1906 to form the Hound Trailing Association, which governs the sport today. There are trails all over Cumbria, from March to October, many of them associated with the big sports meetings, like Grasmere, but mostly they take place on their own. They draw good crowds – not least because it's a betting sport and a good dog can cost up to £300. You often see little huddles of rather furtive-looking farmers standing by the roadsides in out-of-the-way dales, heads together, their hounds at their feet, haggling away, comparing notes, working out strategies.

It takes specialist knowledge to train a good hound, but it takes no knowledge to get pleasure out of watching a trail. The hounds strain at the leash, just as Shakespeare said they did, whining and yelping, till they're released and run towards the trailer, picking up his scent, and then they race towards the distant hills, following the path he's taken. A few dozy dogs might hang around the trailer, sniffing his boots or what's left of the rag, but their owners scream at them to get going after the pack. The hounds soon disappear completely from sight, as they race over the fell tops, as at Grasmere. Other sports continue, down in the arena, till there's a great shout when the first hounds can be seen returning. The owners are supposed to stand behind a line, but a few usually get carried away, straining to get nearer their dogs in their excitement, all of them yelling and whistling and often waving rattles, trying to will their particular dog to be first over the line and win the trail.

There was a bit of fiddling in the old days, with favourites being drugged by rival owners or lured off the course, but naturally, everyone says that's all stopped today. One ploy, in the bad old days, was to rush round and pick up your own dog, when they were out of sight of the officials, then take a short cut across the course, dropping your hound nicely near the finish. Disgusting. With so many spectators today, watching the whole course, and with eagle-eyed officials knowing all the tricks, this is said now to be impossible. A much more complicated trick, which took a bit of bribery, was to get the trailer to lay the trail wearing your boots. Halfway round the trail, he'd pick up the aniseed rag for 200 yards or so, leaving a stretch with no scent. When the hounds all came rushing round, they would grind to a halt, unable to find the trail – while your dog went racing on, following the smell of your old boots. Very cunning. 'Yes,' says Tony. 'You got some rogues in the old days.'

Something went seriously wrong in this year's senior hound trail at Grasmere, a most unusual occurrence. Nearly half the hounds went off on the wrong scent. Some officials blamed sightseers, tramping over the trail and splitting the scent. The Earl of Lonsdale, who was the starter and judge, thought it was the hounds' own fault, some of them trying to be too crafty. 'It looks as if one hound led half a dozen off the scent, thinking he knew the trail better than the trailers. These dogs are known as "guessers". In these circumstances we declared the trail void.'

'It was a real mess-up,' said Tony Bragg. 'I think Screamer would have won. He's had a good season – second at Keswick, third at Patterdale. It was a great shame.'

Perhaps the most important event at Grasmere every year is the Cumberland and Westmorland Wrestling, at least it always *sounds* very important. Fell runners and hound trailers and even gurners are all quite modest in their claims. Only the wrestlers proclaim their champions as *world* champions.

Tom Harrington is at present the best-known name in Cumberland and Westmorland wrestling. He holds three world titles, each at a different weight. Nobody in the history of the sport has held more than that at one time, though there have been champions in the past who have won more matches in one season. Last season he had forty-six wins, including three world titles. Ted Dunglinson, now retired, won fifty-four matches in his best season. So Tom still has some way to go – and he still hadn't achieved his greatest ambition which was to win the heavyweight match at Grasmere Sports.

He's only eleven and a half stone, which is why his record as a heavyweight isn't quite as brilliant as he'd like it to be. He very often competes out of his weight class, trying to win even more titles, wrestling against blokes almost twice his weight. 'I'm supposed to be terribly good at getting out of holds. I'm very nimble on my feet and I've got these long arms. It's not strength in Cumberland and Westmorland that matters most, it's speed. You've got to be quick to get in the right chip at the right time. You give a big man a twist and he's down. Mind you, a big man who knows what to do with his weight, he'll give you a game.'

Tom is thirty-three, with sticking-out flaxen hair and a country-lad complexion. He wears spectacles and doesn't look at all strong or aggressive, more like a rural David Hockney. He's employed as a farm worker on a farm about four miles south of Carlisle.

He must look like a walk-over, for any complete stranger mad enough to challenge him. When Cumberland and Westmorland people talk about having world championships, they really mean it. It is indeed open to the big wide world. The rules are utterly simple. You start by clasping hands behind the neck and shoulder of your opponent. The first one to unclasp his hands or to touch the ground with any part of his body, is the loser. There are no more rules. You can kick if you like, although they tend not to. The skill is in twisting your opponent so that he touches the ground, using the buttock as a lever. The buttock is one of the best-known moves – or chips as the movements are called. You see headlines in the *Cumberland News* like 'Tom's Winning Buttock'.

Judo experts often have a go, or big strong men who've done well in other sports, like boxing or free-style wrestling, but in all Tom's years he's never seen anyone come out of the crowd and do well. 'He might be lucky and get one fall, but they never win. But you have to practise. I've been doing it since I was eight.'

He was born in Loweswater where his father was a tenant

farmer, then they moved to near Bootle in west Cumberland (no connection with the Liverpool Bootle). Tom is one of eleven children, which he thinks was lucky. 'Being a lot of us, we wrustled amongst oursells.' He remembers his father challenging boxers at country fairs. Tom enrolled at Bootle Academy at fourteen. This is not some fancy seat of learning but what the wrestlers call their winter indoor meeting place. The outdoor season, wrestling on grass at village shows, is from May to October. In the winter, they practise inside in local halls.

Cumberland and Westmorland style wrestling goes back at least 400 years. In the last century exhibition bouts were held in London and Paris and drew big crowds but these days it's confined to the northern counties – Cumbria, Lancashire, Northumberland, bits of Yorkshire, and the southern Scottish counties. In a season, Tom goes as far north as Luss on Loch Lomond for their Highland Games, which has a Cumberland and Westmorland section; east to Ponteland near Newcastle; and south to Blackburn in Lancashire. But the greatest number of matches are in Cumbria, especially to the west. In Luss, he has to put on a kilt to wrestle which he says he finds a bit heavy. The opponents tend to be a bit heavy as well, having come from tossing the caber, but they're not usually very fast.

You can wrestle at some shows in jeans and a jumper, but most Cumbrian shows demand the proper costume. Tom would always wear it anyway as he's proud of it. The proper costume is long-john white underpants worn with a velvet centrepiece (this can be a swimming costume, if you're hard up), plus a white vest and socks. Fancy costumes, by which they mean embroidery all over your codpiece, is left to you, but at the big sports, like Grasmere, this is actively encouraged as the public like to see it. At many sports, such as Grasmere, there are extra prizes for the best costume.

You get some fancy pants indeed amongst the wrestlers. (David Hockney would love it.) Absolute strangers, especially the more uncultured element, often jeer and make personal remarks when they first see the wrestlers parade in their heavily embroidered long underpants, but they change their tune when they see the manly skills being displayed.

Tom, wearing his spectacles, slight and hesitant and slender beside the more muscle-bound wrestlers, looks even less like a champion when he first appears in his underpants. He always passes his specs to the referee to keep. 'New folks think I'm being a bit cheeky, as if I think the ref. is blin'.'

Tom's three current world titles were the eleven stone – for which he had to slim down half a stone – which he won last year at the Cumberland Show in Carlisle, the big event in the wrestling year. He had the twelve-stone title which he won at Barbon, just on the Yorkshire border, and the twelve stone which he won at Egremont Crab Fair.

There are seven weights in all – $10\frac{1}{2}$, 11, 12, $12\frac{1}{2}$, 13, 14 and heavyweight – plus two for boys, under fifteen and under eighteen. Each year the ruling body of the sport decides, amongst all the different places holding C. and W. matches, which one will have the honour of staging one of the world champion events. This way, by spreading it out, even little villages can stage a world meeting. The really big glamour shows, like Grasmere, don't stage world champion events. They don't need it to bring in the crowds. But just winning any championship at Grasmere is considered the big time. They usually pay their champs £32 for winning. Smaller shows often pay no more than £1.50 for first prize.

Tom Harrington is technically a professional wrestler as he gets money for it, but he's never made enough in one season to cover his petrol money, what with having to trail round the North of England all summer. But he has got sixty cups he's won outright and can keep for ever.

He hopes he can keep going till he's forty. The really big lads often keep having a go till their fifties. 'They usually turn up just to watch, to meet their old friends, and get roped in to have one last go.' As it's so much a matter of skill, rather than brute force, the old 'uns can still do well. He doesn't care much for wrestling in bad weather, as the grass gets all muddy and clarty. Putting your clothes on afterwards, when they've got all wet, that's the worst part. They don't go in for dressing rooms at many village shows. It's all terribly rural and open air.

During the winter months he practises once a week in Carlisle, at the Carlisle Academy. Now and again he might do press-ups in the byre at work, perhaps skipping in his lunch hour when the cows are out in the field. He went down to Cornwall not long ago with some other C. and W. wrestlers and did some demonstrations at one of their rural shows, asking the champions of the local Cornish wrestling to have a go at their style. Later, their champions came up to a Cumbrian show. Neither beat the other at the other's form of wrestling, but he says the C. and W. wrestlers came nearest.

Farm workers predominate in C. and W. wrestling, as it's essentially a rural sport, but you do get industrial workers and a few teachers. One of the recent Grasmere champions is the present head of the English Department at St Aidan's School, Carlisle, a distinguished school which has produced many distinguished pupils. He's called Roger Robson and he's just become the C. and W. correspondent for the *Cumberland News*, taking over this year from the legendary Clicker.

The sport is in a very healthy condition, and all the big prizes are keenly fought for, but the decrease in the number of little village shows in recent years has meant a decrease in the number of wrestling engagements. At the same time, the big ones, like Grasmere, go from strength to strength. Tom fears that there might also be a decrease in the number of youngsters coming through.

'You need it bred into you. You've got to keep at it, but we lose some very good young lads in Carlisle every year. You breed them up over the winter in the indoor hall, but come the summer and the parents aren't interested in driving them to meetings. Then when the lads themselves turn sixteen they get a bit more money in their pockets and find other things to do. But the big sports are very competitive.'

Tom has worked on farms since he left school at sixteen, moving to his present one, a dairy farm, six years ago. They concentrate purely on milk, which makes for a fairly simple life, but a bit restricting, as someone always has to be there for milking twice a day, all the year round. Tom would really prefer to live out in the country, perhaps try for his own little tenant farm, but his wife is a Carlisle girl and prefers living in the town.

'I like cows. Nothing wrong with cows, but really, I'd prefer sheep. What I'd like to do is manage a little sheep farm. Milking is so tiring. There's alus got to be somebody there. In winter time, we now keep them under cover so I don't even get out in the fields. There's not much freedom, not with cows. Now with sheep, I could get out and stretch my legs, get up on the fells with them, have more freedom.'

It was almost the opposite of what Joss Naylor had said. In his case, he dreamt of moving down the valley to some nice, easier dairy farm. I hadn't the heart to talk to Tom about the economics of sheep farming on the fells, or the insecurity. Perhaps he knows anyway. He just likes to think he might like it, knowing he never will change. It's what you're brought up to.

He had mixed success at the 1978 Grasmere event. He only reached the third round in the heavyweight championship, which was his major aim, being thrown by the eventual winner. In the twelve-stone class he was again thrown by the eventual winner, this time in the semi-final, when he was thrown by his own brother, Joseph. He did, however, win the eleven-stone Grasmere championship. So that was something.

27
THE WORDSWORTH INDUSTRY

A surprise discovery in Carlisle. Jonathan and all the Wordsworths.

THERE ARE TWO VERY FLOURISHING INDUSTRIES IN THE Lakes, tourism and Wordsworth. They're connected, as we know, and they've done a lot to help each other, but the Wordsworth industry is to me the more surprising. Everyone talks about the number of foreign scholars, from Japan and America. Wordsworth seems to be the staple diet of anyone studying English Literature in any of their universities. After Shakespeare he must be the most studied writer in the English language. Just think of all those piles of erudite theses, growing higher every year, enough to reach the top of Scafell Pike. You get people who devote their lives to just a few sections of 'The Prelude' or a few weeks of his life at Dove Cottage.

The only anomaly is the lack of a decent general biography of Wordsworth. I was in the bookshop at Dove Cottage one day and heard an American lady ask the assistant to recommend a biography. She had a master's degree, she said, but had not studied Wordsworth since school. 'I've been asked that question for seventeen years,' said the lady behind the counter. 'The best thing I can recommend is Dorothy's *Journal*.'

There is a massive biography, a two-volume job of some 1264 pages, written by Mary Moorman, the first volume of which came out over twenty years ago, in 1957. It's an excellent piece of research, but it's fifty per cent a history of the poetry, which makes it hard to follow for absolute beginners. The last general biography of his life was some fifty years ago by the American, Professor Harper. The problem is that Wordsworth lived for so long and produced so much. Once an expert gets going, he tends to become a specialist in one area. It's hard then to stand back and see the whole. All the same, I estimate there must be at least ten new books a year on Wordsworth, all of them critical studies of some poem or some element in his poetry.

Why is he so popular? First, William Wordsworth was undoubtedly a great poet and wrote some of the finest poetry in the English language. Also, he wrote some very important poems and had enormous influence, right from the publication of *Lyrical Ballads*, over the style and content of almost every nineteenth-century poet, whether they admitted it or not. And of course it wasn't just poetry – Wordsworth became a symbol of the Romantic Movement which swept across Europe – involving music, art, politics, as well as literature.

And then the Lakes. Through him, the Lakes became a spiritual home for the Romantic Movement, attracting pilgrims from all over the world. But had his home been a Birmingham slum, would the interest in him – however wonderful the poetry – been quite as constant? Liking Wordsworth, you get two nice things for the price of one.

And of course there is the sheer quantity of his writings. Wordsworth was so prolific that there's enough to keep scholars going for ever.

Fashion is another factor in Wordsworth's popularity. He's never been ignored, but he has suffered – perhaps more than other writers – from phases of unpopularity. During the year, Ken Russell did two major TV films on Wordsworth and Coleridge, something he might have done at any time in the last twenty years, but it would seem to be part of a general re-awakening of interest in the Lake Poets. It's almost something that happens out of the air. John Carey, Professor of English at Oxford, says he has noticed a definite swing towards Wordsworth amongst students. In their final year at Oxford, as at most universities, they have to choose a special paper. Ten years ago, the most popular single subject for the Eng. Lit. specialists was D. H. Lawrence. We were then all very interested in working-class culture, industrial conditions, sexual freedoms. Now Wordsworth is the number one choice – he and Coleridge, which is a joint paper, being chosen by around forty per cent of the students. Romance – with or without the capital letter – appears back in fashion. Both the Romantic Movement and the romance of going back to nature is at present very appealing. Conservation is another major concern of today. You can find that too in Wordsworth. There's just so much of Wordsworth, you can find a lot of things, if you look hard enough. (The sonnet I thought I had found at Belle Isle, belonging to Mr Curwen, see chapter one, turned out to be a genuine Wordsworth poem, though one already published. The handwriting has not yet been identified.)

During the time I was working on this book a very important new batch of Wordsworth letters and manuscripts appeared. I became involved in them, in a very minor capacity, and saw at first hand the enormous excitement they generated. The letters have thrown new light on a vital part of Wordsworth's life, but it was the manner of their discovery which provided one of the biggest mysteries for Wordsworth scholars for at least a decade. It almost rivalled the fun that was had out of the Annette scandal, back in the twenties, or the incest allegations, back in the fifties.

They appeared at Sotheby's in July 1977, and were described in the catalogue as an 'unpublished series of letters and important manuscripts of William Wordsworth and his family' and they were said to be 'the property of a gentleman'. Not only were they unpublished, they had hitherto been completely unknown.

The most interesting discovery of all, at least to me, was a series of thirty-five letters, or fragments of letters, between Wordsworth and his wife. Very few such letters exist or have ever been known to have existed. In fact for the period in question, 1810–12, only one letter from Wordsworth to Mary has ever been known. Best of all, they contain love-letters in which Wordsworth writes of his passion for her. 'Every hour of absence is a grievous loss ... the fever of thought and longing and affection and desire is strengthening in me ... last night I suffered and this morning I tremble with sensations that almost overpower me ...'

These love-letters radically alter the view of the relationship between Wordsworth and his wife which many Wordsworth scholars have had for the last ten years. Because so little has ever been known about Mary and William, compared with the reams about William and Dorothy and their love for each other, it's been generally assumed that his marriage to Mary was almost one of convenience. She's been dismissed as a nice lady, a bit dull and certainly not clever or literary, whom William chose relatively late in life, after all his passion appeared spent, to be the mother of his children. It's been thought by some that she was little more than a housekeeper in his life. Her own letters now show her to be a highly intelligent and literary lady. Scholars for decades – having been trying to track down the origin of 'Lucy' and other girls in his love poems, usually deciding they were based on Dorothy – will have to reassess the importance of Mary and the part she played in Wordworth's life and works. And as for all the allegations of incest between William and Dorothy, that will surely have to be reconsidered.

The letters and manuscripts appeared almost overnight at Sotheby's and, according to Jonathan Wordsworth, chairman of the Trustees of Dove Cottage, the experts were all taken very much by surprise. They had little time to organise themselves to make a realistic bid or to work out how on earth such precious material could suddenly have turned up. The prices Sotheby's expected for the Wordsworth material started at £180 for a bread-and-butter letter from Wordsworth to his son, asking him to get him 'one of those new fashioned paletot overcoats'. (I myself put in a bid for this letter, the cheapest sounding item in the sale.) For the love-letters, their pre-sale estimate was £10,000. In the event, they were bought as a collection by Cornell University for £38,500. They got it very reasonably, considering its uniqueness. They were said later to have been willing to have paid up to £120,000 to secure them.

The Dove Cottage Trustees and all the Wordsworth scholars were pleased that the collection wasn't going to be split up but very disappointed that they were leaving the country. However, the Government, in the shape of the Reviewing Committee for the Export of Works of Art, decided to halt their export. It was decided that the Trustees would have until February 1978 to get the money to buy them back from Cornell University. Throughout this, Cornell behaved magnificently and agreed to sell them to Dove Cottage for the price they paid, if Dove Cottage could get the money.

But at the same time, the police were called in to help with investigations into the discovery of the letters. 'I believe that in fact these letters are owned by the Trustees, at least in a moral sense,' said Jonathan. 'All Wordsworth's letters and manuscripts were left first of all to his son William who left them to his son Gordon who in 1934 presented them all to Dove Cottage. At some stage, these letters must have got out of the collection. Everybody thought to begin with that some member of the family must be selling them. We were all suspects. But now the family is in the clear.'

Investigations eventually centred on Carlisle, which was the home of Wordsworth's son William, who was the local sub-distributor of stamps. Naturally, Sotheby's would not reveal the name of 'the gentleman' but Carlisle police, those expert sleuths, tracked the seller down to an un-named Carlisle stamp dealer who denied that there was any possibility of the letters having been stolen from the Wordsworth family.

I was asked by Jonathan Wordsworth if I could try and contact the finder of the letters, using my Carlisle knowledge, as they still desperately wanted to know where they'd all come from, hoping of course that they could prove legal ownership.

One of the Wordsworth family had contacted the dealer, but he wouldn't tell him anything.

It took me some time to find the man and get him to agree that he in fact was 'the gentleman' who had sold them at Sotheby's. He turned out to be a young man of twenty-seven called Steve Murray who, until the previous year, had been a carpet fitter. He said that he had bought the letters for £5.

'It's like winning the pools,' said Mr Murray in his upstairs room above a health food shop. 'I wanted to keep it quiet. Well, there's funny people about. If it was known I had £38,000, someone might have broken in. But now I've got it all invested, I feel a bit happier.'

He hadn't been very happy at being investigated by the police. 'I was really upset about that. They thought the stuff had been stolen and I was handling it. They're my letters. I bought them. The member of the Wordsworth family who came to see me was so mysterious that I didn't trust him. He said he was from the BBC, but he gave me his name, which was Wordsworth, so I told him nothing.'

Mr Murray came by the letters in the normal course of his business, which is buying and selling old stamps and postal markings. It's his custom to advertise for old papers, envelopes, letters, any old salvage that people might have lying around in their attics. Potters, the Carlisle term for tinkers, often bring him bundles they find in demolished houses. He looks at them quickly and gives them £5 out of his back pocket, if they look only vaguely interesting, then he puts them in his shed to sort out later.

He was clearing out this particular sackful, putting the ones with stamps on to one side and the rest ready for the incinerator, when he noticed the name Wordsworth on the bundle he was about to burn and the address Rydal Mount. Not being a literary expert (he left school at sixteen with CSEs), he thought it couldn't be the same Wordsworth, never having heard of Rydal Mount. So a friend went round to Carlisle library and looked up Wordsworth in the reference books. Mr Murray then rang Sotheby's who said don't burn anything else and come down quickly.

Mr Murray had obviously done nothing illegal, but the Wordsworth family and experts were mystified – and still are. Mr Murray had no idea which person sold him the bundle or where they had come from. Nobody since has come forward, but then, if it was a potter, clearing out an old house, he probably doesn't know to this day that his load of rubbish, for which he got £5, was worth a great deal more. 'I'm still not satisfied,' said Jonathan.

Mr Murray's own theory is that the letters got out of the family's hands in the nineteenth century, perhaps taken by someone when they got married. He also thinks, judging by the lack of certain stamps which he would have expected on letters of those dates, that someone in the past had already been through them, looking at their stamp content. If only the exact location could be found, it might lead to further discoveries, which of course is what interests the scholars most of all.

The saga had a happy outcome for Dove Cottage, though they were very worried at first because they already had one Wordsworth appeal currently in hand, to get £130,000 to repair Dove Cottage and rehouse the museum. But there was national publicity about the campaign to buy back the letters and even a rock concert and poetry reading at the Round House in London to raise funds, which shows the interest of young people in Wordsworth. (One of the pop musicians involved had previously been a student, at Newcastle University, of Dr Robert Woof, secretary of Dove Cottage Trustees.)

Money for the letters was raised in time and Cornell graciously agreed to sell them. They are now at the Wordsworth Library, next door to Dove Cottage. They should appear in published form in the next year or so.

Of all the Wordsworth experts today, Jonathan Wordsworth is probably the most qualified, for many reasons. He's not just chairman of the Dove Cottage Trustees, but a Fellow of Exeter College, Oxford, where he lectures, and writes books, on Wordsworth. He's also a descendant of the poet's brother.

There are quite a few direct descendants of Wordsworth around today, the most senior, in blood terms, being William Wordsworth, the poet's great-great-grandson who is directly descended from the poet's son William. He's sixty-six and has spent his working life in the theatre, as a press officer. He's been married four times – one of his wives was Eva Bartok, the film star. There are four other great-great-grandchildren around, plus several others with Wordsworth blood, including of course the French Wordsworths, those descended from Wordsworth's daughter Caroline.

Jonathan Wordsworth is a great-great-great-nephew, being directly descended from Christopher Wordsworth, the poet's brother, the one who became Master of Trinity College, Cambridge. He in turn had clever and successful children (unlike William's own children) one of whom, Christopher, became Bishop of Lincoln. His son John became Bishop of Salisbury. His son Andrew, Jonathan Wordsworth's father, was a teacher at Bryanston School. Jonathan was educated at Westminster and Oxford, did research on the Middle Ages and became a don, only then becoming a specialist on Wordsworth. He is forty-five with four children, Thomas, Charles, Henry and Samuel. He says his mother found it funny and a trifle preposterous, marrying into the Wordsworth family. His own wife has found it just as amusing. 'She pointed out to me early in our married life that I always use the expression The Poet – as if there was only one poet in the world.'

His rooms at Exeter are full of Wordsworth books and mementoes, including a bust of The Poet. His father, as he got older, has come to look like The Poet, as his face narrowed and his nose became more aquiline, but Jonathan so far doesn't bear any family traits.

It was his great-great-grandfather, Christopher, who wrote the official biography of Wordsworth after the poet's death, but was stopped by the family from revealing any details of Wordsworth's illegitimate French daughter. Christopher maintained that people in the streets of London knew about it, but the family still said no and the affair stayed secret for 130 years. Jonathan himself doesn't agree with the theory that Wordsworth was ashamed of himself and so deliberately kept it quiet. 'He told many of his friends, such as Crabbe and Southey, even though it was never made public. He believed that emotion is what mattered. He never turned his back on it.'

The other great area of scandal is the relationship with Dorothy, a topic much discussed since F. W. Bateson's book on Wordsworth in 1954. Bateson was an Oxford Fellow and a tutor in English till he retired in 1969. 'I once met Freddie [Bateson] in the Bodleian Library and asked him straight out if he really thought Wordsworth and Dorothy slept together. He said no, of course not, so I asked him what in God's name is it all about? I still never got a straight answer but I believe that in his wildest dreams he does think they must have done.'

So what does Jonathan himself think? 'Their relationship was extremely intense and there would have been a lot of physical contact. Remember the time they were all going to Wordsworth's wedding. On the journey in the coach, Wordsworth was pillowed on Dorothy who was lying on Mary. It was the habit of the times. Coleridge enjoyed physical contact with all his friends, men and women. That Dorothy should have had sexual feeling towards Coleridge is another matter. She did love him deeply. Byron might have slept with his half-sister but there is no possibility whatever that Wordsworth slept with Dorothy.'

Jonathan has concentrated his study on the poetry and he is the author of *The Music of Humanity – a Critical Study of 'The Ruined Cottage'*, a work which took him eight years to complete. 'The Ruined Cottage' is not one of the Wordsworth poems most people learn at school but Jonathan thinks it is one of his finest. He is about to publish another work, *The Borders of Vision*, mainly about 'The Prelude'. His chief concern has been to get back to Wordsworth's original version of his poems. This appears to be one of the pre-occupations of Wordsworth scholars today, going back to first sources, that and arguing about which are the good poems and which the bad poems. But who knows what is good poetry?

'It's a very dangerous subject. With the Romantics, real creativity always borders on badness. Any sharp awareness of failures would have diminished the chance of success. It's only with people like Eliot, who draws back to write his poetry, that you have poets who are aware all the time about what poetry should be. It was a condition of Wordsworth's way of making poetry that some of it should be bad. A lot of it *is* bad, and unfortunately it's difficult to like the bad Wordsworth the way people can like bad Hardy. And yet he is not only the greatest English poet, aside from Shakespeare, but one of the most varied. "The Prelude" is the only poem in the language that can equal "Paradise Lost", and it has a supporting cast that far outweighs Milton.'

Wordsworth has been parodied and criticised and ridiculed almost from the moment he was published, providing sport for Shelley, Byron and many others. 'Why don't you hire somebody to abuse you,' Wordsworth once remarked to a friend. 'For myself, I begin to fear that I should soon be forgotten if it were not for my enemies.

Wordsworth certainly has not been ignored, either then or now, and implicit in most of the parodies has been knowledge of his work and even affection. Hartley Coleridge did one of the earliest unkind versions of the 'Lucy' poem:

> He lived amidst th'untrodden ways,
> To Rydal Lake that lead;
> A bard whom there were none to praise
> And very few to read.

It was Hartley who first put his finger on the two-sided Wordsworth. 'What a mighty genius is the Poet Wordsworth! What a dull proser is W. W. Esqre of Rydal Mount, Distributor of Stamps.' The most famous version of this thought is of course the one by J. K. Stephen which first appeared in *Granta* in 1891:

> There are two Voices; one is of the deep
> And one is an old half-witted sheep
> And, Wordsworth, both are thine ...

Tennyson referred to the sheep-like verse as the 'thick-ankled' element in Wordsworth, which is neat. The very idea of a Jekyll and Hyde poet is probably another reason why he is still being studied to this day. How could a person of such genius write such bad verse? Meanwhile, research continues, pilgrims gather, passersby come in out of the rain.

28
THE TOURIST INDUSTRY

National Park and national pleasures.

I GOT A TAXI FROM GRASMERE TO WINDERMERE STATION, back to where I began, and the taxi driver said that ten years ago, when he was thirty-three, he used to be an engineer working for General Motors in Liverpool. He'd been to the Lakes on holidays, thought it was magical, and decided that was where he wanted to spend his life, not in a Liverpool factory. He went up to Ambleside, walked into the Information Centre and asked the man behind the counter for advice.

'I'm in industry and want to get out,' he explained.

'Too much stress, is it?' replied the information man.

'That's it.'

'How does it show? A rash behind the elbows, a rash inside the legs?'

'That's it, that's it. How on earth did you know?'

'How do you do,' said the information man, walking forward and shaking his hand. 'I was in the British Aircraft Corporation, Southampton. Join the club.'

The taxi driver had no regrets about giving up his profession. 'I meet old colleagues getting three times as much as I do, but it doesn't worry me. There were forty engineers in my department and, since I left, seven have died, all under the age of forty. If you decide you want to get out and escape to the Lakes, do it *now*. People who wait till they reach retirement age can't really settle. They're the sort who live all their life in Chiswick in a house called Grasmere, then at last move to Grasmere and live in a house called Chiswick. Come when you're young and can get a job.'

The Lake District is full of new-comers, people who've fallen in love with the Lakes and decided to live there, and a surprising number of them come when they're still relatively young, drop-outs from the rat-race who are willing to take any old job. Like Coleridge, Southey, De Quincey, Ruskin, Beatrix Potter, Walpole, Arthur Ransome and thousands more, they feel they will get spiritual uplift from the lakes and fells. There aren't in fact many writers there today, no community of poets or novelists, apart from Norman Nicholson and a handful of specialist Lake District writers. Most of the newcomers are of course artists at heart, even though they may be driving Co-op vans or Mountain Goat buses, selling Kendal mint cake or serving high teas.

It's not just the beauty, it's the security. They moan, once they've arrived, that things are changing, the tourists are ruining everything, things aren't as they were, but as we know, that's been the cry since Wordsworth's day. They also know, deep down, that the Lakes can't really be ruined. They're legally and officially designated part of our heritage. Nothing can alter them. Well, in theory nothing can alter them, not now that they're a National Park.

The National Park is a hard concept. It's neither nationalised, despite the word national, nor is it a park, not in the sense of public park. The owners of the land inside the Park are all private people, like anywhere else, though large slices are owned by bodies like the National Trust or the Forestry Commission, also like anywhere else.

It's a ruling body, first of all, with legal powers to give or refuse planning permission. It's a protection agency, with staff and amenities to look after that area designated as a National Park. Thirdly, it's a propaganda machine, churning out information to help visitors enjoy the amenities, without hindering, so it is hoped, the residents.

National Parks are an American idea. The first was Yellowstone Park, founded in 1872, and they weren't created in England and Wales until relatively recently, not until after the 1949 National Parks Act. The Lake District National Park, one of ten, was created in 1951 and it's the biggest in the country, covering some 866 square miles. Roughly, most of the hill region to the west of the M6 is National Park. It's quite smart to be in the National Park, one feels part of an ancient monument, a listed property, but, on the other hand, it leads to endless palaver when putting on a new kitchen, altering the titles, or in any way changing your house or garden.

The population is small – just over 46,000, and it has remained around that for the last twenty years. It doesn't include Cumbria's biggest town, Carlisle, and it narrowly misses Penrith and Kendal, the two gateways to the Lakes from the M6, nor does it take in the coastal towns like Maryport, Workington, Whitehaven or Barrow. It even makes a little loop to omit Cockermouth. The main centres inside the National Park are Windermere and Bowness with a population of around 8500; Keswick, 5000; Ambleside, 2500; Grasmere, 1000.

The Lake District National Park Special Planning Board, which supervises the Park, has twenty-seven members – eighteen from Cumbria County Council and nine appointed by the

Secretary of State for the Environment. Their total expenditure in 1977 was £800,000 – with £600,000 of that coming from Government and local grants. They made the remaining £200,000 themselves, from car park and camping fees but most of all from Brockhole, their excellent information centre on the shores of Windermere.

It opened to the public in 1969 under its present director, John Nettleton, who beat 330 other applicants for the job. He comes from Carlisle, so he's a Cumbrian lad, compared with many of the possibly more experienced museum people who tended to be southern, and he went to Carlisle Grammar School and University College, Durham. The building was formerly a private house, yet another of those grand mansions with lavish lakeside grounds, built by a Lancashire merchant as his holiday home.

You keep seeing references everywhere to Brockhole, recommendations to visit it, but the scale of it and its exact purpose is never made quite clear, at least I'd never properly understood it. I feared it would be yet another little information bureau, like the local ones the National Park (and the National Trust) open in the season all over the Lake District, full of well-meaning, well-brought-up locals who give the impression they're doing charity work, dishing out leaflets to the ignorant.

Brockhole is a fun palace, an exhibition centre, a modern museum using all the latest audio-visual equipment, designed to tell you about one thing – the Lake District. You might think, if you're actually in the Lake District, why come inside to be told about what's happening outside? It's an experience in itself – and one that shouldn't be left for a rainy day.

'We have three aims: education, information and enjoyment,' says Mr Nettleton, 'and the last one rates very highly.' The gardens are open, including the shore, and you can picnic anywhere or use the cafeteria. The displays I enjoyed most were the flora and fauna, birds and animals, complete with sounds and movement, but they are always introducing new displays, new slide shows and lectures, so it's vital to try and get an up-to-date list of special events before you go. They have almost thirty different slide shows, on different Lake District topics, and the main ones are in a choice of four languages. They also get experts coming in to give talks and do day-long courses.

'The curious come in just to have a look,' says Mr Nettleton, 'then they find they get hooked. They might go to a slide show on sheep, not knowing anything about sheep, then you hear them staying to ask questions about why they see black lambs but no black sheep. Dry stone walling doesn't sound very exciting, but that always fascinates people.'

He has a staff of eleven at Brockhole, plus another dozen or so in the season. The centre costs £134,000 to run – and two thirds of that they bring in themselves. It's now the biggest single attraction in the Lake District, attracting more people than any other fee-paying place. It gets 170,000 visitors a year and, since it opened, one and a half million have visited it. It easily beats the literary houses, such as Dove Cottage or Hill Top, but then so it should, being purposely created for the public's enjoyment.

'We've been lucky in our National Park. The National Trust has been here much longer, but they have the same objectives. In some National Parks, like the Peak District, they have problems with things like grouse shooting and private grouse moors or mineral rights which we don't have here. All the Lakeland fells are virtually open to everyone.'

The National Park also has eleven wardens who wear green jumpers with an oatmeal stripe across the front and grey climbing breeches. Each has about a hundred square miles of Lakeland to look after.

John Wyatt was the only warden in the Lake District when he joined in 1960. He started work as a copy boy on the *Daily Telegraph* in Manchester, till he felt the call of the wilds and came to the Lakes, firstly as a forestry man. Now he is Head Warden with ten full-time wardens under his command, thirty part-timers and 250 volunteers. Their aim is to help the public enjoy the Lakes, which means things like policing Ullswater in motor boats (Windermere is done by real police), teaching map reading, protecting lambs in lambing time, helping to run mountain rescue teams (a voluntary job), patrolling popular walks and picnic places, picking up litter, picking up bodies.

Their police work, which only takes up about three per cent of their time, is the part they like least. They have no legal powers, just heavy persuasion, but they are responsible for about two dozen people a year ending up in court for some offence, such as breaking the speed limit on Ullswater or vandalism. 'We've just had a sudden spate of vandalism, after having had none for a very long time. Four different toilets have been ruined in the last two weeks and every window broken.'

He seemed rather tired the day I met him, at his cottage across Windermere, but then he does have a tiring life. He's also on the National Trust Regional Council and the author of several guide books to the Lakes. Perhaps he was saddened by the lavatory vandals. But on the subject of the future of the Lakes, he immediately brightened.

'All the dire warnings about the huge increase in crowds has not happened. Walkers can still get peace and solitude in ten minutes. It's only the valley floors that get many people. Talking of over-crowding in the Lakes is rubbish. The Lakes can't be all that ruined by people if the eagles have returned. Three pairs have tried to nest here this year, and one has succeeded. And there's the peregrine falcons. We're now the most important breeding ground for them in Europe.

'The litter problem is no worse either, despite the big increase in visitors. We get surprisingly little trouble, when you consider the numbers we have. In 1960, when I first became a warden, police activities took up thirty per cent of my time. Now it's only a tenth of that.

'Rock climbers used to be unhelpful people in the old days. The mountain attracts rugged, aggressive individualists and probably always will. Some of my best friends are mountaineers, but you used to get some disreputable ones, real rebels. Crag rats we used to call them. If you tried to ask them not to go a certain way in order to protect a certain part, they'd soon tell you where to go. Now you'll get a mountaineer ringing up a warden to say he's seen a peregrine on a climbing crag and shouldn't its nest be protected. That's a great change. What's happened in the last eighteen years is that the general public realise that the countryside is being protected for *their* good.'

There are some things people in the Lakes are not too happy about, such as Windscale and the present scheme to raise the height of Ennerdale Water. One wonders if the National Park people, who are good at saying no to a shepherd who wants to convert his barn, will be strong enough when faced with Government bodies. Ennerdale looks as if it's going to be the subject of a public enquiry, now that the National Trust and National Park have come out against the Water Board's plans.

Protection is a difficult business, because the residents and the authorities often have conflicting interests. The tourists also have rights. A natural paradise like the Lakes belongs to everyone and should be available to all. Most tourists are aware of the beauties, even those stuck in their cars all day. Several surveys have shown that the average distance walked by a motorist on a day trip to the Lakes is sixty yards. Just enough to get to a lavatory.

Yet who is to say they shouldn't come to the Lakes? They must love something, or else they wouldn't bother. Their depth of appreciation might be less than those lucky people of inherently good taste, the sort Wordsworth first aimed his guide book at, but something surely must rub off on them as they traipse round Dove Cottage in an apparent stupor. The Lakes are a learning process. They educate all the senses and all sorts of people.

I often thought, during the year, when I was on high with not a trace of man in sight, that this must be the view the Romans had, or the Vikings saw, or this was the path Wordsworth must have taken, but nothing in nature is ever exactly the same from year to year. The natural forests have long since gone. The grass uplands, which took over when the forests were cleared, are now going, as sheep over-eat the good stuff and put nothing back. Bracken is being allowed to spread over huge areas because nobody today can afford the cost of the manual labour, the only real way to keep it down. Becks continue to eat into the fellsides. The weather still works away at the landscape. The new forests have different shapes and different content and attract different flora and fauna. Fields are constantly being drained and burned, exhausted and nurtured, beaten and poisoned, as agricultural practices and patterns develop and change.

Insecticides kill wild flowers and bird life. The price of tungsten goes down and the mines close. The price of trout goes up and they get overfished. Chemicals used in fields get into the streams which get into the lakes and the fish suffer and in turn the fish-eating birds like herons all suffer. Diseases like myxomatosis arrive and wipe out rabbits. Nature is a chain reaction.

Then there's human erosion. Certain paths and walks become too popular and disappear under the strain. New roads and motorways channel new people into new areas. Valleys are flooded for reservoirs. Lakes are expanded. Motor boats pollute the surfaces of the lakes, and everything below. Bus services disappear, more cars arrive, more car parks, more carbon monoxide. Yet more isolation. Villages get cut off. Schools close.

It's not just what we see, it's how we see it. Beauty is beholden differently by different generations. The idea of the Picturesque, which Wordsworth was brought up with, is not the same as our idea of beauty. We don't find Scafell and Dow Crags horrid and horrifying as travellers once did. Views are discovered then dismissed as corny or chocolate box, yet they are the same. We now love white-washed cottages.

Cock fights and bull baiting have gone. Hunting might go, then what would happen to a thriving rural sport, not to mention the foxes. Just fifty years ago, every Lakeland dale had its professional guides and ponies for hire, but now we do our own climbing. The Government could build another atomic power station, or take the present one away. They could withdraw the subsidies from hill farmers and the Herdwicks and the little wool industry and the knitting patterns would all collapse. They could ban orange anoraks, as harmful to the human eye. Second homers might be hanged. Wordsworth might be revealed as a plagiarist (Dorothy wrote everything). Dove Cottage would close its doors and the Japanese gentlemen would concentrate on Stratford. The Lakes are not being ruined, not more than they ever have been, but they are changing, while still remaining. They will always change, so long as they are alive. We want living lakes, not museum pieces. Most of all, we want the Lakes loved and appreciated. That's the best protection.

I could do the whole walk again and see it all differently. The sun might be out on Coniston Old Man. The mist will have cleared from Skiddaw. My second impression might not be my first impression which was what constantly happened during the year. I dismissed Rydal Water, as being as unspoiled as the Serpentine, then grew to love it, seeing it again when it was different and I was different.

I do plan to do it all again, and again. I leave for Caldbeck in the morning. My wellies are all clean. Wordsworth awaits. Or perhaps this time I might buy a pair of big leather boots.

APPENDICES

A: Facts about the Lake District*

Total area 866 square miles
Total population 46,000

1 LAKES

Most experts agree that there are sixteen lakes – the rest are designated as tarns. There are scores of tarns, not all of them with names. Some tarns are quite big – Devoke Water, for instance, is a tarn but it is bigger than Elter Water which is usually given the status of a lake, though it is small and getting smaller as the reeds take over. Windermere, the biggest, is over ten miles long. Elter Water is under half a mile long. The sixteen lakes, roughly in order of size, are:

Windermere
Ullswater
Coniston Water
Derwent Water
Bassenthwaite Lake
Haweswater
Thirlmere
Wast Water
Ennerdale Water
Crummock Water
Esthwaite Water
Buttermere
Loweswater
Grasmere
Rydal Water
Elter Water

2 MOUNTAINS

Scafell Pike	3206 feet
Scafell	3162

* Unless otherwise stated, all facts refer to the area inside the National Park boundary.

Helvellyn	3118 feet
Skiddaw	3054
Great End	2984
Bowfell	2960
Pillar	2927
Great Gable	2924
Esk Pike	2903
Fairfield	2863
Blencathra (Saddleback)	2847

3 TOWNS AND VILLAGES

Windermere and Bowness	8500 population
Keswick	5000
Ambleside	2500
Grasmere	1000
Coniston	1000
Broughton-in-Furness	1000
Hawkshead	700
Patterdale	600
Caldbeck	600

4 CLIMATE

Mean daily temperature: average rainfall: average duration of bright sunshine

Keswick

	Jan.	Feb.	Mar.	April	May	June
Temp. (F.°)	38	39	42	46	51	57
Rain (ins)	6.7	4.2	3.4	3.3	3.2	3.3
Sunshine (hours)	34	56	102	139	192	181

	July	Aug.	Sept.	Oct.	Nov.	Dec.
Temp. (F.°)	59	59	55	49	44	41
Rain (ins)	4.4	5.1	6.8	6.1	6.0	5.8
Sunshine (hours)	146	140	103	72	39	28

Annual rainfall in inches

Seathwaite (head of Borrowdale)	131
Windermere	68.6
Keswick	58.3
Kendal	53
Penrith	34
Carlisle	31

5 LAND OWNERSHIP

It is very difficult to discover who owns the Lake District. Authorities grow. Private estates dwindle. Secrecy prevails. There is complication over what is, and what is not 'ownership', as opposed to land in trust or in common. However, this is my estimated list of land owned in the Lake District National Park in 1978.

National Trust	90,000 acres
North-West Water Authority	40,000
Forestry Commission	30,000
National Park/Local Councils	22,000

The leading 'private' owners, as distinct from 'authorities', include:

Lowther Estates	27,000 (plus 45,000 common land)
Stafford Howard	6000 (plus 6000)
Egremont Estates*	5000 (plus 40,000)
Dalemain Estates	4000
Greythwaite Estates	4000
Rydal Estates	2654

The Lakes

Windermere	surface owned by Cumbria County Council; bed owned by South Lakeland District Council
Coniston	surface owned by Cumbria CC; bed owned by Rawdon-Smith Trustees
Derwent Water	surface owned by Cumbria CC; bed owned by National Trust and local council
Ullswater	surface owned by Cumbria CC; bed owned by National Trust, Dalemain Estates and others
Buttermere ⎫ Loweswater ⎬ Crummock Water ⎭	surface and bed owned by National Trust
Bassenthwaite	Egremont Estates*
Wast Water	Egremont Estates*
Grasmere	Lowther Estates
Rydal Water	National Trust and Rydal Estates
Haweswater	North-West Water Authority
Thirlmere	North-West Water Authority
Ennerdale Water	North-West Water Authority

* In late 1978, due to death duties, the Egremont Estate was being greatly reduced. The common lands round Wast Water were expected to go to the National Trust.

6 TOP TOURIST ATTRACTIONS

In 1977, three million visitors stayed in the Lakes and spent seventy million pounds. The number of day-trippers is not known.

It's unfair to compare attractions, as opening times and seasons vary, attractions differ, some are open air, some inside, some big, some small, some have huge displays, others a couple of unattended rooms, but, nonetheless, here are the leading tourist attractions in the Lake District National Park where fees were charged and heads counted in 1977.

Most-Visited Places

Brockhole National Park Centre, Windermere	170,000
Lowther Wildlife Park, near Penrith	127,000

Most-Visited Houses

Hill Top, Sawrey (Beatrix Potter)	71,000
Dove Cottage, Grasmere (Wordsworth)	53,000
Muncaster Castle, Ravenglass	36,000
Rydal Mount, Ambleside (Wordsworth)	34,000
Brantwood, Coniston (Ruskin)	20,000
Eskdale Mill, Eskdale	18,000
Pencil Museum, Keswick	17,000
Fitz Park Museum, Keswick	12,000
Ruskin Museum, Coniston	9,000
Belle Isle House, Windermere	6,000

Outside the National Park

There are many well-visited places, houses, museums just outside the National Park boundary which are generally classed as Lake District attractions.

Holker Hall, Cartmel	64,000
Tullie House Museum, Carlisle	60,000
Whitehaven Museum	55,000
Levens Hall, Kendal	41,000
Abbot Hall Art Gallery, Kendal	34,000
Lanercost Priory, Brampton	28,000
Lakeland Life Museum, Kendal	25,000
Brougham Castle, Penrith	17,000
Furness Abbey, Barrow	17,000
Wordsworth House, Cockermouth	14,000
Sizergh Castle, Kendal	14,000
Maryport Maritime Museum	11,000

Most-Climbed Mountains
No figures, just guesses, but most experts agree the three most
popular mountains are, in order:

Helvellyn
Scafell Pike
Skiddaw

Three most popular beauty spots:

Friars Crag, Derwent Water
Tarn Hows, Coniston
Air Force, Ullswater

Other Attractions
Steam Railways:
Ravenglass and Eskdale   (tel. Ravenglass 226)
Lakeside and Haverthwaite   (tel. Newby Bridge 594)

7 LAKELAND SPORTS

Grasmere Sports	biggest of all, 10,000 crowds; third Thursday after first Monday in August
Ambleside Sports	Thursday before first Monday in August
Carlisle Great Fair	August, usually last week
Cumberland Show	A Thursday in August
Egremont Crab Fair	Third Saturday in September
Ennerdale Show	Last Wednesday in August
Eskdale Show	Last Saturday in September
Hawkshead Show	First Tuesday in September
Kendal Gathering	Second week in September
Keswick Show	Late summer bank holiday Monday
Patterdale Sheep Dog Trials	Late summer bank holiday Saturday
Penrith Show	A Saturday in July
Wasdale Show	Second Saturday in October
Wigton Horse Sales	Last Wednesday in October

8 NEWSPAPERS
To check dates and places of all shows and events, including
sports, hunts, Cumberland and Westmorland wrestling, hound
trials, sheep dog trials, fell races, it is best to see local newspapers:

Cumberland News Dalston Road, Carlisle
Westmorland Gazette Stricklandgate, Kendal
Keswick Reminder Station Street, Keswick
Whitehaven News Queen Street, Whitehaven

West Cumberland Times Oxford Street, Workington
Cumberland and Westmorland Herald King Street, Penrith

9 USEFUL ADDRESSES
Cumbria Tourist Board
Ellerthwaite, Windermere (tel. Windermere 4444). Invaluable source of countless leaflets and brochures on almost every possible Lakeland topic – accommodation lists, maps, motor routes, houses open to the public, fairs, traditional events, nature trails, boating, cycling, sports, town guides. Send stamped addressed enveloped for latest list of publications, stating particular interest.

National Trust,
Broadlands, Borrans Road, Ambleside (tel. Ambleside 3003). Another invaluable source of leaflets on fishing, camping sites, guides, nature trails and all information to do with National Trust properties.

National Park,
Brockhole, National Park Visitors' Centre, Windermere (tel. Windermere 2231). The National Park produce many little leaflets on many different subjects, all for a few pence – topics include trees, geology, literary associations, climate, fish, plants, birds, mines and minerals, place names, farming. They also print walks round the better-known lakes and valleys, lists of camp sites, caravan sites, etc.

Buses
Ribble – enquiry offices	Ambleside 3233
	Kendal 20932
	Keswick 72791
Cumberland – enquiries	Keswick 72791
Mountain Goat Mini-bus Service	Windermere 4106

Railways
Main line: London Euston to Oxenholme, approx. three and a half hours, tel. (Euston) 01-837 7070
Local line: Oxenholme to Windermere (via Kendal, Burneside, and Staveley); time approx. twenty-five minutes. Local enquiries – Windermere 3025

Youth Hostels
There are thirty hostels in the Lake District. Enquiries:
HQ Trevelyan House, St Albans, Herts.
Lakeland Region, Elleray, Windermere, tel. Windermere 2301

Weather
Ring Windermere 5151 for latest Lakeland weather, including conditions on fell tops.

B: Opinions about the Lake District

1 WAINWRIGHT'S BEST FELLS
Everybody must bow to A. Wainwright in his knowledge and opinions of the fells, having walked 214 of them in thirteen years for his seven classic guides, exploring 2000 routes and covering 10,000 miles (see chapter twenty-three). These are his best:

Six Finest Fells
They are not necessarily the ones he *likes* best – he's omitted Haystacks, for example, as it's too low – but the ones which he considers the finest because of height, commanding appearance, ruggedness, good views.

Scafell Pike
Bowfell
Pillar
Great Gable
Blencathra
Crinkle Crags

Six Best Summits
High vantage points which have a peak of naked rock and a good view.

Dow Crag, Coniston
Harter Fell, Eskdale
Helm Crag, Grasmere
Eagle Crag, Langstrath
Slight Side, Scafell
Steeple, Ennerdale

Six Best Places to be
Places which have exciting situations but can be reached without danger.

Striding Edge, Helvellyn
First Col, Lord's Rake, Scafell
Mickledore, Scafell
Sharp Edge, Blencathra
South Traverse, Great Gable
Shamrock Traverse, Pillar

Finest Ridge Walks
The Fairfield Horseshoe (Ambleside)
The High Street Range (Garburn-Moor Divock)
The Mosedale Horseshoe (Wasdale Head)
Causey Pike–Whiteless Pike

Grisedale Pike–Whiteside
Esk Hause–Wrynose Pass, via Bowfell
The Eskdale Horseshoe (Slight Side–Bowfell)
The Helvellyn Range (Grisedale Pass–Threlkeld)
The High Stile Ridge, with Haystacks
Catbells–Dale Head–Hindscarth–Scope End
The Coniston Round (Old Man–Wetherlam)

2 BONINGTON'S BEST CLIMBS

Most people would also bow, when it comes to climbs as opposed to fell walks, to Chris Bonington, the Everest climber and leader of many British expeditions (see chapter seventeen). He is a Lakeland resident and these are his best climbs and walks:

Favourite Rock Climbs
Great Gable – from the head of Ennerdale, commonly known as
    The Tomb
The Central Buttress of Scafell
Steep Ghyll on Scafell, especially in snow and ice
The great Central Route of Scafell, up Eskdale on the Esk Buttress
Dove Crag in Dovedale, the route known as Don Whillan's route

Favourite Walks
For a really long walk, which can take anything from eight to fourteen hours, depending on your age and on the weather, he recommends a tramp over the tops of the northern fells. Start at Mosedale, where you can park your car, then climb up Bowscale, over the Bannerdale Crags to Blencathra (Saddleback), across and up Skiddaw (if you're really fit), on to Great Calva, on and up Knott, over to High Pike, across to Carrock Fell and then down into the dale once more at Mosedale.

For little walks, of only one or two hours, he likes going up Carrock Fell or High Pike, sitting on the bench at the top, with his back to the Solway, looking at Skiddaw.

3 NICHOLSON'S BEST PLACES

Coming more to earth, these are the nicest lakes, villages and valleys, as chosen by Norman Nicholson, the poet (see chapter nine).

Five Best Lakes
Wast Water. 'Bare and barren, most dramatic.'
Buttermere and Crummock. 'Self-enclosed, looks as if there's no
    way out of it.'
Ullswater. 'It has a special river quality, winding round with
    wooded shores.'
Coniston. 'I like its different reaches.'

Devoke Water. 'It's usually described as a tarn, but it's quite big. You feel it's got left behind by accident since the Ice Age. It's the most desolate stretch of water in the Lakes with no scenic valley beneath. When I wake up in the middle of the night in my home in Millom and it's really wild, I think, my goodness, what can it be like up there?'

Five Villages

Cartmel. 'It's my ancestral home for a start, and has a marvellous Priory, but I like it being a limestone village, with a beautiful setting in a dint in the valley.'

St Bees. 'I like it for the village and headland, Cumbria's finest nesting place for cliff birds.'

Kirkby Lonsdale. 'A delightfully attractive market town.'

Little Musgrave. 'A lovely little village in the Eden Valley, near Brough.'

Ravenglass. 'I thought of choosing Hawkshead but I hate the new car park and the village itself is now almost a stage setting. So I'll pick Ravenglass, a pretty, romantic village with a very good bird life.'

Five Valleys

Duddon Valley. 'Without hesitation this is my favourite place of all. There is such variety, such texture. Every three weeks in the year it's a different place.'

Little Langdale. 'I have so many friends there and have stayed there so often over the years. Considering how well known it is, there's not a lot of traffic. There are no new buildings and the roads have hardly been altered. It's much as Wordsworth knew it. And I'm very fond of Blea Tarn.'

Eskdale Valley. 'The top is very wild and remote. The middle and lower part is granite. It has the same shape as other nearby valleys but inside it's very different.'

Rusland Valley. 'This is a very small valley between Coniston and Windermere, coming down from Grizedale forest. I found a place with the same name in Norway.'

Piel Island. 'I know it's not a valley but I want to include it somewhere. It's a little island off the Furness. Everyone who loves nature should visit it.'

4 BEST PLACES FOR A BUSY DAY

These are my choices. So many people are forced to go in the school holidays and if they're not careful they can get stuck forever in Keswick or Windermere, Ambleside or Grasmere, places worth visiting, but not in the high season, unless you can get there very early in the morning. But even on the busiest bank holiday you can escape all crowds in half an hour if you know the way. Here are ten suggestions.

Wast Water
You have to work your way round the coast to get into it, which keeps the trippers down, but it's the most dramatic and mysterious of all the lakes. Loved by climbers as it's a good, if arduous, way up Gable and Scafell.

Ennerdale
Equally isolated, equally dramatic, but get there quick in case the Water Authority start raising the water level. Dominated by Forestry Commission plantations, so if you hate conifers, don't go, but the forest walks are good and easy and cars are banned.

Buttermere
Much more discovered than the previous two, but very pretty and not too overcrowded, even though you can drive into it from central Lakeland. Don't miss adjoining lakes of Crummock and Loweswater. Park quickly in Buttermere village. Easy family walk round Buttermere lake in two hours or head for heights up Scarth Gap Pass.

Haystacks
There's no need to recommend the famous climbs, like Scafell Pike, Helvellyn and Skiddaw, which must be attempted at some time by all Lakers, but they get very crowded in the season. On a busy day, try Haystacks instead, a smaller fell, loved by the connoisseurs. One of the most beautiful tarns in the Lakes is on top, Innominate Tarn, so called because it hasn't got a name ...

Duddon Valley
As dales go, Borrowdale is probably handsomer and Great Langdale more dramatic, but the Duddon Valley is the prettiest and the least crowded. Follow the valley down from Wrynose Pass towards Broughton-in-Furness and imagine the old days in the Lakes, before pack horses gave way to Cortinas.

Furness Peninsula
Missed by most visitors, as they think the Lake District finishes at Coniston, but the mountains and valleys run straight down to the sea. When the tide comes up, around the Duddon sands, the effect is staggering. Visit Cartmel, Furness Abbey, Piel Isle.

The Northern Fells
People also think the Lakes stop after Keswick. It's true there are no lakes the back of Skiddaw, apart from Over Water (usually

classed as a tarn), but it's still all National Park, probably the emptiest, least touched, least commercialised part of all. You can drive for hours on little, unfenced roads and hardly see an orange anorak. Best villages are Mungrisdale, Mosedale, Hesket Newmarket, Caldbeck, Ireby, Uldale, Orthwaite, then head up for the wild fells.

Ullswater

I personally would avoid Windermere and Derwent Water on a bank holiday, despite the steamers, but Ullswater is too nice to ever miss, as long as you head quickly to the other side, the Howtown side, by boat or road. Start walking from Martindale church, up Boardale, over towards Patterdale, then along the slopes of Place Fell, back along the banks of Ullswater. If I had to choose one walk, that would be it.

Eden Valley

This is slightly out of the National Park boundary, which means it gets overlooked, even though it's lush and very pretty. You'll never believe the M6 is so near. Start at Armathwaite, work south, taking in Nunnery Walks, then to Kirkoswald, Lazonby, ending at Appleby.

Longsleddale

Most visitors come up the M6 from the south and find themselves on the Kendal–Windermere–Keswick A591 rat race before they know what's happened, unaware that there are two one-way valleys right at the beginning of the Lakes, not far from Kendal, easy to sneak into and escape the crowds. Longsleddale and Kentmere are long, narrow valleys which you can drive up, then choose your isolation, heading up the fell side, or to the end and get lost.

5 BEST FOOD

There are 750 hotels in the Lakes and 550 guest houses and bed and breakfast places, offering in all 20,000 beds, so the choice is extensive.

There are two outstanding hotels in the Lake District, however, voted by almost every guide as amongst the top places in the whole of Britain:

Sharrow Bay Hotel, Ullswater   tel. Pooley Bridge 301
Miller Howe, Rayrigg Road, Windermere   tel. Windermere 2536

Your only problem will be getting in – allow at least six days' notice in the summer to book lunch or dinner, six weeks to get a bed. Expect to pay around £30 for dinner, bed and breakfast (1979 prices).

Each is rich, extravagant, stylish, but worth it for the experience, if you can afford it.

I asked the respective proprietors for *their* personal favourite places to eat:

John Tovey of Miller Howe chose:
  Tullythwaite House, Underbarrow
  Sharrow Bay, Ullswater
  White Moss Hotel, Grasmere
  Wine Shop, Coniston
  Port Hole, Bowness

Brian Sack and Francis Coulson of Sharrow Bay chose:
  Tullythwaite House, Underbarrow
  Farlam Hall, Brampton
  Howtown Hotel, Ullswater

Other Recommendations
Parkend Restaurant, Caldbeck   tel. Caldbeck 442
  (My own favourite place to eat, when I haven't got the money or energy for the big two. Stylish, yet relaxing.)
Rothay Manor, Ambleside   tel. Ambleside 3605
Leathes Head House, Borrowdale   tel. Borrowdale 247

Accommodation
The 254 registered farm houses are usually cheapest, but many of the guest houses and small hotels are almost as reasonable. These are the best three I used. In 1979, dinner, bed and breakfast was approximately £8–12.
Nab Cottage Guest House,   tel. Grasmere 311
Rydal Water
Tower Bank Arms, Near Sawrey   tel. Hawkshead 334
Three Shires Inn, Little Langdale   tel. Langdale 215

C: The Lake Poets

WILLIAM WORDSWORTH

1770 Born 7 April, Cockermouth, second of five children
1771 Birth of sister, Dorothy
1778 Death of mother, Ann; moves to relations in Penrith
1779–87 School at Hawkshead Grammar, Windermere
1783 Death of father, John, agent for Lord Lonsdale
1787–91 St John's College, Cambridge
1790 Walking tour of France, witnesses Revolution
1791–2 Returns to France, affair with Annette Vallon in Orleans. Birth of his daughter Caroline
1793–5 London, Wales, Cumberland. First publication, 'An Evening Walk', 1793
1795–8 West Country. Sets up house with sister Dorothy. Meets Coleridge. Writes *Lyrical Ballads* (with Coleridge)
1800 Settles at Dove Cottage, Grasmere, with Dorothy
1802 Marries Mary Hutchinson
1803 Birth of John, first of five children (two die as children)
1808–11 Moves to Allan Bank, Grasmere
1811–13 Moves to the Parsonage, Grasmere
1813 Moves to Rydal Mount, final home. Becomes Distributor of Stamps.
1843 Poet Laureate on death of Southey
1850 Dies at Rydal Mount, 23 April. Buried Grasmere

SAMUEL TAYLOR COLERIDGE

1772 Born Ottery St Mary, Devon
1791–4 Jesus College, Cambridge
1795 West Country with Southey. Marries Sara Fricker. Meets Wordsworth
1800–1803 Moves with his family to Greta Hall, Keswick
1808–10 Lives with Wordsworth at Allan Bank, Grasmere. Leaves Lakes
1834 Dies in Highgate, London

ROBERT SOUTHEY

1774 Born Bristol
1792–4 Balliol College, Oxford
1794 Plans to start commune in the USA with Coleridge and Fricker sisters
1795 Marries Edith Fricker (Coleridge's sister-in-law)
1803 Moves with family to Greta Hall, Keswick, to join Coleridge. Spends rest of life in Lakes
1813 Poet Laureate
1843 Dies at Greta Hall, Keswick. Buried Keswick

THOMAS DE QUINCEY
1785 Born Manchester
1803–5 Worcester College, Oxford
1807 Meets Coleridge and Wordsworth
1808–30 Takes over lease of Dove Cottage from Wordsworth
1818 Editor, *Westmorland Gazette*
1821 *Confessions of an Opium Eater* published
1834 *Recollections of the Lake Poets* published
1859 Dies in Edinburgh

OTHER FAMOUS RESIDENTS (People who were born, died or lived for some time in the Lake District.)
Catherine Parr (wife of Henry VIII), born Kendal 1512
George Fox, founder of the Quakers, lived in Ulverston, 1670–75
George Romney, artist, born Dalton-in-Furness 1734. Died Kendal 1802. Buried Dalton
Fletcher Christian, *Bounty* mutineer, born Cockermouth 1764
John Dalton, atom theorist, born Eaglesfield, Cockermouth 1766
John Peel, huntsman, born and died Caldbeck 1776–1854
John Wilson (alias Christopher North), writer, lived Windermere 1807–15
Percy Bysshe Shelley, lived Keswick 1811–12
Dr Thomas Arnold, headmaster, retired to Ambleside 1834–42
Matthew Arnold, poet, son of Thomas, lived Ambleside 1834–42
Harriet Martineau, writer, lived Ambleside 1844–76
John Ruskin, writer, artist, lived Coniston 1871–1900, died Coniston, buried Coniston
Stan Laurel (of Laurel and Hardy), born Ulverston 1890
Canon Rawnsley, writer, preservationist, lived Keswick 1901–20
Beatrix Potter, children's writer, lived Sawrey 1906–43, died Sawrey
Norman Nicholson, poet, born Millom 1914
George MacDonald Fraser, writer, born Carlisle 1925
Arthur Ransome, children's writer, lived Coniston 1930–67
Sir Hugh Walpole, writer, lived Derwent Water 1932–41, died Derwent Water, buried Keswick
Margaret Forster, writer, born Carlisle 1938
Melvyn Bragg, author, broadcaster, born Wigton 1939

FAMOUS VISITORS
Agricola, Roman governor, campaign in Cumbria AD 79
St Cuthbert, visited Carlisle and district 685
David I, King of Scotland, died Carlisle 1153
Edward I, Hammer of the Scots, died Burgh March 1307
Robert the Bruce, plundered Cumbria 1314
Mary, Queen of Scots, imprisoned Carlisle Castle 1568

Bonnie Prince Charles, captured Carlisle, 1745, marched through
    Cumbria
John Wesley, evangelist, toured Lakes area, 1759
Thomas Gray, poet, travel writer, toured Lakes 1767, 1769
Benjamin Franklin, US statesman, stayed Derwent Water 1772
Charles Lamb, writer, stayed Keswick 1802
William Hazlitt, writer, stayed Keswick 1803
Sir Walter Scott, writer, regular visitor to Lakes 1805–25
Sir Humphry Davy, scientist, stayed Grasmere 1805; Keswick 1833
John Constable, painter, two months in Lakes 1806
George Canning, statesman, visited Lakes 1814, 1825
Robert Owen, reformer, visited Lakes 1817
William Wilberforce, philanthropist, stayed Rydal and Keswick 1818
John Keats, poet, visited Lakes, climbed Skiddaw 1818
Ralph Waldo Emerson, American essayist, visited Lakes 1833
John Stuart Mill, philosopher, stayed Keswick 1833
Lord Tennyson, poet, stayed Bassenthwaite 1835, honeymoon
    Coniston 1850
Branwell Brontë, worked as tutor, Broughton-in-Furness 1840
Charlotte Brontë, writer, stayed Ambleside 1849, 1850
Mrs Gaskell, writer, stayed Ambleside 1850
Charles Dickens, writer, toured Lakes, climbed Carrock Fell 1857
Wilkie Collins, writer, toured with Dickens 1857
Donald Campbell, racing driver, killed Coniston 1967

BIBLIOGRAPHY

Old Guide Books

Almost any old guide book to the Lakes is good fun to read or look at, but the following is a selection of the best, most influential or most interesting.

William Gilpin, *Observations Relative Chiefly to the Picturesque Beauty Made in the Year 1772 in Several Parts of England, Particularly the Mountains and Lakes of Cumberland and Westmoreland*, two vols, 1786.

William Hutchinson, *An Excursion to the Lakes in Westmoreland and Cumberland in 1773 and 1774*, 1776.

Harriet Martineau, *Complete Guide to the Lakes*, 1855.

Ward Lock, *Guide to the English Lakes*, 1891.

Thomas West, *A Guide to the Lakes*, 1780.

William Wordsworth, *Guide to the Lakes*, 1835. (Facsimile edition of 1906 version edited by Ernest de Sélincourt, OUP, 1977, £1.50.)

M. J. B. Baddeley, *The English Lake District*, 1902

Modern Topographical Books on the Lake District

Over 50,000 books have been written about the Lakes, more than on any other comparable region of the British Isles – so the following can only be a very brief selection. They are the ones I enjoyed or found most useful.

A. H. Griffin, *The Roof of England*, Hale, 1968.

Molly Lefebure, *Cumberland Heritage*, Gollancz, 1970.

Molly Lefebure, *The English Lake District*, Batsford, 1964.

Norman Nicholson, *The Lakers*, Hale, 1955.

Norman Nicholson, *Portrait of the Lakes*, Hale, 1963.

John Parker, *Cumbria*, Bartholomew, 1977.

N. Pevsner, *Cumberland and Westmorland*, Penguin, 1967.

A. Wainwright, *Pictorial Guide to the Lakeland Fells*, seven vols, Kendal, 1955–63.

BOOKLETS

'The Lake District National Park', HMSO, 1975, 85p.

'The National Trust in the Lake District', Dalesman, 1975, 40p.

Gordon Manley, 'Enjoy Cumbria's Climate', Cumbria Tourist Board, 40p.

W. R. Mitchell, 'Lake District Sports', Dalesman, 1977, 50p.

Phyllis Whitehead, 'They Came to the Lakes', Dalesman, 1966.

MAPS

The Ordnance Survey maps (1:50000 series) are not detailed enough for walking – and you have to buy seven to cover the whole Lakeland area.

The OS English maps are best (1:25000) of which there are four: SE, NW, NE, SW, price £1.50 each.

The most detailed maps, showing fields, are the OS six-inch maps.

The easiest single map, covering the whole Lakeland National Park area, is the OS Lake District Tourist Map (1:63360), price £1.20.

For beginners, wanting an informative map which puts the whole of Cumbria in perspective, the best is the Cumbria Tourist Board's English Lakeland, Leisure and Holiday Planning Map, price £1.20. On the reverse side it gives a list of Lakeland events, houses, gardens, museums, activities and town centre street plans.

(Note: all prices refer to 1978.)

Books about the Lake Poets and Others

F. W. Bateson, *Wordsworth, a Re-Interpretation*, Longman, 1954.

Kathleen Coburn, *In Pursuit of Coleridge*, Bodley Head, 1977.

Kathleen Coburn (edit.), *Notebooks of S. T. Coleridge*, Routledge and Kegan Paul, 1962–74.

Samuel Taylor Coleridge, *Biographia Literaria*, 1817; edit. George Watson, Dent, 1975.

Thomas De Quincey, *Recollections of the Lake Poets*, 1834; edit. David Wright, Penguin, 1970.

H. W. Howe (revised Robert Woof), *Greta Hall, Home of Coleridge and Southey*, Keswick, 1977.

Margaret Lane, *The Tale of Beatrix Potter*, Warne, 1968 (Fontana, 1970).

Emile Legouis, *William Wordsworth and Annette Vallon*, Dent, 1922.

Mary Moorman (edit.), *Journals of Dorothy Wordsworth*, OUP, 1971.

Mary Moorman, *William Wordsworth, A Biography*, two vols, Clarendon Press. 1957; OUP, 1968.

H. D. Rawnsley, *Reminiscences of Wordsworth among the Peasantry of Westmoreland*, 1882; Dillons, London, 1968.

E. de Sélincourt, *Letters of William and Dorothy Wordsworth*, four vols, OUP. Revised editions 1967–78.

Jack Simmons, *Southey*, Collins, 1945.

Raleigh Trevelyan, *A Pre-Raphaelite Circle*, Chatto and Windus, 1978.

INDEX

WW in index refers to William Wordsworth the poet.

256, 257, 273; and Catharine Wordsworth 76; and Maid of Buttermere 137–8; and Southey 152; at Nab Cottage 267; as editor 256, 257–8; *Recollections of the Lake Poets* 58–9, 73–4, 75, 78, 137

De Sélincourt, Ernest 56, 128

Derwent Water 126, 164–5, 171, 175, 211, 314; ownership 316

Devoke Water 314, 322

Dickens, Charles 207, 328

Dodd, George 173

Domecq, Adele 47

Dove Cottage, Grasmere: Wordsworths at 54–9, 60–1, 72, 73–4, 242, 273; De Quincey at 74–5, 76, 77–8, 256, 257, 273; today 268–9, 270, 272–3, 274–7, 317; bookshop 297; library 302; Trustees 299–300, 302

Dow Crag 65

Drabble, Margaret 275

drugs 58, 72, 258, 273

dry-stone walls 87, 238–9, 310

Duddon Valley 67–8, 80, 83, 263, 322, 323

Dungeon Ghyll Falls 85

Dunglinson, Ted 291

Dunmail Raise 124

Durham University, WW and 205

eagles 311

Eden Valley 324

Edinburgh Review 201

Egremont, Lord 17

Egremont Crab Fair 287, 293, 318

Egremont Estates 316

Elter Water 83–4, 314

English, Mr, of Belle Isle 8, 9

Ennerdale 100–10, 323; forest 102, 103, 104–5; reservoir 106, 240; Water 101, 106–7, 110, 218, 311, 314, 316; youth hostels 105

Esk Hause 118–19

Eskdale Valley 322

Esthwaite Water 19, 75

Examiner 202

Fairfax-Blakeborough, Major 190–1

fell running 91, 92, 96–8; walking 100–1; Guides' Race 288

Fenwick, Miss, of Rydal Mount 261, 264

Flintoft, Mr. of Keswick 163

food 222–4, 225–30, 324–5

Forestry Commission 45, 95, 102–5, 110, 142, 217, 274, 316

Forster, Margaret 327

France, WW in 35, 36–7, 203–4

Freshwater Biological Station 11, 14

Friar's Crag 164

Fricker, Edith (Mrs Robert Southey) 39, 148–9, 154, 156

Fricker, Eliza 149–50

Fricker, Martha 149–50

Fricker, Sarah (Mrs S. T. Coleridge) 39, 40, 57, 148, 149, 150–1; and De Quincey 73; STC describes 154

Frizington 107, 110

Furness Peninsula 323

Fusedale 232–3

Gandy, Norman 163–4

geologists 127–8

Germany, WW visits 41–2

Gidman, Harold, ferryman 12, 14–15

Gilpin, Rev. William, *Observations* 124–5, 130, 329

Goat's Water 65, 66

Gondola, steamer 50, 211–12

Good Food Guide 69

Gosforth 92

Gouldsworthy, Roger 133

Grasmere: WW at 42, 76, *see also* Dove Cottage; Allan Bank 74, 76–8, 129, 278; Parsonage 76, 194; St Oswalds church 194, 265, 278–80, 281; today 277–84; Rectory 280–4; Rothay Hotel 278, 283; Sports 286–95, 318

Graves, John Woodcock 185–6

Gray, Effie (Mrs John Ruskin) 47

Gray, Thomas 123

Great Langdale 83–9

Greta Hall, Keswick: built 148; Coleridges and Southeys at 54, 78,